SECOND EDITION

Customized Version of

MASS
COMMUNICATION

Producers Consumers

BRENT RUBEN · RAUL REIS · BARBARA IVERSON · GENELLE BELMAS

DESIGNED SPECIFICALLY
for
LAURIE FLUKER
TEXAS STATE UNIVERSITY

Kendall Hunt
publishing company

A customized version of *Mass Communications* by Brent Ruben, Raul Reis, Barbara Iverson and Genelle Belmas, designed specifically for Texas State University.

Kendall Hunt
publishing company

www.kendallhunt.com
Send all inquiries to:
4050 Westmark Drive
Dubuque, IA 52004-1840

Printed in the United States of America
10 9 8 7 6 5 4 3 2 1

CONTENTS

THE EVOLUTION OF MASS COMMUNICATION

Laurie Fluker

He was born in the late 1700s in a small town in Tennessee. His mother was Cherokee, and his father, by most accounts, was white. His American name was George Guess, and he grew up without learning how to read and write. George, despite being physically handicapped and uneducated, grew up to be a talented silversmith. He was always intrigued with the manner in which Americans transacted business using their written language. However, Cherokee Indians did not believe that they were meant to read or write. According to their stories, the Great Spirit had given the world red- and white-skinned children. The Spirit had given red-skinned children books (which the Cherokee called talking leaves), and the Great Spirit had given white children bows and arrows (Maloney). One night, a white-skinned child had snuck in while the red-skinned children slept, and the child exchanged the book for bows and arrows (Maloney). Thus, the Cherokee believed that this story proved that Cherokees were meant to hunt and whites were meant to read. The logical progression for most Cherokees was that there was no need for

their people to learn to read or write. George disagreed with this premise.

Despite the doubt of his people, George decided to try to devise a Cherokee system of reading and writing. He dedicated himself to developing a Cherokee syllabary, a series of written symbols that represented syllables in the Cherokee language. George thought that if he could devise such a system, his people would not have to depend on memory to pass on history. He also thought that such a system would ensure Cherokee independence from the white culture (Sequoyah, *Encyclopedia Britannica*). After 12 years of experimentation, George devised a system that would allow his people to read and write.

His alphabet was made up of 86 characters, each representing a sound in the Cherokee language. George knew that his syllabary was effective when he taught his own daughter to read and write. In 1825, the Cherokee nation, which had been doubtful and reluctant, officially adopted George's system, and Cherokee children began to learn the system in Cherokee schools. His system was used to print the *Cherokee Phoenix*, the first Native American newspaper printed in the United States (*Cherokee Phoenix*). The Cherokee Nation later honored George with a silver medal and a lifetime pension (Sequoyah Museum).

Today, most Americans know George Guess by the name that the missionaries of his time gave him, Sequoyah (Sequoyah Museum). It was in honor of this giant man that an English botanist named the large California trees (*The Writing Code*). Sequoyah's significance cannot be overstated. "Never before, or since, in the history of the world has one man, not literate in any language, perfected a system for reading and writing a language" (Sequoyah Museum).

From Storytelling to Printing

This story of Cherokee children is just one example of the kinds of stories told by groups before there was written communication. For centuries in many civilizations, storytelling was the manner in which everyday life was explained, and it was the manner in which history was passed along from generation to generation.

Today, writing systems are crucial to the world; literacy, the ability to read and write, is now essential in most societies. From reading cooking instructions to social networking messages, literacy is the key to successful communication. The sharing and receiving of knowledge are the cornerstones of communication, and there are few places in society where messages are not found. Although critical today, literacy is a relatively young phenomenon. Most historians suggest that the earliest writing dates back approximately 5,500 years; humankind has existed for approximately 150,000 years (*The Writing Code*).

Those early, prewriting civilizations were oral civilizations. They depended on elders to pass on significant lessons and history to their members, and this communication bonded the members. What these civilizations had in common was storytelling, and the more compelling the story, the more likely it was to be remembered. These stories communicated what was acceptable and what was not acceptable; what was expected and what was frowned upon. Patterns of life and customs were established and shared by members of these civilizations, and the stories served to maintain these patterns. In essence, different cultures were developed. *Merriam-Webster Dictionary* defines *culture* as "the customary beliefs, social forms, and material traits of a given racial, religious, or social group." Therefore, in these societies, stories and culture became interwoven.

Over time, some cultures began to use various methods of writing. Sumer, a part of the ancient world found between the Tigris River and Euphrates River, led the way in writing. One of the first methods of writing, developed by Sumerians, is cuneiform, a picture language in which a picture resembled an object being discussed. The pictures were made with an instrument that resembles a current-day stylus for hand-held computer games, so the images were wedge-shaped (*The Writing Code*). The Latin word for "wedge" is *cuneus*, and thus the writing became known as "cuneiform." Paper had not been invented, so Sumerians used clay tablets as a surface for the cuneiform. These tablets ranged in size from small to large, and they were used for a variety of purposes. It was the clay tablets that were found that eventually led to current-day knowledge of this writing system (*The Writing Code*).

Similar to the Sumerian cuneiform is the Egyptian form of writing, hieroglyphs. This ancient writing form was done primarily on walls, particularly the walls of tombs of the great Egyptian leaders. There are more than 2,000 symbols in the original Egyptian hieroglyphics, and with so many symbols, it is doubtful that later civilizations would have been able to decipher the language had it not been for one valuable find.

Napoleon Bonaparte's campaign into Egypt in 1798 gave France the opportunity to bring French scientists and archaeologists to study the ancient country. Perhaps the most valuable find was the Rosetta Stone, found in 1799 in the city of Rashid (called Rosetta by the French). The stone had three sections in two different languages: ancient Egyptian hieroglyphics, a cursive form of Egyptian hieroglyphics, and Greek (Rosetta Stone, *Encyclopedia*

Britannica). Each of the inscriptions described offerings that were to be made to the ancient ruler Ptolemy V of Epiphanes and the lasting contributions he had made to ancient Egypt (Naquin). The inscription ends by detailing how priests were to ensure that sufficient homage was paid to the king through shrines and festivals and "concludes stating that the instructions were to be displayed in stone in the three scripts found on the Rosetta Stone" (Naquin). Several scholars played a part in deciphering the Rosetta Stone; this accomplishment made it possible to understand these ancient forms of writing.

Phoenicia, an ancient civilization located along the coast near present-day Lebanon and Israel, had some of the best merchants and businessmen in the ancient world. Phoenicians are given credit for developing the first syllable alphabet to keep track of their transactions (Phoenician Alphabet). It was the Greeks who ultimately perfected the alphabet around the 800 B.C.E.; this alphabet more closely resembles modern-day alphabets.

Although Egyptians used temple and tomb walls for the purpose of writing, they and many civilizations around the world began to use papyrus, a plant whose slices were strung together. Later, dried animal skins known as parchment became a writing surface. All other surfaces were replaced in the 8th century A.D. when the Chinese developed paper. The world now had writing and paper, but two problems still existed. The first problem was that books had to be handwritten, mostly by religious monks, so books took years to produce. The second problem was that only a few people were educated enough to read or rich enough to buy books. One person's invention would change the world.

The invention was the printing press, and its inventor was Johannes Gutenberg. What he did was create a system of interchangeable metal letters that made it possible to change any printed message easily. Now, printed books were possible, and this change was revolutionary. Prior to Gutenberg's invention, it took scribes 5 years to hand write a Bible. Approximately 50 years after the printing press, 12 million books were published in Europe (*The Writing Code*). Mass communication—the ability to spread information and ideas to massive numbers—had begun.

The Six Information Revolutions

Storytelling is still important in today's society. Writing brought an end to oral cultures. The printing press brought an end to handwritten texts and ushered in the ability to communicate with huge audiences. Eventually, various other mass media are invented, such as newspapers, magazines, radio, and television. These and other media became the primary storytellers in modern society.

Author Irving Fang has suggested that the history of mass communication can be traced to six information revolutions. He defines *information revolutions* as periods of "profound changes involving new means of communication that permanently affect societies, changes that have shaken political structures and influenced economic development, communal activity, and personal behavior" (Fang xvi). These revolutions date back to the beginning of the ancient alphabet, and they continue to modern day. Fang, however, looks at these periods specifically from the perspective of communication.

◆ **The Writing Revolution:** This is the first of the information revolutions that began in Greece during the time of the alphabet, and in Egypt with the use of papyrus. This 8th century B.C. period is notable, according to Fang, because it represents the end of oral civilizations. "With writing used to store knowledge, the human mind would no longer be constrained by the limits of memory. Knowledge would be boundless" (Fang xvii).

◆ **The Printing Revolution:** This is the second of the information revolutions that began in Europe after Gutenberg's invention of the printing press, combined with the Chinese invention of paper. This period brings upheaval to all aspects of society, namely "political, religious, economic, educational and personal" (Fang xvii). Called the Reformation or Renaissance, Fang suggests that this period is the beginning of the modern world.

◆ **The Mass Media Revolution:** This is the third of the information revolutions that began in western

Europe and the eastern part of the United States before and after the 1850s. Technological advances allowed faster and better communication during this period. Samuel Morse sent the first telegraphic message between Washington, D.C., and Baltimore in 1844. Mathew Brady and Alexander Gardner made Civil War photography unforgettable. Education was becoming more common, and newspapers were attractive to the common man (Fang xvii).

◆ **The Entertainment Revolution:** Fang's fourth revolution included Europe and America at the end of the 1800s, and it continues through the 1900s. This is a period of rapid change that is characterized by the Industrial Revolution, the phonograph, radio, and the film industry. Prior to this period, work had consumed most of the time on both continents. However, audiences begin to consume entertainment much more so than ever in history (Fang xvii).

◆ **The Communication Toolshed Home:** This is the fifth information revolution, and it is notable because, for the first time, media began to make tremendous changes in homes. By the middle of the twentieth century, media began "transforming the home into the central location for receiving information and entertainment, thanks to the telephone, broadcasting, recording, improvements in print technologies, and cheap, universal mail services" (Fang xvii).

Of all the technologies available in the home in the 1950s, none compared to television. Although television had debuted at the 1939 World's Fair in New York City, World War II preoccupied America until its end in 1945. In the coming years, the population increased substantially with the birth of the "Baby Boom Generation." The percentage of families who owned television sets also increased substantially. According to author Marie Winn, the percentage of American families who owned television sets in the 1950s grew from 8% in 1950 to 92% in 1964 (Winn). For the baby boomers, children born in America between 1946 and 1964, television would be a mainstay.

Television reached maturity on November 22, 1963, with the coverage of President John F. Kennedy's assassination. For 4 days, the country and the world were riveted to their television sets, watching the burial of the young president, the peaceful transition to a new president, and the investigation into his death. Television proved its worth during this time, and by the end of the coverage, more people trusted television news than print. Television had become the dominant medium of its day, and it was difficult to imagine another medium that could successfully compete.

In the coming decades, television experienced a number of pivotal moments, and some not as beneficial. The History of Television, Film & Video web site includes the following events as some of the most pivotal:

◆ The 1975 SATCOM satellite delivered Home Box Office to homes willing to pay for the privilege.

◆ "Superstation" WTBS in Atlanta became available to cable systems across the country in 1976.

◆ Ted Turner launched the Cable News Network (CNN) in 1980.

◆ Music Television (MTV) debuted in August 1980.

◆ The final episode of M*A*S*H set the record for the program with the largest audience in television history in 1983. It still holds the record.

◆ Apple Computer introduced its Macintosh computer with a groundbreaking commercial in the third quarter of the Super Bowl in 1984.

◆ Australian Rupert Murdoch launched Fox as the fourth television network in 1987.

◆ More than 50% of American homes were wired for cable by 1987. The audiences continued to grow in the coming years.

◆ More than half of all American homes used VHS videocassette recorders (VCRs) by 1988.

◆ Major media companies Time Inc. and Warner Brothers merged in 1989.

◆ In 1989, the television networks lost a large percentage of their audience; they had only 55% of the total television audience.

- More than 90 million people watched O.J. Simpson's "chase" on television in 1994.
- Digital satellite dishes hit the market in 1996.
- Digital video discs (DVDs) became stiff competition for VHS tapes in 2000.
- AOL and Time Warner merge in 2000, becoming the largest such business in the world.
- Cable's prime-time share exceeded network television's share in 2001.
- DVDs outsold VHS tapes in American households by 2004.
- Digital video recorders (DVRs) became available for sell in 2004.
- Blu-Ray DVDs were introduced by Sony in 2006 with large capacity for storage.
- Toshiba introduced high definition discs (HD) to compete with Blu-Ray in 2006.
- A majority of retailers announced they would exclusively sell Blu-Ray in 2008, perhaps signaling an end to HD DVDs.
- Time Warner announced that it would separate from AOL in 2009.

- **The Information Highway:** This is the last of Fang's information revolutions, and it describes the "convergence of computer, broadcasting, satellite and visual technologies" (Fang xvii). As a result of this convergence, the state of all mass media is in flux.

Today's Mass Media Issues

There are a number of factors that now shape mass media during this information revolution. The fact that more and more media are being bought by non-media companies is a major problem. This is called conglomeration. In such instances, persons making decisions in these large corporations have profits in mind, not journalistic integrity. In budgetary matters, reporters, editors, bureaus, and other newsroom entities are often the first to go. All media suffer when this happens.

There are other factors that pose problems for today's media. New media, convergence, media ownership, and the economy are examples of such problems. Any one of these issues would threaten media at any given time. However, when all of these issues confront media simultaneously, the results are traumatic.

New Media

Computers became pivotal during and after World War II by the British and American governments. The digital computer used by the British was Colossus (Copeland). In America, scientists at educational institutions helped developed the Electronic Numerical Integrator Analyzer and Calculator, better known as ENIAC (Copeland). These massive computers can be considered forerunners of the commercial computers later developed. IBM and other companies continued to refine computers for commercial use.

By the 1970s, a number of companies began to offer personal computers. One company that ultimately dominated the personal computer market was Apple Computer. The company was begun by two college students, Steve Wozniak and Steve Jobs, one of whom would continue to be a dominant figure in the technological race in coming years.

With personal computers in place, the scene was set for a network that allowed people to communicate worldwide. The Internet is ubiquitous today, and it has affected every other medium in unparalleled ways. During the first five information revolutions, the media sent messages to audiences, and the audience could accept the message or not accept. Whether it was newspapers, magazines, radio or television, the media were powerful because they were the ones who carefully crafted and shaped the message.

The Internet has drastically changed this dynamic. For the first time, the audience was now able to communicate in ways that were not even envisioned just a few years ago. Now audiences can share digital audio or video content through podcasting. Audiences are free to write a digital diary about a topic that interests them in web logs called *blogs* or video blogs called *vlogs*. Or individuals can now share video through websites such as YouTube. The Internet has made media much more democratic.

There are many aspects of the Internet that have changed American politics, education, and society in general. The following categories are examples of the Internet's influence.

BLOGS

As mentioned, blogs initially described a website that allows an individual to post information in journal style about politics, sports, health, or any other topic of interest to the blogger. The word *blog* was first used in 1997, and many bloggers thought of themselves as experts, or watchdogs for the public. Initially, most of the blogs went unnoticed by the traditional media and by the mainstream public. A few of the better blogs began to be noticed by audiences, and some became sources of legitimate and serious newsworthy content. Once again, traditional media scoffed at the bloggers as amateur journalists.

The situation changed in early December 2002, at the 100th birthday party for Republican Senator Strom Thurmond. Thurmond had run for president in 1948 as a "Dixiecrat," the party that was made up of Southern Democrats who supported segregation. Thurmond lost, of course, and he went on to abandon his segregationist principles and be elected to the United States Senate. He served the longest Senate term in history.

On the night of his birthday party, the incoming Senate Majority Leader, Trent Lott, spoke about Thurmond's 1948 campaign. Lott indicated that his state had voted for Thurmond, and if others had only done so, there would have been fewer problems over the years. Many felt that the statement was racist in nature (Grossman). Lott's comments, however, although televised on C-SPAN, were virtually ignored by mainstream media. The blogs kept the story alive. Four days after the birthday party, Lott apologized for the comments. Two weeks after the party, Lott resigned as Senate Majority Leader. Blogs had gained a measure of respect.

Blogs continued to gain legitimacy in the eyes of journalists and audiences. Today, news organizations, reporters, broadcast anchors, politicians, and many others have blogs. Bloggers are now given press credentials and access in places once reserved for only mainstream journalists. Perhaps the ultimate signal of their acceptance came in February 2009, when President Obama allowed reporter Sam Stein of the *Huffington Post* blog to ask the second question of the president's press conference (Friedman). This was the first time a blogger was given such recognition in a presidential press conference, ahead of other traditional media reporters. Such recognition is not likely to be the last time that newsmakers realize the importance of new media bloggers.

ONLINE SELLING

In September 1995, Pierre Omidyar began a website he called AuctionWeb. He knew he had a winning idea when the only item he had for sale on the site sold. The item was a broken laser pointer, and it sold for $14.83 (eBay). Omidyar changed the name of the site to eBay, and by 2007, the company had 222 million registered users and more than 13,000 employees, and its automotive division had sold more than 2 million passenger vehicles. The eBay corporation acquired PayPal in 2002, the website founded in 1998 that processes payments and monetary transactions for consumers. In 2004, eBay acquired 25% of the classified ad website Craigslist.

Craigslist is the brainchild of Craig Newmark, who worked for IBM for 17 years, and later, for Charles Schwab. Newmark began a personal e-mail list in 1995 for friends that described local events of interest. The number of people increased significantly within the first two years, and most of those using the site were strangers to Newmark. Eventually, job and apartment listings began to be posted. In 1999, Newmark decided to begin an official company, and the result was craigslist. The site began attracting thousands with providing access to advice, jobs, housing, romance, and just about anything else. For many years, Newmark himself scrutinized every message on the site, working hard to discard any offensive items (Wolf). What is really unusual is that most of the postings are free, with only three exceptions. To cover expenses, employers in New York, Los Angeles, San Francisco and fifteen other cities pay for available job postings, usually ranging in price from $25 to $75. New York City brokers pay $10 for apartment listings. Those offering adult and therapeutic services must also pay in order to help authorities keep track of such activities in case of investigations (Wolf). What is astounding to most observers is the site's potential for more profits that Newmark chooses to ignore. The site disdains advertising, and aesthetically speaking, has little to offer. *Wired* magazine recently suggested that normally, such practices would be the kiss of death. However, the lack of competition for craigslist lets the site get away with what others cannot, specifically because of its size and price.

> But seen from another angle, craigslist is one of the strangest monopolies in history, where customers are locked in by fees set at zero and where the ambiance of neglect is not a way to extract more profit but the expression of a worldview (Wolf).

There is no doubt that this business model is working for craigslist. More than 50 million people use craigslist each month, and more than 1 million jobs are posted each month. The site, according to its factsheet, has expanded to more than 700 local sites in 70 countries around the world. Craigslist is available not only in English, but in French, German, Italian, Portuguese and Spanish, and it gets more traffic than either eBay, with 16,000 employees, or Amazon.com, with more than 20,000 employees (Wolf). By stark contrast, Craigslist employs only 30 people, all working as programmers, customer service representatives, or accounting staff (Wolf). Without a sales, marketing or human resource staff, the craigslist employees have no meetings, instead preferring to communicate by sending e-mail or instant messages. Though the website has clearly made Newmark a millionaire, craigslist's true profit margin remains a mystery. He refuses to comment on the site's earnings, but one consultant firm recently estimated that the revenue would probably exceed $100 million in 2009, and if sold publicly, would likely sell for billions (Wolf). What is clear is that Newmark remains insistent that the site will never accept such ads, regardless of the profit potential.

Newmark's philosophy and no-frills website have caught the attention of millions. Writer Douglas MacMillan recently reported that the number of people using online classified ads has more than doubled, from 22% in 2005 to nearly 50% in 2009. Of those online shoppers, 93% were craigslist visitors. In April 2009 alone, 46.5 million people visited craigslist (MacMillan).

Not all of the attention has been positive for craigslist. In April 2009, a Boston University medical student, Philip Markoff, was alleged to have found his victim in the "erotic services" section of craigslist, and later killed her. After the arrest of the suspect, there was a public outcry for craigslist to do a better job of monitoring the kinds of sexually explicit postings. Newmark bowed to the criticism in May, 2009; he announced that the section would be called "adult services" instead, with higher fees to post ads. With Markoff's trial set to begin in early 2011, there will likely be more scrutiny and criticism of craigslist to come.

Another criticism leveled against craigslist is the competition the website has created for newspapers. Many people now choose to advertise in the more than 700 cities that now feature craigslist postings, rather than advertise in the classified section of local newspapers. The choice to post classified ads free on craigslist or post classified ads for a fee in newspapers has left the audience running to the website in droves. This is only one problem that newspapers now face, but this problem alone has been extremely costly. According to *Wired* magazine, newspaper classified ad revenue has decreased by nearly 50% in the last ten years, which equates to a loss of $10 billion (Wolf). This loss, combined with decreased readers, has left newspapers with an uncertain future.

The future of sites such as eBay and craigslist looks bright. eBay continues to expand internationally, and it has strategically acquired or launched other ventures that ensure future profits for the corporation. Though eBay's 25% stake in craigslist was initially seen as fortuitous for eBay, this arrangement is now strained. eBay's influence at craigslist has been greatly reduced, and the two companies are now suing each other (Wolf). Regardless of the outcome of their lawsuits, there is little doubt that momentum is with these new media ventures rather than with old media.

Social Media

It began in February 2004 with a Harvard sophomore who wanted to communicate with friends. Mark Zuckerberg, with roommates Dustin Moskovitz, Chris Hughes, and Eduardo Saverin, may not have foreseen the popularity of their creation, but by the end of 2004, thefacebook.com, its original name, had attracted nearly 1 million users (Facebook). In 2005, the name was changed to Facebook, and there were 5.5 million active users (Facebook). By April 2009,

Facebook boasted 200 million active users (Facebook), which is larger than the population of Japan (Meet the Face Behind . . .).

Zuckerberg dropped out of Harvard, but that has not affected his earnings. He is now worth a reported $1 billion (Meet the Face Behind . . .). Every day, approximately half a million users join Facebook (Meet the Face Behind . . .), and 5 million join each week (Meet the Face Behind . . .). Zuckerberg ran into a problem in early 2009 when he changed announced that Facebook could retain copies of all content on the site. In essence, the announcement suggested that all information, photographs, etc. would be the property of the site, even if it had been deleted by a user. Facebook devotees felt betrayed, and Zuckerberg had to retreat from the announced policy; instead, users were able to create their own policies to govern the website. It appears that Zuckerberg is back on track to be the entrepreneur who impressed *Forbes* magazine, who said that he was "the youngest billionaire on earth and possibly the youngest self-made billionaire ever" (Jones).

The primary competitor of Facebook is MySpace. Brad Greenspan, Chris DeWolfe, and Tom Anderson were pivotal in the early days of its launch in 2003. The website's reputation was enhanced when News Corporation bought it in July 2005. MySpace was the most popular website by 2006. The *Today Show* reported in 2007 that the website had 180 million accounts and that the typical user had 278 online "friends". Teens, in 2007, spent an average of 15 hours per week on the site. MySpace lost its number one spot to Facebook in 2008.

The newest networking phenomenon is Twitter, founded by Jack Dorsey, Biz Stone, and Evan Williams in mid 2006. This site is different in that users are limited to 140 characters in their messages known as "tweets." Basically, the postings answer the question, "What are you doing?" A. C. Nielsen conducted a survey in March 2009 and found that Twitter was the fastest growing site of its kind. "From February 2008 to February 2009, it clocked in at a whopping 1,382 percent growth rate," from 475,000 to 7,038,000 (McCarthy). When looking at the average Twitter visitor in January, Nielsen stated they visited "14 times during the month and spent an average of seven minutes on the site" (McCarthy).

It is no surprise that young people flock to these social networking sites. However, the Pew Research Center says that Boomers are also heading to these sites in large numbers (Strohmeyer). Their presence is also attracting commercial interests because of their buying power. Although younger users are not pleased that their parents are now using these sites simultaneously, the research suggests they are continuing to enjoy the sites (Strohmeyer).

Google and YouTube

Google was founded in September 1998 by Larry Page and Sergey Brin, who are now worth more than $60 billion each (CBS). The two were in a doctoral program together at Stanford University, and their goal was to develop a search engine that prioritized the results based on the information requested. They developed a test site that they named "Google," based on the word *googol*, a number that begins with 1 and ends with 100 zeroes (CBS). The company has never advertised on television, nor have they needed to. From the time they were testing the site until now, word of mouth has made the site successful. The company hires people each week, which is not difficult since they receive around 1,000 resumes a day (McDermott).

One of Google's most strategic moves was the purchase of YouTube in 2006 for $1.65 billion. YouTube was founded in 2005 by Chad Hurley, Steve Chen, and Jawed Karim, all former employees of PayPal. YouTube leads the way as the world's most popular online video-sharing website. "People are watching hundreds of millions of videos a day on YouTube and uploading hundreds of thousands of videos daily. In fact, every minute, ten hours of video are uploaded to YouTube" (YouTube). Since its inception, YouTube has caught the imagination of people through fictional characters such as "lonelygirl15" or through real-life politicians who did and did not understand its simple power. Specifically, a Barack Obama spokesman said that the campaign's videos, made specifically for YouTube, were watched for 14.5 million hours (Miller). The use of this free time was invaluable to the Obama presidential campaign.

As of 2010, YouTube celebrated its fifth anniversary. It is difficult to believe that the website has only been around for five years, but what a remarkable five-year period. The careers of individuals such as Justin Bieber, Susan Boyle, and more recently, Greyson Chance, the 12-year-old boy who rose to stardom by singing Lady Gaga's song "Paparazzi" at his school's festival. Certainly, Judson Laipply ("Evolution of Dance") and Tay Zonday ("Chocolate Rain") credit YouTube for giving them fame. These are, by no means, isolated accomplishments for YouTube. Consider the following statistics about this relative newcomer, taken directly from YouTube's site.

◆ Twenty-four hours of video are posted every minute to YouTube.

◆ YouTube gets two million views a day, double the number of viewers than all three of those watching ABC, NBC and CBS combined in primetime (worldwide numbers for YouTube versus prime-time viewing of Americans alone).

◆ It would take two centuries to watch all of the videos on YouTube.

◆ The average viewer watches YouTube approximately fifteen minutes a day.

◆ Ninety-four of *Ad Ages* top 100 advertisers have run campaigns on Google Content Network & YouTube.

There is no doubt that YouTube has changed the way that politicians run for office, the way in which talent is discovered, and the accessibility to just about anything that interests anyone. The site has come a long way from its initial video of one young man at the zoo.

Here are a few other historical tidbits offered by YouTube on its fifth anniversary.

◆ Nineteen seconds is the length of the first video uploaded to YouTube.

◆ That first video has been played nearly two million times.

◆ The most popular video ever on YouTube is Lady Gaga's "Bad Romance"; it has been viewed nearly two hundred million times.

◆ YouTube is localized in twenty-two countries in 24 different languages.

◆ Seventy percent of YouTube's traffic comes from outside the United States.

◆ Hundreds of millions of videos are watched every month on mobile devices.

Convergence

Technological advancements have now made it easier to access programming in a variety of ways. A decade ago, if an individual missed a given episode of his favorite television program without taping it, the only option was to wait until the network repeated that episode. Now, in most instances, all it takes is Internet access. Broadcasting and cable network websites now often make television episodes available for viewing at any time, on laptop computers, desktop computers, cellular phones, or any other technology with Internet access. Before the development of the videocassette recorder (VCR) and the Internet, audiences were bound to watch television at the time the program was scheduled. There is no longer appointment television, films, etc. This ability to read magazines and newspapers on the Internet (without buying the actual magazine or newspapers), watch television episodes or films, or listen to radio in other ways is called convergence.

NBC Universal (owned by General Electric) and News Corporation (owners of Fox) have come together to make convergence easier for the audience. In 2008, they joined forces to form the website Hulu; this site originally offered programs from NBC and Fox, and other cable properties owned by these companies. The site also makes Sony and MGM films available for viewing (Hoover's). In April 2009, Disney (owners of ABC) announced that they would join in the Hulu venture, offering their program content on the site. This means that three of the four major networks (NBC, Fox, and ABC) now have content on the Hulu website.

CBS will be the lone network excluded in this arrangement. CBS already had a website, TV.com, that began in 2005 (Frommer). The site was a blend of television shows, information, and guides at the time of its inception. In December 2008, CBS announced it would relaunch the website with even more programs and television information. This upgraded site now pits CBS against the partnership of the other three networks.

One additional player in this convergence picture is YouTube. Google will now be offering television and films in a new section of YouTube called "Shows" (Linder). Although there are some television shows now offered on YouTube, these shows are not as varied as the ones offered on Hulu. Sony, Lion's Gate, and CBS are among the corporations that have agreed to provide content for YouTube (Linder).

Research suggests that the television networks are on the right track by making programming available on the Internet. In a recent survey, a large portion of adults reported that they do use the Internet for video viewing. "Twenty-six million adults in broadband homes are watching streaming TV episodes at least once a month, and about 6 million adults in broadband homes pay for premium Web video content on a monthly basis" (Wilson). Television networks need not worry now about the competition since most adults in the survey indicated that they watched on the Internet just to catch up on episodes missed (Wilson).

The handwriting is on the wall as far as convergence is concerned. Television networks now realize that the days of appointment television are over since they are providing opportunities for audiences to watch content on the Internet. The same can be said for magazines, newspapers, and all other media. Convergence is here to stay, but how the media can profit from convergence is still in question.

Media Ownership

Diversity of voices and opinions is valuable, and thus, it would be ideal if there were diversity in media ownership. Unfortunately, more and more media are owned by fewer and fewer entities. The top five media corporations dominate all aspects of the media. They do not own just a newspaper or magazine or radio station. In most instances, these corporations own a variety of media.

The top five media corporations in 2008 were (1) Time Warner, (2) The Walt Disney Corporation, (3) News Corporation, (4) NBC Universal, and (5) Viacom. Not all of these corporations are well known by their names, but their properties are well known.

TIME WARNER

Time Warner is the largest of all media corporations. The company brings together many of the corporations that were impressive individually as well, such as Warner Brothers, Time, Incorporated, and Ted Turner's properties. Time, Incorporated is the largest magazine publisher in the United States, with approximately 125 magazine titles (Time Inc.). "Nationally and globally, Time Inc. titles make their mark. Each month, one out of every two American adults reads a Time Inc. magazine, and more than one out of six who are online visit a Time Inc. website. Every minute, more than 100 Time Inc. titles are sold in the U.S." (Time Inc.).

Warner Brothers Entertainment is the branch of Time Warner that primarily focuses on the film industry. This is not to suggest that Warner Brothers only deals with films. On the contrary, they were responsible for more than 30 television series for the 2008–2009 television season, had 8 straight years (through 2008) of billion-dollar domestic and overseas box office receipts, and enjoyed three of the all-time highest grossing films from Warner Brothers or New Line Cinema, another studio owned by Warner Brothers (Warner Bros.).

Ted Turner is the visionary who brought cable news operations to television. No one had thought of news as a 24-hour possibility until Turner launched Cable News Network in 1980. Most thought it would be a failure, but today, cable news is a mainstay in many homes. Turner also launched WTBS, TNT, Turner Classic Movies (TCM), the Cartoon Network, and CNN Headline News. Several of these networks, such as CNN, TCM, and Cartoon Network, have expanded to other countries. Other brands that Turner Broadcasting System brought to WB were Adult Swim, Pogo, and truTV (Turner Broadcasting).

With just the properties mentioned, it is not surprising that Time Warner is the largest media corporation. However, there are many more properties that are owned by this media heavyweight. The following is a partial list of Time Warner properties. (Time Warner: Who Owns . . .)

◆HBO, Cinemax, WTBS, TNT, CNN, CNN Headline News, Turner Classic Movies, Cartoon Network

- Warner Brothers Studio, WB Television Network, New Line Cinema, Castle Rock Entertainment, Time Warner Cable, Road Runner

- *Time* Magazine, *Fortune* Magazine, *Sports Illustrated*, *People*, *Money*, *Entertainment Weekly*

The Disney Company

The company known for Mickey Mouse is the second largest media conglomerate ("Walt Disney, Hoover's"). Begun by visionary Walt Disney during the 1920s, the Disney Company now owns much more than the animation and theme parks that carry the Disney name. In 1993, Disney purchased Miramax Films, and in 1995, they purchased Capital Cities/ABC. Today, these properties are among many media properties now owned by the company.

The Disney name had the kind of prestige that few companies attain, mostly from the outstanding pen & ink animation that had begun the company. Films such as *Snow White*, *Beauty and the Beast* and *Lion King* are classics, but other non-animated films have also been successful. *National Treasury* and *Pirates of the Caribbean* (created from a successful ride at its theme park) were two examples of highly successful films. Their television efforts were less successful until they struck gold with *Who Wants to Be a Millionaire* in prime time. The game show was so successful that ABC ran it four nights a week. This multiple run diluted the success of it, and it left ABC with few prime-time hits until *Desperate Housewives*, *Lost* and *Grey's Anatomy*.

In 1994, Michael Eisner became the very visible CEO of Disney. Under his leadership, Disney continued to grow. Perhaps one of the best partnerships during Eisner's term was with Pixar, the digital animation company. Under the partnership arrangement, the two companies shared box office receipts and the licensing of products. Their first joint venture was *Toy Story* in 1995. This film was just the beginning of a long line of successes for this partnership. *Toy Story 2*, *A Bug's Life*, *Monsters Inc.*, *The Incredibles*, *Finding Nemo* and *Cars* followed.

Steve Jobs and Pixar

The innovative digital animation company known as Pixar began with the purchase of a computer system created by noted film director George Lucas. Lucas is known for his *Star Wars* and Indiana Jones films that showcase stunning special effects. His company, Industrial Light and Magic, begun in 1975, and is the company that many in Hollywood turn to for the dazzling special effects that only Lucas can give. It was logical that the computer graphics division of Lucasfilm, Ltd. created the hardware that would made digital animation the standard in the industry ("Pixar History").

Steve Jobs is the person who purchased what ultimately became Pixar from Lucas in 1986 ("Pixar Animation..."). Jobs was best known as one of the co-founders of Apple Computers in 1976, and he remained with the company until 1985 (Grobert). It was during his absence from Apple that he purchased Pixar. Over the years, Jobs entered into a joint venture with Disney to allow Pixar to create seven films, beginning with *Toy Story* (Grobert). It was ironic that Disney, known for excelling in the pen and ink animation, would participate in an agreement with Pixar, ultimately known only for digital animation. It is clear now that digital animation has virtually replaced the old Disney method, so though ironic, the venture was fortuitous for Disney.

There had been talks about Pixar merging with Disney, but reportedly, Jobs did not get along with Michael Eisner, the CEO of Disney from 1984 to 2005 (Ritholz). Jobs had decided that *Cars* would be the last film on which Pixar and Disney collaborated (Ritholz). That was until Robert Iger replaced Eisner and became the new CEO for Disney in 2005 (McLean). Jobs and Iger got along well, so few were surprised when in May of 2006, Disney merged with Pixar (McLean). The move was strategically sound for Disney; financially, the deal made Jobs the largest shareholder of Disney (Stern).

In 2007, *Fortune* magazine named Jobs the most powerful person in the corporate world. Under his leadership at Apple, the personal computer became popular. Desktop publishing, unheard of before Jobs, became possible thanks to Apple. The company has introduced a number of other technological wonders, including the laser printer, iPods and iPhones. *Fortune* aptly described what makes Jobs so powerful.

> He has changed the dynamics of consumer electronics with the iPod, and persuaded the music industry, the television networks, and Hollywood to distribute their wares with the iTunes Music Store. With his hugely successful Apple Stores, he gave the big-box boys a lesson in high-margin, high-touch retailing. And this year, at the height of his creative and promotional powers, Jobs orchestrated Apple's entry into the cellular telephone business with the iPhone.
>
> That's five industries that Jobs has upended-computers, Hollywood, music, retailing, and wireless phones. At this moment, no one has more influence over a broader swath of business than Jobs (Schlender).

Jobs has continued to be phenomenally successful. In 2008, 9.7 million Macs were sold. By early 2009, the company had sold 6 billion songs in 6 years to 75 million people. Some projects were put on hold when Jobs took an extended leave of absence in early 2009 because of health issues. There were fears that Jobs' pancreatic cancer, first diagnosed in 2004, may have resurfaced. Since that first health scare in 2004, Apple had always kept information about Jobs' health confidential for good reason. Apple's stock has surged or plunged based on news of Jobs' health. However, in June 2009, Apple announced that Jobs had undergone liver replacement surgery two months earlier, and he returned to work at the end of June, 2009. Predictably, Apple stocks surged, and his return marked even more success for the company.

Following Jobs' return, Apple products continue to be highly successful. Though Apple faced design problems with its iPhone 4G, the various versions of the iPhone have sold billions. The iPad, similar to Amazon's Kindle, sold 1 million units in its first month, and a second million in the second month. By early summer of 2010, the device sold more than 3 million units, considerably more than critics and Apple had predicted. Though Apple had considered later decreasing the iPad's original price, which started at $499, sales would suggest that the price decrease may not be necessary. As it stands, Jobs continues to be perhaps the most valuable individual in business today. He has helped Apple surpass Microsoft as the world's most profitable tech company, and the second most valuable U.S. company behind Exxon Mobil.

Other Disney Holdings

The Walt Disney Company has greatly expanded over the years, in addition to ABC and Pixar. The following is a partial list of media properties owned by Disney ("Walt Disney: Who Owns . . .").

◆ Walt Disney Pictures, Touchstone Pictures, Hollywood Pictures, Miramax Films and Pixar

◆ ESPN (80% ownership in each of the ESPN cable stations), 10 broadcast stations in cities such as Houston, San Francisco, Chicago, Los Angeles and New York, Disney Channel, ABC Family, SOAPnet, as well as partial ownership of A & E, History Channel and Lifetime

◆ Walt Disney Imagineering, Disneyland, Walt Disney World Resort, Tokyo Disney Resort, Disneyland Resort Paris, Hong Kong Disneyland, Disney Vacation Club, Disneyworld

◆ Walt Disney Records, Hollywood Records, Lyric Street Records

◆ Magazines, radio stations, publishing companies, and other media-related industries

News Corporation

Australian Rupert Murdoch is the genius behind News Corporation. By the time he bought his first U.S. media property, Murdoch had already amassed an entire media empire in both Australia and England. He had inherited two Australian papers in 1953, and he moved from there to purchase British media in the 1960s ("News Corporation: Who Owns. . ."). He bought his first U.S. media property in the 1970s with the purchase of the *San Antonio Express News* ("News Corporation: Who Owns . . ."). He continued expanding his empire into Asia in the 1980s ("News Corporation: Who Owns . . ."). His company, News Corporation, is now the third largest media corporation ("News Corporation, Hoover's").

News Corporation's American media purchases have been extremely impressive, spanning media from film to television to print media. More recently, he has expanded to online media as well. The following list provides merely a few of the American media properties owned by News Corporation ("New Corporation: Who Owns . . .").

◆ Fox Broadcasting Company, Fox News Channel, Fox Business Network, Fox Sports Channel, FX, Fox Sports Net, 30 television stations (owned and operated)

◆ 20th Century Fox, 20th Century Fox Television, Fox Searchlight Pictures, Fox Television Studios, Blue Sky Studios

◆ *New York Post, Wall Street Journal, The Weekly Standard*

◆ Dow Jones, HarperCollins (publishing), MySpace.com, Los Angeles Kings (40%), Staple Center (40%), FoxSports.com, AmericanIdol.com, Fox.com, Rotten Tomatoes

Rupert Murdoch

According to Fortune magazine, the second most powerful person in business is Rupert Murdoch. His media empire that now includes four continents, with more than 25 newspapers outside the United States ("News Corporation: Who Owns. . ."). It is his ambition, combined with his money and savvy, which make Murdoch a serious force in media.

One of his most successful ventures was the creation of Fox Broadcasting Company. The last serious attempt to become the fourth major television network, competing against NBC, CBS and ABC, had been the DuMont Television Network, but that attempt had been at the inception of television in the 1940s and 1950s. That network ceased operations in the mid-1950s. No one had since been successful at obtaining such a distinction until Murdoch. In the late 1980s, Fox went to low-power, independent stations in various cities around the country asking them to give some time on Sunday evenings only to try Fox programs. Among the programs offered on Sunday night were *21 Jumpstreet, The Tracey Ulmann Show* (featuring animated quick skits starring a dysfunctional family with an obnoxious son), and *Married with Children*. Eventually, Fox expanded to seven nights of programming, with programs ending at 9 p.m. each night (CST). *The Simpsons, The X-Files, 24, Ally McBeal, Melrose Place,* and *Beverly Hills, 90210* have been some of the most popular Fox programs over the years. In *Living Color,* the 1990s comedy produced by Keenen Ivory Wayans, began the careers of Jim Carrey, Jamie Foxx, Jennifer Lopez, and Carrie Ann Inaba. National Football League games came to Fox during the 1990s, and it seemed that Fox had the formula for success. *American Idol,* the ultimate talent show for singers, has garnered millions of viewers in each of its eight seasons on Fox. The reality program has been among the top ten programs viewed each year, and its contestants have gone on to win a number of awards, including the Grammy and Academy Awards.

Fox now has the number one cable news network, a newly launched business network, in addition to its other television properties. However, it is not the broadcasting networks that Murdoch is proudest of. In 2007, Murdoch felt that he had finally achieved the pinnacle of American media properties when he purchased Dow Jones, a package that included *The Wall Street Journal,* the oldest newspaper in the country. It is clear that Murdoch intends to continue to be a major player in American media.

General Electric (NBC Universal)

General Electric (GE) has an impressive history in America, dating back to the times of Thomas Edison. The company was one of several companies to form the Radio Corporation of America (RCA) in 1919 ("General Electric: Who Owns . . ."). In 1926, RCA created the National Broadcasting Company (NBC). In the coming decades, GE and RCA parted ways, so it was ironic that in 1985, GE purchased RCA for $6.3 billion, and thus acquired NBC. In 2003, GE announced a merger with Vivendi Universal, the corporation that brought the Universal theme parks, Universal Pictures, and other properties to the deal. The name of the newly merged group was NBC Universal, with GE owning 80% of the new company ("General Electric: Who Owns . . .").

GE is a major corporation with varied interests in addition to NBC Universal. The following is a partial list of GE's holdings beginning with their media properties ("General Electric: Who Owns . . .").

◆ A number of television stations in major cities such as New York, Los Angeles, San Diego, Miami, Chicago, Philadelphia, and Washington

◆ Several Telemundo (Spanish-language) stations in cities such as Miami, Houston, Los Angeles, New York, Chicago, San Antonio, Denver, Phoenix, and Puerto Rico

◆ CNBC, MSNBC, Bravo, USA, Sci-Fi, Oxygen

◆ Universal Pictures (film studio) and Universal Parks & Resorts

◆ GE Aircraft Engines, GE Consumer Products, GE Insurance, GE Medical Systems, GE Plastics, GE Transportation Systems

In December, 2009, General Electric announced that Comcast Corporation, America's largest cable operator and internet home provider, would be acquiring NBC Universal for $30 billion. If approved by Congress, this will be a joint venture with Comcast owning 51 percent, and GE owning 49 percent. Comcast would bring the cable properties it owns, which include E Entertainment and the Golf Channel, and GE would bring not just NBC, but its other cable channels that include MSNBC, CNBC, USA, Bravo and SyFy. The change in ownership will allow Comcast, already extremely successful in its cable ventures, to get

involved with the content side. The change for the NBC network would be fortuitous since that network's ratings have steadily declined over the last few years.

NBC Universal

NBC Universal ranked fourth among powerful media corporations in 2008 (Hoover.com). The NBC television network has, over the years, had a great deal of success with programming. During the 1950s, NBC hired an innovative head of programming, Sylvester "Pat" Weaver, who felt that there should be programming available early in the morning and late at night for audiences. His solution was the creation of *The Today Show* and *The Tonight Show*, two programs that set the standard for these genres ("Weaver").

The network continued to garner critical acclaim and audience loyalty over the years with programs such as *I Dream of Jeannie, Chico and the Man, Sanford and Son, The Cosby Show, A Different World, Seinfeld, Cheers, Family Ties, L. A. Law, St. Elsewhere, Hillstreet Blues, Miami Vice, 3rd Rock from the Sun, The Office, ER, Law & Order* and *Heroes.*

More recently, NBC has faced a number of challenges in its programming. The network faced a difficult decision in 2009 when Jay Leno's contract expired. Leno, the 17-year host of *The Tonight Show*, was still the highest rated late night talk show. However, NBC had promised Conan O'Brien that his many years as talk show host of *Late Night with Conan O'Brien*, the program following *The Tonight Show*, would be rewarded. O'Brien was tapped to replace Leno in the coveted spot as the new host of *The Tonight Show*. NBC's dilemma was evident when rumors surfaced that ABC was extremely interested in having Leno establish a new late night talk show on their network to compete with O'Brien on NBC and Letterman on CBS. NBC's solution was to offer Leno a prime-time talk show each weeknight from 9–10 p.m. Central time. O'Brien began his stint on *The Tonight Show* in June, 2009, and Leno's show premiered in the fall of 2009. Audiences for O'Brien's show slumped after weeks on the air, and audiences for Leno's show never satisfied the network affiliates. The experiment had been a dismal failure, and in January, 2010, few were surprised when NBC announced that Jay Leno would be returning to *The Tonight Show*, and O'Brien would be leaving NBC with a healthy amount of money for him and his staff. The entire debacle was a public relations nightmare for the network, and Leno was portrayed as the villain. O'Brien has seemingly bounced back with the announcement of the November, 2010 debut of his new one-hour program on TBS. This five-year deal will not only bring a large young audience to late-night TBS, it will also be financially lucrative for O'Brien since he will own the rights to his program (Flint). The good news for NBC: Leno's audience is steadily increasing. The bad news: the audience has lost most of its young viewers, with the audience's current median age of 56 (Carter).

Another dilemma that NBC faces is its low standing in the ratings war. Some NBC favorites, such as *Heroes*, lost viewers in the 2008 season, and the show fired a number of previous writers in an effort to attract viewers back to the program. The changes were perhaps too little, too late; *Heroes* was cancelled in May, 2010. It is unclear what the change in ownership to Comcast will mean for the struggling network. The one thing for sure is that there is nowhere to go but up. If NBC's historic track record is any indication, the network will likely climb back as a major competitor.

Viacom Incorporated

Viacom is not a name that is as well known as Disney, but it is, likewise, a major media corporation. Its holdings include broadcast and cable television networks, radio stations, Internet properties, as well as book publishing, film production and film distribution ("Viacom: Who Owns . . ."). Though Viacom ranked as the fifth media corporation in 2008, it is the media giant that reaches an extremely diverse audience ("Viacom, Hoover's"). Its broadcast network, Columbia Broadcasting System (CBS) is one of the most watched networks, thanks in large part to its *CSI*

franchise. CBS draws an older audience, but Viacom's cable holdings ensure that the corporation reaches a large young audience. All of the major cable music networks are owned by Viacom. Whether it is Music Television (MTV) or MTV2, or Black Entertainment Television (BET) or BET J, or VH1 or VH1 Classic, or County Music Television, Viacom owns each.

Sumner Redstone is the founder of Viacom and its Executive Chairman of the Board of Directors ("Redstone"). The 86-year-old mogul has been a major figure at Viacom and CBS for many years. Under Redstone's leadership, Viacom Incorporated now owns multiple media properties ("Viacom: Who Owns . . .").

◆ Nickelodeon, Nick at Night, TV Land, Noggin, Spike TV (the first network for men), Comedy Central, Logo (a network for gay, lesbian, bisexual and transgender audiences), The Movie Channel, Showtime

◆ Paramount Pictures, Paramount Home Entertainment, Dreamworks Studio, Paramount Vantage, MTV Films, Nickelodeon Movies, Home Entertainment

◆ Simon & Schuster, Blockbuster, Infinity Broadcasting, Xfire, Atom, Addicting Games, Gamerailers, Harmonix, Neopets, Parents Conflict, Quizilla, Rhapsody, Shockwave

◆ Syndication rights to *Roseanne*, *A Different World*, *I Love Lucy*, *Perry Mason*, *The Twilight Zone*, and *The Cosby Show* (Syndication refers to the selling of rights to air a program.)

The Economy

News of businesses closing, going bankrupt or struggling is not unusual in 2009. The result for mass media is fewer advertising dollars. Less advertising would be difficult for media, but once again, less advertising, more competition, and an audience gravitating to new media have all created a crisis. According to research done by Pew, just about one of every five journalists who worked in the newspaper industry in 2001 is likely gone now ("Journalism.org"). The recession has, at the very least, doubled the revenue losses in 2008 ("Journalism.org").

What is clear is that the media must find new ways to finance and reinvent their operations. What is not clear is whether the executives who have been in charge, who had ample opportunity to make changes along the way, are the ones who can make these changes happen now.

Works Cited

"Apple IPad Sales Show Little Signs of Slowing." *Reviews, News, and Opinion About Personal Technology by Harry McCracken & Friends | Technologizer*. Web. 12 July 2010. *http://technologizer.com/2010/06/01/apple-ipad-sales-show-little-signs-of-slowing/*.

Arango, Tim. "The New York Times Log In." *The New York Times - Breaking News, World News & Multimedia*. Web. 28 May 2010. *http://www.nytimes.com/2009/12/04/business/media/04nbc.html?_r=1&pagewanted=print*.

Arrango, Tim. "25 most powerful people in business - Rupert Murdoch (2) - FORTUNE." *Business, financial, personal finance news - CNNMoney.com*. Web. 1 July 2009. *http://money.cnn.com/galleries/2007/fortune/0711/gallery.power_25.fortune/2.html*.

"The Art and Architecture of the British Renaissance." *Welcome to Nicholls State University - Thibodaux, Louisiana*. Web. 14 Apr. 2009. *http://www.nicholls.edu/art-dhc/*.

"At Five Years, Two Billion Views per Day and Counting." *YouTube Blog*. Web. 28 May 2010. *http://youtube-global.blogspot.com/2010/05/at-five-years-two-billion-views-per-day.html*.

Buskirk, Eliot Van. "5-Year-Old YouTube Tops Networks' Primetime With 2 Billion Views | Epicenter | Wired.com." *Wired News*. Web. 28 May 2010. *http://www.wired.com/epicenter/2010/05/five-year-old-youtube-tops-networks-primetime-with-2-billion-views/*.

Carter, Bill. "Leno at Top of Late Night TV, With Older Viewers - NYTimes.com." *The New York Times - Breaking News, World News & Multimedia*. 11 Apr. 2010. Web. 28 May 2010. *http://www.nytimes.com/2010/04/12/business/media/12late.html?src=mv*.

"Cherokee Phoenix archives." *The Online Books Page*. Web. 14 June 2009. *http://onlinebooks.library.upenn.edu/webbin/serial?id=cherokeephoenix*.

Copeland, Jack. "A Brief History of Computing." *Alan-Turing.net*. Web. 29 May 2009. *http://www.alanturing.net/turing_archive/pages/Reference%20Articles/BriefHistofComp.html#computer*.

"Craigslist | about Factsheet." *Craigslist Classifieds: Jobs, Housing, Personals, for Sale, Services, Community, Events, Forums*. Web. 27 May 2010. *http://www.craigslist.org/about/factsheet*.

"EBay Media Center: About eBay." *EBay Media Center: Overview*. Web. 13 June 2009. *http://news.ebay.com/about.cfm*.

"Facebook CEO Mark Zuckerberg." *The Today Show*. NBC. Austin, TX, 27 Feb. 2009. Television.

"Factsheet | Facebook." *Welcome to Facebook! | Facebook*. Web. 19 June 2009. *http://www.facebook.com/press/info.php?factsheet*.

Fang, Irving E. *History of mass communication six information revolutions*. Boston: Focal, 1997. Print.

Flint, Joe. "Conan Will Have Ownership of His TBS Show | Company Town | Los Angeles Times." *Top of the Ticket | Bill Clinton Was White House Conduit to Sestak in Failed Bid to save Specter. Next, Bill Tries to Rescue Blanche Lincoln | Los Angeles Times*. Web. 28 May 2010. *http://latimesblogs.latimes.com/entertainmentnewsbuzz/2010/04/conan-obrien-ownership-tbs-show.html*.

Friedman, Jon. "Obama's New Best Friend: Huffington Post - CBS News." *Breaking News Headlines: Business, Entertainment & World News - CBS News*. Web. 22 June 2009. *http://www.cbsnews.com/stories/2009/02/20/business/marketwatch/main4814633.shtml*.

Frommer, Dan. "CBS Going After Hulu With TV.Com (CBS)." *The Business Insider*. Web. 20 June 2009. *http://www.businessinsider.com/2008/12/cbs-going-after-hulu-with-tvcom*.

"General Electric: Who Owns What |." *Columbia Journalism Review*. Web. 29 June 2009. *http://www.cjr.org/resources/index.php?c=ge*.

Grobart, Sam. "While You Were Out: Apple's Years With and Without Steve Jobs." *The New York Times - Breaking News, World News & Multimedia*. Web. 1 July 2009. *http://www.nytimes.com/interactive/2009/01/22/technology/20090122_JOBS.html*.

Grossman, Lev. "Meet Joe Blog - TIME." *Breaking News, Analysis, Politics, Blogs, News Photos, Video, Tech Reviews - TIME.com*. Web. 13 June 2009. *http://www.time.com/time/magazine/article/0,9171,1101040621-650732-1,00.html*.

"History of Television." *High-Tech Productions Professional Worldwide Video and DVD Services*. Web. 15 July 2009. *http://www.high-techproductions.com/historyoftelevision.htm*.

"Hulu - Company Description - Hoover's." *Company Information from Hoover's including business reports and profiles*. Web. 28 June 2009. *http://www.hoovers.com/hulu/—ID__159434--/free-co-profile.xhtml*.

Jones, Del. "Forbes: Zuckerberg Youngest Self-Made Billionaire." *Campus Entrepreneurship*. Web. 5 June 2009. *http://campusentrepreneurship.wordpress.com/2008/03/06/forbes-zuckerberg-youngest-self-made-billionaire/*.

Journalism.org- The State of the News Media 2009. Web. 20 June 2009. *http://www.stateofthemedia.org/2009/narrative_overview_intro.php?cat=0&media=1*.

Linder, Brad. "YouTube goes Hulu, adds TV, movies." *Download Squad*. Web. 1 July 2009. *http://www.downloadsquad.com/2009/04/17/youtube-goes-hulu-adds-tv-movies/*.

"MacDailyNews - Apple Surpasses Microsoft to Become World's Biggest Tech Company, Second-most-valuable U.S. Company." *MacDailyNews - Apple and Mac News - Welcome Home*. Web. 12 July 2010. *http://www.macdailynews.com/index.php/weblog/comments/25385/*.

MacMillan, Douglas. "Craigslist Fuels Online Classified-Ad Surge - BusinessWeek." *BusinessWeek - Business News, Stock Market & Financial Advice*. Web. 5 June 2009. *http://www.businessweek.com/technology/content/may2009/tc20090522_861316.htm*.

Maloney, Ann. "Sequoyah." *RootsWeb.com Home Page*. Web. 26 May 2009. *http://www.rootsweb.ancestry.com/~oknowata/Sequoyah.htm*.

McCarthy, Caroline. "Nielsen: Twitter's growing really, really, really, really fast | The Social - CNET News." *Technology News - CNET News*. Web. 6 July 2009. *http://news.cnet.com/8301-13577_3-10200161-36.html*.

McDermott, Tricia. "Defining Google - 60 Minutes - CBS News." *Breaking News Headlines: Business, Entertainment & World News - CBS News*. Web. 10 June 2009. *http://www.cbsnews.com/stories/2004/12/30/60minutes/main664063.shtml*.

McLean, Prince, and Jade Kasper. "AppleInsider | Jobs and Iger comment on Disney's acquisition of Pixar." *AppleInsider | Apple Insider News and Analysis*. Web. 26 June 2009. *http://www.appleinsider.com/articles/06/01/24/jobs_and_iger_comment_on_disneys_acquisition_of_pixar.html*.

"Meet the Man Behind Facebook - Oprah.com." *Oprah.com - Live Your Best Life - Oprah.com*. Web. 16 June 2009. *http://www.oprah.com/article/oprahshow/20090313-tows-facebook-zuckerberg*.

Miller, Claire C. "How Obama's Internet Campaign Changed Politics - Bits Blog - NYTimes.com." *Technology - Bits Blog - NYTimes.com*. Web. 4 July 2009. *http://bits.blogs.nytimes.com/2008/11/07/how-obamas-internet-campaign-changed-politics/*.

Mintz, Jessica. "Apple CEO Steve Jobs at Work Again - AOL Money & Finance." *Money - AOL Money & Finance*. Web. 1 July 2009. *http://money.aol.com/article/apple-ceo-steve-jobs-at-work-again/536120*.

"Myspace." *The Today Show*. Austin, TX, Feb. 2007. Television.

Naquin, Adrienne. "The Discovery and Decipherment of the Rosetta Stone at the British Museum." *Welcome to Nicholls State University - Thibodaux, Louisiana*. Web. 15 June 2009. *http://www.nicholls.edu/art-dhc/surveyessays/rosetta.htm*.

"NBC Universal - Hoover's." *Company Information from Hoover's including business reports and profiles*. Web. 28 June 2009. *http://www.hoovers.com/nbcuniversal/—ID__159434—/free-co-profile.xhtml*.

"News Corporation Description - Hoover's." *Company Information from Hoover's including business reports and profiles*. Web. 28 June 2009. *http://www.hoovers.com/newscorp/—ID__159434—/free-co-profile.xhtml*.

"News Corporation: Who Owns What |." *Columbia Journalism Review*. Web. 29 June 2009. *http://www.cjr.org/resources/index.php?c=newscorp*.

O'Brien, Timothy. "Craig Newmark Interview: A Brief History of Craigslist - O'Reilly Broadcast." *Community | O'Reilly Media*. Web. 16 June 2009. *http://broadcast.oreilly.com/2008/12/craig-newmark-interview-a-brie.html*.

On, Clicking. "25 Most Powerful People in Business Rupert Murdoch (2) - FORTUNE." *Business, Financial, Personal Finance News - CNNMoney.com*. Web. 25 May 2009. *http://money.cnn.com/galleries/2007/fortune/0711/gallery.power_25.fortune/2.html*.

On, Clicking. "25 Most Powerful People in Business - Steve Jobs (1) - FORTUNE." *Business, Financial, Personal Finance News - CNNMoney.com*. Web. 25 May 2009. *http://money.cnn.com/galleries/2007/fortune/0711/gallery.power_25.fortune/*.

"Phoenician Alphabet." *Phoenician Encyclopedia: A Bequest Unearthed, Phoenicia and the Phoenicians, Punic, Canaanites — Encyclopedia Phoeniciana*. Web. 6 June 2009. *http://phoenicia.org/alphabet.html*.

"Pixar Animation Studios — Company History." *Connecting Angel Investors and Entrepreneurs*. Web. 13 July 2009. *http://www.fundinguniverse.com/company-histories/Pixar-Animation-Studios-Company-History.html*.

"Pixar History." *Pixar Animation Studios*. Web. 12 July 2009. *http://www.pixar.com/companyinfo/history/index.html*.

Quittner, Josh. "Can Apple Survive Without Jobs? TIME." *Breaking News, Analysis, Politics, Blogs, News Photos, Video, Tech Reviews - TIME.com*. Web. 1 July 2009. *http://www.time.com/time/magazine/article/0,9171,1870502-2,00.html*.

"Redstone, Sumner -." *The Museum of Broadcast Communications*. Web. 15 July 2009. *http://www.museum.tv/eotvsection.php?entrycode=redstonesum*.

Ritholtz, Barry. "Jobs and Eisner - Barrons.com." *Financial Investment News - Stock Investing News - Investment*

News - *Barrons.com*. Web. 13 June 2009. *http://online .barrons.com/article/SB107550935532116897.html*.

"Rosetta Stone — Britannica Online Encyclopedia." *Encyclopedia - Britannica Online Encyclopedia*. Web. 15 June 2009. *http://www.britannica.com/EBchecked/topic/ 509988/Rosetta-Stone*.

Sandoval, Greg. "Craigslist CEO on how 'adult' section will change site | Digital Media - CNET News." *Technology News - CNET News*. Web. 14 July 2009. *http://news.cnet.com/8301-1023_3-10239947-93.html*.

Schlender, Brent. "25 most powerful people in business Steve Jobs (1) - FORTUNE." *Business, financial, personal finance news - CNNMoney.com*. Web. 1 July 2009. *http://money.cnn.com/galleries/2007/fortune/0711/gallery .power_25.fortune/*.

Serjeant, Jill. "NBC Ends Late Night Wars: Conan Is Out, Leno Is Back | Reuters." *Business & Financial News, Breaking US & International News | Reuters.com*. 21 Jan. 2010. Web. 28 May 2010. *http://www.reuters .com/article/idUSTRE60K30N20100121*.

"Sequoyah (Cherokee leader) — Britannica Online Encyclopedia." *Encyclopedia - Britannica Online Encyclopedia*. Web. 26 May 2009. *http://www.britannica.com/EBchecked/ topic/535250/Sequoyah*.

"Sequoyah." *Infoplease: Encyclopedia, Almanac, Atlas, Biographies, Dictionary, Thesaurus. Free online reference, research & homework help*. Infoplease.com. Web. 15 May 2009. *http://www.infoplease.com/ce6/people/A0844467 .html*.

Sequoyah Museum: The Sequoyah Birthplace Museum. Web. 26 May 2009. *http://www.sequoyahmuseum.org/*.

Stern, Meiera. "Pixar-Disney Merger Casts An Uncertain Spell - AppleMatters." *AppleMatters.com - A serious yet irreverent look at all things Apple*. Web. 13 June 2009. *http://www.applematters.com/article/pixar_disney_merger _casts_an_uncertain_spell/*.

Strohmeyer, Robert. "Are Baby Boomers Killing Facebook and Twitter? | Pew Internet & American Life Project." *Pew Internet & American Life Project*. Web. 15 July 2009. *http://www.pewinternet.org/Media-Mentions/2009/Are-Baby-Boomers-Killing-Facebook-and-Twitter.aspx*.

"Time Inc." *Time Warner*. Web. 20 June 2009. *http://www .timewarner.com/corp/businesses/detail/time_inc/index.html*.

"Time Warner: Who Owns What |." *Columbia Journalism Review*. Web. 15 June 2009. *http://www.cjr.org/ resources/index.php?c=timewarner*.

"Turner Broadcasting." *Time Warner*. Web. 20 June 2009. *http://www.timewarner.com/corp/businesses/detail/turner_ broadcasting/index.html*.

"Viacom: Who Owns What |." *Columbia Journalism Review*. Web. 1 July 2009. *http://www.cjr.org/resources/ index.php?c=viacom*.

"The Walt Disney Company - Company Description - Hoover's." *Company Information from Hoover's including business reports and profiles*. Web. 28 June 2009. *http://www.hoovers.com/disney/--ID__159434--/free-co-profile.xhtml*.

"The Walt Disney Company: Who Owns What |." *Columbia Journalism Review*. Web. 29 June 2009. *http://www.cjr.org/resources/index.php?c=disney*.

"Warner Bros. Entertainment." *Time Warner*. Web. 20 June 2009. *http://www.timewarner.com/corp/businesses/ detail/warner_bros/index.html*.

"Weaver, Sylvester (Pat) -." *The Museum of Broadcast Communications*. Web. 6 July 2009. *http://www.museum.tv/ eotvsection.php?entrycode=weaversylve*.

"What Happened to Alleged Craigslist Killer Philip Markoff? - Crimesider - CBS News." *Breaking News Headlines: Business, Entertainment & World News - CBS News*. Web. 28 May 2010. *http://www.cbsnews.com/ 8301-504083_162-20006029-504083.html*.

Wilson, Carol. "Telco TV: Online video, prime-time TV both growing." *TELEPHONY Online | Convergence, Connectivity, Clarity*. Web. 6 June 2009. *http://telephony online.com/iptv/news/telco-tv-online-video-1111/*.

Winn, Marie. "The Plug-In Drug by Marie Winn." *Marie Winn's Home Page*. Web. 26 July 2009. *http://www .mariewinn.com/plugin.htm*.

Wolf, Gary. "Why Craigslist Is Such a Mess." *Wired News*. Web. 27 May 2010. *http://www.wired.com/ entertainment/theweb/magazine/17-09/ff_craigslist ?currentPage=all*.

"The Writing Code |." *PBS*. Web. 1 June 2009. *http:// www.pbs.org/thewritingcode/*.

YouTube - Broadcast Yourself. Web. 22 May 2009. *http: //www.youtube.com/t/fact_sheet*.

"YouTube Facts & Figures (history & Statistics) | Website Monitoring Blog." *Website Monitoring - Availability Monitoring by SITEIMPULSE*. Web. 28 May 2010. *http://www.website-monitoring.com/blog/2010/05/17/ youtube-facts-and-figures-history-statistics/*.

MASS COMMUNICATION EFFECTS

Raul Reis

Chapter Objectives:

◆ Understand the impact of the Payne Fund Studies on mass media research

◆ Explain how researcher's ideas about the effects of mass media changed over time

◆ List and describe different theories of mass communication effects

◆ Describe how violence in media affects society, specifically children

◆ Understand the process of mass media research

Introduction

Have you ever wondered what influences have helped to shape the person you are today? Your family, friends, education, and socio-economic status have undoubtedly had some affect on the way you think, feel, or act in certain situations. You may feel you have a quick temper because your family fought a lot while you were young. Or you may believe you have a hard time concentrating on schoolwork because you didn't get enough help with reading while in elementary school. Have you ever considered that some of your feelings and actions are affected by mass media? Perhaps your short temper is the result of violent video games or your short attention span the result of excessive television watching.

Over the last century, communication scholars have participated in extensive research and analysis to determine how mass media affects us as individuals and as a society and how it will shape our future. Still the influences and consequences of mass media are not fully understood. It is clear that mass media affects us in some way, but *how* and to what degree is yet to be determined. In this chapter we will explore the history of mass communication effects and examine the findings and theories of communication scholars that explain how the mass media impacts our lives.

History of Mass Media Research

The impact of mass media on the public has been a subject of interest for communication scholars for many years. From the rise of print publications to the gradual introduction of radio, film, television, and the Internet, the effects of mass media on society have been closely study by psychologists, sociologists, and social psychologists.

PIONEERS IN MEDIA RESEARCH

Pioneering researchers from the early 20th century created theories that laid the groundwork for much of how we conceptualize the effects of media today. Charles Horton Cooley was one of the first social psychologists to establish such theories on the effects of mass media. In works such as *Human Nature and Social Order* (1902) and *Social Organization* (1909), Cooley attempted to explain the role of communication in society. In his studies, Cooley unveiled two opposing ideas. On one hand, Cooley saw new media as a way to encourage individuality by supporting ideas and customs that follow a person's self-interest. For example, if a person has political views that are not popular in his or her community, media can introduce that person to other like-minded individuals and give validation to unique ideas. On the other hand, new media limits the distribution of new ideas and customs, therefore leading to assimilation. For example, the type of language used in a widely distributed newspaper may, over time, become accepted as the universal dialect for a region, and all local dialects may disappear. Cooley explains that people have an innate desire to be alike and new media gives people information on how others talk, dress, and feel.

Cooley solved his paradox by determining that there are two different kinds of people: one that embraces isolation and one that is drawn to choice. Additionally, Cooley feels modern media fosters isolation and obliterates choice. Meaning, over time media will gradually eliminate the things that make us unique as individuals, communities, races, and nations. This process creates a universal understanding that although individuals may look, dress, or behave differently, we are all still extremely similar. For example, by watching a television show with homosexual characters such as *Will & Grace*, viewers can learn that homosexuals deal with the same life issues as heterosexuals. This type of effect can have a positive impact on society, as it promotes tolerance and acceptance. However, it can also have a negative effect. Since we learn about such a large variety of people, we only have the capacity to develop a superficial understanding and concern for other people. We are unable to learn about others in detail because we are overloaded with information.[1] Therefore, while a syndicated sitcom may help heterosexuals learn to view homosexuals as equals, heterosexuals may never take the time learn about the personal and political issues such as gay rights that are important to the homosexual community. Cooley's theories were mostly based on the effects of print media. However, his studies inspired other researchers as new types of media emerged.

THE START OF EXTENSIVE STUDY

During the 1920's the motion picture industry propelled itself into American culture. With the introduction of full length feature films like Charlie Chaplin's *The Kid* (1921) and *The Gold Rush* (1925), viewing a movie at a local theater became a common pastime for adults and children. The experience of sitting in a theater and watching a movie was like no other media at the time. Unlike newspapers and books, which only appeal to one sense, the movie-going experience activated multiple senses. The growing popularity of motion pictures caused the Motion Picture Research Council to question the amount of influence this new medium was having on audiences. This concern prompted one of the largest research projects ever conducted in an effort to understand the relationship between a medium and a specific audience. Established in 1928, the **Payne Fund Studies** was a series of 13 studies conducted to examine the various aspects of potential effects of motion pictures on individuals, specifically children. The studies were funded by grants from the Payne Fund and were executed by some of the most well-know social scientists of the day. The

Payne Fund Studies focused on children because at the time millions of children were frequently attending movies—typically more than one a week. The Saturday matinee was a fun and inexpensive form of entertainment for young boys and girls, as many families did not have radios or televisions in their homes at the time.

Each of the Payne Fund studies was developed to address a specific question. To determine the type of content displayed in motion pictures, qualitative analysis of 1500 movies, produced between 1920 and 1930, was used to place movies in specific categories of content. Ten categories were established: children, history, comedy, crime, love, sex, mystery, travel, war, and social propaganda. The results showed over three-fourths of films dealt with only three thematic categories—crime, sex, and love. A majority of films also displayed the use of tobacco and liquor (materials that were illegal during the period of prohibition). To determine who was viewing this content, census and survey data was used to identify the ages and sex of individuals attending movies.[2]

Well-known educator Edgar Dale studied the movie attendances of over 50 Ohio communities in order to estimate the size and composition of the audiences. He used this information to project estimates for the entire nation. Dale found that children five to eight years were attending movies on a regular basis and school-age children were frequent moviegoers—attending more movies per week than adults. Dale also determined that boys attended more often than girls.[3]

Once researchers understood the type of content involved in motion pictures and who was exposed to it, the next step was to determine if audiences actually retain the information embedded in motion picture content. Over three years, nearly 3,000 children and adults were tested on various types of information presented in films. They found that even children as young as eight years old acquired a substantial number of ideas from movies. In fact, retention rates were high among all age groups. Subjects were tested at six weeks and again at three months after seeing the films. In some cases, subjects tested six months after seeing the films showed even higher levels of retention. This supported the concept of the **sleeper effect**—the idea that information can sit dormant in our subconscious and emerge over time. Investigators concluded that movies provided a special learning format that caused an unusually high retention of factual information when compared to the acquisition of facts in standard laboratory experiments.

One of the more sophisticated investigations in the Payne Fund Studies involved the process of determining whether these retained ideas create an emotional response. Researchers used laboratory studies to first measure the emotional levels of a group of children before the group viewed a series of films. The children's emotional levels were then measured after they viewed the films. Researchers' test found that most children displayed emotional responses such as anger, fear, sadness, and excitement after viewing the movies. The studies determined that the increase in emotional responses was directly related to the content in the viewed films. Meaning, motion pictures create an emotional response in children.

The most challenging part of the Payne Fund Studies was determining whether motion pictures caused children to act on their increased emotions. Through extensive study, researchers found that children who frequently attended movies also demonstrated declining morals, delinquent behavior, lower intelligence, and a number of other factors. These results lead to a complex question: does frequent movie attendance lead to unsophisticated behavior or do unsophisticated children go frequently to the movies? Unfortunately, the authors of the studies were unable to answer the question. They concluded that there was no simple cause-and-effect relationship between movie attendance and delinquent behavior. They did determine that there is a reciprocal relationship—movies do have an effect on children, but the children that are most likely to attend the most violent and aggressive movies are also most likely to participate in delinquent behavior.

While the Payne Fund Studies were unable to find definitive answers to all of the questions the studies posed, the series of studies did make the groundbreaking discovery that adults and children learn from media and that what they learn affects how they live their lives. This discovery changed the way the academic community viewed communication and new media. A number of the Payne Fund studies documented effects that would be restudied in research on other forms of media such as radio and television in later decades.

WAR OF THE WORLDS

By the time the Payne Fund Studies published its findings on the effects of motion pictures, a new form of media was being examined. During the 1930s radio became an increasingly popular outlet for news and entertainment for American families. Millions of listeners tuned in each evening to hear news reports and radio programs. In 1938, one particular radio programmed changed the way social psychologists viewed media's influence over human behavior. On October 30, the CBS radio aired an episode of *The Mercury Theater of the Air* in which theater director Orson Welles adapted HG Wells's classic science-fiction novel *The War of the Worlds*. The novel's plot involved the invasion of Martians and the destruction of major cities. In order to condense the novel into a one-hour radio broadcast, much of the introduction was told through fictional news bulletins that "interrupted" regularly scheduled programs.

About 12 million listeners tuned in for the show, however some listeners were not aware the program was fictional. The production value for Welles' broadcast was top-notch for the time. It had excellent special effects, professional actors, and realistic dialog, and in turn, caused many uninformed listeners to believe the invasion was real. They evacuated their homes, flooded police stations with concerned calls, and spread alarm among friends and family members. Reality eventually sank in after a few hours, and the radio network came under heavy attack. CBS issued an apology for the program. Soon after, the Federal Communications Commission (FCC) published guidelines against the practice of mixing fictional stories and news information. During the weeks following Welles' broadcast, press stories described numerous accounts of terror among listeners. While the exact number of people involved in this mass hysteria is unclear, it is estimated that as many as 6 million people believed Martians were invading the planet at the time of the broadcast.

The confusion that *The War of the Worlds* created was a dramatic demonstration of the power of radio. Hadley Cantril and a group of fellow broadcast researchers at Princeton University were compelled to understand what caused so many people to panic when the circumstances of the report were so unlikely to take place. Through interviews and observation, the group attempted to identify the individual characteristics that caused a person to panic or not to panic. This was the first time communication researchers describe the types of people and the types of conditions that lead to panic. While Cantril's early studies supported the idea that individuals with a low level of education were most likely to believe the broadcast was real, his later studies revealed the phenomenon was more about a person's suggestibility than education. The characteristics of high suggestibility were found to be a lack of self-confidence, a sense of fatalism, a tremendous amount of personal worry, and strong religious beliefs. While these characteristics alone do not explain a listener's reaction to the radio program, together they identify the individuals most likely to perceive the broadcast as a critical situation and are therefore more susceptible to panic.[4]

MEDIA AS A SUPER POWER

Cantril's conceptualization of media effects focused primarily on the psychology rather than the sociological aspects of the relationship between the media and society. During the early stages of media research (1900 to 1940) many thought media was a powerful force and could directly affect the views and behaviors of the public. Political scientist and communication theorist Harold Lasswell formed the analogy of the hypodermic needle off of this belief. The **hypodermic needle model** suggests that media can "inject" the public with whatever thoughts and opinions the media manipulators want inscribed.[5] The concept is far-fetched by today's standards, but at the time the direct access media had to the public was new and unfamiliar. For the first time, messages could enter people's homes and workplaces and release information that was unfiltered by human interaction.

Because researchers felt the public was highly susceptible to the influence of media, they attributed the Nazi's gain of power to the extensive and intelligent use of radio, film, and print media. In Germany during the 1930s, the Nazi political party used posters, pamphlets, and radio programs to promote the party's ideas and agenda. Mass communication played an important role in both World War I and

The Public Opinion Quarterly

The American Association of Public Opinion Research (AAPOR) was founded in 1947 by a group of researchers interested in understanding the public's response to media. The organization was founded under the idea that if we can develop a better understanding of how the public feels, we can develop and implement programs that promote peaceful living. The AAPOR developed the *Public Opinion Quarterly*, which became an official journal in 1948. It was the first university journal on mass communication. Leading researchers such as Harold D. Lasswell, George H. Gallup, and Paul F. Lazarsfeld were central to the advancement of the AAPOR and the history public opinion research.[7]

World War II, as many nations, including the United States, used **political propaganda**—widely distributed pieces of communication used to harness support for political objectives—to encourage patriotism among one's own country or hatred for an enemy. Lasswell published many works on the subject of propaganda and politics, and was eventually given the task of organizing the Wartime Communication Study for the US Library of Congress. He became famous for posing the question—"who says what in which channel to whom with what effect?—in his studies.[6] This question, which was essentially a formula, prompted researchers to examine the various facets of media effects research instead of focusing on how one thing affects another.

MEDIA AS A LIMITED POWER

After the end of both world wars, communication researchers began to change their views on the power of media. New types of studies demonstrated that media did not have as much influence over society's actions and opinions as a whole as previously thought. During the 1940s, Austria-born American sociology Paul Felix Lazarsfeld and his colleagues at Columbia University pioneered the use of scientific survey to understand the influence of mass media on public opinion. He was interested in examining the impact of newspapers, magazines, radio, and motion pictures on the voting habits of Americans. Lazarsfeld conducted a large-scale study that used statistical information to gauge the change in the public's views. Initially Lazarsfeld thought that exposure to mass media messages could sway a voter's decision. However, the results of his study determined that media had little effect on voter's opinions. He found that political party affiliation was far more influential than media content. While most voters follow the campaigns through media sources such as newspaper and radio, they gave most of their attention to the content that supports their political affiliation.

This concept gave rise to the selective perception theory. The **selective perception theory** states that individuals respond and perceive media messages differently, based mostly on their own personal needs and interests. Instead of affecting groups the same way, the effects of media messages would be personalized, depending on what people *selected* to retain. This process of selective recall was basically in place to gratify the individual needs of each audience member.

Later, Lazarsfeld joined forces with researcher Elihu Katz and used the selective perception theory to develop the **uses and gratifications theory,** which placed even greater influence on personal needs and individual uses of the media to define how messages affected audiences. As the name implies, uses and gratifications theory places great emphasis on the personal gratification each individual gets from the media to explain why and how we select the messages we consume and how those messages affect us.[8]

Lazarsfeld and Katz's findings helped them develop the **two-step theory.** This theory proposed that media messages first influenced economic and political power elites, or opinion leaders, who later propagated them through interpersonal contact or by using the media themselves. Thus, instead of directly affecting the masses, messages were first processed by opinion leaders, who gave them their own spin before they were disseminated to a larger public. Popular in the 1950s and 1960s, this theory lost some of its power once media channels multiplied and popular access to this multitude of channels became more of a reality.[9]

The Technological School

In addition to theories suggesting that mass communication products have a *direct* effect on consumers, there are others proposing that this influence is significant but *indirect*. One such group of theorists has focused its research efforts on the impact of the media themselves rather than on the messages they convey. These researchers have been termed the "medium theorists," and together form what could be called *the technological school*. Proponents of the technological school do not dismiss the idea that particular messages may have various effects on particular individuals, audiences, or behaviors. They contend, however, that the most substantial impact of mass communication lies in the more general and indirect effects of different communication technologies (including writing, printing, and electronic media) on modes of thought, patterns of human interaction, and the structure of societal institutions.

Because of its origins, this line of thought is sometimes also called the Toronto School.

This emphasis can be summed up by the saying that "the medium is the message." Marshall McLuhan, author of this memorable phrase, was one of the earliest, and certainly the most widely known of the medium theorists, and he and his mentor, Harold Innis, did much to highlight this point of view. Innis argues that Western culture has been deeply influenced by the spatial bias and cognitive processes associated with print media, which he believes has promoted cultural complexity, but also confusion and alienation.

By saying that "the medium is the message," McLuhan was attributing to any particular medium (books, television, and now the Internet) the power not only to shape and influence the message itself, but also the power to determine how the audience would interpret that message. If you think about the producers' side of the mass media, when putting together their media products TV journalists and documentarians will be much more influenced by the power of the image than will be newspaper journalists working on the same story. In this sense, much of a journalist's message is shaped by the medium he or she is working in. On the other hand, the medium is the message also means that, as audience members, our perception of a message, or a news story to stay with the same example, will be extremely influenced by the medium through which that message is reaching us.

McLuhan shared with Innis the conviction that communication media are extensions of the human mind and body. He considered modern electronic media to be a sort of extension of the human nervous system, an extension that circles the globe and establishes a network of interpersonal involvements that he referred to as a "global village" an aphorism that has been widely used to describe the Internet, which was widely adopted and popularized only decades after McLuhan coined that emblematic phrase.

Joshua Meyrowitz and Manuel Castells are other thinkers who have made major contributions to the technological school of thought in media effects. Meyrowitz's book *No Sense of Place* (1985) examines the influence of electronic media on the construction of particular kinds of cultural environments in which our roles and behavior patterns are played out. In Castells' massive three-volume book *The Information*

Age (1997), Castells deals with the social, political, economic, and cultural impact of the so-called information society on our daily lives. In the trilogy's second volume "The Power of Identity," he focuses particularly on how new media and new technologies are changing the ways in which we organize and define ourselves.

A MODERN LOOK AT MEDIA EFFECTS

Towards the end of the 20th century, some researchers started to look at media effects from a new angle. They began to examine not just how the public is affected by the media, but how the pubic *thinks* they are affected by the media. Born in the early 1980s, the **third-person effects hypothesis** states that people tend to believe media messages influence others more than themselves. It claims that as audience members, we resist to the idea that we can be directly affected by messages, and instead tend to believe that other people are always more influenced than we are. This hypothesis is still very favored in mass communication research, and many studies have been published that tend to confirm it. Born out of the third-person effects hypothesis, a more recent model, called the **indirect-effects model** states that people tend to perceive the effect that media messages have on others and then react to their perception. For example, we would hear so much about a popular show such as *Dancing with the Stars* or *American Idol*, that even if we are not fans we would assume that those shows are very influential on audiences, and might be tempted to "jump on the bandwagon" so that we won't be left out.[10]

Important Issues in Media Effects

In psychological theory, **social learning** involves learning behavior that is controlled by environmental influences rather than by inherent or internal forces. Modeling is a typical result of social learning. **Modeling** is a type of learning that occurs when

an individuals observes the actions of others to gain information on how to behave. You probably participate in modeling on a daily basis. In class you may notice your peers diligently taking notes. Regardless of whether or not you use class notes to study, you may start taking notes simply because it seems like appropriate behavior for the setting. While it seems bizarre, many of the choices you make every day are based on modeling the behavior of others rather than making an internal decision. For example, you look out the window of your home and notice that most people outside are wearing jackets. Without going outside to test the temperature for yourself, you decide that since everyone is wearing jackets it must be cold and you put on a jacket before leaving the house as well.

Children are active participants in modeling. American psychologist Albert Bandura was one of the pioneers of modeling theories. He conducted numerous studies showing that when children observe the actions of others they learn many forms of conduct. Behaviors such as sharing, aggression, cooperation, social interaction, and disappointment are picked up from the individuals in their environment.

VIOLENCE

Bandura's insights into the learning habits of children lead him and many other psychologists to question the effects of the media, more specifically television, on the behavior of children. If children learn to be aggressive or introverted from the people in their environment, it is possible that they can learn similar behavior from the people on their television set.[12] Research on the effects of violence in the media has been controversial. Two types of theories have been proposed. One suggests that a child's urge to participate in violent behavior can be diverted by watching violent behavior on television. In other words witnessing violence lessens the drive to commit violence. Under this theory, a young girl who watches a cartoon character play a violent prank on another character will be less likely to play a violent prank on a classmate. The second theory suggests that viewing violent behavior actually increases the drive to participate in violent activities. Following Bandura's idea of modeling, children model their behavior after the images they see on

Bandura's BoBo Doll

In 1961, Albert Bandura conducted an experiment to study the effects of viewing violence on children. Bandura used 36 boys and 36 girls enrolled in Stanford University Nursery School whose ages ranged from 3 to 5 years old. The subjects were divided into eight experimental groups and 24 subjects were put into a control group. The experimental groups were shown a video that displayed an adult model hitting, throwing, and kicking an inflatable doll called a Bobo doll, as well as using aggressive language. After viewing the video, the children were left in a room by themselves with the same BoBo doll and other toys. The children were told all of the toys were there for them to play with. The study showed that the majority of the children who were exposed to the aggressive video played with the Bobo doll and repeated much of the same violent behavior and language displayed in the video. Other parts of Bandura's study showed that the Bobo doll video encouraged some subjects to participate in other aggressive acts such as gun play and harsh language.[11]

TV. Under this theory, the same little girl that witnessed the prank simulated in a cartoon would be more likely to initiate a similar prank on a classmate.

Violence in the media, especially on television, has been a concern since the medium became popular, in the 1950s. A great deal of effects research has focused on violence in the media, where researchers have gone back and forth between a more critical position, which says that media violence has a great influence on causing aggressive behavior on consumers; and a "limited effects" position, which is still concerned with the impact of violent messages but sees their influence as more moderate.

In the late 1960s two governmental commissions—the National Commission on the Causes and Prevention of Violence, and the Surgeon General's Scientific Advisory Committee on Television and Social Behavior—undertook a series of research studies. On the basis of laboratory experiments and field studies, the Surgeon General's committee concluded, somewhat cautiously, that viewing violence on television contributes to violent or aggressive behavior in viewers. Just how much this influence really amounts to is still a point of disagreement for specialists. In general, most studies have supported that there is a causal relationship between watching violent programming and acting aggressively.

In the past 15 years, the discussion about violence in the media has gained even more strength on the basis of the popularity of video games and hip-hop music. In the early 1990s, Congress once again focused its attention on violent rap lyrics, denouncing artists such as Ice T for what they saw as the aggression and incitement contained in lyrics for rap songs such as "Cop Killer." In the late-1990s, the attention shifted to the violence in video games. Incidents such as the Columbine and Arkansas school shootings led parents, educators, and other groups to argue that the extreme violence contained in some video games was influencing children to behave more aggressively.

Violence in the media is a compelling and contentious subject for both consumers and researchers. Some feel the media is often used as a scapegoat for other causes of violence in our society. It is often easier to blame a popular video game for an increase in firearm related deaths than blame the government's policy on gun control. Still no person can deny that there is a substantial amount of violence in the media today. The average child under the age of 14 is exposed to 11,000 murders on television in their lifetime.[13] According to The National Television Violence Study, nearly 2 out of 3 TV programs contained some violence, and average about 6 violent acts per hour.[14]

Many theories have been developed to explain the various effects of mediated violence on audiences. The **catharsis theory** claims media outlets such as television can ease children's urges to participate in violent behavior. According to the theory, mediated violence allows aggressive people to discharge their anger vicariously through the media images, therefore lessening aggressive behavior. The concept of the catharsis theory dates back to Aristotle and the ancient Greeks. In his work *Politics*, Aristotle stated that viewing tragic plays allows people to release emotions related to negative feelings such as grief, rage, and fear.

Other theories of media effects claim that media changes society's perception of violence. Television is often used to express the collective stories of our culture. From the life of spoiled high school students in California to the gritty intricacies of the judicial system, many television shows, whether fact or fiction, attempt to interpret a cultural story. The **cultivation theory** views television as a main source of storytelling for heavy viewers (those who watch more than four hours of television a day). Because these viewers look to television instead of their own experiences to shape their views of the world, their beliefs about society are warped and often less favorable than reality. This theory grew out of the work done by George Gerbner and his colleagues in the Annenberg School of Communications at the University of Pennsylvania. Since the late 1960s, Gerbner and his group have measured the amount of violence in prime-time television programming and tried to correlate that to the perception that television viewers hold about "real-life" violence. Gerbner associates this altered perception with

mean world syndrome, a condition in which a person interprets the world as a far more dangerous place than it is in reality. For example, individuals who watch numerous hours of dramatic entertainment such as *CSI: Miami* or *Law & Order* may feel that the murder rate in this country is much higher than it is in reality. By producing a yearly Violence Profile, the group, also known as the Cultural Indicators Project, tries to establish a causal link between watching television and how we perceive reality.

Cultivation theory proposes that in the long term, television "cultivates" or shapes the way in which we see the world, creating a homogenous and fearful society. Findings from this research tend to support the view that the more television (or violent programming) people watch, the more distorted their perception of the real world or real-life violence will be.

A study done by the American Academy of Pediatrics focused its attention on violent video games, noting that the most popular video games tend to have "behavioral scripts" in which players not only are rewarded for their violent actions, but also learn to act in a way that goes from choosing a violent scenario to resolving that conflict through the use of violence. Video games have been accused of encouraging children and young teens to commit real-life crimes, and in some cases they are used as a form of defense in court (see side bar).

While the judicial system is not ready to accept violent video games as the primary cause of violent behavior, many professionals are. David Walsh, a child psychologist, believes that exposure to violent video games can cause teenagers to participate in violent behavior. He supports his beliefs with research conducted by the National Institutes of Health, which shows the brains of teenagers are not fully developed. According to Walsh, the impulse control center of the brain, the section that helps us think ahead, control urges, and consider consequences, is under construction during the teenage years. When this low level of control is combined with a continuous flow of violent images, Walsh believes teenagers are capable of violent behavior without fully understanding the consequences. Walsh admits that other risk factors such as a troubled upbringing can contribute to violent behavior, but violent video games heighten the impulses of those troubled teenagers.[15]

Grand Theft Causes Grand Crime?

Shortly after the shoot 'em up video game Grand Theft Auto released its third edition, the same violence glamorized in the video game emerged in real life on the streets of Fayette, Alabama. On June 9, 2003, 18-year-old Devin Moore was charged with three counts of murder for allegedly shooting two police officers and a dispatcher while fleeing a police station. Moore was in the process of being booked for auto theft when he grabbed an officer's gun, fired fatal shots, and escaped in a stolen police cruiser. After he was arrested and arraigned, Moore pleaded not guilty by reason of mental defect. He blamed the combination of the abuse he endured as a child and the influence of playing Grand Theft Auto for his violent behavior.[16] On August 2005, a jury determined Moore was guilty as charged. While the jury did not believe that the video caused Moore to murder three people, the victims' relatives did. Attorney Jack Thompson filed a civil lawsuit on behalf of the relatives of the shooting victims against Sony Corp., the makers of Grand Theft Auto. The wrongful death suit claimed that Sony and other video game retailers were liable for the deaths of the officers because they created and distributed a game that encourages violent behavior. After a lengthy process, the civil case was dismissed.

A more recent study focused on violent images in music videos, especially music videos made available online by cable channels such as MTV, BET, VH1, and Country.com. The study found that 185 out of 951 videos analyzed (16.4%) contained acts of violence. Although the proportion found was relatively low, the author of the article was troubled by the kind of violence portrayed, where 76% of all violent acts were assisted by the use of weapons. The study also found that hard rock (72% of videos) and hip-hop/rap (48% of videos) were the musical genres where violence was more often committed.[17]

The vast majority of studies analyzing violence in the media point toward three general areas of concern:

1. *Increased levels of aggressiveness.* Children and teenagers, especially boys, who are exposed to heavy levels of media violence, tend to perceive real-life violence as the natural, accepted way to resolve conflicts. Most of these children also tend to act more aggressively when they are playing or having other types of social interaction[18].

2. *"Mean world" syndrome.* A steady diet of violent media over a long period of time tends to cultivate in users the perception that the real world is a "mean and violent" place, which might lead to feelings of anxiety, alienation, and depression.

3. *Desensitization.* Refers to the widely tested hypothesis that constant exposure to violent messages might lead to a loss of sympathy for victims, less proactive involvement in preventing/stopping violence, and a general perception of violence as a normal occurrence.

SEX AND PORNOGRAPHY

The production and consumption of sexually explicit material such as books, magazines, and videos is a worldwide business of enormous dimensions. The

Internet and other digital technologies such as DVDs added new ways to make pornographic material even more widespread and accessible. But while many consumers enjoy a regular diet of such material, others find it distasteful, obscene or corrupting.

With a wide range of views concerning what is offensive and what is not, what is pornographic and what is simply erotic, what has artistic merit and what does not, it is obviously difficult to formulate definitions or a widely accepted concept of obscenity. Even the courts have a very hard time determining clear limits or legal concepts that could be applied across the board.

Such concerns have led Congress to dedicate a whole section of the Telecommunications Act of 1996 to the issue of pornography on the Internet. The courts have subsequently struck down some of these rules as unconstitutional and conflicting with the protections warranted by the First Amendment.

Despite the legal ramifications, the discussion rages on about the potential harmful effects of pornographic messages in the mass media. Research on the functions and effects of sexually explicit material in the media began in earnest with the establishment in 1970 of the Presidential Commission on Obscenity and Pornography. Since that time a good deal of study has been done on the various aspects of this issue, including the influence of pornography on the image and treatment of women and on the relationship between the sexes, on the physiological effects of viewing such material, and on the possible relationship between pornography and violent crimes such as rape and murder and other forms of aggressive behavior.

More recently, a great deal of criticism has focused on the depiction of women on hip-hop lyrics and music videos. Many feminists and other media critics have argued that those lyrics and videos often degrade women and present them as subservient to men. Others have focused their attention on popular video games, which they accuse of objectifying and stimulating violence and aggressive behavior toward women, many times presented in a very sexual manner.

Analyses of the content of pornographic materials have provided some evidence that messages of the supremacy of men over women are often present. Other research indicates that viewing pornography can contribute to attitudes of increased acceptance of violence toward women. Other studies, however, show that sexually explicit material portraying men and women as partners or equals can educate and help to reduce antisocial attitudes. Although some studies indicate a relationship between high rates of availability and/or consumption of pornography and high rates of rape, a causal relationship has never been found, so it would be premature to say, on the basis of this research, whether, or how, one causes the other.

A study done recently showed that 83% of the most popular TV shows among teenagers in 2001–2002 had sexual content, while on average each hour of programming contained 6.7 scenes with sexual references.[19] In the same study, only 1% of shows containing sexual behavior focused on the risks or negative aspects of it, while only 3% of scenes analyzed discussed sexually transmitted diseases or pregnancy. A similar study argues that exposure to high dosages of sexual content might not only stimulate sexual behavior in children, but also artificially age them, accelerating their developmental stages and making children act between 9 and 17 months older than their actual age.[20]

ETHICS AND ANTISOCIAL BEHAVIOR

Other concerns with potentially harmful effects of media come from those who worry that some messages might be eroding traditional ethical values, thus stimulating antisocial behavior. Some media critics argue that negative media messages are so pervasive that they might be creating a sense of alienation and frustration in younger generations, manifested in a disregard for commonly accepted cultural traditions and societal rules, and leading to apathy, cynicism and nihilism. Religious leaders often raise similar concerns.

Other critics note that pervasive and widespread media use might lead to a society that places excessive importance on materialism, appearances, and the consumption of material goods. These critics see the preponderance of commercial media messages as an indication that mass communication has lost its power to educate and socialize, or at least that younger generations are being socialized into a community that sees them only as potential buyers. Many media literacy programs have been developed and adopted by educators concerned with these potentially harmful media effects.

Education and Socialization

Questions concerning the educational, cultural or social impact of mass media have been discussed and debated for centuries. In ancient Greece, Plato warned that writing weakens the mind and destroys the memory. In the fifteenth century, similar complaints were leveled against printing, though many people defended it as an unprecedented means for distributing and increasing knowledge. From the birth of electronic media on, the focus has been on television.

Studies have shown that people who spend a great deal of time watching television have lower Intelligence Quotients or IQs than people who spend less time doing so. However, more recent studies have shown that children who spend a limited amount of time watching television (two hours per day, on average), actually perform better academically than children who do not watch TV at all.[21] It is uncertain from both sets of studies if there is a causal relationship between television viewing and intellectual performance. Our understanding of the relationship between reading behavior and TV viewing also remains uncertain. Some studies have found a positive correlation over time among younger viewers, while other studies have shown that adults who spend no time reading watch much more television than those who read. Similarly, the nature of the connection between viewing and both academic performance and educational aspiration has not yet been unraveled; so many factors—such as grade level, gender, television content, and type of school subject—seem to be implicated in this complex relationship.[22]

On the positive side, researchers have also studied the effects of so-called educational programming, such as *Sesame Street*, and found that not only the content of these programs can help children strengthen certain cognitive abilities such as problem solving, reasoning, language, and arithmetic skills, but also that the form or style of presentation can stimulate the development of other important mental operations. The research also suggests that the educational impact of television viewing is affected by the nature of the family and social relationships prevailing in the child's environment.[23]

Quite a bit of media research has examined the ways in which people, including children, use communication messages in the socialization process. Researchers have investigated the influence of media such as television, music, movies, and videogames on the development of personal identity and on the association of certain attitudes and behavior patterns with particular sexes, ages, races, and occupations.[24] If so much of what we know about the world comes from the media, researchers are interested in finding out how much impact the content of these messages have on the socialization process, our personalities, and the development of our worldviews.

In general, media messages tend to reflect and perpetuate gender and ethnic stereotypes, for example. Scientists want to know how much of these stereotypes affect our perception of reality. Many of the men and women characters appearing on television present somewhat stereotyped male and female images. Various studies have shown that children, who are heavy television viewers, when asked whether certain activities or occupations would be associated with women or with men, gave answers more in line with television stereotypes than did lighter viewers.

Research also indicates, however, that programs with characters in atypical occupational roles can educate children away from the traditional sexual stereotypes. Additionally, it has been found that boys almost always choose male characters as ideal role models, and that girls sometimes choose female characters but also often choose male ones.[25]

A similar situation happens with ethnic stereotypes. Content analyses of television programming have shown the lack of ethnic diversity on mainstream television programs, as well as the presence of harmful ethnic stereotypes, or yet the association of particular ethnicities with certain occupations. Studies have shown that people who are heavy television viewers, or who rely heavily on television for information about the world, tend to associate some ethnic minorities to stereotypical behaviors presented on television.

Careers in the Field

The career of a researcher may not seem very exciting when compared to that of a television news anchor, advertising copywriter, or other high profile positions involving mass media, however, the work of a researcher can unveil some thrilling theories that affect the way the whole world perceives media. Researchers that exam the effects of mass media on society typically have degrees in sociology or psychology. They may work for private organizations, academic institutions, or large corporate conglomerates.

A person interested in sociology and computer science may enjoy a career as a research assistant at a telecommunications firm. Through various methods of research, such as conducting surveys, observing real life situations, creating laboratory simulations, or studying historical documents, a telecommunications researcher can learn how people react to new technology in media. This information can effect the way cellular communications companies design and release their products. It can also effect a city government's decision to install WiFi in all city buildings.

Because researchers study why we behave a certain way and the forces that motivate our actions, their findings provide answers to important questions. Does text messaging harm our language skills? Does prolonged use of the Internet cause children to be antisocial? While as a researcher you may not be able to respond to all questions with definitive answers, you can uncover interesting revolutions that better our understanding of how media affects our lives.[26]

Chapter Summary

◆ The Payne Fund Study was the first large scale study of media effects
◆ In the 1940, researchers started to look at the sociological and psychological aspects of media effects
◆ Children adapt skills through social learning, and are therefore susceptible to media images
◆ Violence in television is major issue in media research

Glossary

catharsis theory—a theory that claims media outlets such as television can ease children's urges to participate in violent behavior

cultivation theory—a theory that views television as a main source of storytelling for heavy viewers

hypodermic needle model—a theory that suggests that media can "inject" the public with whatever thoughts and opinions the media manipulators want inscribed

indirect-effects model—a theory that states people tend to perceive the effect that media messages has on others and then react to their perception

mean world syndrome—a condition in which a person interprets the world as a far more dangerous place that it is in reality

modeling—a type of learning that occurs when an individuals observes the actions of others to gain information on how to behave

payne fund studies—a series of 13 studies conducted to examine the various aspects of potential effects of motion pictures on individuals, specifically children

political propaganda—a widely distributed pieces of communication used to harness support for political objectives

social learning—the process of learning behavior that is controlled by environmental influences rather than by inherent or internal forces

selective perception theory—a theory that states that individuals respond and perceive media messages differently, based mostly on their own personals needs and interests

two-step theory—a theory proposed that media messages first influenced economic and political power elites, or opinion leaders, who later propagated them through interpersonal contact or by using the media themselves

third-person effects hypothesis—A theory that states that people tend to believe media messages influence more others than themselves

uses and gratifications theory—a theory that placed even greater influence on personal needs and individual uses of the media to define how messages affected audiences

Discussion Questions

1. How does media affect the way you live your life?
2. How does media both encourage and discourage individuality?
3. What are you thoughts on the hypodermic needle theory? Do you think media has the ability to "inject" people with ideas?
4. Do you think violence in television can cause violent behavior in children?
5. Think about the two step theory. Do you think most people get the majority of their information directly from media sources or do they base their opinions off of the opinions of others?

Supplemental Web Sites

National Youth Violence Prevention:
http://www.safeyouth.org/scripts/faq/mediaviol-stats.asp
Statistics on violence in the media.
American Association of Public Opinion Research:
http://www.aapor.org/
Facts and statistics on public opinions.
Video: Bandura's BoBo Doll Experiment
http://video.google.com/videoplay?docid=-4586465813762682933
Video footage of Bandura's subjects.

Endnotes

1 John Downing, Denis McQuail, Ellen Wartella, *The SAGE Handbook of Media Studies* Thousand Oaks: California, 2004.
2 Garth S. Jowett, Ian C. Jarvie, Kathryn H. Fuller, *Children and the Movies: Media Influence and the Payne Fund Controversy* Cambridge Press January 1996.
3 Shearon Lowery, Melvin Lawrence DeFleur *Milestones in Mass Communication Research: Media Effects* Longman Publishers USA, 1995

4 Hadley Cantril, Hazel Gaudet, *The Invasion from Mars: A Study in the Psychology of Panic*, Princeton: Princeton University Press, 1940.
5 Carrol J. Glynn, Susan Herbst, Garrett J. OKeefe, Robert Shapiro, *Public Opinion* Westview Press
6 Armand Mattelart, Michele Mattelart, James A Cohen, Susan Gruenheck Taponier *Theories of Communication* Sage Publishing, Thousand Oaks: CA 1998.
7 American Association for Public Opinion Research, History, at http://windowsxp-privacy.net/?id=198760161.
8 76.pdf in folder, referencing work by Katz and Lazarsfeld
9 (USED 76.PDF BALL-ROKEACH)
10 (thirdperson.pdf)
11 Albert Bandura, Dorothea Ross, Sheila A. Ross "Bandura: Transmission of Aggression Through Imitation of Aggressive Models" 1961 *Journal of Abnormal and Social Psychology*, 63 575–582.
12 social learning." Encyclopedia Britannica. 2008. Encyclopedia Britannica Online. 31 Oct. 2008 at http://www.britannica.com/EBchecked/topic/551304/social-learning.
13 Daniel Chandler, "Television Violence and Children's Behavior" December 22, 2004 at http://www.aber.ac.uk/media/Modules/TF33120/tv-violence_and_kids.html.
14 The Kaiser Family Foundation, Key Facts, Spring 2003 at http://www.kff.org/entmedia/upload/Key-Facts-TV-Violence.pdf.
15 "Can a Video Game Lead to Murder?" *CBS News* March 6, 2005 at http://www.cbsnews.com/stories/2005/03/04/60minutes/main678261.shtml
16 AP, "Teen Charged in Ala. Cops Shooting" *CBS News* June 9, 2003 at http://www.cbsnews.com/stories/2003/06/07/national/main557477.shtml
17 (Aikat 2004).
18 (citation could be cites 23–26 in publichealth.pdf article.)
19 (ref. 84, cited in sexualbehavior.pdf)
20 (Collins et al, ref. 110 in sexualbehavior.pdf)
21 (ref. From Media Lit book).
22 (36 ref.).
23 (37 in ref.).
24 (ref. 38).
25 (39).
26 Sociological Careers Open to MAs and PhDs: Teaching, Research, and Practice. American Sociological Association at http://www.asanet.org/cs/root/leftnav/careers_and_jobs/sociological_careers_open_to_mas_and_phds_teaching_research_and_practice

3

THE MEDIA AS ENTERTAINMENT

Laurie Fluker

The media in America have many roles. They inform, enlighten, delight, aggravate, enrage, encourage, excite and motivate those who interact with them. One of the most important roles of mass media is the entertainment function that they serve. Before the twentieth century, most Americans had little time to do much more than work. However, the Industrial Revolution made work much more efficient, and the Revolution gave workers the ability to capitalize on their leisure time. The need for relaxation tools became a vital aspect of everyday life, and the media were there to fill that need.

There are both positive and negative aspects to this dominant and changing role of mass media in our society. On the positive side, psychologists suggest that individuals must have some outlet of relaxation in order to cope with the stresses in their lives. On the negative side, critics complain that the media primarily supply a tasteless product with little redeeming value. Critics suggest that the media waste opportunities to enlighten and enrich their audiences. Yet others argue that the entertainment function is simply one aspect of the media that helps

to balance the other functions, and thus it makes the seemingly negative more palatable.

Whatever people think of media, there are now many new media outlets to enjoy. There were once just the traditional media from which people could choose, such as newspapers, books, magazines, films, radio and television. These traditional media have now merged with new media, such as computers, videogames, iPods and cell phones, to compete in the entertainment realm. Media convergence is now the name of the game, and the lines have blurred in terms of when and where people will choose to access media content. Henry Jenkins, in his work *Convergence Culture*, succinctly describes this phenomenon. He says it is the "flow of content across multiple media platforms, the cooperation between multiple media industries, and the migratory behavior of media audiences," that is most prevalent, and that these audiences are not necessarily loyal to any particular media to entertain them (p. 2).

The bottom line is that people enjoy being entertained and told a good story, and they will invest in whatever technology will make the entertainment more accessible. This fact is not new, and since the inception of media, audiences have gravitated to the newest medium on the market.

Newspapers as Entertainment

Some have called newspapers the most novel product of the printing press. In the American colonies, the first attempt at a newspaper was Benjamin Harris's *Publick Occurences, Both Forreign and Domestick* in 1690. Harris was a logical person to begin a newspaper since he owned a bookstore and was himself an author. His first and only edition was a lively account of bloodthirsty Indians and the lustful escapades of British royalty. His writing style did not meet with approval from the government authorities, and he was forced to end his publication and flee America. Though his paper did not have the continuity required of a true newspaper, Harris did understand that the medium had to give its audience something of interest.

The newspapers that followed Harris's paper were, for many years, published with the permission of government authorities, and they lacked the entertaining writing style of Harris. Benjamin Campbell's *Boston News-Letter*, first published in 1704, became the first continuously published paper in the colonies. Campbell was the postmaster for Boston, and so it was logical that he would have access to a great deal of information. Though his writing style was boring, the *News-Letter* met the needs of his audience. Campbell continued publishing the paper after his stint as postmaster, so the next postmaster had to begin his own paper.

James Franklin, the brother of Benjamin Franklin, began publishing the *New England Courant* in 1721. Franklin's paper mimicked the style of London newspapers, which were much more exciting than Campbell's style. Franklin also included the writings of some of the best authors of the day, such as James Fennimore Cooper. One of the most prolific contributors to the paper was a writer named Silence Dogood, the widow of a minister. Silence Dogood wrote fourteen letters complaining about the unlimited power of the government. What James Franklin did not know was that his brother, Benjamin Franklin, was actually Silence Dogood, and this was the beginning of a prolific writing career for young Ben. The *New England Courant* lasted until 1726. For five years, the paper had given readers much more than the boring fare of other papers of the day (*http://www.ushistory.org/franklin/courant/silence dogood.htm*).

Throughout the 1700s and into the 1800s, only the wealthy could afford to get access to the newspapers. Newspapers were sold on a subscription basis, so the common workingman was left out until Benjamin Day decided to sell newspapers on a per issue basis. With each issue costing only a penny, the *New York Sun*'s debut in 1833 represented the beginning of the "penny press." This paper, and other similar papers to follow, began to emphasize stories about crime and sex, thus creating an entirely new readership. The penny press did not provide a great deal of news or a great deal of truth, but these papers provided entertainment for the common man.

Horace Greeley improved on the penny press formula with his *New York Tribune*. Greeley liked the idea of the newspaper being inexpensive, but he felt that the common man deserved a better product that was more ethical and truthful. Greeley saw to it that the paper was just as entertaining, and he tackled relevant issues of the day such as slavery and capital punishment. The *Tribune* was nicknamed the "Great Moral Organ," and it proved that penny papers could be not only entertaining, but also ethical and truthful (*http://www.u-s-history.com/pages/h150.html*).

The end of the 1800s ushered in the age of Joseph Pulitzer and sensationalism that brought a great deal of entertainment to the common man. This period was dubbed "yellow journalism" because of the toothless, grinning cartoon character, the Yellow Kid, found in Pulitzer's *New York World*. The paper established a separate sports department, promotional coupons, cartoons and an expanded Sunday edition. It also, featured sensationalized stories. Although Pulitzer provided excellent news coverage in addition to sensationalized content, he was never proud of his role during this period of "yellow journalism." To compensate for this, Pulitzer established a prize in his will, the Pulitzer Prize, to be given each year in recognition of the best in journalism and other fields (*http://www.pulitzer.org/history.html*).

The early twentieth century was the time that the public's need for entertainment popularized the tabloid-style newspaper. Graphic photographs characterized the 1920s, a decade of "jazz journalism." New York papers such as the *Daily Mirror* went out of their way to be as sensational and lurid as possible. These papers made no pretense of being respectable. Instead, they sought to be "true confession" newspapers, making this period a sensational stage similar to previous times. The graphic photography only added to the effect. Though tabloids were popular during this period, most did not last beyond the 1920s (*http://ehub.journalism.ku.edu/history/1920/1920.html*).

After the 1920s, the public still found entertainment in newspapers through comic strips. Pulitzer's paper had used full-page comics, and the comic sections continued to expand over the years. H. C. "Bud" Fisher's *Mutt and Jeff*, begun in 1907, was the first successful daily comic strip in syndication. The two characters were extremely appealing to the common man because they were working class men whose lives paralleled the lives of the readers. Other comic strips such as *Little Orphan Annie, Tarzan* and *Dick Tracy* were introduced in the following years (*http://www.toonopedia.com/muttjeff.htm*).

The Depression and World War II brought an end to sensationalism in newspapers. The world had become too complicated to waste time on sensationalized stories. Newspapers helped interpret the international issues facing the country and reported on the New Deal policies of President Franklin Roosevelt. This interpretative characteristic of newspapers continued and remains a permanent part of the newspaper industry today.

A new and entertaining newspaper debuted in 1982 that combined short news stories with bold color, and it provided newspapers with a very different look. The newspaper industry did not warmly accept *USA Today*, begun by Gannett Company, because it seemed to have more in common with broadcast newscasts than with other newspapers. Over the years, *USA Today* strengthened its news division, but it kept the bold colors. This innovative paper has influenced the look of other newspapers, which now use more pictures and more color, and these innovations have led *USA Today* to become the #1 daily newspaper in the country with a circulation of 2.3 million (*http://www.hoovers.com/usa-today/—ID__115987—/free-co-profile.xhtml*).

Magazines as Entertainment

The magazine industry in America began in the 1700s, but it was not until the late 1800s that the medium began to flourish. The cost of magazines by the latter 1800s had risen to thirty-five cents per issue, and few could afford such a high price. Magazine publishers began to realize that if they reduced the magazine prices, circulation would rise quickly and more than compensate for the lower prices. Magazines such as *Munsey's, McClure's* and *Cosmopolitan* benefited most from the reduced prices, providing quality products at reasonable prices for more readers to enjoy.

The majority of magazines from the late 1800s into the twentieth century focused on and was marketed to women. *Ladies Home Journal, McClure's, Good Housekeeping* and other magazines addressed issues that mothers and homemakers were facing. In addition, recipes, short stories and advice columns were regular staples that provided entertainment in these magazines. Some of these magazines remain popular today by continuing to use the same successful formula from the late 1800s (*http://www.britannica.com/EBchecked/topic/482597/history-of-publishing*).

By the 1950s, entertainment magazines became much more specialized in content, and publications for different demographic groups began to become more popular. *Playboy* was founded in 1953 with men as the target audience. The national version of *TV Guide* was first published in 1953 for television viewers. This pattern of specialized publications remains the basic pattern of the magazine industry today (*http://www.cybercollege.com/frtv/mag2.htm*).

In 1974, Time Inc. began a new type of entertainment magazine. People magazine was a blend of celebrity news, human interest stories and impressive photography also used in other Time Inc. publications, such as *Time* and *Sports Illustrated* (*http://www.time.com/time/magazine/article/0,9171,944778,00.html*). The success of *People* led the way for the emergence of similar publications. *US Weekly* began in 1977, and Time Inc. also began *Entertainment Weekly* in 1990. The popularity of such publications has proven that there remains a significant audience for entertainment fare in the magazine world. The magazines have also spawned television programs such as *Entertainment Tonight* and *Access Hollywood* that are broadcast versions of the magazines.

Perhaps the most sensational publications in recent history are a hybrid of newspaper tabloids and magazines, having the look of a newspaper with content that resembles magazines. *The National Enquirer* is the most popular of these publications (*http://www.fundinguniverse.com/company-histories/EnquirerStar-Group-Inc-Company-History.html*). Begun during the tabloid age of the 1920s, the *Enquirer* became more noticeable in the 1970s with the exclusive cover picture of Elvis Presley in his coffin. In the 1990s, the *Enquirer* obtained exclusive pictures of Princess Diana after her death, but it opted not to use the photos for fear of a negative backlash from its audience. In recent years, the *Enquirer* has become much tamer in its coverage of celebrities. Its primary competition, *The Star,* began in 1974. In the 1980s, the *Enquirer's* parent company, American Media, purchased it (*http://www.media owners.com/company/americanmedia.html*).

While a large number of magazines are geared toward entertainment, it is important to understand that many more magazines have a different emphasis. Magazines are diverse in nature and in purpose, and thus we should not group these publications into one category.

Books as Entertainment

Books in colonial America were not meant to be entertaining. The Puritans brought the first printing press to America for educational and religious purposes. The intended audiences were only men, the wealthy and the well educated. For the most part, books either were *for* educated people or used *to* educate people.

This changed in the latter part of the 1800s when dime novels became popular. Similar to the penny newspapers, dime novels allowed books to be affordable. The content in the dime novels was also similar to the penny papers; crime, scandal and romance were the popular themes. Eventually detective stories and western adventures also became popular with the public. The popularity of dime novels diminished when other forms of media, specifically magazines and films, became more exciting to audiences (*http://www-sul.stanford.edu/depts/dp/pennies/home.html*).

During the twentieth century, various authors brought readers back to utilizing books as entertainment with a variety of types of novels. Though paperback books had been around since the 1800s, it was not until 1939 that they again became popular. Pocket Books reintroduced paperback books that year, followed by Bantam Books (*http://paperbarn.www1.50megs.com/Paperbacks/msg6.htm*). The renewed popularity of the paperback was largely due to both its entertainment value and its economic value to the common reader. The publishing company Dell also introduced the smaller version of paperback books during this period. Millions of paperback books sold in the coming decades, making the paperback a permanent staple in the publishing industry (*http://paperbarn.www1.50megs.com/Paperbacks/msg7.htm*). Eventually, a sophisticated marketing strategy developed, distributing hardcover books first, followed later by paperback versions. By 1960, paperback books outsold hard cover books, and this trend continues today. The romance novel rejuvenated in 1972 when Kathleen Woodiwiss published *The Flame and the Flower* as an original paperback (*http://www.kathleenewoodiwiss.com/*).

Today, books provide a tremendous variety of genres and authors. Many books have become extremely popular in print and thus have stimulated interest in film and television adaptations. Audio books now available have become extremely popular with some audiences. Finally, e-book devices now make reading a lot more convenient for mobile readers. All of these innovations ensure that books will remain a viable entertainment outlet for audiences.

Films as Entertainment

The moving image seemed revolutionary when audiences were introduced to the film industry. A number of inventors designed the equipment necessary to project continuous motion and eventually entertain the masses. In America, Thomas Alva Edison opened his Black Maria studio in New Jersey to film individuals through his *kinetoscope* camera. His equipment did not allow mass viewing of his films. Instead, patrons had to peek into a machine one at a time to see the films (*http://www.essort ment. com/all/movie thomasedi_rcgn.htm*). French inventor Louis Lumiere designed a camera, the *cinematographe*, which was much more mobile than Edison's camera. Lumiere used the camera to film outdoor scenes and then, after filming, to project the moving images to mass audiences (*http://www.britannica.com/EBchecked/topic/1403398/Lumiere-brothers*). Eventually, technology became sophisticated enough to film and display unified stories with a plot.

The first unified film in America to entertain audiences was Edwin S. Porter's *The Great Train Robbery* in 1903. The approximately ten-minute film was choppy compared to today's films, but this film established many firsts. It was the first western film, the first film to shoot on location, the first narrative film and the first film to utilize camera angles and editing to establish the mood (*http://www.britannica.com/EBchecked/topic/471087/Edwin-S-Porter*). Although this film was exciting, it paled in comparison to the masterpiece released in 1915.

We can consider D. W. Griffith's *Birth of a Nation* the first blockbuster film, and it remains one of the most impacting, influential and controversial films in the history of the industry. It tells the story of the Civil War South victimized by the Northern army and violent black people (*http://www.filmsite.org/birt.html*). The film presents the Ku Klux Klan as heroes, and this controversy has marred the historical significance of the film. *Birth of a Nation* was the first full-length film (three hours long), the first to have music especially composed for the film, the first film to have a director in charge of production and the first film to utilize the movement of a camera (*http://www.filmsite.org/birt.html*). This film was the most expensive and the most popular film in the industry until 1939 (*http://www.filmsite.org/birt.html*).

Warner Brothers Studio added sound to films in the mid-1920s, and films continued to get more spectacular and entertaining for audiences (*http://www.filmsite.org/jazz.html*). Perhaps the greatest year of filmmaking was 1939, when films such as *Gone with the Wind*, *The Wizard of Oz*, *Mr. Smith Goes to Washington*, *Stagecoach* and *Of Mice and Men* released. The film industry appeared to be giving the audiences exactly what they wanted—pure entertainment.

The film industry was not prepared for the competition that television created in the 1950s. Studios viewed television as a temporary novelty, but it soon became clear that television was a permanent fixture. In addition, the American courts had determined that Paramount and the other film studios had to divest themselves of the theaters that exhibited their films due to anti-monopoly laws. Hollywood no longer had the power they had enjoyed in previous decades. They were forced to reinvent the film industry and to produce television programs.

The coming decades were innovative years for the film industry. Up and coming directors such as Steven Spielberg, Quentin Tarantino, Spike Lee and others brought a new perspective to the film screen. Director George Lucas was not only responsible for *American Graffiti* and the *Star Wars* films; he also brought outstanding special effects to the industry through his company, Industrial Light and Magic. The computer animation of Pixar Studios made "Buzz Lightyear" and "Nemo" favorite film characters. In addition, audiences could rent, buy or pay for a single viewing of films, which helped with their popularity.

Now, in the twenty-first century, studios fully understand the importance of and symbiotic relationship with television. Most of the major studios own or share ownership with television broadcast or cable networks. Walt Disney is the parent company of the American Broadcasting Company (ABC) as well as the Disney Channel and ABC Family. Rupert Murdoch owns News Corporation, which in turn owns Fox Network, Fox News Network, FX Network, My Network TV and Fox Sports. Viacom controls MTV, VH1, BET, Nickelodean, Nick at Night, Comedy Central, Country Music Television and TV Land. Time Warner's holdings include Cable News Network, TNT, WTBS and part ownership of The CW network.

These major media conglomerates, along with others, remain heavily involved in all aspects of the entertainment media. Author Henry Jenkins, in his book, *Convergence Culture*, suggests that the new media have a different philosophy today:

> Whereas old Hollywood focused on cinema, the new media conglomerates have controlling

interests across the entire entertainment industry. Warner Bros. produces film, television, popular music, computer games, Web sites, toys, amusement park rides, books, newspapers, magazines, and comics (Jenkins, p. 16).

These owners will make decisions about media entertainment content for a very long time. It is not clear how their involvement will seemingly affect the content. What we do know is that the decisions about our entertainment will include fewer and fewer voices.

Radio and the Recording Industry

In 1877, Thomas Edison invented the phonograph, a machine that allowed owners to play musical recordings. The phonograph became the first technological medium available in the home. Its development ensured that audiences who could not afford to see live performances could hear these performers in their own comfortable environments.

The phonograph was a novelty until radio became available in American homes. Radio was the first broadcasting medium designed for household usage, and the timing was perfect for it. In the 1920s when radio became available, the country was experiencing tremendous change. The post World War I years brought Prohibition, women's right to vote and ultimately the Great Depression. As the audience looked for ways to escape from their troubled lives, radio found a place in their homes. Going out to the movies became an expensive proposition, and staying home to listen to radio became a cheap alternative form of entertainment.

The original structure of the radio networks was very similar to the structure of television networks today. The Radio Corporation of America (RCA), General Electric (GE), Westinghouse, American Telegraph and Telephone (AT&T) and United Fruit joined forces to form the National Broadcasting Company (NBC). RCA president David Sarnoff supervised two NBC networks, NBC Red and NBC Blue. The NBC Blue network eventually became the American Broadcasting Company (ABC). The other major network of the time was Columbia Broadcasting System (CBS), owned by William Paley, a tobacco tycoon. These major radio companies (NBC, CBS and ABC) each eventually expanded to television.

Radio programming in its early days was similar to television programming today. Music was available on radio, and musical programs mostly featured classical and semi classical music. Dramas also became popular fare on radio. *The Eveready Hour* and *Great Moments in History* were two dramas that entertained large audiences (*http://www.answers.com/topic/the-eveready-hour?cat=entertainment*). One of the most famous dramas of the time aired on CBS. Orson Welles and his troupe of actors enacted an adaptation of the H. G. Wells novel, *War of the Worlds*. CBS had gained an outstanding reputation for its news coverage, and audiences had grown accustomed to trusting the network's coverage of events. Therefore, when the entertainment drama had fictitious news reports about Martians landing in New Jersey, many in the audience thought that the drama was authentic. Many listeners were terrified, and some actually fled their homes. The power of this entertainment medium was now fully understood on that night before Halloween in 1938 when the program aired (*http://news.nationalgeographic.com/news/2005/06/0617_050617_warworlds.html*).

Another type of drama also found a place on radio. Episodic daytime shows with recurring characters were extremely popular. These stories followed the lives of individuals whose problems seemed worse than the problems of the listening audience. Soap manufacturers, primarily Procter & Gamble, were the main sponsors of these dramas. As a result, these broadcasts became known as "soap operas," and they remain among the favorite daytime programs on television today (*http://www.museum.tv/archives/etv/S/htmlS/soapopera/soapopera.htm*).

Comedy shows, similar to the vaudeville stageact traveling shows of the time, became extremely popular. Initially, the comedy focused on jokes or gags, commonly referred to as "slapstick." This type of comedy eventually matured to fifteen-minute comedy shows.

The most popular comedy on radio was the brainchild of performers Freeman Gosden and Charles Correll in 1928. These two white performers provided the voices of two black characters, Amos Jones and Andy Brown, and their daily exploits at the "Fresh-Air Taxicab Company." *Amos 'n' Andy* became the first syndicated radio program, sold to stations across the country for airing. In spite of the negative stereotyped portrayals of African Americans in the program, it remained popular throughout its years on radio. It was so popular that some cities reported all activities coming to a standstill while the program aired (*http://www.otr.com/amosandy.html*). When television debuted, the program successfully transferred from radio to television.

Amos 'n' Andy was not the only program to leave radio and move to television. Television robbed radio of many precious programs, and radio was left to scrounge for entertainment that would bring audiences back. Instead of the dramas and comedies, radio began to emphasize music. The recording industry and radio became dependent on one another, as radio primarily played music by those musicians whose music sold well. Radio also became fragmented, with music for different demographic audiences played on different stations. Amplitude modulation, or AM, was originally the dominant bandwidth. Later, frequency modulation, or FM, became the more popular bandwidth. Today satellite radio is striving to become as popular as the standard AM and FM radio.

Radio remains one of the most dominant of all entertainment media. Though radio does not hold the place in the home it once held, it remains a medium that is attractive to a diverse audience. Whether it's talk radio or shock jocks or sports programs, radio continues to deliver quality entertainment.

Television as Entertainment

Television's first decade was the 1950s. This was perhaps television's most innovative period. Game shows, situation comedies, Sunday talk shows, morning shows, soap operas and westerns were all mainstays on the television schedule in those early years. For the first time, audiences had entertainment in their homes that combined sight, sound and motion, and they loved it. The three major networks, NBC, CBS and ABC, all had programming designed to attract both viewers and advertisers.

One of the most groundbreaking programs of the time was *I Love Lucy*. Lucille Ball had been a Hollywood actress when CBS asked her to create a television program that paralleled her real-life marriage to Cuban musician Desi Arnaz. Ball insisted that CBS allow her real-life husband to play the role of her husband on *I Love Lucy*, and eventually CBS agreed. It was the first television situation comedy, the first television program to portray an interracial couple and the first to have a multiple-camera setup. While all of these accomplishments are impressive, the agreement that Arnaz made with CBS to put the *Lucy* episodes on expensive film stock and for the couple to keep the rights to each episode were the most pivotal. At the time that the series began, there was no such thing as syndicated television, or rather programs rerun for profit. The deal made the married couple two of the most successful actors in Hollywood history (*http://www.museum.tv/archives/etv/I/htmlI/ilovelucy/ilovelucy.htm*).

Not everyone was thrilled about the entertainment possibilities of television. Broadcast journalist Edward R. Murrow had built an excellent reputation on his news coverage at CBS, but he also hosted an entertainment program that took audiences into the homes of current-day celebrities. Murrow was thus keenly aware of both worlds, and he warned an audience of news journalists early on to beware of the entertainment side of the new medium (*http://www.turnoffyourtv.com/commentary/hiddenagenda/murrow.html*). With today's network newscasts competing with tabloid and gossip shows for an audience, it appears that Murrow was right on target.

The 1960s were tumultuous years for America, and television reflects that. The assassinations of John F. Kennedy, Martin Luther King, Robert Kennedy and Malcolm X made television news a powerful genre. The Vietnam War and the Civil Rights Movement came into audience homes nightly. The other genres continued to be popular as well, but news became an accepted and necessary entity in network programming.

Cable television debuted in the 1970s, and television found it was in competition with itself. Audience members migrated to the vast array of choices available on cable, even though they had to pay for the right. Cable continued to expand over the years, and now hundreds of channels are available with just about every type of programming imaginable. Not only must television networks compete with cable, there is also satellite television. Network television executives have had to struggle to find entertainment programming to bring the viewers back to the networks.

Two television genres have proven quite popular in recent years, one for daytime television and one for primetime or evening programming. Reality courtroom shows with the judge as the star now occupy a large portion of daytime programming across the nation. The current trend in court shows began in 1981 with Judge Joseph Wapner and *The People's Court*, which lasted an impressive twelve seasons (*http://www.metnews.com/reminiscing.htm*). The show made executives realize that the genre could be a successful draw for entertaining audiences.

Judge Judith Sheindlin's court show, *Judge Judy*, debuted in 1996, and it quickly became apparent that she would be a judge unlike any other (*http://www.the futoncritic.com/news.aspx?id=20080129cbs04*). Her nononsense, in-your-face style made her the highest rated judge on television. Though she has her critics, Sheindlin has managed to maintain a loyal viewing audience. In 2007, she signed a multi-year deal that will keep her on the airwaves through the 2011–2012 television season (*http://www.thefuton critic.com/news. aspx?id=20080129cbs04*). It is therefore not surprising that the number of judge shows has increased to a crowded field that includes not only Sheindlin, but also Judges Joe Brown, Greg Mathis, Marilyn Milian, Alex Ferrer, Christina Perez and Glenda Hatchett.

Reality programs have also become a mainstay in primetime television. MTV ushered in this modern-day version of reality television in 1992 when it brought seven young strangers to live together under the same roof. *The Real World*, celebrating its twentieth season in 2008, proved that a program with no script, no writers and just human interaction could attract large viewing audiences. Over the years, the various broadcast and cable networks have introduced more and more reality television programs, ranging from talent to cooking to modeling to survival shows. A sign of just how successful this entertainment genre actually became was evident in the 2000-2001 television year when the Emmy Awards for outstanding television programs created the "reality television" category (*http://www.realitytvworld.com/news/american-idol-leads-reality-tv-emmy-awards-field-with-8-nominations-4215.php*).

Television remains one of the most popular of all the entertainment media. It is true though that its audience has decreased over the years, and now television must continue to find programming that will bring audiences back. However, the audience can now be more particular about where and when they view that programming. As entertaining as television is, it simply is no longer the big kid on the block.

Other Technologies as Entertainment

Today, there are many different kinds of technology available to entertain audiences. Computers, the Internet, videogames, cellular phones and MP3 players now bring entertainment programming to audiences at their leisure. These new media only complicate what once was a very simple relationship between the media and their audiences. Media owners are scrambling to ensure that they stay in step with what the audience wants.

One company that has been extremely successful in giving audiences the entertainment they desire in the last decade is Apple Inc. Apple had already made its name in the computer market during the last quarter of the twentieth century. However, in 2001 Apple introduced the first iPod, a digital audio player that allowed users to purchase and store media content. Apple later set up the iTunes store, which allowed customers to purchase songs as well as television and movie shows via the Internet. As of the summer of 2007, iTunes had become "the world's most popular online music, TV and movie store featuring a catalog of over 5 million songs, 550 television shows and 500 movies" (*http://www.apple.com/pr/library/2007/07/31itunes.html*). Apple continues to be an innovator in the consumer electronic industry, having recently unveiled the iPhone and other versions of the original iPod.

The recent convergence of old and new media will be difficult to sort out. Hollywood writers led a strike in 2007–2008 because audience members could now get the writers' work in numerous ways without profiting the writers. The audience is now accustomed to getting its media in a variety of ways, and Hollywood writers were still being paid as if content was available exclusively in the original medium. The audience has tasted this freedom, and putting the genie back in the bottle will be hard. Author Henry Jenkins predicts a dominant role for future audiences. "There will be no magical black box that puts everything in order again. Audiences, empowered by these new technologies . . . are demanding the right to participate within the culture" (p. 24).

tomorrow. What is in vogue today may well be passé tomorrow. Entertainment will continue as a nebulous concept that is always in flux. The media will attempt to give the audience what they think the audience wants, but the ultimate decision will continue to lie with the audience. If content fails to entice the audience, something more entertaining will replace it. As audience tastes continue to change, this is one thing that will never change. Regardless of whether the medium is newspapers, books, magazines or even film, television, radio or newer technologies, people will always enjoy being entertained and told a good story.

Conclusion

All media struggle to bring the most entertaining content possible to their audiences. However, a medium that is extremely hot today may not be so

Works Cited

Jenkins, Henry. *Convergence Culture: Where Old and New Media Collide*. New York: New York University Press, 2006.

BOOKS

Laurie Fluker

Joanne was born to be a writer. She had begun writing at the age of six, and she often dreamed of being a successful writer. She did not come from a family of writers. Her parents had both served in the military, and they married when they were only nineteen years old. Joanne was the first child born into this marriage, and not quite two years later, her sister, Di, was born.

Joanne and Di did not get along during their childhood, but there were occasions when Di listened to young Joanne practice her storytelling. As the girls aged, their family moved various times, meeting new people with each move. In one particular neighborhood, Joanne became friends with a brother and sister who lived nearby, whose name Joanne liked immensely. Their name, Potter, remained a name that Joanne favored for many years.

As an adult, Joanne finished college and worked in various jobs. She continued to think about her writing and on a train ride one afternoon in 1990, she thought of writing about a boy who did not realize he was a wizard. Without a pen and paper, Joanne brainstormed for hours about her idea. When she finally made it home that evening, she began writing

The Philosopher's Stone, and Joanne continued to write about the boy she named Harry. Over the next few years, Joanne moved to Portugal and married. Joanne's marriage yielded one daughter. The marriage did not last very long, but Joanne had a beautiful child when she moved from Portugal to Scotland in 1994.

Rather than return to the work world, Joanne decided to finish her novel instead. As a single parent, she lived on public assistance and wrote her book in longhand in Scottish coffeehouses during her daughter's naps. She ultimately received a grant to finish her work, and she later found an agent and a publisher. When the time came to publish the novel, Joanne's publisher decided to use Joanne's initials rather than her full name to ensure that the fact that a woman had written the adventure did not disturb young boys. Since Joanne had no middle name, she chose to use the initial K, from her favorite grandmother, Kathleen. In the end, *Harry Potter and the Sorcerer's Stone* (in Britain, the title was *Harry Potter and the Philosopher's Stone*), was a phenomenal success, and J.K. Rowling is now said to be the richest author in history.

The Origin of Books

Books are the oldest of all mass media. When we think of books, we think of sophisticated finished products with nice covers and hundreds of pages. This assumption is deceptively simple. A number of civilizations contributed to what we now think of as books. Sumerians developed clay tablets considered the predecessors of books. Greeks perfected the alphabet, and the Chinese developed paper. The Chinese also had developed a press machine, but they used their machine for artwork. It is not until the development of the printing press that books, as we know them today, came to exist.

In England, prior to the development of the printing press, people had to hand copy books. For many years, Catholic monks were the ones who painstakingly copied work, mostly religious in nature. These hand-written books were thus only available to the church and to the wealthy. This arrangement worked well for those in power, as commoners had to depend on these persons' interpretations of the writings. Thus the development of the printing press would cause a great deal of upheaval in English society.

Johannes Gutenburg

It was a simple man who brought about this upheaval in the 1400s and revolutionized society. Johannes Gutenberg, born in 1400 in the city of Mainz, Germany, was a man who dreamed of getting rich. Gutenburg never fulfilled those dreams, moving from one job to another, one city to another, never staying with any particular job very long. He began as a goldsmith, initially producing religious charms. Gutenburg understood the importance of the Catholic Church to its members, so he spent a great deal of time exploiting the members' faith. He eventually began printing indulgences, a piece of paper that the Catholic Church sold to its members to absolve them of their sins. Once again, Gutenburg thought this scheme would make him wealthy.

In 1455, Gutenberg devised the brilliant idea to convert an old Roman wine press into a printing press. Even though he did not invent the printing press, he was the first to use individual, interchangeable lead letters, utilizing his skills as a goldsmith. Prior to Gutenberg, people carved full pages on wooden blocks and printed page by page. In 1456, Gutenberg printed his first book, the Bible. His Bible had two columns, and the printing was beautifully ornate like the writing of his day. Still extremely expensive, each copy of the Bible that Gutenberg sold cost the equivalent of an average worker's wages over three years. He was never able to sell enough of the Bibles to satisfy his financial backers, so they eventually foreclosed on him and repossessed his printing press.

Over the next three decades, printing presses spread throughout Europe. This did not please King Henry VIII and the Catholic Church. The government set up mandatory laws that printers had to gain prior approval before printing anything. The Church, fearing widespread knowledge it could not control, set up the very first office of censorship in Mainz, Germany in 1485. It is no coincidence that the city that led to the birth of the printing press was also the city that gave birth to censorship. However, it was too late. Gutenberg had begun a revolution that was to give rise to the Protestant Reformation and many political upheavals in centuries to come. Gutenberg, himself, never gained good fortune; he died bankrupt.

The History of Books in America

When English colonists arrived in America, they had little time to think about books. They established the southern colony of Jamestown to find riches in the new land. These colonists found little more than mosquitoes, hostile natives and strife. The northern colonies they founded were different, and the religious sect known as Puritans began one particular colony.

Puritans had come to the new world to seek religious freedom, which they had not had available to them in England. They made the Massachusetts Bay Colony extremely organized and self-sufficient. They also had to work long hours, from sunrise to sunset, to achieve their goals. However, they prized education for the men in their society, so it is not surprising that only six years after they began the colony, they established Harvard College in 1636. They needed a printing press to produce the religious materials necessary for an education, so in 1638 they established the first press shop in America, known as the Cambridge Press. The first book printed in the colonies was *The Bay Psalm Book*, also called *The Whole Booke of Psalms*. Most of the books printed in America for decades to come were religious in nature until the 1700s when Ben Franklin published *Poor Richard's Almanack*, a collection of witty poems and stories still quoted today. Franklin was also responsible for publishing *Pamela* in America, a novel written by British author Samuel Richardson. *Pamela*, a controversial story about a maid who struggled to remain virtuous and moral, was the first novel reprinted and sold in the colonies.

The 1800s were extremely successful years for the book industry. Major publishing houses became established, and some of the most popular American authors wrote their classic novels during this century. James Fennimore Cooper wrote *Last of the Mohicans* (1826); Mark Twain wrote *Huckleberry Finn* (1884); and Nathaniel Hawthorne wrote *The Scarlet Letter* (1850). Better technology, improved literacy rates and new developments all led to more success for the industry. Erastus and Irwin Beadle introduced "dime novels" in 1860, paperback novels that sold for five or ten cents. Detective, Western and romance stories were popular genres for these books aimed at young, working-class individuals.

Continued growth of the publishing houses that had begun in the 1800s characterized the modern book publishing industry of the twentieth century. In the first half of the century, authors such as F. Scott Fitzgerald, John Steinbeck and Ernest Hemingway brought their unique styles of writing to novels. African-American writers experienced success during this time as well. W. E. B. Du Bois, one of the founders of the National Association for the Advancement of Colored People (NAACP), published *The Souls of Black Folk*. Booker T. Washington, founder of Tuskegee University, also published a number of works.

During the 1920s and 1930s, African-American poets and book authors were extremely prolific in an area of New York City known as Harlem. The period became known as the "Harlem Renaissance," and authors such as Langston Hughes, Countee Cullen, and Zora Neale Hurston became well known. Other black book authors continued to flourish in the 1940s and 1950s. Richard Wright wrote *Native Son*, his indictment of racism. Ralph Ellison's *Invisible Man* has made many readers understand life in a black man's world. James Baldwin's autobiographical *Go Tell It on the Mountain* describes his life as the son of a minister in Harlem.

The latter half of the century was even more successful for African-American authors. Alex Haley, Toni Morrison, Alice Walker and Maya Angelou have all had books on various best-seller lists. Several of their works have turned into blockbuster films or highly rated television movies. *Roots*, written by Haley, sold an impressive five million books over eight years. One hundred and thirty million people viewed *Roots*, the television mini-series, over an eight-night period.

A number of twentieth century Latino authors have risen to prominence in the last three decades. Laura Esquivel is one such author. A native of Mexico City, Esquivel wrote *Like Water for Chocolate* in 1990. The novel is an unusual blend of a Mexican girl's story of forbidden love, combined with recipes. The novel was so successful that it became a film in 1993 and ultimately the largest grossing foreign film in America. In 1994, Esquivel received the ABBY award given by the American Booksellers Association to the book they most liked to sell (*http://mostly fiction.com/latin/esquivel.htm*). The book is a worldwide success, translated into thirty languages and selling millions of copies (*http://mostlyfiction.com/latin/esquivel.htm*).

Several other Latino authors have found success with their first novels. One particular Latino novelist experienced success as far back as 1972. U.S. born Rudolfo Anaya wrote *Bless Me, Ultima*, and although the book has received periodic challenges, critics credit the novel with establishing the modern Latino literature movement. Chilean born Isabel Allende is another popular Latino author. In 1985, Allende's first novel, *House of the Spirits*, was published. Sandra Cisneros, born in Chicago, was successful with her debut novel, *The House on Mango Street*, in 1984.

Like Water for Chocolate was not the only novel successfully converted to a film. Other authors also capitalized on the trend. Ian Fleming's series of books about British spy James Bond was extremely popular and translated to equally successful films. Stephen King, Michael Crichton and John Grisham have made millions of dollars first from their books and then from the film adaptations.

Book Categories

Authors write books for different groups of individuals and for different purposes, and the content differs accordingly. To this end, we divide books into a number of categories. The primary categories are trade books, professional, religious, university press, elementary and high school, college, subscription reference, mail order and book club.

Most readers are more accustomed to trade books because this category sells the greatest number of books. Trade books can be hard cover or paperback, fiction or nonfiction. They can cover a wide range of interests, and, thus, we sometimes refer to them as general interest books.

Professional books, as the name suggests, are books written for persons in a given profession. Doctors and lawyers are examples of professionals who have a special interest in books dedicated to their fields. There will always be a need for professional books because some individuals will be entering the field while others will want to remain abreast of the latest information in their field.

Religious books include any books that focus on any aspect of the religions in the world. Such books would include the Bible, spiritual guides and hymnals. In recent years, religious books have become extremely popular. One such book is Rick Warren's *The Purpose-Driven Life*, with more than twenty-four million copies sold by 2006. The book received unexpected attention when in 2005 a kidnap victim in Georgia read the book to her captor, an escaped felon. The felon soon after turned himself into authorities.

University press books are usually scholarly books written for or by educators and mass-produced by publishing houses associated with colleges or universities. The audience for university press books is understandably small in comparison to those who read general public books and textbooks.

Textbooks represent one of the most lucrative categories of books for publishing houses. They sell on the elementary, middle and high school levels as well as selling on the college and university level. For the kindergarten to high school levels, local school districts or states make decisions about which books to use. College and university textbooks include books used at all higher education institutions. College and university textbooks are often written by college professors and usage decisions are usually made at the institution itself.

Subscription reference books are books of information such as dictionaries, encyclopedias or other general interest publications purchased directly from the publisher rather than from a book retailer. Mail order books are those bought and sold through the mail. Book club books include all kinds of books sold and sent by these membership associations to their members, usually at a discount rate. Most book clubs charge a fee for their membership privileges.

The Birth of the Book "Superstore"

In 1873, Charles Barnes began selling books from his home in a small town in Illinois. Forty-four years later, Barnes' son moved the business to New York and joined forces with G. Clifford Noble, thus establishing Barnes & Noble. Still later, they purchased their Fifth Avenue store in New York City, and this bookstore location became known around the world for its excellence. In the 1960s, Leonard Riggio decided to open a bookstore that catered to university students. He opened a store in New York, and later opened six other college bookstores. Riggio later acquired the flagship Barnes & Noble.

Barnes & Noble continued to make innovations in the bookselling world. In 1974, the company purchased advertising time on television, the first

Book Trivia

What is the longest title of a book?

The longest title, written by Davide Ciliberti of Italy in 2007, has 1,433 characters and 290 words. The book is about the peculiarities of the field of public relations. The full title: *Per favore dite a mia madre che faccio il pubblicitario lei pens ache sono un Pierre e che quindi regalo manciate di free entry e consumazioni gratis a chi mi pare, rido coi vips, I calciatori le veline e le giornaliste, leggo Novella e mi fotografano I paparazzi, entro nel prive slatando la coda, bevo senza pagare, sono ghiotto di tartine e gin tonic, ho la casa piena di oggetti di design, conosco Paris Hilton, Tom Ford ed Emilio (www.guiness worldrecords.com).*

What is the book held in the left hand of The Statue of Liberty?

What she is holding is not a book. It is actually a tablet inscribed with the date of the Declaration of Independence from Britain, July 4, 1776. The date on the tablet is in Roman numerals.

What is the most valuable comic book of all time?

Though there are a number of valuable comic books, many think Action Comics #1 from June 1938 is the most valuable. Why? It was the first of the superhero genre, and it was the debut of Superman. In 2003, someone offered one million dollars for a near-mint copy, though no one has discovered such a copy (*http://www.answers.com/topic/first-appearance-1*).

What is the world's longest novel?

According to Guinness World Records, *A La Recherche Du Temps Perdu* (in English, *Remembrance of Things Past*) by Marcel Proust's is the longest novel. It is a thirteen-volume work with 9,609,000 characters (*http://www.bookspot.com/ask/longestbook.html*).

---

bookseller to do so. In 1975, the company became the first bookseller to offer books on the *New York Times* bestseller list at a discount rate. During the 1980s, Barnes & Noble acquired B. Dalton Bookseller, Doubleday Book Shops and BookStop, which further positioned them as the preeminent bookseller. In the 1990s, Barnes & Noble continued to improve on the "superstore" concept by selling not only books, but also a large inventory of

music, DVDs and Starbucks coffee. Such innovations now make Barnes & Noble a shopping experience for its customers.

During the midst of the Depression, in 1933, Lawrence Hoyt opened a rental library that was so successful it grew to 250 locations within fifteen years. In 1962, he opened his first independently owned bookstore, naming it Walden after Henry David Thoreau's book. In 1981, Waldenbooks became the first chain of bookstores to have stores located in all fifty states.

In 1971 in Ann Arbor, Michigan, brothers Tom and Louis Borders opened their first bookstore, Borders. The location was small, with just two rooms, and the inventory consisted of only used books. The store eventually expanded to a large, national bookstore, and Borders added a large variety of new books to their sales inventory.

Both Waldenbooks and Borders ended up under the same company. In 1992, Kmart acquired Borders and Waldenbooks and later merged the two. In 1995, Kmart was having financial problems of its own, and it allowed Borders to buy itself out.

Today, the true "superstores" that remain are Barnes & Noble and Borders-Walden, now known as the Borders Group. Barnes & Noble is the largest bookseller in the world, with approximately seven hundred locations in all fifty states. The Borders Group is the second largest chain of stores. It has opened many locations around the world, and its largest location, sixty thousand square feet, is in Malaysia. However, in 2007, the Borders Group announced that they would be refocusing and reinventing their company, beginning with the sale of their subsidiaries in the United Kingdom and Ireland.

Anatomy of a "Bestseller"

The word "bestseller" is deceptive. The common assumption is that if a book makes it to a recognized bestseller list, it has to have sold a certain number of copies. This is not necessarily the case. There are instances when a book makes it to such lists when it sells well in a given market. In fact, proclaiming that a book is a "bestseller" is many times nothing more than an excellent marketing ploy that publishers use to sell their books. A select few authors will write books that sell in extremely large numbers, but there are vast numbers of obscure authors whose works will simply not sell in large numbers. So if a book sells well in a tiny city, the book industry may well dub it a bestseller all around the country. The

purpose of a bestseller book list is to make money for the book industry, along with the newspapers and magazines that publish the lists. It is clear from the sheer number of bestseller lists that have cropped up over years that these lists are influencing book buyers.

The one bestseller list that has gained a great deal of prestige is the *New York Times* Bestseller List. Few people know how the newspaper qualifies books for its lists since they keep the actual formula a secret. What is known is that the *Times* editors choose thirty-six titles they believe could be best-selling titles, and they also poll three thousand bookstores across America. They ask the stores to give the sales numbers for the chosen titles and to identify books that are selling fast. The *Times* bestsellers list comes from that information. If a book does not make the list one week, it may well make the list the following week. They never divulge the polled bookstores because publishers might try to influence the sales of particular titles at those particular stores. This has happened in the past.

The Wall Street Journal and *USA Today* publish other notable bestseller lists. A number of newspapers publish regional bestseller lists. In general, all of these papers "call some local stores (they won't say which ones), ask what's selling (without asking for proof), and utilize a secret formula whereby they give more weight to sales from bigger stores". Therefore, the next time you see a bestseller list, you will know to view this list with a bit of skepticism.

The Best-Selling Books in History

You might be asking yourself, "Are there really any bestselling books?" There are, in fact, many books that people have read for many years in America and in other countries around the world. However, just because a book *seems* popular, is it truly one of the best-selling books in history? There are a number of lists circulating that claim to contain the definitive bestselling books in history, and *Mental Floss* magazine published one of these in 2007. This list includes the titles, the author names and the number of copies sold (if known). Here are the top fifteen bestselling books in history according to *Mental Floss* magazine.

1. *The Bible* (6.7 billion copies)

2. *Quotations from Chairman Mao*, Mao Tse-Tung (900 million)

3. *The Qur'an* (800 million)

4. *Xinhua Zidian* (Chinese dictionary first published in the 1950s; 400 million)

5. *The Book of Common Prayer*, Thomas Cranmer (number unknown)

6. *Pilgrim's Progress*, John Bunyan (number unknown)

7. *Foxes Book of Martyrs*, John Foxe (number unknown)

8. *The Book of Mormon*, Joseph J. Smith, Jr. (123 million)

9. *Harry Potter and the Sorcerer's Stone*, J.K. Rowling (107 million)

10. *And Then There Were None*, Agatha Christie (100 million)

11. *The Lord of the Rings*, *J.R.R. Tolkien* (100 million)

12. *Harry Potter and the Half-Blood Prince*, J.K. Rowling (65 million)

13. *The DaVinci Code*, Dan Brown (65 million)

14. *Harry Potter and the Chamber of Secrets*, J.K. Rowling (60 million)

15. *The Catcher in the Rye*, J.D. Salinger (60 million)

One quick look at this list will explain just how significant J.K. Rowling is as an author. She is the only author with more than one book in the top fifteen. What is even more astounding is that the other three Harry Potter titles occupy the sixteenth, seventeenth and eighteenth best-selling books on this list. These six books do not include her seventh and last book, *Harry Potter and the Deathly Hallows*, released later in 2007 after the publication of the *Mental Floss* list. Just a few hours after the publishers announced the July 2007 release date of the book to the general public, a full five months in advance, the

last Potter book became the top-selling book on both Amazon.com and the Barnes and Noble lists. It is likely that since the seventh Potter book is the last in the series, it too will likely command a spot on the top fifteen bestseller list in history.

A Decade of Change

We can view the 1990s as a decade of true bestsellers, a revolutionary period for the book industry. The book superstores, as previously discussed, were omnipresent. John Grisham's *The Firm* and *The Pelican Brief*, Michael Crichton's *Jurassic Park* and *The Lost World* and others left impressive works in books and at the box office. The O.J. Simpson trial spawned a number of "instant" books, or books written quickly to capitalize on a media sensation for a particular event.

Although the popularity of some of these books was meteoric in their own rights, none of this compared to what three individuals did to affect the book publishing industry. J.K Rowling, Oprah Winfrey and Jeff Bezos changed the reading habits of millions of individuals. Rowling's prolific writing style lured readers into the world of a young wizard. Winfrey not only told her audience to read, but she also told them what to read; they obeyed. Bezos made it really simple for people to acquire the books they wanted. So began this decade of change.

J.K. Rowling

J.K. Rowling is not just an impressive writer who captured children's imaginations in her seven-book series about Harry Potter. She is much more than that. A writer for *Entertainment Weekly* summed it up by saying:

> In an era of videogame consoles, online multiplayer 'environments,' and tinier-is-better mobisodes, minisodes, and webisodes, she got people to tote around her big, fat old-fashioned printed-on-paper

books as if they were the hottest new entertainment devices on the planet.

Rowling's first book, *Harry Potter and the Sorcerer's Stone*, hit America in September of 1998. The next year, Rowling followed up her first book with two more books in the series: *Harry Potter and the Chamber of Secrets* (released in America in June 1999); *Harry Potter and the Prisoner of Azkaban* (released in America in September 1999). That same year, these first three installments of the Harry Potter series were the top three books on the *New York Times* bestseller list, prompting the *Times* to create a bestselling list for children's literature. By the summer of 2000, the first three books had earned nearly $480 million, and had sold more than 35 million copies in thirty-five different languages.

Rowling followed up with *Harry Potter and the Goblet of Fire*, the fourth in the series, released simultaneously in Great Britain and America in July 2000. By 2003, the year of the fifth book's publication, Rowling's reputation worldwide was already a proven formula. *Harry Potter and the Order of the Phoenix* had a first print run of an astonishing 8.5 million copies in America, with 5 million copies sold on the first Saturday after its release. Barnes and Noble sold 286,000 copies of the *Phoenix* in just one hour. The sixth book, *Harry Potter and the Half-Blood Prince* (July 2005) continued to break records. It sold 9 million copies in Britain and in America within the first twenty-four hours. Selling 6.9 million in the United States alone, the *Half-Blood Prince* averaged 250,000 sales per hour on the first day. The final installment, *Harry Potter and the Deathly Hallows* (July 2007), was the most impressive. The first print run was 12 million in the United States. It sold 8.3 million copies in America on its first day and 2.65 million copies in Britain. *Deathly Hallows* sold an average of 5,000 books per minute, 300,000 per hour the first day. It officially became the fastest-selling book in history ("Potter" setting all-time records, *www.cnn.com*, July 24, 2007).

All of these accomplishments were quite impressive, but Rowling's years were replete with challenges. In 2002, Nancy Stouffer sued Rowling for plagiarism. Stouffer had written a book in 1984, *The Legend of Rah and Muggles*, and one of her characters was Larry Potter. The judge in the case ruled that Stouffer had lied to the court and dismissed her case. In 2003, Rowling and her publisher sued a Dutch publishing company that prevented the sale of a book whose main character, a girl wizard, was too similar to Rowling's character.

Perhaps the most famous challenging obstacle to Rowling has come from religious persons who consider the magic celebrated in the Potter series anti-Christian. People have banned and challenged books for many years, so this challenge to Rowling was nothing new. What was new was that no other book had been this popular with both children and adults alike. The challenge, although well publicized, was not successful.

Entertainment Weekly named Rowling the "2007 Entertainer of the Year." Why? Here's their explanation:

> The numbers, after all, are so much fun to tally and goggle at: $15 billion (the estimated total revenue generated by the Harry Potter industry); nearly 400 million (the number of Potter books sold worldwide); $4.49 billion (the total worldwide box office gross of the five Harry Potter films, allowing the series to zip past *Star Wars* and the James Bond films this summer to become the most lucrative movie franchise in history). And let's not forget 1, 2, 3, and 4: the places Rowling holds on the list of the fastest-selling books in the not-very-long history of measuring fast-selling books.

Oprah Winfrey

Oprah Winfrey's longstanding television talk show has enjoyed extreme popularity for many years. In 1986, The Oprah Winfrey Show became the highest rated talk show in all of television history ("Showbiz Tonight," 2/6/08). The show became a perfect platform in 1996 for Winfrey to begin a new feature segment she called "Oprah's Book Club." In that year, she chose three novels, and in 1997 chose eleven novels. Initially, Winfrey wanted to keep her choice private until her show revealed the featured book. She did not even tell publishers of her choice until very late in the process. However, the publishing industry could not possibly keep up with the demand from audience members and viewers who immediately sought to purchase the novel chosen. Winfrey finally had to cave in to the demands of publishers. She agreed to give publishers advance notice of her choice with the understanding that no one would disclose the information before her show aired. Eventually, they added a sticker to all chosen books indicating they were "Oprah Book Club" recommendations. The Book Club was so popular that whenever she announced the selections, the books instantly became bestsellers, selling millions of copies. Winfrey's influence was such a phenomenon in the publishing industry it became known as "the Oprah effect."

Winfrey allowed viewers to join her book club online, and approximately one million have registered as members. With these numbers, it is not surprising that her recommendations are so valuable.

In 1997, *Newsweek* named her the most important person of books and media. In 1999, The National Book Foundation chose her for its 50th Anniversary Gold Medal. The Association of American Publishers gave her its highest award, the "AAP Honors".

Not all members of the publishing community have embraced Winfrey's praise. In 2001, Winfrey chose *The Corrections* by Jonathan Franzen for the book club. Franzen expressed concerns that her recommendation might jeopardize his novel's place in the industry, likening her logo to a "corporate" endorsement (*www.cnn.com*). Winfrey withdrew the recommendation, and because of the lost financial potential, no other author since has turned down her endorsement.

Perhaps the most publicized problem with the book club was her choice of James Frey's *A Million*

Little Pieces in October 2005. The book was supposed to be a non-fiction memoir of his years as an alcoholic, drug addict and criminal. Next to the Harry Potter book in that year, Frey's book sold more copies in the U.S. than any other title, 1.77 million, and most of those sold after the airing of Winfrey's show. Later the discovered occurred that Frey had created portions of his non-fictional memoir. Initially, Winfrey continued to back Frey under pressure. However, it became clear that she had to denounce Frey and his lies. In January 2006, Winfrey publicly chastised the author and his publisher. Before the end of 2005, Frey's book had made $4.3 million; it made another $1.5 million after he had admitted to lying in the book. The "Oprah effect" was in full motion as even Winfrey's anger helped make the book more popular.

What are Winfrey's personal favorite books among the 63 books chosen over the years? Her Website states that *The Grapes of Wrath* (John Steinbeck), *Sula and The Bluest Eye* (Toni Morrison), *I Know Why the Caged Bird Sings* (Maya Angelou) and *To Kill a Mockingbird* (Harper Lee) are her all-time favorites.

Jeff Bezos

Jeff Bezos had a lucrative job at a New York City investment firm in the summer of 1994, and in an instant, he quit that job and moved to Seattle. This young man decided that he wanted to begin a bookstore, but not your typical bookstore. Instead, he wanted to sell books over the Internet. He had originally taken the idea of one-stop book shopping via the Internet to his employers, but they were not ready for such a plan. Although detractors tried to dissuade him, Jeff Bezos would not give up his dream.

That dream became Amazon.com, and his decision was a wise one. Bezos decided to stock his shelves with a million titles, an inventory more than six times that of the largest physical bookstore. In July 1995, Bezos opened Amazon.com to the world, and within a month, it had sold books in forty-five foreign countries and all fifty states. It was not just that the site had so many titles available to sell. In

addition, Bezos offered customers the opportunity to purchase books easily, to review their choices and to receive an e-mail order confirmation. Over time, Amazon began offering clothing and other consumer goods online. In 1999 when *Time* magazine named Bezos "Man of the Year," customers bought $15 billion worth of his goods. Bezos served as the chief executive officer and president of his company.

As if changing the way and where we shop for books were not enough, Bezos and Amazon introduced their first Kindle at end of 2007. The Kindle is an electronic reading device that allows customers to download books, newspapers and magazines at the customer's leisure. The first Kindle was capable of storing approximately two hundred books, with more possible if stored on a memory card. In early 2009, Bezos announced the more updated e-book reader, the Kindle 2, which is slimmer, lighter and sleeker than its predecessor. The newer model has a longer battery life, is easier to read, and can now convert text to audio so that books can now be read to owners by way of a digital voice. One of Kindle 2's main attractions is its wireless connectivity using the Sprint data network that allows customers to search and download books.

The Kindle was not the first e-book device. Sony introduced its first electronic reading device, the Sony Librie, in Japan in 2004. That device, which was only available to read in the Japanese language, failed to catch on. In 2006, Sony introduced the PRS 500 Sony Reader, which was much more successful than the Librie and available in English. Sony has since released newer versions of its Reader, and its newer version is slightly smaller and lighter than the Kindle 2. However, the number of books available through Sony's e-book store is not as large as the number of books available through Kindle 2's store. The Reader's screen is not as attractive as the Kindle 2's screen, and the Reader's storage of 350 books compares unfavorably to the Kindle 2's storage of 1,500 books. One advantage that the Reader has is that one of its versions has a touchable screen, and the Kindle 2 does not.

The 2010 introduction of the Apple iPad has predictably brought more attention to the e-book reader market. The iPad has a larger screen than its competitors, and the screen is not only a touch screen, it's a color screen. The color screen makes a huge difference when viewing color newspaper and magazine

Amazon's 5 Best Books of the Millennium

1. The Lord of the Rings   J.R.R. Tolkien
2. Gone With the Wind   Margaret Mitchell
3. To Kill a Mockingbird   Harper Lee
4. The Catcher in the Rye   J.D. Salinger
5. Harry Potter and the Sorcerer's Stone   J.K. Rowling

The 10 Most Frequently Challenged/Controversial

1. Scary Stories (Series)   Alvin Schwartz
2. Daddy's Roommate   Michael Willhoite
3. I Know Why the Caged Bird Sings   Maya Angelou
4. The Chocolate War   Robert Cormier
5. The Adventures of Huckleberry Finn   Mark Twain
6. Of Mice and Men   John Steinbeck
7. Harry Potter (Series)   J.K. Rowling
8. Forever   Judy Blume
9. Bridge to Terabithia   Katherine Paterson
10. Alice (Series)   Phyllis Reynolds Naylor

(*http://www.ala.org/ala/oif/bannedbooksweek/bbwlinks/100mostfrequently.cfm*)

2009 Top Five Book Sales (Adult Nonfiction)

1. Act Like a Lady, Think Like a Man   Steve Harvey (Amistad Press)
2. Glenn Beck's Common Sense   Glenn Beck (Threshold Editions)
3. Liberty and Tyranny: A Conservative Manifesto   Mark Levin (Threshold Editions)
4. Outliers: The Story of Success   Malcolm Gladwell (Little Brown and Company)
5. Going Rogue: An American Life   Sarah Palin (HarperCollins)

(Source: The Nielsen Company)

2009 Top Five Book Sales (Adult Fiction)

1. The Lost Symbol   Dan Brown (Doubleday Books)
2. The Shack   William P. Young (Windblown Media)
3. The Time Traveler's Wife   Audrey Niffenegger (Harvest Books)
4. The Associate   John Grisham (Doubleday Books)
5. The Guemsey Literary and Potato Peel Pie Society   Mary Ann Shaffer (Dial Press)

(Source: The Nielsen Company)

2009 Top Five Book Sales (Juvenile)

1. New Moon   Stephenie Meyer (Little, Brown Young Readers)
2. Breaking Dawn   Stephenie Meyer (Little, Brown Young Readers)
3. Eclipse   Stephenie Meyer (Little, Brown Young Readers)
4. Twilight   Stephenie Meyer (Little, Brown Young Readers)
5. The Last Straw   Jeff Kinney (Harry N. Abrams, Inc.)

(Source: The Nielsen Company)

pictures or online videos. The iPad has 16, 32 and 64 GB storage, much more than the Kindle 2 and the Reader. The battery life for the iPad is 10 hours, not as impressive as Kindle 2's one-to-two week battery life. Apple has partnered with several of the largest publishing companies to ensure extensive book availability, but as of now, the Kindle Store inventory easily outnumbers all others with 450,000 titles available. However, what sets the iPad apart from its competitors is that it is not only an e-book reader, it is also a device that will allow its customers to watch movies, play games, read e-mail, store photos and use all the iPhone applications, in addition to WiFi and Bluetooth capabilities. The iPad is essentially a game system, with many of the capabilities of a laptop computer that includes an e-book reader. The iPad price begins at $499, more expensive than either of its competitors, so for those customers who prefer to simply read books, the choice seems to be the Kindle 2.

Rowling, Winfrey and Bezos are three individuals who either innovatively wrote, defined or sold us books that made us want to return to loving books in general. Their influence will continue to have a powerful impact upon the book industry well into the future.

Ethical Issues in the Book Industry

We have already discussed James Frey's ethical dilemma, but he is not the only author to cross the line of ethics in the book industry. Kaawa Viswanathan, a Harvard sophomore, received a $500,000, two-book deal at age seventeen from Little, Brown publishers. Her book, *How Opal Mehta Got Kissed, Got Wild, and Got a Life*, seemed unusually similar to another author's work. Megan F. McCafferty accused Viswanathan of using passages from McCafferty's book, *Sloppy Firsts*. Eventually, Little, Brown pulled Viswanathan's book from the shelves and cancelled her two-book deal.

More recently in 2008, Margaret Selzer wrote her non-fiction memoir, *Love and Consequences*, that described her life as a foster care mixed child raised in South-Central Los Angeles who ran drugs for the

Bloods gang. The problem was none of it was true. Margaret was an all-white girl who never lived in foster care. Investigation proved other assertions false, forcing the author to apologize.

Situations such as these suggest that some authors will take liberties with the truth in order to achieve success. It is clear that publishers will need more vigil when it comes to researching the assertions of their authors.

The Future of the Book Industry

The book industry is the most specialized of all mass media. Books will rarely be as popular as television programs, films or even magazines. A case in point is one of Amazon's top books of the millennium, *Gone with the Wind*. Margaret Mitchell's great work was so powerful that some have suggested that the book may have spurred the Civil War. It took forty years for the novel to sell 21 million copies, compared to 55 million who watched the first half of the movie version in a single evening of its television debut (Rawlins).

In spite of this, books remain a pivotal part of our society. **Kindles, Readers and iPads** will make book reading more convenient, but nothing will replace the empowering feel of a book in the hands of the reader.

Works Cited

"Apple IPad Sales Show Little Signs of Slowing." *Reviews, News, and Opinion About Personal Technology by Harry McCracken & Friends | Technologizer.* Web. 12 July 2010. <http://technologizer.com/2010/06/01/apple-ipad-sales-show-little-signs-of-slowing/>.

"Barnes & Noble Booksellers." *Barnes & Noble, Inc.* Web. 09 Dec. 2008. <http://www.barnesandnobleinc.com/our_company/history>.

"Best-Selling Books of 2009." *MarketingCharts: Charts and Data for Marketers in Web and Excel Format.* Web.

08 July 2010. <http://www.marketingcharts.com/ print/ top-books-of-2009-11540/>.

"BGIView - Borders - Books, Music and Movies." *Borders - Buy Books, Used Books, Music, DVDs & Blu-ray Online*. Web. 15 Dec. 2008. <http://www.borders.com/ online/store/BGIView_aboutus>.

"Book Publishing - Part I - The Early History." *CyberCollege Index Page for Free TV Production and Mass Media Course*. Web. 09 Dec. 2008. <http://www.cybercollege .com/frtv/book1.htm>.

Clark, Judy. "Laura Esquivel: Like Water for Chocolate: The Law of Love: Like Water for Chocolate: Book Review." *Mostly Fiction Book Reviews*. Web. 09 Dec. 2008. <http://mostlyfiction.com/latin/esquivel.htm#bio>.

"Complete List of Oprah's Book Club Books - Oprah.com." *Oprah Winfrey's Official Website - Live Your Best Life - Oprah.com*. Web. 08 July 2010. <http:// www.oprah.com/oprahsbookclub/Complete-List-of-Oprahs-Book-Club-Books>.

Ganapati, Priya. "Showdown: Kindle 2 vs. Sony Reader | Gadget Lab | Wired.com." *Wired News*. Web. 09 July 2010. <http://www.wired.com/gadgetlab/2009/ 02/showdown-kindle/>.

Harris, Mark. "2007 Entertainer of the Year: J.K. Rowling | J.K. Rowling | 1 | Flashback: 2007 | Books | Entertainers of the Year | Entertainment Weekly." *Entertainment Weekly's EW.com | Entertainment News | TV News | TV Shows | Movie, Music and DVD Reviews*. Web. 10 Dec. 2008. <http://www.ew.com/ew/ article/0,,20152943_20153269_20162480,00.html>.

"Harry Potter and the Deathly Hallows: Information from Answers.com." *Answers.com: Wiki Q&A Combined with Free Online Dictionary, Thesaurus, and Encyclopedias*. Web. 20 Dec. 2008. <http://www.answers .com/topic/harry-potter-book-seven>.

"Harry Potter Book Topples U.S. Sales Records - Business - U.S. Business - Msnbc.com." *Breaking News, Weather, Business, Health, Entertainment, Sports, Politics, Travel, Science, Technology, Local, US & World News- Msnbc.com*. Web. 6 Jan. 2009. <http://www.msnbc.msn.com/id/ 8608578/>.

"IPad - See the Web, Email, and Photos like Never Before." *Apple*. Web. 08 July 2010. <http://www.apple .com/ipad/>.

"J.K. (Joanne) Rowling Biography, plus Links to Book Reviews and Excerpts." *BookBrowse.com: More than 20,000 Book Reviews, Reader Reviews, Critic's Reviews, Book Excerpts and More*. Web. 15 Dec. 2008. <http://www.bookbrowse.com/biographies/index. cfm/author_number/334/JK-Joanne-Rowling>.

"MacDailyNews - Apple Surpasses Microsoft to Become World's Biggest Tech Company, Second-most-valuable U.S. Company." *MacDailyNews - Apple and Mac News - Welcome Home*. Web. 12 July 2010. <http:// www.macdailynews.com/index.php/weblog/comments/25385/>.

"Mental_floss Blog » The All-Time Best-Selling Books." *Mental_floss Magazine - Where Knowledge Junkies Get Their Fix*. Web. 20 Dec. 2008. <http://www .mentalfloss.com/blogs/archives/5886>.

On, Clicking. "Final Harry Potter Book Sells 8.3M Copies in First Day - Jul. 23, 2007." *Business, Financial, Personal Finance News - CNNMoney.com*. 23 July 2007. Web. 15 Dec. 2008. <http://money.cnn.com/2007/07/23/news/ companies/scholastic_potter/index.htm>.

Oprah Winfrey's Official Website - Oprah.com. Web. 20 Dec. 2008. <http://www.oprah.com/index.html>.

Rawlins, Gregory. Cambridge: MIT, 1996. Print.

Rawlins, Gregory J. E. *Moths to the Flame: the Seductions of Computer Technology*. Cambridge, Mass.: MIT, 1996. Print.

Sony USA. Web. 08 July 2010. <http://www.sony.com/ index.php>.

"Waldenbooks." *Employment - Search Job Employment Opportunities by Company Name - Monster.com*. Web. 15 Dec. 2008. <http://company.monster.com/waldenbooks/>.

Way, The. "Kindle vs IPad Review « Kindle Review – Kindle 3 Review, IPad Review." *Kindle Review – Kindle 3 Review, IPad Review*. Web. 09 July 2010. <http://ireaderreview. com/2010/01/27/kindle-vs-ipad-review/>.

NEWS

Genelle Belmas

Chapter Objectives:

◆ Identify the characteristics that define newsworthiness

◆ Describe the concept of gatekeeping

◆ Identify several common criticisms of the news media

◆ Explain the effects of special interest groups and individual activists on news organizations

◆ List the seven adjectives that describe what modern consumers look for in news

Introduction

What is news? If you have ever wondered what makes the cut to be printed in the newspaper, to be broadcast on your television, or to appear on your favorite news Web site, you've wondered about **newsworthiness.** News judgment is something that most news professionals take years to define and refine. It isn't something that comes from reading a textbook or writing a few news stories.

Characteristics of News

Why is one item "news" when another item doesn't qualify? There are several characteristics used to measure an item's newsworthiness.

TIMELINESS

The item is current. A century or more ago, when news came by ship and other early modes of transportation, timeliness was not a factor. If a story was new to the reader, then it was considered news. Today, with virtually instantaneous electronic transmission of information, news is perishable. Editors who are confronted with a day-old story must find a different perspective or a new way of presenting it.

PROXIMITY

The item happened nearby. If two children are killed in a fire in distant city, it is only of mild interest. But if it happened in your town, you wonder "Have I ever passed that place? Is it somebody I might know?" Likewise, a high-school basketball team's victory might get front-page coverage in the weekly paper serving the local area. Even the local daily paper, which might cover dozens of suburban communities, will most likely determine that the basketball team's story doesn't interest enough readers to merit a position on the front page. This is evidence that today's news is moving more toward the **hyperlocal**—perhaps within a few blocks of your city or town—than ever before.

HUMAN INTEREST

The item is a compelling example of humanity. You hear a story on the radio about a little girl who fell down a well in a faraway state. The fact that she is still alive and hundreds of rescuers are racing against the clock to save her life touches the hearts of listeners and keeps the story in the media for three days until she is brought out alive. This is an example of a basic human interest story. With human interest stories, proximity isn't as important as the ability of consumers to identify with the people involved in the story.

CONSEQUENCE

The item affects the reader. The incredible fact that the death, injury, or capture of thousands in the Iraq war of the 2000s did not initially attract much attention in the U.S. news media can be attributed to the inability of the consumer to fathom what difference it all made. The war featured more prominently in the news, however, when it continued to last longer than most Americans expected or wanted to experience. In contrast, the report of a car-bombing that kills two people in strife-torn Northern Ireland will get news coverage because millions of Americans have Irish ancestors. In this case, the news item affects a fairly large group of readers and would therefore be considered newsworthy.

DISASTER

The attributes of a disaster are related to consequence but of greater magnitude. When two hijacked airplanes crashed into the World Trade Center in 2001, destroying the structure and killing thousands, it was the horror of calamity that produced an audience. Follow-up articles, or "second-day stories," which described the miraculous escape of workers from the Twin Towers, can be classified as human interest stories. **Sidebars,** or secondary articles running alongside the main article, explained the timeline of the tragedy or the technical details of the collapse of the towers.

PROMINENCE

The people involved are well known. If you or your neighbors give a party, it probably will not be reported in the news. However, if several film stars are invited to a dinner at the White House, we can all read or hear every detail about what was served, who wore what, and what was said by everyone of importance. We may bemoan what feels like non-stop coverage of the lives of celebrities, but many of us watch and read and consume.

NOVELTY

The item is unusual. "If man bites dog, that's news," according to the old saying. When a hobbyist builds a boat in his basement and then can't remove the boat without tearing down the house, that, also, is newsworthy.

CONFLICT

The item is an example of individuals' inability to get along. Stories about divorce, charges of political corruption, the arrest of a bombing suspect, the assassination of a foreign political figure, or a movie star's angry complaints about a film critic are all considered news.

Gatekeeping

As you read in the previous section, there are several characteristics used to determine whether an item is newsworthy. **Gatekeepers** are the individuals who help shape the news by applying these characteristics and making this determination.

All producers function as gatekeepers. From all the information available, a small amount is selected and most items are rejected. Sources for a news story recount what they remember—or choose to remember—and thus are the first gatekeepers. Reporters sift through their notes and recollections, selecting the details that will make the story complete, accurate, and interesting. Editors then scan all the stories prepared by their reporters or offered by the wire services to select enough material to fill the page or the time allotted in the news broadcast. The consumer is the final gatekeeper, choosing what news to absorb and what items to skip or ignore.

The Internet affects gatekeeping. On one hand, gatekeeping is more important in in Internet news because, increasingly, readers have a limited amount of time to absorb information. On the other hand, gatekeeping is less important in that if a reader cannot find what he or she wants or needs on one site, there are thousands more that could have the desired information.

All those who have studied gatekeeping understand that utility is the first and foremost reason for letting a news item pass. If the perception is that the audience wants or needs the information, the news item is likely to be accepted for publication or broadcast. If an item fits a pattern—that is, it looks like information previously used, so it is judged to be newsworthy—it may get the green light. If the information is unusual in a way that intrigues the gatekeeper, and if the perception is that the item also will amuse, astonish, or intrigue the audience, it may be considered newsworthy. In other words, any gatekeeper, while applying standard criteria, also makes a personal judgment that a story is worth sharing with the consumer.

Criticisms of the News Media

By knowing the characteristics of newsworthiness and understanding the concept of gatekeeping, you will gain a better understanding of how the news media operate. However, you may still be wondering about some of the common criticisms of the media. For example, are the media biased? Do the media sensationalize news stories to attract a larger audience? Do the media invade individuals' privacy? These criticisms, as well as several others, are discussed in the next few sections. Although each of the criticisms that follows is based on a partial truth, it's important to understand that each criticism is also based on selected information that may reflect only a particular point of view.

"THE NEWS MEDIA ARE BIASED."

Anyone who has attended an event and then read or heard an account of it in the news is aware that reporters usually choose to focus on one aspect of a story. If that aspect happens to be something that we don't feel was the main point, we may come to the conclusion that the reporter was biased. This is especially true if the account appears to favor the "other side" in a story that concerns politics or controversy.

Because reporters tend to be younger than the average consumer, and because their task of exposing wrongdoing tends to place them in an antiestablishment stance, many people perceive that reporters have a **liberal bias.** That is, they are seen as left-leaning politically and champions of the underdog oppressed by a bureaucratic society. There may be some truth in that assumption on a case-by-case basis, but as mass communication researcher and theorist Ted Glasser suggests, the American press is inherently a **conservative** institution, despite the occasional liberal bent of a reporter. Glasser argues that journalists follow the status quo; they accept and participate in the conservation of society's dominant values, and they proceed from an underlying assumption that the American value system is "right." Nevertheless, journalists and consumers often find themselves at odds when it comes to understanding the role of reporter or editor.

"THE NEWS MEDIA ARE TOO QUICK TO JUMP ON THE BANDWAGON."

The pressure of competition causes editors to demand that their reporters obtain the latest information and report it even if they are not 100 percent certain of the facts. From the journalists' points of view, facts can be added to later versions of a story as they become known. But a story that later proves largely in error is not quickly forgotten by consumers. When a Northwest Airlines MD-82 jet crashed immediately after takeoff from the Detroit airport in August 1987, people were quick to speculate about the cause of the crash. A CBS reporter told Dan Rather on the CBS Evening News program that "my best guess... is that it was a catastrophic failure of the engine, that it literally exploded." Similar speculation among journalists, witnesses, and airport personnel was reported as apparent fact by many major newspapers and broadcast stations. However, the National Transportation Safety Board investigators eventually found that the cause of the accident was something entirely different—most likely the flightcrew's failure to extend the plane's flaps and slats prior to takeoff.[1] Endless examples of this type have soured consumers, yet the media appear unable to resist rushing on air or into print with unproven information in the hope that they will be perceived positively as being the first to report. Unfortunately, this pressure has only increased with the proliferation of online news.

"THE MEDIA ARE CARELESS WITH INFORMATION."

On any given day, a newspaper might contain at least a few "typos" (typographical errors) as well as some erroneous facts. For example, suppose a reporter erroneously refers to a "set shot" as a "hook shot" in covering a basketball game. Or perhaps the sportscaster on TV mistakenly reports that Chicago won a baseball game when the graphic on the screen says Atlanta was the winner. Or the "crawl" on the bottom of the television screen includes a misspelled word. As a consumer, you forgive a few of these errors, but when you see your own name misspelled in print or when you know from experience that someone was misquoted, it becomes easy to mistrust all reporting. When faced with this criticism, the majority of editors would most likely respond that newspapers and broadcast reports prepared under deadline pressure are subject to error, and that the media should be judged for the vast amount of information they transmit correctly.

"THE MEDIA USE SENSATIONALISM TO ATTRACT AN AUDIENCE."

A scantily clad actress on a magazine cover sells more copies than the portrait of a political leader. During "sweeps weeks," when broadcast ratings are determined, feature stories on prostitution, runaway children, and spousal abuse suddenly receive heavy promotion and extended air time. These are the facts of economic life of the popular news media; in other words, the charge is true. Some media consciously sensationalize the news at all times to attract a wide audience. Publishers counter such criticism by saying, "That's what sells newspapers." Broadcasters can see ratings increase after they report on a sordid story of vice or crime. The audience, as you have seen, helps decide whether the media will continue to use sex and sensation to attract and hold its attention.

"THE MEDIA ARE AIMED AT THE LOWEST COMMON DENOMINATOR OF SOCIETY."

Because the mass media need to attract large audiences to increase funding from advertisers, there is a natural tendency to write and report so that everyone can understand the information. Many television news programs present relatable reporters, weather forecasters, and sportscasters who joke with one another during the half-hour program so the experience is pleasant and painless for all. As long as the mass media remain a predominantly commercial enterprise committed to securing the largest possible audience, aiming low intellectually is to be expected.

"THE MEDIA INVADE THE PRIVACY OF INDIVIDUALS."

The widow of a police officer slain in the line of duty weeps uncontrollably at her husband's graveside. The television camera brings her grief into our kitchen; we cannot escape the sound of her sobs or the vision of her total breakdown. Many viewers might consider this an invasion of privacy. However, a journalist might counter, "Grief is natural; it does not reflect negatively on anyone." Besides, the image of a murder's impact on one family may have the positive effect of spurring society to action in fighting crime and violence. Most journalists, however, would not defend the colleague who enters someone's home under false pretenses to obtain, perhaps by theft, pictures from the family album of a crime victim. Few condoned the actions of the freelance photographer who hounded Jacqueline Kennedy Onassis and her children on the streets outside her home to the point where a judge forbade him to come within close camera range.

As you have read, the criticisms discussed in the previous sections have some truth to them. But does this mean all news is tainted? Should we mistrust everything we read, see, or hear? Well, not necessarily. Partly as a result of wire services dominating the production and distribution of news for use in smaller papers throughout the nation and in other parts of the world, the "objective" story—one that is free of political bias from the publisher and free of personal bias from the reporter and editor—became a hallmark of journalism. It became a code taught in journalism schools, and the myth of "objectivity" permeated journalism training. Although the myth of journalistic objectivity was accepted throughout much of the twentieth century, today it must be examined seriously. Consider these questions about "objective" news reporting:

◆ Is there a reporter who does not filter information through a set of values developed over time, assigning greater meaning to some facts than others?

◆ Does the practice of assembling news articles by quoting spokespeople (with differing viewpoints from either side of an issue) guarantee lack of bias?

◆ Are journalists somehow better trained and equipped to sort through and select the facts than judges, clergy, teachers, parents, and lawyers?

The critical consumer necessarily develops a situational understanding of just how objective the news media are, can be, and try to be. In other words, the savvy media consumer does not rely solely and unshakably on one news source but tries to sample many different sources and ideas to put together the best possible picture of the news.

Consumer Action

Consumers are not passive receivers of information. The consumer's response to information constitutes **feedback,** or new information created in reaction to the original information. That feedback often influences the producer of mass messages. Although consumer feedback takes many forms, it is commonly presented by special interest groups and individual activists who act as spokespeople for unorganized groups. These groups and individuals can apply pressure to news organizations that is similar to legal and political threats. Formal and informal mechanisms also exist for delivering individual complaints to the producer, and the media organizations themselves sometimes attack their competitors.

SPECIAL INTEREST GROUPS

Special interest groups include church organizations, politically oriented groups, and coalitions that form around individual issues. In the early 1980s, Reverend Jerry Falwell's "Moral Majority" coalition of religious organizations sought to focus attention on all forms of mass media information that they felt were unwholesome and not suitable for American families. In addition to presenting their views on various religious radio and television programs sponsored by groups belonging to the coalition, the Moral Majority engaged in letter-writing campaigns to legislators and congressional representatives who they felt would be sympathetic to their conservative point of view. They also mounted a grassroots campaign aimed at influencing the Federal Communication Commission (FCC). Currently, a group of concerned individuals in Los Angeles called the Parents Television Council is very active in monitoring broadcast television for indecent content and in encouraging its members and others to speak out to the FCC by complaining when the broadcast media shows indecent content.

Although most special interest groups claim to represent "public opinion" and to be acting for the good of society, producers of mass communication information must decide which complaints are really in the public interest and which represent a special point of view. As an aide to the National Advisory Commission on Civil Disorders noted, "The problem is made harder by the fact that accusations of bias against the media are often based on the bias of the audience itself."

MEDIA CRITICS

Media critics play a role in monitoring the performance of the press. *The Washington Journalism Review*, published at the University of Maryland journalism school, monitors press coverage of affairs centered in the nation's capital. The *Columbia Journalism Review*, published at Columbia University's journalism school, is known for its "Darts and Laurels" department, which praises examples of good reporting and editing, but criticizes sloppy or biased journalism. *The Quill*, published for members of the Society of Professional Journalists, presents analysis of news coverage by individual newspapers or stations as well as the entire profession's performance on important issues. Regional press reviews are published in several major cities, and magazines such as *New York* and *The Atlantic Monthly* regularly publish articles examining the role of information producers.

INDIVIDUAL CONSUMER ACTION

Individual consumer action can be accomplished in many ways, including the simple actions of turning off the TV or canceling a subscription to a publication. These types of actions do not let the producer know what your specific complaint might be but, if enough people carry them out, these actions can affect the media. For example, a reduced viewing audience may spell the end for a banal television program. A newspaper that no longer satisfies the needs of its audience may see a reduction in profits.

The Federal Communications Commission's license renewal mechanism guarantees that broadcast stations pay attention to complaints received from their listeners and viewers, although individual written response to complaints is not required. Newspapers, although not required by law or regulation to handle feedback in any particular way, print letters to the editor on the editorial page. Most newspapers also print corrections as a way of rectifying mistakes and providing readers with an opportunity to differ with views expressed by others, including the paper's editorial board. The National Advertising Division of the Council of Better Business Bureaus in New York receives consumer complaints about advertising, as does the Federal Trade Commission in Washington. The first is an independent association supported by merchants and manufacturers; the second, of course, is a government agency. All the major television networks maintain audience service departments in their headquarters to respond to viewer concerns about network programming and news. Manufacturing and service companies are sensitive to individual complaints about their advertising messages, particularly at the local level. Some media organizations employ ombudsmen or reader representatives to serve as direct connections with the public.

Trends in Newsgathering and Reporting

What consumers want, and what news organizations are scrambling to deliver, is up-to-the-minute content provided in the format they want and the ability to interact with that content. News organizations of all sizes must take into account the increasing sophistication of their audiences. "Shovelware" Web sites, where content from the daily paper or broadcast is dumped wholesale online, are no longer acceptable. Now, online content is developed solely for the online news experience, complete with audio and video, links to additional information, and discussion boards. In fact, the development of content for all the products of the news organization has resulted in at least one newspaper renaming its "reporters" as "content providers," signaling the movement toward a new way of thinking about the delivery of news.

So, what trends typify this new way of thinking about newsgathering and delivery? In the next sections, you'll read about seven adjectives that describe news consumers' expectations and desires.

DIGITAL

By definition, a digital system has a set of discrete values, in the form of binary numbers (ones and zeros). In contrast, an analog system has a continuous range of values. Think about a digital thermometer and an older mercury thermometer. A mercury thermometer might tell you that it is 72 degrees F, but a digital thermometer might reveal that it is a bit warmer than 72, maybe 72.2 or 72.3 degrees F. The digital thermometer is able to show you nuances that the mercury one cannot. Listening to an analog radio, you might hear pops and clicks and snaps of static and interference. A satellite radio's music, on the other hand, is clear and uncluttered.

Digital formats have a lot of benefits over their analog counterparts. In addition to being less susceptible to noise and other interferences, digital material can be compressed into smaller sizes for easy sending and downloading. Content in digital format can be duplicated and shared easily without loss of quality. This particular feature has affected recording companies. In 2007, the number of CDs sold fell to 511.1 million after peaking at 942.5 million in 2000, according to the Recording Industry Association of America.[2]

Some forms of mass media embraced digital technology earlier than others. For example, compact disks have largely replaced vinyl records for most consumers (although purists insist than vinyl recordings are warmer and more true to the music), and digital cameras have been around in some form since the 1980s. News media, however, have been somewhat slower to adapt.

"Going digital" for a news media organization means more than simply using digital cameras and developing a Web site. As one commentator suggests, having a Web site does not make a newspaper a master of electronic publishing any more than buying a hammer and saw makes one a master carpenter.[3] There is a need to shift the organization's entire view on what it means to be a news supplier. But going digital is the necessary first step in achieving some of the other expectations from consumers.

CUSTOMIZABLE

In the age of TiVo, Sirius radio, and iPods, most consumers no longer want a "one size fits all" news experience. They want to listen to books on their iPods or in their cars, they want to skip television commercials, and they want to be able to customize the information and news they get and how they get it. Most major newspapers and broadcast stations offer consumers the option of subscribing to email newsletters or summaries that feature various topics such as breaking news, entertainment, or sports.

Search portals have taken customization of the news experience seriously. At Yahoo! users can customize their My Yahoo! page to include local news, national news, TV listings, weather, maps, and shopping. iGoogle has similar customization options; users can add a joke of the day, a daily sudoku puzzle, or a module to search YouTube for videos. Users can even change the layout of their page. In addition, users are encouraged to create their own "gadgets" for use on the iGoogle site and for sharing with others quickly and easily. They can feature their own pictures, quotes, and journals.

The downside of customization is that if users choose only news they know they want, they may miss out on important news in other areas. For example, if a subscriber only selects news about fashion and entertainment, that subscriber might miss out on breaking news or local news stories that might ultimately affect that user's life more deeply than the latest runway designs.

IMMEDIATE

Do you want news delivered to you as soon as possible? If so, you can set up your computer to receive RSS feeds on news headlines or podcasts. You may have heard the term "podcast" or seen podcasts available for downloading on iTunes. A **podcast** is a digital audio or video media file that can be

News at Seven

The concept of personalized news isn't new, but this method of delivery is. Students at Northwestern University's Intelligent Information Laboratory have developed a personalized news system with news delivered by *avatars* (computer-generated images of people) that users can customize.

According to the Web site, "News at Seven is an automatic system that builds personalized news shows. It finds the news you are interested in; edits it; finds relevant images, videos, and external opinions; and then presents it all using a virtual news team working in a virtual studio. News at Seven is a uniquely compelling experience that can present traditional news—augmented with supplemental images, videos, and opinions from the blogosphere—all without human intervention."[4]

The interface permits total customization. Users select topics of interest, and the software behind the Web site searches for information about that topic, edits it to broadcast story length, and has the avatars speak it with appropriate inflection.

Not everyone is thrilled about this avatar-driven innovation. But with the option to include news feeds from users' MySpace and Facebook pages along with local, national, and international news, News At Seven may draw the next generation of Web users.

downloaded to a user's computer or MP3 player for listening or viewing at the consumer's leisure. Early podcasts were developed by former MTV veejay Adam Curry, who still publishes his podcast, "Daily Source Code." There is software that allows you to receive updated headlines or podcasts as soon as they are published online. The creator of the podcast sets up a web feed, often in a format called RSS, or "Real Simple Syndication." Those who wish to receive the information may subscribe to the web feed using software called an RSS reader or **aggregator.** As soon as the Web site or podcast is updated, the site sends out a notification to the aggregator, which shows the subscriber that there has been an update and lets the subscriber access the new information quickly and easily. Aggregators are built in to My Yahoo!, iGoogle, and other portals. Users can also download software such as Juice or Newsfire RSS

to aggregate their feeds. In addition, iTunes permits its users to subscribe to podcasts and other web feeds.

RSS feeds fit the need for custom information delivered when and where users want it. Apple reports over 100,000 podcast episodes on iTunes alone, covering a wide range of topics such as travel, cooking, current events, technology, and sports.

If customized emails with breaking news, podcasts, and RSS feeds don't fulfill the need for immediacy in news consumption, how about news alerts to your cell phone? Text messages from the local newspaper or broadcast station can be sent to users' cell phones to inform them about anything from inclement weather to breaking news. Anywhere there is a digital media device, there can be news.

Making a Podcast

Making a podcast is easier and less expensive than you might think. All you need is a computer with an Internet connection, a microphone, and software to save and edit your podcast. Then you need to determine a way to publish it so that others can hear.

There are several free applications that exist to record your voice. Audacity is popular because it's easy to use, has a lot of advanced features, and it's free. You can download the application online. Audacity has versions for Windows and Macintosh platforms, as well as Linux and other operating systems. Microsoft Windows has a free utility built in called Sound Recorder that will also do the job, although you will need to convert the saved file from .wav to .mp3 format. Macintosh users can use GarageBand or other Mac utilities.

Do you want to add some music? There are several online sources for music that's free to add to podcasts and for which users need not pay royalties. Check out PodSafe Audio and Podsafe Music Network for background music. (Never use music from your own personal collection without obtaining explicit permission; you don't want to be in violation of the creator's copyright.)

Once you've created your podcast, you need to upload it to a publicly accessible server (your university probably has server space set aside for all students). Once you've done that, you need to create an RSS feed so that interested listeners can find your file. You can code that by hand using one of a number of tutorials online, or you can use a free service such as Cosmic Scripts to help you out. Upload that RSS file to your server and publish in iTunes or elsewhere; directions for publishing to iTunes are on the site. If you don't want to publish using RSS, you can just email your podcast to your friends and family or post it on your Web site as an .mp3 file for anyone to download.

What about personal uses for podcasts? Record a message for a friend and email it for a more personal birthday greeting. Place the microphone in front of your elderly grandfather or aunt and encourage him or her to talk about the past. Write and record a review of the latest indie band you're into and email it to the band (with permission to post on their own Web site, if you want).

INTERACTIVE

The word that perhaps best summarizes the entire Web 2.0 experience is "interactive." No longer satisfied with letting news elites and professionals remain removed from discussion and feedback, users want to talk back to the media in ways they have never been able to before. Most news organizations have some kind of feedback forum in the form of online message boards or discussions on individual news stories.

Users create news as well. **Blogs,** a combination of "web" and "log," can take a number of different forms, from personal diaries to commentaries on current events or any other imaginable topic. Regularly updated and often deliverable to users via RSS or other web feeds, blogs exploded in the late 1990s. Roughly ten years later, Technorati, a Web site devoted to monitoring happenings on the web, tracked nearly 113 million blogs.[5] Anyone can start a blog using free online services such as LiveJournal or Blogger. You have also participated in creating content if you've ever uploaded a video to YouTube or have a social networking page on a site like MySpace or Facebook.

News organizations are following the trend of interactivity, too. Typical of news organizations taking advantage of readers with cell phone cameras or video cameras, CNN has a section of its webpage called "iReports," where CNN viewers can submit video footage or photos of "news happening before their eyes." If they desire, viewers can allow the use of their recordings on CNN's Web site or cable TV shows. Then, users can write about the news item on the iReports blog and discuss it with other viewers.

CONVERGED

The buzzword *convergence*, as Webster's defines it, is "the merging of distinct technologies, industries, or devices into a unified whole."[6] From the consumer's perspective, convergence means convenience. For example, a subscriber to the *Los Angeles Times* might receive a copy on the doorstep in the morning and also read breaking news and updates online all day. At *Time* magazine's Web site, you'll find more than just the copy from the printed magazine. There is Time On The Go, where you can go to mobile.time.com and get information delivered to your handheld device.

Consumers expect more than just bare facts; they want the history of the event, additional photos and commentary, full text of interviews with key sources, audio and video of events as they happen, and links to additional information. Convenience for consumers also means that one company provides all the telecommunications services a user requires for one fee—and one monthly bill. For example, several companies offer Internet, cable, and telephone service for one monthly subscription fee.

The notion of convergence also means that the distinctions between print, broadcast and online media are fading and blurring. Professionals working in the news industry must be conversant with all media forms; the traditional print reporter must be ready to shoot video for the Web site, or the broadcast reporter may be asked to write copy for dissemination online or in an email alert. Journalism schools and departments around the country are responding to the need of the news industry for entering news professionals to have basic training in all forms of mass communication, not just the one in which they plan to work.

HYPERLOCAL

Large cities such as New York and Los Angeles are home to millions of residents. How can one media organization hope to provide news to interest and inform all of them? The answer is to break the city down into smaller pieces and provide news on a hyperlocal, or community, level. News of interest to those living in one community, defined ethnically, geographically, or in some other way, may not be of interest to the residents of another community. Your student newspaper and broadcast station are examples of hyperlocal media because they serve and are of interest to your university community.

The community journalism movement, is one way of engaging in hyperlocal journalism. In many of these community journalism publications, citizens play an active role in creating and disseminating news of importance to them and their communities. For example, the city of Bakersfield, California not only has a daily city newspaper, *The Bakersfield Californian*, but several other smaller publications. *The Northwest Voice* is tailored toward residents of northwest Bakersfield; *The Southwest Voice*, for residents of southwest Bakersfield; and the *Tehachapi News*, for residents and businesses of Tehachapi, a small city outside Bakersfield. All three hyperlocal publications allow and encourage citizens to post their own photos, stories, blogs, commentary, and news.

Interested in blogs about your local community? Look for placeblogs! Placeblogger.com is a searchable directory of local placeblogs. What is a placeblog? According to Placeblogger, "A placeblog is an act of sustained attention to a particular place over time. It can be done by one person, a defined group of people, or in a way that's open to community contribution. It's not a newspaper, though it may contain random acts of journalism. It's about the lived experience of a place."[7] Placeblogs, then, are less about the goings-on of a community and more about what makes the community unique, important, and authentic.

Another form of hyperlocal media is **low-power FM stations,** or LPFM. The Federal Communications Commission authorized licenses for these hyperlocal radio stations, which cover only two to four miles, in 2000. According to the Media Access Project, an organization that advocates and supports LPFM, the benefits of this type of radio are significant:

◆ LPFM stations are truly local and by law the applicants for the license must be within 10 miles of the transmitter.

◆ They are affordable, costing as little as $10,000 for equipment.

◆ Because they are non-commercial, LPFM stations aren't driven by a profit motive and must be educational (broadly defined) in nature.

◆ They are diverse because no single corporation can own more than one LPFM license.

An example of LPFM radio is WRYR, 97.5 FM (We aRe Your Radio), serving the eastern and western shoreline communities of the Chesapeake Bay in Maryland. Its goal is to promote intelligent growth and environmental sustainability, and its programming includes local news, health and lifestyle information, and music. The Media Access Project reports that there are currently over 250 of these LPFM stations on the air, with more on the way.

UBIQUITOUS

The word "ubiquitous" means "everywhere," and that's where consumers want their media to be. News appears on your cell phone, online, in the newspaper, on the television. You may want your music in your car, on your iPod, in your cell phone, and on your computer. Some news organizations, like National Public Radio, feature software that you can install on your computer that will deliver news to your desktop, customizable with RSS feeds.

Consumers want to have their media and watch it too, and they can with **placeshifting**—consuming live, recorded, or stored music, television shows, or other media on a remote device, either online or over a data network. Similar to the **timeshifting** that DVRs or VCRs do, recording a show for later consumption, a placeshifting system lets you watch your show or listen to your music from anywhere in the world. If you were on a business trip and did not want to miss a local team play, you could placeshift the show to your computer and watch it in your hotel room.

Ever wanted to go to a Web site you knew you'd bookmarked on your home computer but were at a computer lab or a friend's house? Use a **social bookmarking** site, like del.icio.us or Digg. A social bookmarking site is an online place to store favorite sites, share them with others, and see what others are storing. Another element of Web 2.0, social bookmarking organizes information with tags—a term or word associated with the information—to enable classification and searchability.

Information Glut?

Call it information glut, information overload, or infobog. It all adds up to the same thing: too much information, too few editors, too little time. As David Shenk wrote in his book *Data Smog*, "We thrive on the information, and yet we can also choke on it." Billions of emails are sent each day. Think about how many times you answer your cell phone, check your email, or turn on your MP3 player.

Alvin Toffler coined the term "information overload" in his 1970 book *Future Shock*. In that book, Toffler defines "future shock" as how a person reacts to too much change in too short a period of time. As he put it, "Much that now strikes us as incomprehensible would be far less so if we took a fresh look at the racing rate of change that makes reality seem,

Careers in the Field

As you have read in this chapter, news continues to evolve as new and different formats emerge. Today, not only are there jobs available at traditional newspapers and TV and radio broadcast stations, there are also positions at online newspapers and magazines. News media outlets employ a variety of professionals, such as news anchors, news correspondents, reporters, editors, camera operators, and photographers. According to the U.S. Bureau of Labor Statistics, job growth in news-related professions is expected to be limited over the next several years, with little or no change in the availability of jobs.[9]

sometimes, like a kaleidoscope run wild. For the acceleration of change does not merely buffet industries or nations. It is a concrete force that reaches deep into our personal lives, compels us to act out new roles, and confronts us with the danger of a new and powerfully upsetting psychological disease." What can we do about it?

Dr. Danna Walker, a professor of journalism at American University in Washington, D.C., gave an assignment to the freshmen in her "Understanding Mass Media" course. She asked them to be electronic media-free for 24 hours. She asked students to avoid using electronic media, such as cell phones, MP3 players, the Internet, computer games, and radio, but allowed students to read books, magazines, and newspapers. After the "e-media fast," many students reported that they felt some relief at not having their cell phones ring at inopportune times. They spent time with their families. They read books. They cleaned their rooms. They recognized that silence, while golden, is hard for them. Most students were used to having two or more electronic media devices (for example, the TV and the Internet) on at the same time or they felt disconnected. They realized that the way they kept in touch with many of their friends was through instant messaging or social networking sites.

One of Dr. Walker's students wrote in the reflection paper, "A day without electronic media showed me how dependent society and I were upon it. Without that distraction, I can discover new things in the real world, or at least be more productive. Neil Postman was right when he said that American society has become obsessed with the trivial and the minute."[8]

Chapter Summary

◆ The characteristics of newsworthiness include timeliness, proximity, human interest, consequence, disaster, prominence, novelty, conflict. The more of these characteristics that can be found in a story, the more likely the news medium is to decide that the audience will be interested in the story.

◆ Gatekeepers are those who help shape the news by determining which stories or facts are newsworthy and which are not. Examples of gatekeepers include eyewitnesses (who provide their recollection of a particular event), reporters (who decide which details to include in a story), editors (who might need to revise stories for length), and even consumers (who determine what news to absorb and what to ignore).

◆ There are several common criticisms of the news media. Some consumers claim that the media are biased. Others might say that news organizations frequently sensationalize stories to increase the size of their audience. Another common criticism is that reporters routinely invade individuals' privacy. Although these criticisms are all based, in part, on truths, it's also important to understand that they may also be based on a particular point of view.

◆ Special interest groups and individual activists can apply pressure to news organizations that is similar to legal and political threats. Feedback from these groups and individuals often influences the producers of mass messages.

◆ Modern consumers are interested in news that is in a digital format, customizable, immediate, interactive, converged, hyperlocal, and ubiquitous.

Glossary

aggregator—a tool, built into a portal such as My Yahoo! or iGoogle, that shows the subscriber when there has been an update to a Web site or podcast to which the user subscribes

blogs—a combination of the words "web" and "log," which can take a number of different forms, from personal diaries to commentaries on current events or any other imaginable topic

conservative—having right-leaning political ideals

feedback—new information created in reaction to the original information

gatekeepers—the eyewitnessnes, reporters, editors, and consumers who help shape the news by determining whether an item is newsworthy

hyperlocal—pertaining to a single community, defined ethnically, geographically, or in some other way

liberal bias—having left-leaning political ideals

low-power FM stations (LPFM)—hyperlocal radio stations, which transmit over only two to four miles

newsworthiness—a news item's level of interest to the general public; determined by characteristics such as timeliness, proximity, and consequence

placeshifting—consuming live, recorded, or stored music, television shows, or other media on a remote device, either online or over a data network

podcast—a digital audio or video media file that can be downloaded to a user's computer or MP3 player for listening or viewing at the consumer's leisure

sidebars—secondary articles running alongside the main article in a print news story

social bookmarking—an online place to store URLs to favorite Web sites, share them with others, and see what others are storing

timeshifting—using DVRs or VCRs to recording a show for later consumption

Discussion Questions

1. How has the Internet affected the concept of gatekeeping?
2. How will the role of journalism in a democracy be fulfilled in this age of customizable, digitized, commercialized, convergent news?
3. The chapter discussed whether it's possible for the media to remain truly objective. Is the entire journalistic system biased by virtue of its situation in the free enterprise system where information is packaged for sale? Why or why not?
4. What is the difference between ubiquitous and convergent media?
5. Should blogs be considered a form of news? Why or why not?

Supplemental Web Sites

Center for Citizen Media: *http://citmedia.org/*
Northwest Voice: *http://www.northwestvoice.com/*
Media Access Project: *http://www.mediaaccess.org/*

Endnotes

1. "Northwest Airlines, Inc., McDonnell Douglas DC-9-82, N312RC, Detroit Metropolitan Wayne County Airport, Romulus Michigan, August 16, 1987," NTSB Report Number AAR-88-05, adopted on 5/10/1988, National Transportation Safety Board, *http://www.ntsb.gov/publictn/1988/AAR8805.htm*, Accessed September 8, 2008.

2. "2007 Year-End Shipment Statistics," Recording Industry Association of America, *http://www.riaa.com/keystatistics.php?content_selector=keystats_yearend_report*, Accessed September 8. 2008.

3. "Adopting a Digital Mindset," *Poynter Online*, Feb. 16, 1999, *http://www.poynter.org/content/content_view.asp?id=5672&sid=26*, Accessed September 8, 2008.

4. "About the Project," News at Seven, *http://www.newsat-seven.com/about.php*, Accessed September 8, 2008.

5. "Welcome to Technorati," Technorati Media, *http://technoratimedia.com/about/*, Accessed September 8, 2008.

6. "convergence," Merriam-Webster Online Dictionary, 2008, *Merriam-Webster Online*, *http://www.merriam-webster.com/dictionary/convergence*, Accessed September 8, 2008.

7. "What's A Placeblog?" *Placeblogger.com*, *http://www.placeblogger.com/faq*, Accessed September 8, 2008.

8. Danna L. Walker, "The Longest Day," *Washington Post Magazine*, August 5, 2007 p. W20

9. "News Analysts, Reporters, and Correspondents," Bureau of Labor Statistics, U.S. Department of Labor, *Occupational Outlook Handbook, 2008–09 Edition*, *http://www.bls.gov/oco/ocos088.htm*, Accessed September 8, 2008.

NEWSPAPERS

Genelle Belmas

Chapter Objectives:

◆ Understand the historical development of newspapers in the United States as well as the evolution towards other news media.

◆ Identify minority newspapers and understand their purpose.

◆ Define and distinguish different forms of journalism such as jazz journalism and investigative journalism.

◆ Identify current trends in newspaper publication including online texts.

Introduction

While sipping coffee in the local cafe, you are fairly likely nowadays to see the people around you staring at a computer screen. They're scrolling through pictures with a click of the mouse or responding to an email from a friend. It's even expected that some of them will be reading the news. But what are the chances that you see someone sitting next to you, coffee in one hand, and a newspaper in the other?

Those people who read a newspaper daily or even if those who just pick one up from time-to-time are not alone. According to the Project for Excellence in Journalism, 51 million people on average still buy a newspaper, and overall 124 million still read them.[1] To paraphrase Mark Twain, the report of newspapers' death is an exaggeration. Yet it is probably not news to the majority of people that newspaper readership is in decline. In 2006, according to the same report, circulation fell 2.8 percent for daily newspapers and 3.4 percent for Sunday editions for the six months ending in September compared to that period a year earlier.

But there are bright spots for newspapers. Online readership continues to grow, and newspapers are continuing to take advantage of the Internet's content delivery opportunities to provide timely and complete coverage.

Consumers are the newspaper's final editors, whether online or offline. They select what interests or affects them. Most newspaper readers have definite personal agendas that cause them to jump from department to department. They are able to do this because of the way the modern newspaper is organized. The investor moves quickly to the stock market listings, and then checks out stories that tell what companies are introducing new products or considering merger offers. The sports fan can't be bothered with anything else until the scores and plays of last night's games have been absorbed. This is true online as well. Many newspaper websites allow the reader to personalize the newspaper reading experience and can deliver content that interests each reader in the ways that reader wants, via email, a website, or both.

But newspapers had a long and rich history before they ever hit the Internet. From the earliest news sheets to today's newspaper websites with audio and video content, newspapers continue to deliver the news with the same mission they have always had – to provide important information to interested individuals.

The Evolution of the American Newspaper

Newspapers began as a mere "sideline" enterprise for printers and gradually developed into the main source of a fresh commodity called news. They now contain news that is a notice of current events in local areas as well as far-flung places. The news is of interest to readers not only for its usefulness but also for its unusualness. For well over a century the print medium enjoyed this role until the age of electronic media changed the way people receive news.

BROADSHEETS: A PROFITABLE SIDELINE

Until the early 1700s, few printers gave any thought to being the purveyors of the tidbits of trivia and gossip and happenings about town. These forms of communication were usually passed throughout the community by word of mouth. Printing was a slow and laborious process that did not lend itself to speedy distribution of the latest talk. Also, governments did not look with favor on those who disseminated frivolous information that they had not approved.

Yet when a technology is available, **entrepreneurs** will think of ways to use it to cater to the public. As a society forms, expands, and has more time and money to spend, a market develops for new products. In colonial America, these conditions occurred in the early 1700s. Previously, the presses worked hard until books and government publications had been printed and then stood quiet. Eventually, printers realized they had a salable commodity in the letters they received from Europe. This was particularly true when the communications dealt with **calamity**, changes in government, or rumors about people remembered from "the old country." Excerpts from these European letters were a staple of a new kind of publication, the earliest form of newspaper. These printings were called **broadsheets,** so named because they were single-page impressions made from the full width of the printer's press.

Other broadsheets arrived from England, and printers on this side of the Atlantic quickly combed them, as well as other periodicals, for tidbits of information that would interest colonial readers. The concept of "reporters" was to come much later. Printers merely relied on what they could crib from other sources or what walked in their door in the form of gossip from friends and employees. This information was set in columns of type, without illustration, graphic devices, or anything but the most rudimentary headlines. The broadsheets were printed in quick impressions on the single page, or, at most, four pages when a single sheet was folded. These papers were sold at the printer's counter or hawked outside in the street by an apprentice or a child. Because broadsheets were printed only on one side of the paper people often wrote the latest news on the reverse side before passing the text onto their neighbors.

EARLY COLONIAL NEWSPAPERS

The publication usually acknowledged as the first newspaper in the colonies was *Publick Occurrences Both Foreign and Domestick*, published in Boston in

1690 by Benjamin Harris. In form, it was a newspaper. The content, however, was offensive to the government because of its disrespect for the established order. It never had a chance to become a periodical because it was banned instantly by the governor.

True newspapers, appearing with regularity, can be traced to the introduction of the *Boston News-Letter* in 1704. The publisher, John Campbell, was the postmaster; thus, he not only had government approval, but he could also distribute his publication through mail. Early in its publication, the *Boston News-Letter* consisted mostly of news from England and stories about British politics. Campbell's paper was technically government "approved," however, its content was of little interest to the people. Consequently, it never achieved the success of later endeavors such as the *Boston Gazette*, introduced in 1719. That paper was printed by Benjamin Franklin's older brother James on behalf of Campbell's successor as postmaster, William Brooker.

When James Franklin decided to publish the *New-England Courant* on his own in 1721, newspapers were beginning to play a larger role in the community. They mixed information from the town and neighboring villages with essays, opinion pieces, columns, and even "exposés." Both of the Franklin brothers were men who were not afraid to take risks. Benjamin willingly operated the irreverent paper on the occasions when James found himself in jail for an indiscretion.

Eventually Ben Franklin left Boston, finding Philadelphia more to his liking. There he took over the *Pennsylvania Gazette* and molded it into a lively, entertaining, literate, and provocative flagship paper for a chain of small local newspapers in eastern Pennsylvania. Newspapers were springing up and dying quickly, but Franklin showed that the medium could survive and become dependable as a conduit for information and ideas. Under Franklin's command, the *Pennsylvania Gazette* was the most successful paper in the colonies. Part of the success can be attributed to the inclusion of political cartoons, many of which Franklin himself wrote. One such cartoon, *Join, or Die*, shows a snake divided into eight pieces, each depicting one of the colonies. This cartoon was Franklin's way of telling his readers that they must be united.

Probably the greatest contribution of the colonial newspapers was the forum they provided for discussion of the important issues that seeded the revolution. The *Federalist Papers*, written by John Jay, Alexander Hamilton, and James Madison, saw light of day in various newspapers to which they were distributed by the authors. These 85 essays called for the ratification of the United States Constitution, a topic that was under much debate across the country. The authors explained how the new government would operate, thus showing the people why ratification was beneficial and necessary. For example, Federalist No. 84 opposed the Bill of Rights. In it Hamilton states his fears that it would be considered a list of the only rights Americans had, therefore limiting their power and freedom. The *Federalist Papers* originally appeared in three New York newspapers. They were later additionally distributed in other states, though publication outside New York was irregular. It would be misleading to call the colonial newspapers a true mass medium because they circulated primarily to the literate populace who had both leisure time and money to spend on publications. It was several decades after the American Revolution and the founding of the new republic before cheap newspapers were read by the average citizen and were considered a necessity for keeping in touch with the world.

Early American newspapers were highly **partisan**; that is, they followed political party lines and published vitriolic critiques of other perspectives. The Republican viewpoint was highlighted by Philip Freneau's *National Gazette* and Benjamin Franklin Bache's *Aurora* (published by Benjamin Franklin's grandson). The editors of these publications were critical of the presidency of John Adams. Isaiah Thomas' *Massachusetts Spy* and Noah Webster's *American Minerva* (later *The Commercial Advertiser*) supported Federalist political positions.

THE 1800S: DEVELOPMENT OF THE POPULAR PRESS

The introduction of the **rotary press**, with its revolving cylinders printing at many times the speed of **flatbed press**, made possible the cheap mass production of newspapers. In 1833, Benjamin Day founded the daily *New York Sun*, and within a few years he was using the new technology to produce 30,000 copies each day. The paper sold for a mere penny (in relative value, about the equivalent of what we spend for a daily newspaper today). Thus began the era of the **penny press**, the first truly popular newspapers. By 1835 there were 1,200 newspapers in the United States.

Just two years after Day founded the *Sun*, James Gordon Bennett introduced the *New York World* and combined the technology used by Day with a new technique called reporting. He sent people out on the streets to visit the police halls, to observe comings and goings at the piers, and to chronicle the daily occurrences of a busy commercial city. With the New York dailies providing a model, daily newspapers sprang up in major cities around the country in the mid-1800s.

Bennett's success with the *Herald* led to competition. Horace Greeley founded the *New York Tribune* in 1841, hiring the legendary managing editor Charles A. Dana to oversee the news-gathering operation while Greeley concentrated on developing the editorial page's interpretive function. A decade later, in 1851, Henry J. Raymond founded *The New York Times* and emulated *The Times* of London in offering foreign coverage, in-depth reporting, and serious-minded editorials. *The New York Times* continues today as the paper that sets an example for completeness in **public affairs reporting**.

After the rotary press, other new technologies wrought similar changes to the newspaper industry, resulting in circulation increases for ever-improving products. One was the **wire service**, which brought stories from afar by telegraph to newspapers that shared the costs. The first, the **Associated Press** (AP), was formed in 1848 by six New York newspapers as a way to reduce the expenses caused by duplicated efforts to obtain news from afar. Duplication of effort on local stories was viewed as useful because each paper was competing for an exclusive report on events that directly affected its readers. The formation of the AP also served to widen the horizons of smaller papers that could not afford their own correspondents around the country and abroad.

Wars speed the development and use of technology. The value of the telegraphic wire services in speeding news from the Civil War battlefronts to the big-city newspapers was a spur to readership and circulation. Faster printing methods were developed that enabled papers to increase daily circulation and offer large Sunday editions with preprinted feature

sections. Newspapers in the South and the Midwest grew and improved as they fed the readers' appetite for information about the war. Following the war, westward expansion led to growth of newspapers in the mountain and Pacific states. By the 1870s the New York newspapers were rivaled in quality by important regional papers such as Joseph Pulitzer's *St. Louis Dispatch*, the *Chicago Tribune* edited by Joseph Medill, William Allen White's *Emporia Gazette* in Kansas, the *Courier-Journal* in Louisville, and the Portland *Oregonian*.

THE INVERTED PYRAMID

With the invention of the telegraph in 1844 came a new kind of reporting. Previously a newspaper article might not get to the actual news until the very end of the writing. The background would come first and lead to the real noteworthy information. The telegraph, when it was first used, was considered expensive. During the Civil War, newspapers were shelling out high costs to get the latest news via telegraph. This caused a shift in writing known today as the **inverted pyramid.**

The inverted pyramid style of writing begins an article with the most important information. Everything you need to know about the story comes in the first paragraph of the article. The details come after in the body and conclusion. This is illustrated by the larger base of a pyramid on top, narrowing to a point at the bottom.

THE ABOLITIONIST PRESS

In the years leading up to the Civil War, a robust **abolitionist** press arose, dedicated to fighting slavery and supporting efforts to free slaves. The abolitionists were social radicals and used their newspapers to create a network for advocacy, information, and support. In Boston, William Lloyd Garrison's *Liberator* was one of the longest-lived and best-known of the abolitionist newspapers. Garrison, provocative and fiery, wanted immediate emancipation of the slaves. His incendiary articles provoked both the northern states that wanted a compromise solution to the slavery issues, and the southern states that the status quo benefited.

Garrison's colleague was Frederick Douglass, an escaped slave whose master's wife had broken the law by teaching him to read. Douglass gave speeches about his experience as a slave and published several autobiographies. His newspaper, *The North Star*, had as its motto "Right is of no Sex—Truth is of no Color—God is the Father of us all, and we are all brethren." Differences in opinion about the anti-slavery movement and particularly about the U.S. Constitution caused a split between Douglass and Garrison, resulting in Garrison believing *The North Star* to be a competitor to his *Liberator*. After the Emancipation Proclamation abolished slavery in 1862, Douglass went on to help with Southern reconstruction. Sadly, when Douglass' home in Rochester, New York burned in 1872 (a suspected arson), an entire run of *The North Star* burned with it.

The abolitionist press was not without its enemies. In 1837, Elijah Lovejoy, publisher of the abolitionist newspaper *Alton Observer* in Alton, Ill., was shot to death in his publishing warehouse by an angry mob. His printing press was destroyed and thrown into the river – the fourth press for the *Observer* to have met such a fate. The *Alton Observer* was the third of Lovejoy's newspapers to be shut down. He had written in the *Observer*, "We distinctly avow it to be our settled purpose, never, while life lasts, to yield to this new system of attempting to destroy, by means of mob violence, the right of conscience, the freedom of opinion, and of the press."

EARLY MINORITY PAPERS

The earliest African-American owned and operated newspaper in the United States was *Freedom's Journal*, published in New York by John Russwurm and Samuel Cornish from 1827 to 1829. An abolitionist paper, it published calls for an end to slavery, as well as served as a newspaper of record for the New York black community. Events such as lynchings as well as more positive news like births and marriages in the African American community were reported. *Freedom's Journal* circulated in 11 states, the District of Columbia, Haiti, Canada, and some European countries. By the start of World War I, the African Americans had yet another newspaper, the *Chicago Defender*. During the war, the paper used its influence to encourage African Americans in the United States to move north. Editorials, articles, and cartoons showed the benefits of a move while

the paper included train schedules and job listings. Today there are multiple African American newspapers including *New York Amsterdam News, St. Louis Sentinel, and Omaha Star.*

The *Cherokee Phoenix* was published from 1828 to 1835 and was the first Native American newspaper. Its purpose was to publish both laws and documents of the Cherokee nation as well as to print news. Published by Elias Boudinot, the newspaper changed its name to The *Cherokee Phoenix and Indian Advocate* in 1829 to reflect the need to be more inclusive of other tribes. Started in New Echota, Georgia, the capital of the Cherokee Nation, a newspaper of the same name is now published in Tahlequah, Okla. Independent American Indian newspapers today include *News from Indian Country* published since 1986 in Hayward, Wis., and *Indian Country Today*, from Canastota, NY.

Serving the early Hispanic immigrant population in New York were *El Mercurio de Nueva York* (1829-1830) and *El Mensagero Semanal de Nueva York* (1828-1831). According to one researcher, from the 1850s through the 1870s, San Francisco supported the longest running and most financially successful Spanish-language newspapers in the United States. These papers helped new immigrants adjust to their new homes and covered news from home. Other large-city daily Hispanic newspapers included two Los Angeles papers, *La Opinión* (founded in 1926) and *El Heraldo de México* (1915); San Antonio's *La Prensa* (1913); and New York City's *La Prensa* (1913). In Tampa, Fla., Cuban tobacco workers started a labor newspaper, *La Federación*, in 1899.[2]

PHOTOGRAPHY ILLUSTRATES THE STORIES

Before and during the Civil War, sketches made by artists and reproduced through **woodcuts** generally served as pictorial representation of the events reporters wrote about. An artist would draw an image in reverse on a wooden block, and engravers would cut out the design, which could then be inked and pressed. Thus, the scenes from the battlefields existed for most Americans as a result of pen and ink work.

Newspapers were limited to publishing duplications of these woodcuts, but readers were unsatisfied.

Underground Press in the United States

In many countries, the term **underground press** is used in reference to publications that are illegal. Governments in other countries have been known to forbid the printing of newspapers and magazines that they feel are inappropriate. In the U.S., this is not the case. Because of the First Amendment, there are very few reasons the government can shut down a publication.

In the U.S. the term underground press typically refers to an independent publication, such as a newspaper, mostly those that focus on unpopular themes, or counterculture issues.

Possibly one of the best known underground newspapers is the *Village Voice* of New York. The paper was started by Dan Wolf, Ed Fancher and Norman Mailer in October of 1955. It was then, and still is today, known for its no-holds-barred reporting. It has published news about New York politics, the writings of authors such as Allen Ginsberg, and even has a section with advice on sex and a list of "adult services." Other underground publications in the United States include the *Boston Phoenix*, *Chicago Reader*, *Seattle Gay News*, *The Black Panther*, *New Age*, and *Bay Guardian*.

They increasingly wanted more realistic visuals of the battles going on throughout the country. Photo documentation of the epic struggle between the Union and the Confederacy by the renowned Mathew Brady, as well as other artists, was widely exhibited after the war. This helped spur interest in the use of the photograph to capture true images of important events.

In the 1870s the first use of photographs by newspapers heralded the day when totally realistic representation became a basic part of visual news coverage. By the 1890s, the techniques had been developed for **halftone engravings** – the system for translating photos into small "dots" – and photos began to appear regularly in the New York newspapers. Efficient production of newspapers with photographs came when the printing press was able to reproduce halftone images at the same rate as pages without images. The real ability for speed and efficiency, however, came with wire transmission of photography. Wire transmission was not possible until 1924, and it was 1935 before AP established a regular Wire photo network to supply pictures to its members.

YELLOW JOURNALISM

By the end of the nineteenth century, a distinct pattern emerged among major city newspapers: strong-headed owners built booming businesses out of newspapers by sensationalizing stories concerning crime, abnormal behavior, and government wrongdoing. These newspapers complemented their coverage of human behavior with an eagerness to crusade against wrongs in government, while lauding the spirit of the common working person who plunked down a penny or two for a copy.

The era provides us a term still used to describe journalistic excesses. **Yellow journalism** is any sensational attempt at selling newspapers by depicting the seamier side of life, such as prying into the lives of celebrities or sex scandals involving government officials. The term comes from a comic strip, "Hogan's Alley," which featured the "Yellow Kid," a child dressed in a yellow gown who mocked upper-class customs and rituals. The strip was originally popularized in Joseph Pulitzer's *New York World*. The Yellow Kid was so popular that his face graced every kind of item from cookie tins to soap to cigarette packs. Among the stunts and gimmicks favored by Pulitzer to sell papers was the sponsorship of Nellie Bly's around-the-world trip in quest of the fictional 80-day record popularized by Jules Verne in his book *Around the World in Eighty Days.*

William Randolph Hearst is the publisher most often associated with this period of the first press barons. His *New York Journal* attempted to outdo Joseph Pulitzer's *World*. He even hired the "Yellow Kid" cartoonist, R.F. Outcault. Legends abound of the lengths to which Hearst went to buy, plant, or control a story. His competition with Pulitzer to dramatize and place blame for the sinking of the battleship *Maine* in Havana Harbor in 1898 fed the flames of nationalism that led to involvement in the Spanish-American war. Hearst is reputed to have told his photographer covering the rumored conflict, "You supply the pictures, I'll supply the war." Elected to Congress in 1902, Hearst lusted for higher power – perhaps even the presidency of the United States – but his romantic life, personal spending, and ruthless control of his enterprises worked against his ambitions. Orson Welles's classic film *Citizen Kane* is a barely fictionalized account of the excesses of Hearst.

During the yellow journalism era, banner headlines, the comics, puzzles, sports sections and other innovations were developed to please the consumer.

Newspapers in the Twentieth Century

While newspapers peaked as a mass medium about 1900, yellow journalism has never entirely gone away. As long as there were three or more competing newspapers in the big cities, at least one stayed with the tradition of printing sensational headlines and pictures of bathing beauties.

When magazines developed the exposé story – *McClure's* ran a critical look at Standard Oil by Ida Tarbell in 1902 followed by Lincoln Steffen's series, "Shame of the Cities" (1903-1905) – newspapers followed suit with articles that exposed wrongdoing and corruption. An angry President Theodore Roosevelt labeled the practice **muckraking**. Other famous muckrakers include Nellie Bly, who wrote "Ten Days in a Mad-House," chronicling an 1887 stay at Blackwell's Island, an asylum for the insane in New York, and Upton Sinclair, whose 1906 book *The Jungle*, written about Chicago meat-processing plants, caused public outrage that resulted in the passage of the Meat Inspection Act and the Pure Food and Drug Act of 1906.

One of the resurgences of yellow journalism came in the 1920s, when several new **tabloids** were published in New York City, each trying to outdo the other with crime stories, lurid photographs, coverage of scandals involving the rich and famous, and sex escapades. The period came to be known as the era of **jazz journalism** because it seemed in tune with the raucous music of the time. Muckraking became more sophisticated and eventually gained a more respectable label: **investigative journalism**.

The economic woes brought on by the Great Depression cut heavily into newspaper profits and effectively ended the last major wave of yellow journalism's popularity. Nevertheless, as recently as the 1970s, Australian publisher Rupert Murdoch was buying tabloids and injecting them with new doses of yellow journalism – stories about the "killer bees" advancing on the United States from South America, for example – in an attempt to hold readers lured away by television and other entertainment media.

Supermarket checkout "newspapers" such as *The Star* and *The National Enquirer* use modern-day yellow journalism with their headlines proclaiming "Elvis Is Living with Martians" and "Baby Kicks Twin out of Womb." Even though the sensational tabloids aren't really newspapers at all in the traditional sense, as they do not focus on conventional news coverage, some researchers suggest that while the headlines of many tabloid stories are sensational, the content is often presented rationally. For example, a story headlined "Woman Pregnant for Twelve Years" described a woman who carried a dead fetus

Women Journalists in the Twentieth Century

Ida Tarbell and Nellie Bly both made names for themselves as journalists in the twentieth century. Their fame, however, did not come easily. They are just two examples of women who were able to succeed in a world that was dominated by men.

Ida Tarbell never chose to write about the challenges of becoming a professional woman. That does not refute the fact that she constantly found out the troubles of being a woman during this time period. When she went away to Allegheny College, she was surrounded by men. She was the only female student in her class, all of her professors were male, and there were no dormitories for female students.

During this time period, women were expected to marry and take care of a family. Those that did manage to get through school and have a career faced many challenges. Female journalists were expected to write about being a homemaker. Both Ida Tarbell and Nellie Bly refused to abide by this ideal. For example, Ida Tarbell wrote about corruption in the oil industry. Also, in 1911, Nellie Bly became the first woman to cover the Eastern Front in WWI.

for 12 years.[3] One company, American Media, owns 65 percent of supermarket tabloid titles, including the *National Enquirer*, the *Globe*, the *National Examiner*, the *Sun*, the *Star*, and *Weekly World News*. The company also owns health and fitness magazines *Shape* and *Men's Fitness*.

NEWSPAPERS OF RECORD

Beginning in 1896, under the leadership of Adolph Ochs, *The New York Times* started to carve out a niche for itself as the "newspaper of record," first for its city, and then for the entire nation. Increasingly, newspaper publishers saw that they could ensure profitability by offering readers a responsible information package based on reporting of public affairs in the circulation area, along with a mix of national and international news, sports, entertainment features, social news, and coverage of local business.

The "newspaper of record" plays the role of an agenda-setter, helping decide which issues will move to the forefront of national debate. In addition to *The New York Times*, newspapers that have attracted national audiences include the *Washington Post*, *The Wall Street Journal*, the *Los Angeles Times*, and the *Christian Science Monitor*. Many newspapers grew into roles as leading voices in their state or region: the *Atlanta Constitution*, the *Chicago Tribune*, the *Des Moines Register*, and the *Miami Herald* are examples.

THE OPINION FUNCTION

In the nineteenth century, flamboyant editors used their news columns to wage political battles and attempt to influence national debate. Increasingly in the twentieth century, the opinions of the publisher, editors, columnists, and letter-writers were reserved for the editorial page. Editorials will often be followed by Letters to the Editor, where readers can respond to the opinions as well as the actual news presented by the newspaper. Expanded space was made available for exchanges of views in the "op-ed" (opposite editorial) page and even in entire opinion sections, especially in Sunday newspapers. Herbert Baynard Swope of *The New York Evening World* is said to have created the first modern op-ed page in 1921. The National Conference of Editorial Writers (NCEW) was founded in 1946 to foster appreciation of the role of editorial pages among both journalists and readers.

JOURNALISM AS A PROFESSION

Movies and plays in the 1920s and 1930s portrayed newspaper editors and reporters as chain-smoking, hard-drinking, coarse, street-wise individuals driven by an obsession to yell "Stop the presses... I've got a scoop!" While the portrait offered by the classic farce *The Front Page* was not entirely fictional, the reality was that newspaper editors and reporters in the twentieth century were beginning to view themselves as professionals rather than craftsmen. Far from the "ink-stained wretches" of the nineteenth century, journalists in the twentieth century adhered to a model of social responsibility – turning to professional education and codes of ethics to improve their images. Rather than looking for the sensational angle, the social responsibility model encouraged the press to provide truth and accuracy to the public it serves.

The American Newspaper Publishers Association (ANPA), formed at the end of the nineteenth century as a trade association, emerged in the twentieth century as an organization dedicated to improving newspapers through its research institute, regular publications focusing on business practices and law, and an information service for the profession. In 1909, Sigma Delta Chi was formed as a secret fraternity on the DePauw University campus in Greencastle, Ind., only to emerge as an association serving the needs and interests of working journalists. Now known as the Society of Professional Journalists (SPJ), it holds an annual convention, publishes a monthly professional magazine, and lobbies for freedom of the press. Student chapters exist all over the country to support student press efforts. Interestingly, the organization voted to admit women sixty years after its creation, in 1969.

Both SPJ and the American Society of Newspaper Editors (ASNE), formed in 1922, have a code of ethics governing behavior by journalists. The ASNE's Canons of Journalism, issued a year after formation of the organization, is a code of conduct for journalists and a ringing statement of principles that include protection of the freedom of the press and the people's right to know. The ASNE has a number of standing committees that monitor journalistic practices, issue publications, and work for professional standards.

The Newspaper Guild, the journalists' trade union, also is concerned with improving the profession. Tired of working long and odd hours for little pay, journalists formed the guild in the 1930s. Today, however, only some 32,000 of the nearly half-million employees of newspapers are guild members, and in the days of automation and computers, the union poses virtually no strike threat to publishers. Wage increases accepted by the union in the 1980s actually lagged behind gains made by other professional workers.

While membership in all these journalism organizations is voluntary, they speak for the field, advance its welfare, and have enhanced its respect.

USA TODAY: THE FIRST TRULY NATIONAL NEWSPAPER

Until the Gannett Co., Inc. introduced *USA TODAY* in the fall of 1982, newspapers were the only non-national medium in the United States. Also, the United States was one of the few countries in the world without a national newspaper. *The Wall Street Journal* and *The New York Times* have editions that circulate throughout the country, but it can be argued that both are specialized papers appealing to a specialized audience rather than true national newspapers aiming at the widest number of potential readers.

USA TODAY, while it circulates throughout the nation, does not function as a strong editorial voice in the nation's political and social arena. What it does well, however, is to provide capsulated information that can be digested quickly by busy consumers with an interest in national trends. The paper is as much a "databank" as a news vehicle. Easy-to-understand color graphics put statistics and facts in a form that can be read quickly.

USA TODAY Celebrates Its Silver Anniversary

On September 15, 2007, *USA TODAY* celebrated its 25th anniversary. Revolutionary in its birth, with short articles and an emphasis on fast information delivery, *USA TODAY* is now solidly entrenched as a national newspaper. With four consistent sections – News, Money, Sports and Life – *USA TODAY* has become a staple in hotels, airports, and other places where the public gathers.

Pollster Lou Harris suggested to Al Neuharth, the founder of *USA TODAY*, the basic premise of the paper. He showed Neuharth the *New York Times* and *Wall Street Journal* and said, "Here I've got two that are very dull and very grey and very good ... But if you want to grab the television generation you've got to transfer from the tube to print a lot of the stuff that the TV generation likes on the tube. It's pretty simple."

The newspaper is in many ways a reflection of its creator. Neuharth's premise of a "journalism of hope," an emphasis on good news, is still the premise today, although perhaps not quite as unabashedly. So is Neuharth's mandate that women and minorities should appear on the front page above the fold every day. Perhaps the most notable impact *USA TODAY* has had is that over half the newspapers in the United States have been redesigned to imitate its use of full-color photographs and lavish "spot color" graphics around boxes and charts.

According to one commentator, *USA TODAY* is better poised than its national competitors to go digital. Because of how users read Web pages, moving around quickly from link to link and story to story, and because of how they tend to skim rather than read entire long stories, *USA TODAY*'s small-bite formula suits a digital platform better than a lengthy *New York Times* article. The paper's come a long way from punsters' jokes that it would win prizes for "Best Investigatory Paragraph."[4]

Printed as a newspaper, *USA TODAY* has much in common with the online databases that busy executives use to keep abreast of the latest trends and developments.

Detractors have called it "McPaper" because while it is cheap, convenient, and easy to find in any urban area, its brief stories are to traditional journalism what a fast-food burger is to steak.

Initially, advertisers warmed slowly to the new medium, not sure exactly what it was and how it served its audience. Other newspapers, however, were quick to imitate the colorful graphics and quick-reading charts, starting with the giant multicolored weather map.

Not content with merely inventing a new national medium, Al Neuharth, who shepherded the project from drawing board to financial success, said he envisions an information network that includes television, radio, computer databases, and virtually any other medium into which information gathered by the Gannett system can be channeled. More than any other publisher, he appears to have realized that the newspaper in the twenty-first century will be just part of a complex information system. The headline in *Advertising Age* on *USA TODAY's* fifth anniversary offered a prognosis for the new style of newspaper: "Here to Stay."

USA TODAY's short stories, informational graphics, and approach to news heralded the new age of newspapers – one that is built on adapting to fast-changing media preferences and savvy media consumers.

NEWSPAPER OWNERSHIP AND CIRCULATION

Until recently newspapers were predominantly an independent medium in terms of ownership. Many were still the property of the heirs of their founders – family-run papers as small as the smallest weeklies and dailies and as large as *The New York Times*. Most chains had no more than a dozen small- or medium-sized papers and were regionally concentrated.

That pattern has changed. In the United States, Gannett Co., Inc. owns 85 daily newspapers, including *USA TODAY*, and nearly 850 nondaily publications, with a combined daily paid circulation of approximately 7.2 million. *USA TODAY's* circulation alone is approximately 2.3 million. The company is the largest newspaper publisher in the United States. Knight-Ridder, the second-largest publisher with 32 daily newspapers, was purchased by the McClatchy Company in 2006, which then sold about half of the papers to other buyers. McClatchy also sold its largest remaining newspaper, the *Minneapolis Star Tribune*, in 2007.

Worry about Gannett's dominance of such a large segment of the newspaper market, especially when the circulation of *USA TODAY* is included, has been voiced by many critics of American journalism. To date, however, admiration for Gannett's ability to run

papers profitably has far overshadowed serious concern about any desire to control the market.

Criticism of another ownership trend has been much louder: the purchase of newspapers by owners who appear merely to want to squeeze profits out of them, with little concern for quality or the integrity of the product. The acquisition of papers across America, including the floundering *New York Post*, by Rupert Murdoch was viewed with alarm by many journalists who decried his formula of crime coverage, sensational reporting, and gossip as news. Many advertisers were wary of the lowest-common-denominator audiences attracted by such newspapers. Similar cries were heard when Murdoch acquired the *Wall Street Journal* in late 2007 – an acquisition whose outcome and effects have yet to be seen. But at the beginning of the 1990s, critics grudgingly conceded that Murdoch and deceased British "press lord" Robert Maxwell saved many newspapers that might otherwise have died.

The phenomenon of newspapers being sold to other newspapers is viewed as a consolidation of power within the industry. Of even greater concern to some is the sale of newspapers to broadcast media companies that want to diversify, and to noninformation producers who buy into the information business. The president of the Newspaper Guild, the union for reporters and lower-level editors, warned of the dangers of "an industry dominated by bankers and big investors" as well as the threat of concentrated media power being used for "political propaganda purposes."

In 1970, newspaper publishers convinced Congress to pass the Newspaper Preservation Act. This enabled them to cut costs—and save failing newspapers by merging business and printing operations (but not news and editorial operations) in cities where newspaper competition still existed. Both small and large papers have taken advantage of the law. In 2007, there were twelve **joint operating agreements** in effect, permitting two newspapers, one considered to be "failing," to share business and operating costs – an exception to usual antitrust laws. Early in 1990, Detroit's two 650,000-circulation papers, the *Free Press* and the *News*, finally got the go-ahead to join business operations. This came only after a lengthy legal battle. As the nation's ninth- and

Table 6.1

TOP 25 DAILY NEWSPAPERS BY CIRCULATION, SEPTEMBER 2007[5]

Newspaper	Sep. 30, 2007	Sep. 30, 2006	% Change
USA TODAY	2,293,137	2,269,509	(+1.04%)
The Wall Street Journal	2,011,882	2,043,235	(−1.53%)
The New York Times	1,037,828	1,086,797	(−4.51%)
Los Angeles Times	779,682	775,765	(+0.50%)
Daily News, New York	681,415	693,423	(−1.73%)
New York Post	667,119	704,011	(−5.24%)
The Washington Post	635,087	656,298	(−3.23%)
Chicago Tribune	559,404	576,131	(−2.90%)
Houston Chronicle	507,437	508,091	(−0.13%)
Newsday	387,503	410,578	(−5.62%)
The Arizona Republic	382,414	397,295	(−3.75%)
The Dallas Morning News	373,586	404,652	(−7.68%)
San Francisco Chronicle	365,234	373,805	(−2.29%)
Boston Globe	360,695	386,417	(−6.66%)
The Star-Ledger, Newark, N.J.	353,003	363,100	(−2.78%)
The Philadelphia Inquirer	338,260	330,622	(+2.31%)
Star Tribune, Minneapolis	335,443	358,887	(−6.53%)
The Plain Dealer, Cleveland	334,195	336,940	(−0.81%)
Detroit Free Press	320,125	328,719	(−2.61%)
The Atlanta Journal-Constitution	318,350	350,159	(−9.08%)
The Oregonian, Portland	309,467	310,805	(−0.43%)
St. Petersburg (Fla.) Times	288,807	288,679	0.04%
The Orange County Register	278,507	287,204	(−3.03%)
San Diego Union-Tribune	278,379	304,334	(−8.53%)
St. Louis Post-Dispatch	265,111	276,677	(−4.18%)

tenth-largest newspapers by circulation, both Gannett's *News* and the then-Knight-Ridder's *Free Press* were losing money for the parent companies. The joint operating decision did not solve the papers' problems. Advertisers rebelled against sharply increased advertising rates. Subscribers complained about a joint Sunday edition that combined sections and features from each of the papers. All factions could agree that the merger had one benefit: 2,000 jobs were saved because neither of the papers had to fold.

Regardless of ownership, newspapers are largely declining in circulation. As seen in Table 6.1, circulation of daily newspapers declined by an average of 2.6 percent between 2006 and 2007 Sunday circulations dropped an average of 3.5 percent. However, the Audit Bureau of Circulations, recognizing that its circulation measurement tools penalized the newspaper business, piloted a new method of determining circulation that takes into account more than just paper pages delivered.

A Truer Method of Assessing Newspaper "Reach"

In late 2007, after releasing circulation data for newspapers that showed another significant decline, the Audit Bureau of Circulations announced changes in the assessment of newspaper circulation. The new scheme will permit newspapers, over the next three years, to be considered paid regardless of the price paid for them; "other paid" copies, like those purchased by sponsors or provided to schools, will become known as verified (nonpaid); and there will be a new paid-circulation category for hotel and employee copies. For most of its existence, the ABC focused just on paid circulation, the distribution of paid physical copies.

The ABC also released Audience-FAX, a new section to its FAS-FAX circulation reports, which accounts for both print and online readership, unduplicated combined readership and monthly unique users. According to the ABC, "Audience-FAX is the latest step in a multilevel industry initiative to answer advertisers' needs for measurement data that fully reflects newspapers' full reach and audience. The combination of readership and online audience data reflects a more complete picture of a newspaper's total audience and enables advertisers to truly gauge the impact of a newspaper in the community it serves."

Participation in Audience-FAX is voluntary, and currently about 30 percent of daily newspapers who participated in FAS-FAX are trying out the new metric. Audience-FAX is a combined effort of the ABC, Scarborough Research and the Newspaper Association of America. The companies say the metric is still a work in progress but believe that it more accurately reflects the "full reach" of newspapers instead of merely limiting circulation counts to paid physical copies.

Newspapers Today: "Innovate or Die"

The message is clear, say many media watchers. If newspapers cling to antiquated notions of what news is, how to design it, and how to deliver it, they will perish. Yet in some ways the notion of what has to be done is startlingly similar to what has always been done. As *Atlanta Journal-Constitution* editor Julia Wallace said in a posting to a media blog: "We have four clear jobs: Grow digital. Reinvent print. Create more regular local enterprise (distinctive content) that readers cannot get elsewhere. Improve our news and information gathering."[6] Most reporters would tell you that they are always looking for new ways to localize news stories and improve their information-gathering techniques. Most of what has changed, then, is digital. But that is a lot of change.

In his book *Faster: The Acceleration of Just About Everything*, James Gleick writes, "We believe that we possess too little time: that is a myth we now live by. What is true is that we are awash in things, in information, in news, in the old rubble and shiny new toys of our complex civilization, and – strange, perhaps – stuff means speed." The challenge for newspapers, and in fact every form of mass media, is to get useful information to its users quickly and efficiently.

Early personal delivery technology included attempts by some newspapers to fax abridged copies of their papers to consumers as early as 1938, when the *St. Louis Post-Dispatch* used its radio station to send a "Radio Edition" to printers at the homes of its staff. In the 1930s and 1940s more papers experimented with faxed newspapers; the *New York Times* still publishes TimesDigest (formerly TimesFax), a daily compilation of articles that is sent to hotels, cruise ships, corporations and Navy ships and bases. However, the technology didn't catch on, partially due to the high expense of the equipment.[7]

Yet today's newspapers publish online as well as traditional print copies, and consumers have taken to this technology – which is not much different than daily faxes – in droves. Today's newspaper editors are

No More Paper Newspapers?[10]

Amid the cries of "Reinvent or die," "Go digital" and "Paper's a thing of the past," several Harvard researchers are finding that paper isn't likely to go the way of stone knives and bearskins – and that newspapers should not necessarily depend on the Internet for salvation.

Harvard media critic William Powers, in the provocatively titled research paper "Hamlet's BlackBerry: Why Paper is Eternal," suggests that paper has many charms that a website does not. Paper is tactile; you can write on it, underline and highlight things; it is less distracting than reading content on a website, where readers might be distracted by links and flashing colors. Moreover, it's easier on the eyes than reading a screen (as any researcher will tell you!). Therefore, readers may go to the Web for fast bits of information like sports scores and weather, but for longer reads, paper's where it's at.

In his paper, "Creative Destruction: An Exploratory Look at News on the Internet," Harvard researcher Thomas E. Patterson found that while traffic to national newspaper websites is continuing to grow, as is traffic to broadcast television and alternative news sites, visitors to daily newspapers in big cities and smaller towns are not coming in droves. He predicts that local newspapers will have trouble keeping their current readers, much less attracting new ones.

What does this pair of studies suggest? The need for more research to confirm or deny the findings. Why do we care? If newspapers go, there goes a lot of the investigative journalism that American democracy needs to survive. It isn't just about saving journalism – it's about watching the government.

just as likely to be worried about **RSS feeds**, page hits and blogs as they are about crafting the best headline for the top news story. The Internet has forced newspapers to rethink how they deliver their content. According to Nielsen//Net Ratings, the top-visited newspaper website, the *New York Times'* site, got 13,857,000 unique visitors in the six months from March to August 2007. Those readers looked at 27 pages per visit on average and spent an average of 20 minutes and 20 seconds on the site.[8] Moreover, research suggests that those who visit websites are "power users" – they are intensive Internet users who spent more time online than their peers, are likely to shop and make purchases online, and are younger, better-educated and more affluent.[9] It stands to reason that newspapers would want to cater to these users and their purchasing power.

NEWS DELIVERY

Marc Gunther wrote in 2007 that reporters at the *Washington Post* have become "platform-agnostic," which means that they realize that their content must be accessible in many different ways. Readers of the *Post*, noted Gunther, can experience news in many different ways and from many different perspectives: "They can join a lively global debate about religious faith, read hyper-local coverage of a fast-growing Virginia county, or watch daily video programs from the digital magazine Slate." The traditional business model of newspapers, driven by advertising revenue, is not as viable as it once was.[11] To survive, newspapers must reinvent themselves, and do so quickly.

Newspapers continue to experiment with different ways to deliver their content. Early newspaper websites were simply mirror images of what the print edition contained; they earned the dubious label of "shovelware" or "dumpware" because the tendency was to put everything online instead of culling through the chaff for the wheat. Usability studies suggest that people browse Web pages differently than they browse printed products. Newspapers began to adjust to the notion that they had to edit material to go online as closely and carefully as the content that went into the printed product. They must also consider how to best design their home pages to maximize usability and access. Instead of looking like a traditional front page of a newspaper, with a few stories "above the fold," the home page of a newspaper's website will have more links and less actual content, to entice the user into clicking and reading.

According to AOL's third annual "Email Addiction" survey conducted in July 2007, the average email user checks email five times a day, and 59 percent of those with portable devices like Blackberries check every time they get a new message.[12] How can newspapers take advantage of that email addiction? Some deliver a morning email to their subscribers with headlines at a glance, followed by regular email notifications of news stories, customized to the user's preference. For example, subscribers can choose to receive the *Los Angeles Times'* daily summary, "Top of the Times," and may select additional email notifications or newsletters on topics like breaking news, food and drink, and travel. The *New York Times* offers both morning and afternoon summaries and other customizable alerts.

Want the news on your phone? Many newspapers have cell phone and Blackberry-friendly versions of their websites. Newspapers are also taking advantage of Web 2.0 features like blogs, podcasts, syndication, and other interactive, user-created technologies that will be discussed in depth in Ch. 11.

TALKING BACK AND PERSONALIZATION

Traditionally, newspapers were a one-to-many medium. Readers could talk back in the letters to the editor feature or the op-ed pages, but this process took time. Also, editors could choose not to publish letters or articles on topics they did not like or that were critical of the news organization.

Many newspaper websites provide the option for readers to comment on stories, often in discussion board format. Readers can share their thoughts and ideas, usually subject to limitations on libel or profanity, related to the story. Many newspapers also permit discussion in the blog sections of their websites.

Newspapers also recognize that users want choices. As noted above, subscribers to the *Los Angeles Times'* email digest service can customize their topics and delivery options to their individual tastes. The idea of creating one's own newspaper dates to 1992 and an experiment by a class of freshmen at the

Newspapers Go Niche[13]

Newspapers have traditionally tried to reach the largest audience possible. However, with readership declining, many papers are finding that it may be helpful to cater to a more narrowed audience. A niche newspaper may well turn out to be the best plan to counter the fall in print readers.

The tabloid Quick is aimed at a younger audience. Everything in the paper has a bit of attitude, even the weather. Instead of giving temperatures, the paper tells its readers what to wear. This approach is an attempt to make reading the paper more entertaining, in the hopes that younger readers will get into the habit of reading a daily newspaper.

The Chicago Tribune launched their niche paper, RedEye, in 2003. Their approach to gaining a new audience includes punchy headlines and attractive photography. "The idea was to try some approach to attract this hard-to-attract demographic group to the newspaper reading habit," said Don Wycliff, the Tribune's public editor.

Many have feared that these niche papers, especially the ones daily papers offer for free, would take away readership. The general feeling is that most young readers who pick up these tabloids would not be readers of the wider publication. And hopefully, by engaging young readers, these newspapers gain readers for the future.

Massachusetts Institute of Technology's Media Lab. The class assignment was to provide a news service for potentially homesick new freshmen at MIT by gathering news from their hometowns. The class developed fishWrap, a personalized news service that received data from the student, like hometown and special interests, and searched online wire services for stories matching that data. Users could refine their news each time they accessed fishWrap.

While most newspaper websites do not allow for that level of customization, and the newspaper staff usually prefers to retain control of how its home page is delivered, there can be no doubt that readers will continue to demand increased personalization options and turn to news outlets where that customization is possible. Community journalism sites permit residents in a very local area to participate in discussions about issues affecting areas no larger than city blocks – perhaps the height of customized, personalized, hyper-local content.

Careers in the Field

The newspaper industry is a great field for individuals who excel at collecting information, writing, and editing. It is also good for people who enjoy having something new to focus on every day. Since the news is always changing, what you work on will always be new. Positions at a newspaper include reporters, writers, and editors. You might also find positions for layout design. Today you could even work on the newspaper's website doing design or maintenance. There are also many opportunities on the administrative side of the industry in departments such as public relations, marketing, or ad sales.

To start your career in the newspaper industry, you may only need to look to your school. Most universities and colleges have an on-campus publication that is developed by students. You may also try to find an internship at your local paper. Having experience will help you develop a portfolio, a collection of all the news stories you have written. This is especially important if you want to work as a reporter or a writer. Hiring papers will want to see what you are capable of doing.

Chapter Summary

- The first newspapers in America were one-sided printings called broadsheets that reported news from England.
- Colonial, minority, and abolitionist newspapers all included information that was involved in revolutions for their target audience.
- The introduction of the rotary press made possible the cheap mass production of newspapers.
- Yellow journalism became popular as an attempt to sell newspapers by depicting the seamier side of life.
- *USA TODAY's* short stories, informational graphics, and approach to news heralded the new age of newspapers – one that is built on adapting to fast-changing media preferences and savvy media consumers.
- Today, newspapers are continuing to take advantage of the Internet's content delivery opportunities to provide timely and complete coverage.

Glossary

abolitionists—people who believed in getting rid of slavery

Associated Press—a cooperative news agency in the United States

broadsheets—an early newspaper consisting of single-page impressions made from the full width of the printer's press

Calamity—great misfortune or disaster

entrepreneurs—the person who organizes, manages, and assumes the risks of a business or enterprise

flatbed press—a printing press that uses a flat surface for the type against which paper is pressed, either by another flat surface acting against it or by a cylinder rolling over it

halftone engravings—an engraving used to reproduce an illustration, created by a series of dots

inverted pyramid—journalistic style of writing where an article begins with the most important information

investigative journalism—a type of reporting in which reporters deeply investigate a topic of interest, often involving crime, political corruption, or some other scandal

jazz journalism—the journalism style of the roaring twenties, named after its energetic fashion and well illustrated tabloid layout

joint operating agreements—permitting two newspapers, one considered to be "failing," to share business and operating costs

muckraking—a term associated with a group of American investigative reporters, novelists, and critics from the late 1800s to early 1900s, who investigated and exposed societal issues such as conditions in slums and prisons, factories, insane asylums, sweatshops, mines, child labor and unsanitary conditions in food processing plants

partisan—a firm adherent to a party, faction, cause, or person

penny press—cheap, tabloid-style papers produced in the middle of the 19th century.

public affairs reporting—journalism that informs readers, listeners and viewers about ongoing events and activities

rotary press—a printing press in which the images to be printed are curved around a cylinder

RSS feeds—a family of Web feed formats used to publish frequently updated works in a standardized format

tabloids—newspapers that tends to emphasize sensational stories and gossip columns

underground press—independent publications that focus on unpopular themes, or counterculture issues

wire service—an organization of journalists established to supply news reports to organizations in the news trade: newspapers, magazines, and radio and television broadcasters

woodcuts—an artistic technique in printmaking in which an image is carved into the surface of a block of wood

yellow journalism—a type of journalism that downplays legitimate news in favor of eye-catching headlines that sell more newspapers

Discussion Questions

1. Discuss the evolution of gossip and seedier stories in newspapers. What events help explain the introduction of gossip? What does the desire for these stories say about the change in readership?

2. Analyze newspapers as a means to insight revolution, including abolitionist papers and underground presses. How does the media lend itself to spreading individualized messages? What are the differences between revolutionary papers in the colonial period and those that exist nowadays? What explains the changes?

3. Identify the distinguishing factors between the various forms of journalism including public affairs reporting, yellow journalism, jazz journalism and investigative journalism. How do the differences explain the aims of the paper publishing the news pieces?

4. Discuss how Letters to the Editor changed the way people use newspapers. How do they bridge the gap between reader and reporting? How does this communication explain the natural progression towards online news?

5. Analyze the status of newspaper readership. Is online readership the solution or does it only give key headlines? Can newspapers find a way to start a resurgence in print readers?

Supplemental Web Sites

Audit Bureau of Circulations (ABC) www.access-abc.com

Newspaper Association of America http://www.naa.org

Newspaper Association of America Foundation http://www.naafoundation.org

Business of Performing Audits Worldwide (BPA) www.bpaww.com

American Society of Newspaper Editors http://www.asne.org/

Society of Professional Journalists http://www.spj.org

National Conference of Editorial Writers http://www.ncew.org/

Editor and Publisher http://www.editorandpublisher.com

Cherokee Phoenix www.cherokeephoenix.org

The New York Times www.nytimes.com

Around the World in 72 Days http://digital.library.upenn.edu/women/bly/world/world.html

Endnotes

1 "The State of the News Media," Retrieved from *http://www.stateofthenewsmedia.com/2007/narrative_new spapers_intro.asp?media=3*

2 Nicolás Kanellos, "Recovering and Re-constructing Early Twentieth-Century Hispanic Immigrant Print Culture in the US," *American Literary History* 2007 19(2):438-455

3 Andrea Parrot; Joan Ormondroyd, "Can a Woman Really Be Pregnant for Twelve Years? Or Is Scholarly Learning Possible from Reading the Tabloids?" *Teaching Sociology*, Vol. 20, No. 2. (Apr., 1992), pp. 158-164

4 *Edmonton Journal* (Alberta), "Revolutionary USA Today turns 25; Rivals mocked, then copied easy-to-read newspaper for the TV generation," September 14, 2007, pg. E6; John K. Hartman, "Assessing *USA TODAY* As 25th Anniversary Approaches," *Editor & Publisher*, September 6, 2007, Retrieved from *http://www.mediainfo.com/eandp/news/article_display.jsp?vnu_content_id=1003635101.*

[5] *Editor and Publisher*, November 5, 2007, from Audit Bureau of Circulations data

[6] Carla Kimbrough-Robinson, "News groups must innovate or die," *Quill*, April 2007, p. 37

[7] George Mannes, "Delivering the FAX," *Invention & Technology Magazine*, Spr. 1999, Vol. 14, No. 4, *http://www.americanheritage.com/articles/magazine/it/1999/4/1999_4_40.shtml*

[8] Newspaper Association of America Nielsen//NetRatings Retrieved from *http://www.naa.org/TrendsandNumbers/Newspaper-Websites.aspx#spotlight-Top-100-Newspaper-Websites*

[9] Brent Stahl, "Power Users 2006: An Engaged Audience for Advertising and News," June 2006, *http://www.naa.org/TrendsandNumbers/~/media/PDFs/Power_users_2006%20pdf.ashx*

[10] Kelly Toughill, "The discreet charm of newsprint," *Toronto Star*, September 8, 2007, p. AA6.

[11] Marc Gunther, "Hard News," *Fortune*, 8/6/2007, Vol. 156, Issue 3

[12] *http://press.aol.com/article_display.cfm?article_id=1271*

[13] Alison Miller. "Niche papers use 'attitude' to target new readers," The American Society of Newspaper Editors, April 19, 2004

MAGAZINES
Lawrie Fluker

John was born in Arkansas City, Arkansas, in 1918. He was raised in this small, rural city at a time when the school systems in Arkansas were completely segregated. As an African American, John's educational choices were limited, so there were no high schools for him to attend in his small community. To compound his family's troubles, John's father died when he was only eight years old, and John and his mother were left struggling and on welfare. By the time John finished the eighth grade, his mother had remarried, and she decided to move to a community where her son could continue his education. Chicago became their new home, and John moved smoothly into DuSable High School, where his classmates included Redd Foxx and Nat King Cole. John's hard work and skills helped him shine in high school as the student council president and as editor of the school's newspaper and yearbook.

John received a scholarship to attend the University of Chicago, and while going to college, he began working at the black-owned Supreme Liberty Life Insurance Company. One of John's duties was to collect African-American news and information to compile in a weekly digest for the company's president. John thought the idea of such

a compilation would also be useful to the community, and his work at the life insurance company proved that black-owned businesses, when well run, could thrive. John decided to try his hand at a publication similar to *Reader's Digest*, with stories compiled on African Americans. Many tried to discourage John, but his mother, as always, believed that he could turn it into a profitable business. His mother allowed John to use her furniture as collateral for a $500 loan, and in November 1942, John published his first issue of *Negro Digest*. The magazine became a success, and it prepared John for his next publication.

John had been interested in two particular magazines, *Life* and *Look*. Both were known for their beautiful photographs, and John believed that such a publication for African Americans would be extremely successful. In November 1943, John published the first issue of *Ebony* magazine, a sophisticated blend of beautiful photography and African-American success stories. He followed up in 1951 with *Jet* magazine, a small, fit-in-your-pocket publication that highlighted African Americans in the news at the end of each week. *Jet* went on to become the number-one news weekly for African Americans. Whereas all of John's magazines were successful, none was as successful as *Ebony*, which, in its 67th year, now boasts more than 12 million readers per month.

John Johnson went on to open his own book publishing company and television production company; to organize the Ebony Fashion Fair, the largest traveling fashion show in the world; to create Fashion Fair Cosmetics, a line of cosmetics for African-American women; and he purchased three radio stations. In 1996, President Bill Clinton bestowed the Presidential Medal of Freedom to John Johnson, and Arkansas later inducted him into the Arkansas Business Hall of Fame. As a multimillionaire, John Johnson died in 2005, the 60th anniversary year of *Ebony*. Not a bad life for someone who began with so little.

British Magazines

Magazines are as commonplace today as newspapers, but historically, magazines came into existence many years after the first newspapers. The first English-speaking magazine appears to have been published in London in 1704 by Daniel Defoe, the author of *Robinson Crusoe*. His magazine, *Review*, was published as frequently as most newspapers, two to three times a week, but its content was similar to magazines. The publication had essays covering political, trade, and religious issues, and it was published until 1713. Though the publication is not well known today, it appears that Defoe's *Review* led the way for other magazines to follow.

Two other such publications arose in London in the years following the birth of *Review*. The *Tatler* was founded by Sir Richard Steele in 1709. Steele's concept for his magazine was much more laid-back than Defoe's concept. The *Tatler* stationed reporters in coffeehouses throughout London, and then published essays based on the news and gossip derived from the coffeehouse conversations. Although this material was of great interest to the people, the magazine lasted only two years. Steele then joined forces with Joseph Addison to start *The Spectator* in 1711, yet another periodical devoted to entertaining essays and discussions about friendship, morals, and manners.

The first time the term *magazine* was used in a magazine title was in London in 1731. It was there

that Edward Cave founded *The Gentlemen's Magazine*, a monthly publication that included a variety of subjects and authors. Cave understood exactly what intelligent readers wanted to read, and he provided that for them in his publication. Other similar publications had been attempted, but none had the success of Cave's magazine. Cave also had a sophisticated distribution system, which meant that The *Gentlemen's Magazine* was read throughout the English-speaking world, and the publication lasted until 1907. Two men in the American colonies watched Cave's publication with great interest.

American Colonial Magazines

The colonists tried to establish media similar to what they had been accustomed to in England. Once newspapers were established in America, it was only logical that magazines would follow. The Bradford family proved to be pivotal in the American colonial printing business, both in newspapers and in the magazine industry.

William Bradford was one of the original colonists on the *Mayflower* and a devout Puritan. His writings about the founding of this country remain as history, particularly his work *On the Plantation*. Bradford also began the printing family dynasty, introducing the first New York newspaper. His son, Andrew Bradford, a competitor of Benjamin Franklin's, went on to establish the first newspaper in Philadelphia; then in 1741, he founded the first magazine in the new colonies, the *American Magazine*. It was a monthly magazine that published only three issues, but it will forever retain its status as the first magazine in America.

Three days after *American Magazine* debuted, Benjamin Franklin introduced his magazine, *General Magazine*. Franklin's publication lasted only three months longer than Bradford's, a total of six months, never really attaining any distinction other than being a close second for colonial magazines. Ironically, it was Franklin who had a lasting influence on the magazine industry. This had little to do with his *General Magazine*, however. Instead, his influence was based on the one-year-old seminal newspaper he acquired in 1729, the *Pennsylvania Gazette*.

Franklin's successful *Gazette* began as a four-page newspaper, with a large volume of profitable advertising and ultimately, the largest circulation of any other paper in the Philadelphia area. Franklin retained his leadership role with the paper for almost two decades until he retired. The paper continued and changed its name in 1821 to *The Saturday Evening Post*. In 1897, Cyrus H. K. Curtis purchased the publication, and employed George Horace Lorimer as editor from 1899 to 1936. Under Lorimer's leadership, the *Post* grew from 2,000 copies sold per year to 3 million copies. The *Post* remained a weekly publication until 1969. Since then, there have been intervals when the *Post* ceased publication, but without a doubt, it remains one of the most important magazines in American history, all stemming from Benjamin Franklin's early success.

Women's Magazines

As magazine publishing continued in the nineteenth century, some magazines began to cater to specialized audiences. Louis Godey began publishing *Godey's Lady's Book* in 1830 in Philadelphia, one of a handful of women's magazines at the time. Most of these types of magazines did not survive, but such magazines began to draw women into the medium in large numbers.

Godey's publication was one of the few that was successful. Its emphasis was on fashion, and the magazine used engraved, colored fashion drawings as its mainstay. There were also patterns that women could use to sew their own fashions at home. The surviving fashion drawings from *Godey's* provide documentation of women's fashions of the day. In addition to fashion, well-written stories and essays were included in each issue. Some of the greatest authors of the time wrote for the magazine, and *Godey's* had issues that exclusively highlighted women authors. The publication reached the pinnacle of its success before the Civil War, and it had proven that women were a viable audience for magazines.

In the coming decades, seven pivotal magazines were founded with women as their primary audiences.

These magazines were referred to as the "Seven Sisters," and they were among the most successful magazines of the 19th and 20th centuries.

The oldest of the Seven Sisters was *Good Housekeeping*, founded in 1859 in Massachusetts featuring articles of interest to women. From its inception, the magazine fought for consumers, particularly as it pertained to false claims from advertisers. In 1900, the magazine began investigating products and alerting customers about product dangers. Over time, the Good Housekeeping Research Institute was formally opened, and the magazine began refusing to advertise any product it had not tested to prove the accuracy of the advertising claims. Within years, the magazine created the "Good Housekeeping Seal of Approval" that provided a warranty, directly from the magazine, for the products determined to be well made. The Hearst Corporation purchased *Good Housekeeping* in 1911, and the magazine's stellar reputation continued to be enhanced as the magazine led the way in such issues as safe milk, proper food temperatures, smoking hazards, car safety belts, and other major issues. *Good Housekeeping*, to this day, continues to be one of the most popular magazines in the market. As of 2009, it ranked fifth in circulation in America.

The second of Seven Sisters founded was *McCall's* magazine. It was founded in 1873 under another name, but later changed its name to *McCall's* for its owner, James McCall. McCall, a tailor by trade, saw the magazine as a vehicle for selling his dress patterns. When he died 11 years after the magazine was founded, his widow took over the management. The magazine languished at the turn of the 20th century until the 1920s, when the editors decided to reach out to more educated and affluent female readers by providing information to the modern woman. Prestigious women throughout the decades were guest writers, and the magazine's prestige continued to grow. During the 1990s, however, circulation began to drop as magazine competition increased. Therefore, it was not all that surprising when talk show host Rosie O'Donnell chose to enter the magazine world and partner with the owners of *McCall's* in 2000. In doing so, O'Donnell followed predecessors Oprah Winfrey and Martha Stewart, who had both been making their mark in the magazine world. The historic magazine was renamed *Rosie's*, but the magazine could not seem to tap into O'Donnell's popularity. In the opinion of most analysts, what resulted was a joint venture that

Table 7.1

TOP 15 AMERICAN MAGAZINES BY CIRCULATION (2009)

1. *AARP, The Magazine*	9. *Family Circle*
2. *AARP Bulletin*	10. *Game Informer Magazine*
3. *Better Homes and Garden*	11. *People*
4. *Reader's Digest*	12. *Time*
5. *Good Housekeeping*	13. *Taste of Home*
6. *National Geographic*	14. *Sports Illustrated*
7. *Woman's Day*	15. *Cosmopolitan*
8. *Ladies Home Journal*	

SOURCE: http://www.stateofthemedia.org/2010/magazines_industry_overall.ph

was ill-advised to say the least. Initially, there was a spike in circulation, but as time passed, O'Donnell and the editors began to have public disputes over editorial control. O'Donnell issued her resignation in 2002, but that did not end the problems. In 2003, both the magazine parent company and O'Donnell sued each other for breach of contract. Allegations were made throughout the trial, and each side was tarnished as a result. In the end, the judge dismissed both cases, but the magazine did not survive. In 2002, after serving American women for more than 125 years, *Rosie* ceased publication. It is the only one of the Seven Sisters that did not survive.

Ladies Home Journal, founded by Cyrus Curtis in 1883, is the third magazine of the Seven Sisters publications. Cyrus and his wife, Louisa Knapp Curtis, had worked together on a farm magazine that included a women's section. When it became clear that more subscribers were interested in that section rather than the farming articles, all other material was dropped, and it became the *Ladies Home Journal*. The magazine became synonymous for its "Can This Marriage Be Saved?" column that featured the stories of troubled married couples each month, combined with advice from a marriage counselor. This and other columns helped boost the circulation of *Ladies Home Journal* to 1 million copies a month by the turn of the 20th century. Today, the magazine ranks eighth in circulation in America.

The four remaining of the Seven Sisters magazines were founded in the 20th century.

1. *Redbook* was founded in Chicago in 1903 by a group of retail merchants. It is the only one of the remaining Seven Sisters that is not in the top 10–ranked magazines in circulation in America today.

2. *Better Homes and Gardens* was founded in 1922 by Edwin Meredith. This is the best-selling general interest magazine in America today, ranked third in overall circulation, being outsold only by *AARP The Magazine* and *AARP Bulletin*. (See Table 7.1.)

3. *Woman's Day* was founded in 1931 as a free supplement to shoppers at the A&P stores. It currently ranks seventh in circulation in America.

4. *Family Circle* was founded in 1932 as a publication sold in American grocery stores. It currently ranks ninth in circulation in America.

Post-Civil War Magazines

Women's magazines were not the only popular magazines after the Civil War. Magazines, in general, were becoming more popular, owing in large part to better postal rates, less expensive printing costs, and growing audience literacy. Literary magazines were published by book companies, primarily with the intent of publicizing and generating interest in upcoming books. These magazines would publish an excerpt of the books, making the public anxious to read more. The following are the four most popular literary magazines of the 1800s.

1. *Harper's Monthly* was begun in 1850 by New York publishing company Harper & Brothers.

2. *The Atlantic Monthly* was founded in Boston in 1857 by a group of successful authors of the time. Harriet Beecher Stowe, John Greenleaf Whittier, and Ralph Waldo Emerson were among the founders.

3. *Scribner's Magazine* was founded in 1870 by the New York publisher Charles Scribner & Sons. It was reported that the company spent $500,000, a huge sum at the time, to set up the magazine to effectively compete with *Harper's Monthly* and *The Atlantic Monthly*.

4. *The Century Magazine* was founded in New York in 1881. After Charles Scribner died, *Scribner's Magazine* was renamed *The Century Magazine*; therefore, this was not truly a new publication.

Literary magazines were extremely popular with affluent audiences, and they were expensive, usually costing between 25 and 35 cents. A number of less expensive magazines were founded, starting with *McClure's Magazine* in 1893, which cost 15 cents. *McClure's* led the way not only in offering more affordable magazines, but in a new movement called *muckraking*.

Muckraking Magazines

The turn of the 20th century saw increased political and social reporting, as well as in-depth investigative reporting. President Theodore Roosevelt compared the investigative journalists of the time to a character in John Bunyan's literary work, *Pilgrim's Progress*. The character was someone who was always negative and constantly looking downward in the muck. Roosevelt believed that the journalists, whose work had uncovered all matter of evil, dwelled too much on the negative. Although Roosevelt never used the term *muckraker*, his comparison led the journalists of the time to be nicknamed muckrakers.

McClure's led the way as one of the most prominent of muckraking magazines of the time. Journalist Ida Minerva Tarbell wrote insightful investigative articles on the company Standard Oil for *McClure's*, while journalist Lincoln Steffens wrote about corruption in

St. Louis politics. Other notable muckraking magazines included *Cosmopolitan*, *Harper's Weekly*, the *Nation*, and *Collier's*. By the 1920s, audience interest in muckraking had declined, and other subject matter replaced this kind of reporting.

Post-World War I Magazines

Many of the magazines on the market today began in the early 20th century. After the muckraking period, general interest magazines dominated the market for a number of reasons. After World War I, these magazines provided news, entertainment, and beautiful photographs to the masses. These magazines were the television of the time, and large audiences flocked to these publications. *Time*, *Reader's Digest*, and *The New Yorker* are excellent examples of post–World War I magazines.

TIME MAGAZINE

Time was first published in 1923 by Briton Hadden and Henry Luce, both graduates of Yale University. The intent of the magazine was to summarize the news each week in a manner that was understandable yet interesting to its readers. From its inception, *Time* summarized its stories into capsules in different departments, such as news in the nation, news about people, news in the arts, and the like. In January 1927, *Time* chose Charles Lindbergh as its first "Man of the Year," a distinction given to the individual the magazine feels has had the most effect on news for the previous year. They have continued to choose a person of the year each year since 1927. (See Table 7.2.) Some individuals have been named Person of the Year twice, but President Franklin D. Roosevelt is the only individual to have been given the honor on three occasions. Other notable choices include Adolf Hitler in 1938, Joseph Stalin in 1939, and You (everyone in control because of the Information Age) in 2006. In 2009, *Time* magazine ranked 12th in American magazine circulation.

Table 7.2 **TIME MAGAZINE "PERSON OF THE YEAR," 1927–2009**

1. Charles Lindbergh, 1927
2. Walter Chrysler, 1928
3. Owen Young, 1929
4. Mohandas Gandhi, 1930
5. Pierre Leval, 1931
6. Franklin D. Roosevelt, 1932
7. Hugh Samuel Johnson, 1933
8. Franklin D. Roosevelt, 1934
9. Haile Selassie, 1935
10. Mrs. Wallis Warfield Simpson, 1936
11. Generalissimo & Mme Chiang Kai-Shek, 1937
12. Adolf Hitler, 1938
13. Joseph Stalin, 1939
14. Winston Churchill, 1940
15. Franklin D. Roosevelt, 1941
16. Joseph Stalin, 1942
17. George Marshall, 1943
18. Dwight D. Eisenhower, 1944
19. Harry Truman, 1945
20. James Byrnes, 1946
21. George Marshall, 1947
22. Harry Truman, 1948
23. Winston Churchill, 1949
24. American Fighting Man, 1950
25. Mohammed Mossadegh, 1951
26. Elizabeth II, 1952
27. Konrad Adenauer, 1953
28. John Foster Dulles, 1954
29. Harlow Herbert Curtice, 1955
30. Hungarian Freedom Fighter, 1956
31. Nikita Krushchev, 1957
32. Charles De Gaulle, 1958
33. Dwight Eisenhower, 1959
34. U.S. Scientists, 1960
35. John F. Kennedy, 1961
36. Pope John XXIII, 1962
37. Martin Luther King, Jr., 1963
38. Lyndon B. Johnson, 1964
39. General William Westmoreland, 1965
40. Twenty-Five and Under, 1966
41. Lyndon B. Johnson, 1967
42. Astronauts Anders, Borman, and Lovell, 1968
43. The Middle Americans, 1969
44. Willie Brandt, 1970
45. Richard Nixon, 1971
46. Nixon and Kissinger, 1972
47. John Sirica, 1973
48. King Faisal, 1974
49. American Women, 1975
50. Jimmy Carter, 1976
51. Anwar Sadat, 1977
52. Teng Hsiao-P'ing, 1978
53. Ayatullah Khomeini, 1979
54. Ronald Reagan, 1980
55. Lech Walesa, 1981
56. The Computer, 1982
57. Reagan and Yuri Andropov, 1983
58. Peter Ueberroth, 1984
59. Deng Xiaoping, 1985
60. Corazon Aquino, 1986
61. Mikhail Gorbachev, 1987
62. Endangered Earth, 1988
63. Mikhail Gorbachev, 1989
64. The Two George Bushes, 1990
65. Ted Turner, 1991
66. Bill Clinton, 1992
67. The Peacemakers, 1993
68. Pope John Paul II, 1994
69. Newt Gingrich, 1995
70. Dr. David Ho, 1996
71. Andy Grove, 1997
72. Bill Clinton and Kenneth Starr, 1998
73. Jeff Bezos, 1999
74. George W. Bush, 2000
75. Rudolph Giuliani, 2001
76. The Whistleblowers, 2002
77. The American Soldier, 2003
78. George W. Bush, 2004
79. Bill Gates, Melinda Gates, & Bono, 2005
80. You, 2006
81. Vladimir Putin, 2007
82. Barack Obama, 2008
83. Ben Bernanke, 2009

SOURCE: http://history1900s.about.com/library/weekly/aa050400a.htm

READER'S DIGEST

Reader's Digest was begun by DeWitt Wallace, the son of a minister, who wanted an upbeat magazine with articles culled from other publications. Although the idea did not appeal to numerous publishers, this miniature magazine caught the imagination of a large and loyal audience. Its pages were glossy, unlike the other publications that originally had pages made of rough-textured paper. In 1947, *Reader's Digest* became the first magazine to exceed 9 million in circulation. The magazine accepted no advertising until 1955, relying instead on its subscriptions. Newsstand sales were also added in 1955. It still accepts no cigarette advertising, which harkens back to the conservative philosophy of its founder. *Reader's Digest* has remained remarkably resilient, charging as much as $100,000 for a full-page color advertisement. The magazine ranked fourth in circulation in 2009.

THE NEW YORKER MAGAZINE

Harold Ross founded *The New Yorker* magazine in 1925. The magazine was begun initially for a New York audience, but its outstanding and accurate profiles, insightful articles, witty cartoons, and excellent fictional stories have made the magazine extremely popular even outside of New York City. The magazine does not carry news articles; instead, it gives the readers entertaining features that cannot be found in other magazines. Shirley Jackson's "The Lottery" and James Thurber's "The Secret Life of Walter Mitty" are among the short stories the magazine has published over the years. The magazine also made history in 1962 by publishing Rachel Carson's *Silent Spring* over three issues, which enlightened readers about the sensitive ecosystem. *The New Yorker* has no deadlines for its reporters, and no limit on the number of words used. Instead, the magazine just expects good writing.

Men's Magazines

By the 1900s, the most desired demographic audience for magazines was women. The 1930s seems to be the decade that proved that men also had an interest in the medium. Men's fashion was the emphasis of *Apparel Arts* magazine, begun in 1931 in New York City. At a cost of $1.50, the magazine's purpose was to provide information on the latest men's fashions to retailers who sold men's clothing. This information was passed on to customers, and fabric samples were included to help with decision making. *Apparel Arts* was not only popular with retailers; customers would often leave the stores with the magazine. The magazine's founder, David Smart, and the magazine's editor, Arnold Gingrich, saw the potential for a men's fashion magazine. The result was one of the most enduring men's magazines of the twentieth century.

ESQUIRE

The popularity of *Apparel Arts* directly led to the founding of *Esquire* magazine in the summer of 1933 in Chicago. The name was chosen by the editor's secretary when a letter was addressed to the editor, "Arnold Gingrich, Esq." *Esquire* sold for fifty cents a copy, and its issues included stories and columns from some of the most well known writers and professionals of the time. Author Ernest Hemingway and boxer Gene Tunney wrote stories for the very first issue. Over the years, F. Scott Fitzgerald, J. D. Salinger, and Truman Capote were among the well known authors featured in the pages of *Esquire*. The artwork of Alberto Vargas became synonymous with the magazine. Vargas was a gifted painter whose beautiful *Esquire* portraits of pin-up girls became known as the "Varga Girls." The tasteful pin-up photos, its fashion emphasis, and the excellent literary pieces made *Esquire* one of the most popular men's magazines from its inception. It was the first of the classy men's magazines, and others would follow.

Playboy

Hugh Marston Hefner was a young staff member at *Esquire* magazine during the time that the magazine was published in Chicago. In 1950, *Esquire* moved its offices to New York, but Hefner stayed in

Chicago to begin his own publication. In December 1953, Hefner borrowed enough money to publish his magazine, initially called *Stag*, but changed the name to *Playboy* prior to publication. The first woman chosen for the cover was Marilyn Monroe, long before she became a Hollywood icon. The first issue was not numbered, nor did it have Hefner's name on it since Hefner was unsure if there would be a second issue.

Of course, there were many issues to follow, with Hefner making the decision to make his publication classy but lustier than *Esquire*. The nude centerfolds became a staple of the publication, and in-depth interviews with celebrities, politicians and historical figures were also mainstays. The magazine began an entire Playboy industry that ultimately included nightclubs and products in all other media. Its best-selling issue was the November 1972 issue, and its largest issue was the 414-page January 1979 issue. Hefner's health problems led him to step down in the 1980s as CEO of the company. He was replaced by his daughter, who led the company from 1988 to 2008. Hefner remains editor-in-chief of the magazine, and in its 57th year, Hefner has successfully maneuvered through the decades of criticism for the magazine's portrayal of women. *Playboy* is now facing a financial crisis, as most magazines are, but it remains the best-selling men's magazine on the market.

GQ

Apparel Arts, the retail publication that preceded *Esquire*, was revamped and introduced again in 1958 to *Esquire* subscribers as a fashion supplement. It was distributed quarterly, and the name was changed to *Gentlemen's Quarterly*. It continued to be published by Esquire, Inc. until 1983 when the magazine was sold to the large publishing company Conde Nast, and the company changed the name of the publication to *GQ*. The new publishers kept the fashion emphasis, but it also began to publish articles of interest to men. Soon, *Esquire* and *GQ* became direct competitors, and by 1993, *GQ* began to outsell *Esquire*. Today, *GQ* still has a large circulation, but other magazines such as *Maxim* and *FHM* are giving the magazine strong competition.

Men's Magazines Today

There are many men's magazines today from which to choose. The many versions of Bob Guccione's *Penthouse* provide adult entertainment much like *Playboy*. *Sports Illustrated* is an example of a publication that features primarily sports information, and its best-selling issue annually is the one that features swimsuit models. In contrast to these examples, many of the most popular men's publications do not include lusty material. Men's magazines focusing exclusively on cars, fitness, health or sports are all quite popular. Of course, online men's magazines are also attempting to find large audiences. It is clear that magazines are no longer intended for women readers only.

Post World War II Magazines

America changed a great deal after World War II. The population has become much more urban and mobile, and the country became much more industrialized and consumer driven. In terms of media, television came on the scene, and general-interest magazines such as *Saturday Evening Post* seemed dull to audiences. *Collier's*, a mass circulation magazine begun in 1888, had weathered the end of the muckraking era, but it could not effectively compete with television. It became the first such magazine to declare bankruptcy and cease publication in 1957. The handwriting was on the wall for the general-interest magazines, and the only way to survive and compete with television was to become more specialized.

The magazines that began and survived after World War II and on through the end of the 20th century were the specialized magazines such as *TV Guide*, *Rolling Stone*, *People*, and *O* magazine.

TV GUIDE

TV Guide was begun in 1948 by Walter Annenberg as a publication with television listings for New York City. By the 1950s, it became apparent that the new medium was going to be remarkably popular. In 1953, the publication was converted to a national publication, and by the end of that year, it boasted 1.5 million subscribers. For many years, *TV Guide* was the publication with the highest circulation, later competing with *Reader's Digest* for the number-one spot. However, as the Internet became a force, fewer people watched television, and still fewer relied on *TV Guide*. Over the years, adjusting to the changing marketplace, *TV Guide* added a website and a television network that initially scrolled television listings. In 2005, the owners of the magazine changed from its original small format to a full-size national magazine that would downplay the television listings and add more entertainment stories. Now, the magazine, website, and network are all owned by different entities, all still using the iconic *TV Guide* name.

ROLLING STONE MAGAZINE

Jann Wenner was a student at the University of California Berkeley in the mid-1960s. It was there that he began writing a music column for the university newspaper, the *Daily Californian*, focusing on his favorite artists of the time, Bob Dylan, the Beatles, and Mick Jagger. The 20-year-old Wenner decided to drop out of college to begin his own publication. He borrowed $7,500 from friends and family, and on his birthday in 1967, launched *Rolling Stone*, named in honor of the Muddy Waters song of the same name. Becoming profitable in its sixth year, it successfully became the voice of a new generation. *Rolling Stone* now boasts 12 million readers, and it is the preeminent magazine to combine both youth and music. Wenner now owns three other magazines, one of which is *Us Weekly*. His company is now said to be worth $250 million, 30,000 times his initial $7,500 investment.

PEOPLE MAGAZINE

People magazine was begun by Dick Durrell and Matthew Maynard in 1974 by Time Inc., the parent company of *Time* magazine. As a matter of fact, the "People" section of *Time* magazine had become so popular that the company decided to try the subject area as a magazine of its own. It showed a profit within two years, and it reached a circulation of more than 2 million within five years. By the 1990s, the magazine ranked only behind *TV Guide* in the amount of money it generated in advertising revenues and circulation.

People magazine capitalizes on America's fascination with celebrities, and most of the stories revolve around entertainment and sports personalities. Other human interest stories are also combined in each issue. After a 1995 edition featuring Tejano star Selena sold out, *People en Espanol* was begun the following year. *Teen People* was another version, but met with little success and lasted only eight years. There is currently an Australian version of the magazine as well.

Today, *People* generates more revenue than any other magazine on the market. Though that is impressive, it is the number of similar magazines and entertainment television programs that have been created as a direct result of *People* that makes this magazine so astounding. Magazines such as *Entertainment Weekly* and *Us Weekly*, along with television programs such as *Entertainment Tonight* and *The Insider* likely have *People* magazine to thank for their existence. There is no doubt that this single magazine has changed the market for celebrity news in remarkable ways.

O MAGAZINE

Most people thought that an Oprah Winfrey magazine similar to her television talk show would likely be profitable. It is unclear if anyone, including Winfrey herself, had any clue just how successful such a magazine would be. In May 2000, Winfrey, in partnership with Hearst publications, launched her glossy, self-titled magazine. *O* is simply a print version of her successful talk show, and after only seven issues, it became the most successful start-up magazine in the history of the magazine industry (do not forget that magazines date back to colonial times). The magazine was named *Ad Week's* "Start-Up of the Year in 2001"; *Advertising Age* named it the "Best Magazine of the Year" and the "Best Launch of the Year" in 2001; and in 2007, the American Society of Magazine Editors gave it the "National Magazine Award for Leisure Interests" as well as the "Best Magazine Cover of the Year: Best Service Cover."

During the 10 years since *O* launched, 8,000 magazines were published, and of those, only 40 percent lasted for five years ("Oprah's Big Weekend"). After 119 outfits and 74 hairstyles, Oprah is still thriving in magazine business ("Oprah's Big Weekend").

produces original reporting with contributors such as Meghan McCain and Condoleezza Rice. By September 2009, the *New York Times* reported that *The Daily Beast* had reached 3 million unique visitors per month (Rich).

Online Magazines

Just as it has impacted all other media, the Internet has also affected the magazine industry. Most magazines have Internet websites that usually offer Internet access to the print magazine articles. Some offer additional services on such sites, and many readers now turn to the electronic versions of their favorite magazines in addition to or rather than the print versions. The traffic on the websites of popular magazines can be extremely heavy, as is the case of *Sports Illustrated*, with more than 500,000 individual page views a month.

However, four online magazines, known as webzines, lead the way in the electronic magazine business. One of the first webzines was *Salon*, begun by David Talbot in 1995. The magazine's emphasis is on breaking political news, but the site also includes other topics, with information updated daily. The site is now a combination of free articles and premium articles that require a paid subscription to access.

Salon's primary competitor is *Slate*, a webzine begun in 1996 by Michael Kinsey. Initially owned by Microsoft, the site is now owned by the *Washington Post*. As with *Salon*, *Slate* struggled to determine how to make a profit with its Web offering. In 1998, the website attempted to become a subscription-based site only, but less than a year later, it returned to a completely free site. It has garnered an excellent reputation for its political coverage, though it is criticized for its liberal leanings.

The Huffington Post and *The Daily Beast* are two of the most recent webzines. *The Post* was launched in 2005 by Arianna Huffington, also primarily a political news website with liberal leanings. *The Daily Beast* is a website begun by seasoned magazine editor Tina Brown in 2008. While *The Beast* is a news aggregator, much as the *Drudge Report*, it also

The Future of Magazines

Supporters of magazines point to the fact that magazines continue to capture advertisers as an indication that magazines still hold an important place in media. However, many advertisers are moving rapidly to the Internet, as more readers are now becoming Web viewers. As more emphasis is placed on "going green," magazines' use of paper is coming under more scrutiny.

For now, there is a silver lining for the magazine industry. According to the 2009–2010 *Magazine Handbook*, a publication of the Magazines Publishers of America, four out of five adults still read magazines in spite of the large variety of other media options. The amount of advertising dollars spent in magazines is still higher than all other media, with the exception of television, which it ties. Consumers enjoy advertising in magazines more than in any other medium, and they like the portability and sharability of magazines. As digital technology improves, however, there is no predicting the future of print magazines.

Works Cited

"A New Yorker Timeline." *The New Yorker*. 02 June 2010. Web. 29 May 2010. *http://www.newyorker.com/magazine/timeline*.

"About | Saturday Evening Post." *Saturday Evening Post | OFFICIAL WEBSITE*. Web. 3 Dec. 2009. *http://www.saturdayeveningpost.com/about*.

"Defoe's Review 1704–13 / Major Works." *Pickering and Chatto Publishers - Shop Site*. Web. 01 Dec. 2009. *http://www.pickeringchatto.com/major_works/defoe_s_review_1704_13*.

"History of Publishing." *Encyclopedia—Britannica Online Encyclopedia*. Web. 15 Dec. 2009. *http://search.eb .com.libproxy.txstate.edu/eb/article-28689*.

"History of the Good Housekeeping Research Institute – Consumer Safety History—Goodhousekeeping.com." *Diet Plans—Healthy Recipes—Haircut Pictures—Cleaning Tips—Goodhousekeeping.com*. Web. 3 Dec. 2009. *http:// www.goodhousekeeping.com/product-testing/history/good- housekeeping-research-institute-history? click5main_sr*.

"History of TIME—Archive Collection—TIME." *Breaking News, Analysis, Politics, Blogs, News Photos, Video, Tech Reviews—TIME.com*. Web. 14 Dec. 2009. *http://www.time.com/time/archive/collections/0,21428,c_time_ history,00.shtml*.

"Jann S. Wenner | Biography." *Jann S. Wenner | Home*. Web. 31 Dec. 2009. *http://www.jannswenner.com/ Biography/*.

"John H. Johnson, a Standard for Black Businesses. | African American Registry." *The Black Box | African American Registry*. Web. 20 Nov. 2009. *http://www. aaregistry.org/historic_events/view/john-h-johnson-standard- black-businesses*.

"Johnson Publishing Company | About JPC | John H. Johnson | Biography." *Johnson Publishing Company | Home*. Web. 21 Nov. 2009. *http://www.johnsonpublishing. com/assembled/about_johnson_biography.html*.

"Muckraking." *Spartacus Educational—Home Page*. Web. 20 Dec. 2009. *http://www.spartacus.schoolnet.co.uk/ Jmuckraking.htm*.

"National Women's History Museum: Women with a Dead-line." *National Women's History Museum—NWHM*. Web. 4 Dec. 2009. *http://www.nwhm.org/online-exhibits/women- withdeadlines/wwd24.htm*.

"Oprah's Big Weekend—ABC News." *ABCNews.com— Breaking News, Politics, Online News, World News, Fea- ture Stories, Celebrity Interviews and More—ABC News*. Web. 15 May 2010. *http://abcnews.go.com/GMA/ video/oprahs-big-weekend-10596532*.

Rich, Motoko. "Daily Beast Seeks to Publish Faster." *The New York Times* [New York City] 29 Sept. 2009. Print.

"Scribner's Magazine." *Spartacus Educational—Home Page*. Web. 30 Dec. 2009. *http://www.spartacus.schoolnet. co.uk/USAscribners.htm*.

"TIME's Man of the Year List." *20th Century History*. Web. 30 Dec. 2009. *http://history1900s.about.com/ library/weekly/aa050400a.htm*.

Web. 01 June 2010. *http://www.magazine.org/advertising/ handbook/Magazine_Handbook.aspx*.

RADIO

Barbara Iverson

Chapter Objectives:

◆ Discuss the early history of radio and how it was influenced by contributions from Heinrich Hertz, Guglielmo Marconi, Lee DeForest, Edwin Armstrong, and David Sarnoff.

◆ Outline the transition of the radio from military equipment to home entertainment device in the 1920s.

◆ Explain why individual radio stations began forming networks in the 1920s and 1930s.

◆ List the first four major radio networks.

◆ Discuss how the rise of talk radio affected AM radio.

◆ Discuss Edward R. Murrow's contribution to radio news broadcasting.

◆ Explain the impact of the Radio Act of 1927.

◆ Discuss how the Telecommunications Act of 1996 has affected radio as we know it today.

◆ Identify forms of global radio.

◆ Explain how the emergence of satellite radio, CPB stations, Internet radio, and podcasts have altered the ways in which people listen to radio.

◆ Identify two factors that currently limit job growth in radio broadcasting.

Introduction

Radio is one of the oldest mass media in society. Over time, technology and public policy have caused radio's function and purpose to change. What was once just a few bleeps sent from one ship to another is now crystal clear voices communicating around the world. Although radio waves float freely though the air, the contents of those waves are highly restricted. There are government regulations about who can own radio stations and who controls subject matter over the airwaves, in addition to economic models that dictate who pays and who makes money. These factors help determine how radio fits into a society.

In commercial radio, what news, information, and entertainment the audience wishes to hear and how they choose to receive that content have an influential role in how radio functions as well. The attention of an audience did—and can—create a "golden age" for the medium. However, just as quickly, a shift in attention can end one.

To talk about radio, we need to know that **radio**, from a technological standpoint, means telecommunication modulated by electromagnetic waves. However, *radio* also may refer to radio programming, modern music radio, the radio industry, or radio stations in general. All these meanings of *radio* inform our understanding of radio as a mass medium.

Today there are more than 16,000 AM radio stations, 26,000 FM stations, and 1500 shortwave radio stations in the world. In addition, over 3 million people subscribe to satellite radio. As we'll explore in this chapter, modern radio only vaguely resembles the original concept of wireless electromagnetic transmissions. These days, people are as likely to be listening to what they call "radio" on an MP3 player, a computer, or via satellite transmission in their cars as they are to be listening to an AM/FM receiver.

A Historical Overview

It's hard to believe that what started as a few taps of Morse code in 1901 grew into the diverse multimedia outlet that is today's radio industry. Indeed, the history of radio is an ongoing story of vision, ingenuity, and rapid technological advancement.

BIRTH OF A MEDIUM—1888–1912

Although radio as we know it today has only been around for a little over a century, radio waves have been present as long as planets have orbited the sun. However, it took the innovative thinking of many scientists and inventors to make sense of these invisible waves. German physicist Heinrich Hertz was the first to prove the existence of radio waves in the late 1880s. His experiments proved that, like light,

radio waves are a type of electromagnetic wave.[1] **Electromagnetic waves** are movements of energy that can travel at the speed of light in a free space detached from wires. Soon after Hertz made these discoveries, scientists were eager to find a way to use radio waves to carry sounds, including voices.

As a young man, Guglielmo Marconi read about Hertz's work and began conducting his own experiments in a quest to develop wireless telegraphy. By 1901, Marconi had transmitted the first radio message across the Atlantic Ocean—Morse code for the letter "S." Over the next several years, radio came to be used as a form of ship-to-shore communication. In 1912, wireless operators were onboard both the *Titanic* and the ship that rescued its survivors, the *Carpathia*. Marconi's technology allowed radio operators to transmit information about the disaster and ask for assistance before the *Carpathia* reached its port in New York City.[2]

Meanwhile, Lee De Forest was developing his own innovations for radio, including the **Audion**, a device that he patented in 1907. De Forest's device was used to convert radio frequency into audio frequency, so sounds could be transmitted and amplified. The Audion made live broadcasting possible and later became a key component of all telephone, television, and radar systems before the invention of the transistor.[3] Although some admirers refer to De Forest as the "father of radio," some critics of his time claimed that he merely patented many ideas that others had generated.[4]

Ironically, De Forest brought similar claims against another pioneer of early radio, Edwin Armstrong. In 1912, Armstrong took De Forest's invention of the Audion one step further by devising a way to improve the amplification by a thousandfold, so the sound generated could be heard across a room. The most impressive part of Armstrong's take on the Audion—later named the regenerative circuit—was that it could serve as an oscillator as well as a receiver. This allowed the device to both generate and obtain radio waves. Shortly after receiving a patent for his idea, he crossed paths with De Forest, who claimed ownership of the idea. Although De Forest eventually won a lengthy legal battle on the basis of a language technicality, Armstrong is still credited with the invention.[5]

As illustrated by De Forest and Armstrong, the development of radio in its earliest forms depended on the ingenuity and, at times, fierce competitiveness of pioneering scientists.

FROM WORK TO PLAY, TOOL TO TOY

Radio communications were a vital link in the military chain of command during World War I. This caused the U.S. government to place heavy restrictions on radio broadcasting. At the end of World War I in 1918, many of those restrictions were lifted and radio broadcasting was ready to take on a new purpose. David Sarnoff, a Russian immigrant who had worked for the Marconi Company during the war, had a vision of radio as a home entertainment device. Sarnoff believed that radio could bring music into the home in a way no one else had imagined. He also envisioned a radio receiver in every home. Sarnoff's tenacious efforts helped him rise to fame as one of the first on-air radio personalities and a leader at Radio Corporation of America (RCA).[6]

A radio in every home was a visionary idea for a time when there was no mass communication beyond print brought directly to the individual. KDKA, the first commercial radio station, which began broadcasting in 1920, changed all that. It featured music and entertainment, but it also carried the election returns for the 1920 presidential election.

The main downfall of radio was the high operating costs. Running a broadcasting station required strong financial backing but realized little or no profit. However, as radio stations began to rise in popularity and value, businesses started to view radio as a good platform for advertising. Eventually, advertising became the primary means of support for radio broadcasting in the United States.

As its popularity grew, large corporations wanted to get into the business of radio. In 1926, Sarnoff brought together the resources of RCA, General Electric, and Westinghouse to purchase WEAF in New York. WEAF eventually became the anchor station for the National Broadcasting System (NBC). NBC soon swelled to 25 stations nationwide and became the first broadcasting network. In 1927, NBC was able to broadcast the Rose Bowl from California to New York through the use of long-distance wire telephone lines. Fans from coast to coast could hear the football game for the first time.

Still, music was the "killer app" that Sarnoff believed would make radio a household necessity. From the beginning, the success of radio and the success of music recording industries have been intertwined. Americans bought radios so live music could be delivered directly into their homes. In turn, radio spurred the sales of records, as listeners sought out their favorite songs or bands after hearing them on the radio. Sarnoff's hunch that broadcasting and music recording would influence one another over time turned out to be accurate.[7]

REPORTING AND NEWS RADIO

Although much of radio programming in the 1920s and 30s revolved around music and entertainment, there was an interest in radio news as well. In addition to the 1920 KDKA broadcast of the election, news events such as presidential inaugurations, baseball's World Series, and aviator Charles Lindbergh's safe landing in Paris after his solo flight across the Atlantic were broadcast on the radio. However, regular newscasts didn't catch on until the mid-1930s. These first newscasts consisted of summaries of the headlines from the morning newspapers read over the air.

Newspaper publishers feared that radio would lure their audiences away, and many refused to print radio schedules in the early years. The newspaper publishers blocked the press associations (AP, UP, and INS) from selling news for radio broadcasts until the 1940s.

The radio networks understood the potential of broadcast news and began to create syndicates and the capability for reporting national and global events. With the start of World War II, radio became the most important link between the public, Washington, D.C., and the rest of the world. With their loved ones thousands of miles away, listeners tuned in to the familiar voices of correspondents who reported from abroad to "bring home" news of the war to the United States.

Edward R. Murrow of the Columbia Broadcasting System (CBS) was in Europe when the war began. He quickly assembled a team of reporters to report nightly to London on the progress of the war. Honest, urgent, and live at the scene, these broadcasts came to define broadcast news for decades.

In the new medium of radio, there were no models for reporters to follow. Murrow didn't have formal training as a journalist. He thought that made it easier to report for radio because he didn't have to unlearn anything before jumping into radio reporting.

One of his innovative broadcasts features the sound of British civilians entering an air-raid shelter. Murrow set the microphone on the ground to record the quiet, orderly footsteps that reinforced his words about the courage of the average citizen during the London Blitz.

Murrow and his team of reporters, called his boys, set an example at CBS that became the model for all the networks. Investigative reporters and political correspondents adopted the blunt style of the reporter, microphone in hand, who steps up to politicians, generals, corporate leaders, or John Q. Public and asks the tough questions, demanding to know the truth. This style came to define hard-hitting journalism and also migrated to television with Murrow and his protégés.

FROM NOVELTY TO NETWORK

Due to the influence of World War I (1914–1918) and the Great Depression (1929–1939), the structure of radio broadcasting developed under different economic and social conditions than those that exist today. The radio industry was based on a different set of assumptions about programs, producers, technology, and consumers.

Newspapers were the dominant medium at the time of radio's introduction into the world of mass communications. Radio stations had to find **economies of scale** through the wire services that allowed companies to pool their resources in order to extend their coverage. Creating these networks also allowed stations to share the expense of producing and transmitting content. Juggernauts of the industry quickly emerged.

After NBC was created, the company formed two semi-independent radio networks, the Blue Network (WJZ) and the Red Network (WEAF). The Red Network flourished and, by 1938, carried 75 percent of NBC's commercial programs. The askew performance of the two networks prompted NBC to sell the Blue Network, which eventually became the American Broadcasting Company (ABC), in 1943.[8]

Shortly after NBC's conception, a cigar-business owner named William S. Paley combined the United Independent Broadcasters and the Columbia Phonograph Company to create the Columbia Broadcasting System (CBS). A businessman at heart, Paley strove to turn a struggling radio network into a success. The key to this accomplishment was advertising. He offered free programming to affiliated stations if those stations would designate slots of airtime to network shows that were sponsored by advertisers. Paley's gimmick helped CBS expand from 22 stations in 1928 to 144 stations over the course of a decade. Although CBS produced many successful radio shows that featured stars such as Fred Allen, Bing Crosby, and Kate Smith, the network's repertoire grew considerably after Paley's raid of NBC's talent pool. Paley was able to coerce stars such as Jack Benny, George Burns, and comedy duo Amos 'n' Andy to join the CBS network. This attack hurt NBC even more when the age of television approached, as these personalities proved to be as popular on the screen as they were on the air.[9]

Not all radio networks were created to compete on a national level. In 1934, the Mutual Broadcasting System (MBS) was developed as a cooperative network shared by WOR in New York, WGN in Chicago, WLW in Cincinnati, and WXYZ in Detroit. Unlike the larger networks, MBS had no production studio or centralized corporate owners. The network catered mostly to small, rural markets and carried popular programs such as the *The Lone Ranger* and *The Green Hornet*.[10]

The rise of radio networks gave way to a new generation of radio listeners. No longer a system of amateurs broadcasting to a puny local audience, radio became a medium to which people from all over the nation could connect and enjoy the same entertainment, share information, and exchange opinions. In 1935, two out of three homes had a radio set, and broadcasting could be heard 24 hours a day. By 1950, there were radio sets in 40 million homes, and 63 percent of Americans claimed radio as their primary source for news. This era of initial excitement and respect for the medium is often referred to as the "golden age" of radio. However, the golden age came to gradual extinction as radio became a victim of its own growth. More stations meant more competition, and a swollen market meant less revenue to go around.[11]

THE RISE OF FM

Although Lee De Forest criticized Edwin Armstrong for being an unoriginal thinker, Armstrong proved himself as an inventor with the creation of frequency modulation (**FM**) broadcasting. Unlike standard amplitude modulation (**AM**) broadcasting, which varies the amplitude, or power, of radio waves to create sound, FM varies the frequency of radio waves across a wide band of frequency, creating a clearer sound.[12] Still, AM radio dominated the broadcast band until the 1960s. Although the technology for the static-free sound of FM broadcasting had been around for nearly 30 years, concern for sound quality did not equal the concern for bandwidth exertion. Finally, in 1961, new Federal Communications Commission (FCC) regulations opened up more bandwidth on the FM dial. The combination of newly introduced stereo sound, the transistor radio, and high-fidelity records helped FM radio become the home for music.

As a larger audience began to tune in, FM stations became more specialized. Tailored formats such as easy listening or rock and roll started to emerge. Baby boomers, who were becoming teenagers during FM's emergence, could listen to music specifically targeted to their generation. FM radios were showing up in people's homes, cars, and even in their hands. In the early 1960s, Japanese electronics company Sony perfected the transistor radio with the TR-63. The small, stylish, and battery-powered FM radio could be carried in a front shirt pocket. The transistor radio allowed people to stay connected to music, news, and entertainment while on the go, similar to the way MP3 players do today.

As contemporary music continued to change throughout the 1960s, station formats became more experimental. DJs started to do more than just play records; they indulged in political debates over controversial issues such as the Vietnam War, civil rights, and the draft.[13] The "free-form" format of FM stations helped shape the music and politics of the 1960s and 70s. This mini renaissance for radio faded as baby boomers aged and as FCC rule changes in the 1990s made it easier for large corporations to purchase multiple independent stations.

TALK RADIO

AM radio was shedding audience in the 1970s, as the best music migrated to FM. In the 1980s, however, the talk format caught on and flourished, revitalizing AM radio. The AM frequencies that couldn't handle high-fidelity audio well were fine for transmitting the sound of the human voice. The 1987 repeal of The Fairness Doctrine (see Callout Box from pg. 235 on Section 315) further hastened the rise of talk radio. Previously, the Fairness Doctrine had required broadcasters to balance shows in terms of their political points of view. The idea was that the need for the public to have access to a variety of viewpoints outweighed commercial needs of broadcasters. With the law's repeal, however, political commentators such as Rush Limbaugh could bring a blend of news, entertainment, and partisan analysis to AM. Although the politically charged broadcasts of commentators such as Limbaugh often spark controversy, they also attract listeners. Talk radio is the top choice for about 15 percent of the radio audience, and it dominates AM radio today. Listeners are mostly male, but otherwise fairly diverse.[14]

Rules and Regulations

From the beginning, the radio industry has been subject to a variety of government rules and regulations. As times and technology have changed, so too have many of the rules governing the medium.

THE EARLY YEARS

Signal interference arising from broadcasts airing on the same frequencies is a technical issue requiring a large-scale solution. Unless a station was granted a "clear channel" to broadcast on the same frequency across the entire country, radio stations from different locations broadcast on the same frequencies. Trouble arose when stations strayed into each other's frequencies or when their signals were too powerful. The result was static, dissonance, and disgruntled audiences.

In the United States, radio was a commercial affair almost from the beginning. Herbert Hoover served as Secretary of Commerce under presidents Harding and Coolidge before being elected president in 1928. He favored the allocation of radio frequencies to large corporations as a solution to the problems of interference, ownership, and funding.

In 1923, three kinds of stations were created by allocating bands of frequencies (see "How Radio Frequencies Work"). These included high-power "clear" channels, medium-power channels, and low-power channels. The Radio Act of 1927 set up the Federal Radio Commission (FRC) with responsibility for regulating radio frequency usage. In 1928, the FRC's General Order 40 shifted most radio stations' frequencies so that 23 of the first 25 clear channels were assigned to affiliates of NBC. Formed in 1926, NBC had 48 affiliate stations, sold "sustaining" programs to affiliates, and broadcast "sponsored" programs produced by advertisers such as the American Tobacco Company.

The FRC's favoritism toward commercial interests gave rise to a radio reform movement beginning in 1930. An examination of the impact of radio and newspaper publishing on democracy in 1934 by the Hutchins Commission helped lead to the establishment of the FCC to replace the FRC. Many of the problems identified by the Hutchins Commission—such as the distortion and neglect of news coverage by large corporations and the control of news by advertising and commercial interests—remain relevant today.

The ownership caps and other rules and regulations put in place by the FCC in 1934 grew out of the Hutchins Commission recommendations. This 1934 legislation, updated by amendments, still influences policy today.[15]

How Radio Frequencies Work

A radio wave is an electromagnetic wave propagated by an **antenna**. Radio waves have different **frequencies**, and by tuning a radio receiver to a specific frequency, you can pick up a specific signal.

When you listen to a radio station and the announcer says, "You are listening to 91.5 FM WRKX, The Rock!" what the announcer means is that you are listening to a radio station broadcasting an FM radio signal at a frequency of 91.5 megahertz, with FCC-assigned call letters of WRKX. **Megahertz** means "one million cycles per second," so "91.5 megahertz" means that the transmitter at the radio station is oscillating at a frequency of 91,500,000 cycles per second. Your FM (frequency modulated) radio can tune in to that specific frequency and give you clear reception of that station. All FM radio stations transmit in a **band** of frequencies between 88 megahertz and 108 megahertz. This band of the radio spectrum is used for no other purpose but FM radio broadcasts.

In the same way, AM radio is confined to a band from 535 kilohertz to 1,700 kilohertz (kilo meaning "thousands," so 535,000 to 1,700,000 cycles per second). So an AM (amplitude modulated) radio station that says, "This is AM 680 WPTF" means that the radio station is broadcasting an AM radio signal at 680 kilohertz, and its FCC-assigned call letters are WPTF.

Common frequency bands include the following:

♦ **AM radio:** 535 kilohertz to 1.7 megahertz

♦ **Shortwave radio:** bands from 5.9 megahertz to 26.1 megahertz

♦ **Citizens band (CB) radio:** 26.96 megahertz to 27.41 megahertz

♦ **Television stations:** 54 to 88 megahertz for channels 2 through 6

♦ **FM radio:** 88 megahertz to 108 megahertz

♦ **Television stations:** 174 to 220 megahertz for channels 7 through 13

Every wireless technology you can imagine has its own little band. There are hundreds of them! For example:

♦ Garage door openers, alarm systems, etc.: around 40 megahertz

♦ Standard cordless phones: bands from 40 to 50 megahertz

♦ Baby monitors: 49 megahertz

♦ Radio-controlled airplanes: around 72 megahertz, which is different from...

♦ Radio-controlled cars: around 75 megahertz

♦ Wildlife tracking collars: 215 to 220 megahertz

♦ MIR space station: 145 megahertz and 437 megahertz

♦ Cell phones: 824 to 849 megahertz

♦ New 900-MHz cordless phones: obviously around 900 megahertz!

♦ Air traffic control radar: 960 to 1,215 megahertz

♦ Global Positioning System: 1,227 and 1,575 megahertz

♦ Deep-space radio communications: 2,290 megahertz to 2,300 megahertz

Why is AM radio in a band at 550 kilohertz to 1,700 kilohertz, while FM radio is in a band at 88 to 108 megahertz? It is all completely arbitrary, and a lot of it has to do with history.

AM radio has been around a lot longer than FM radio, and frequency allocation for AM radio occurred during the 1920s.

Television stations were largely nonexistent until 1946, which is when the FCC allocated commercial broadcast bands for TV. By 1949, a million people owned TV sets, and by 1951 there were 10 million TVs in America.

Courtesy of howstuffworks.com

THE 1980S AND BEYOND

As a result of further technological developments in the telecommunications industry, such as the introduction of cable television, the FCC continued to update its rules and regulations over the years. In the 1980s however, President Reagan began actively moving to deregulate industries. His efforts had their greatest impact on radio with the Telecommunications Act of 1996, which President Clinton signed into law. This act includes many sections and deals with television, cable, telephony, radio, and more. Its impact on broadcast radio in the United States has been far-reaching.[16]

Before 1996, corporations were not allowed to own more than 40 radio stations. Deregulation in the 1980s and 1990s, however, relaxed these limits. Business strategists sought to make money by consolidating smaller independent companies into large corporations. By exploiting economies of scale, giant corporations produced economic gains for their stockholders.

After the deregulation in 1996, media consolidation snowballed in AM and FM radio in the United States. Today, six companies own the majority of the nation's radio broadcasting frequencies and therefore dominate broadcast radio. These **oligopolies** exert economic dominance over radio and related media enterprises such as advertising, performance venues, and recording contracts for music artists and merchandizing. Clear Channel, one of just a handful of companies that control most of broadcast radio frequencies, aggressively acquired stations when the ownership limit was relaxed, and today they control over 1,200 radio stations nationwide.[17] They dominate broadcast radio in 100 of the 112 major media markets.[18]

Increased media consolidation led to a decline in FM radio's individuality and local character. Most owners were increasing the number of ads per hour and decreasing the number of songs in their playlists. Restricted playlists with as few as 100 songs became commonplace. In 2005, on Clear Channel stations, commercials took one minute in five of typical broadcasts. Audiences began to turn away from programming that trailed in importance to advertising.

PUBLIC INTEREST ROUSES FCC

Although the Telecommunications Act of 1983 did remove many of the regulatory controls on commercial radio, the broadcast airwaves continue to belong to the public, and the FCC still retains responsibility for regulating them.

In 2003, the FCC moved to relax the rules on media ownership further. This may have been a tipping point, because public outcry calling for limits on media concentration was fierce. Nearly 3 million people contacted the FCC calling for media reform in 2003. The issue brought together groups from both the left and the right, including the National Rifle Association, Common Cause, MoveOn.org, the Traditional Values Coalition, and Mediareform.org.

The matter went to court. There was no further relaxation of ownership limits, and the FCC decided not to appeal the matter. As a result, the FCC had to rewrite its policy pertaining to serving local interests and promoting access to the airwaves by diverse groups.[19]

Developments and Issues in Contemporary Radio

The radio industry has experienced dramatic changes in the recent years. For us in the 21 century, the consumer is king of mass media. With digital media and broadband networks, consumers can get content wherever, whenever, and however they want. Broadcasting is giving way to **narrowcasting** in radio, as well as other mass media. The question isn't AM or FM, nor is it what station to tune in. Today's listener wants "me media" that provides whatever content he or she wants at the time and place demanded by the listener. Today, radio transmissions are often "narrowcast" to listeners on demand.

SATELLITE RADIO

The rise of **satellite radio** in recent years marks an important development in the radio industry. Subscribers to satellite networks pay a monthly fee and get access to commercial-free programming, some of it directly from broadcast radio, and other stations that are only heard via satellite.

Satellite radio operators have made deals with car manufacturers so that all new vehicles have built-in satellite radio receivers, and most come with a complimentary subscription to the first several months of satellite radio.

Portable satellite radios are also available. These devices can download and play individual songs like MP3 players can, as well as play programming streams from satellite radio.

Other listeners time shift their favorite radio programs by subscribing to RSS (real simple syndication) feeds that automatically download the most recent episodes of a program to their computer and transfer the segments to their MP3 players.

In 2006, **shock-jock** Howard Stern moved to satellite radio. The move was closely watched throughout the radio business. He commanded an audience of 10 million with his morning show on FM radio. Following crackdowns on profanity over the airwaves from regulators and the threat of fines or censorship from his employer, Stern decided to make a decisive move off the public airwaves and onto subscription radio broadcast via satellite. With his move from FM broadcast radio to satellite radio, his new employer SIRIUS saw its subscription base rise above the 3-million mark.

In the past several years, satellite radio subscriptions have continued to increase. After the 2008 merger of SIRIUS and XM, the combined company had over 18 million subscribers.[20] That same year, a study conducted by the digital technology research firm Parks Associates predicted that by 2012, satellite radio subscribers would increase to 39 million.[21]

PUBLIC BROADCASTING

More than 26 million people listen to Corporation for Public Broadcasting (CPB) stations and support news shows like "All Things Considered," long-form radio entertainments like "This American Life," and a variety of musical offerings on public radio stations through pledges. The audience for CPB had remained steady, but has declined slightly between 2004 and 2005. Competition for listener attention is fierce, and the hours per day that individuals can engage with mass media can't expand indefinitely. It may be inevitable that as more varied devices are available, the number of listeners in the audience for any one device may decrease.

INTERNET RADIO AND PODCASTING

Innovative radio broadcasting stations of all kinds are presenting supplemental content via downloads for listeners who have special interests. News radio 780, one of the only all-news AM radio stations still broadcasting, has put press conferences and uncut interviews on its Web site where listeners can listen, download, or subscribe to news of their choice. The Internet has allowed the station, and others like it, to reach audiences far beyond their over-the-airwaves reach.[22]

Nowadays, even individuals with computers and inexpensive software can provide competition for listeners. It is simple to create online music or talk programming. Digital audio, such as **podcasts** (digital recordings of radio broadcasts or similar programs made available on the Internet),[23] can be uploaded to the Internet and downloaded for listening on computers or MP3 players. This is yet another form of competition for the attention of listeners.

REVENUES AND RATINGS

Radio revenues are dependent on advertising. But how do radio stations know how large the audience is for various programs, and how do advertisers verify that the claims made by station owners are correct? They turn to Arbitron Inc., an "international media and marketing research firm serving radio broadcasters, radio networks, cable companies, advertisers, advertising agencies, outdoor advertising companies, and the online radio industry in the United States, Mexico, and Europe."[24] In a joint venture with VNU, Inc., Arbitron provides media and marketing research services including market **ratings** to broadcasters and advertisers.

Radio shows are programmed around a set of genres. A **genre** is a style. Like any other fashion or any other style, music genres go in and out of popularity with audiences. Arbitron also provides data on audience demographics for different genres and for various **dayparts**.

The amount of money that broadcasters can use for advertising time is tied to ratings. Arbitron and similar companies provide ratings information for major markets. These resources provide an interesting way to learn about radio and are essential for those who intend to pursue a career in radio.

RESPONDING TO COMPETITION

With satellite radio, Internet radio, and podcasting bursting onto the media scene, there are suddenly many more alternatives for the listening audience.[25] To stay in business, the radio industry looked to new formats as a way to be competitive in a world in which competition comes from the Internet, MP3 devices, cell phones, or anyone who has a computer with a microphone and Internet connection.

In 2002, an alternative format called "Jack" was trademarked in Canada. With the slogan "Playing what we want," "Jack" stations typically have a playlist of 1,000 songs. They are classified as variety or adult hit by radio research companies.[26]

By 2004, "Jack," "Bob," and even "Dave" radio, based loosely on the "random shuffle" concept, were taking over American airwaves. Several of these alternatives to the Clear Channel cyberjock model began to advertise fewer commercials per hour. Although they denied they were responding to the competition, Clear Channel moved to reduce the number of commercials on its stations in 2005.

In addition, companies such as Clear Channel responded to mounting competition by seeking to cut expenses by achieving economies of scale. Clear Channel is a leader in using **voice-tracking** software to customize their programs to make it sound as if the DJs are actually local residents. With digital equipment, local traffic and weather information can be interlaced into a broadcast from a single point, like Clear Channel's San Antonio studios. When the broadcast goes out across the airwaves, listeners think the DJ is local because of the customized traffic and weather segments. The use of cyberjocks cuts the cost of producing radio shows, but at the same time it can rob the airwaves of diverse voices and local perspectives.[27] Other changes evolve from the consolidation of radio ownership.

Beyond National Boundaries: Global Radio

Although radio is an old medium, it is still one of the most vital forms of communication outside the United States. There are about 44,000 radio stations in the world according to the CIA World Factbook, and only one in three of these is in the United States.

THE BBC

In the United States, the airwaves were largely put into commercial use. In the United Kingdom, the British Broadcasting Corporation BBC, or the "Beeb" as it is called by millions of listeners, was established with public support and a royal charter in the 1927.[28] The effort to keep the BBC independent of commercial and government influence was led by John Reith, the BBC's first general manager, who believed in "an independent British broadcaster able to educate, inform, and entertain the whole nation, free from political interference and commercial pressure."[29]

In 1937, the BBC established a network designed for its empire and the rest of the world, which is called the World Service today. The BBC was broadcasting television by 1936, but had to suspend television broadcasts during World War II.

The coronation of Queen Elizabeth in 1952 drew the largest audience in BBC history and set the stage for television to become the premiere broadcast format. BBC programming was solid, but competition from Independent Television (ITV) captured many viewers during the 1950s and 1960s. In the 1970s, the BBC linked with the Open University to create the University of the Airwaves. In the 1980s, Margaret Thatcher's government cut back funding, but the BBC streamlined and in the 1990s launched the highly respected BBC Online. By January 2005, BBC Internet radio listenership had jumped 70 percent from the previous year, with a total of over 7 million listeners.[30] Today, the BBC Web site and Internet radio broadcasts continue to gain an audience.

SHORTWAVE BROADCASTS

Many radio stations that are widely accessible are shortwave broadcasts. Shortwave signals can be aimed at the earth's ionosphere. When they strike the ionosphere, they bounce back to Earth and can skip from one part of the globe. This is called the skywave effect, and it helps the waves continue or propagate over long distances.

Solar emissions can affect the reflectivity of the earth's atmosphere, but if conditions are right, a shortwave radio in the United States can pick up stations from Africa, Asia, Australia, and East Asia.

Avid shortwave listeners are known as Dxers from the old telegraph term meaning "Distance." They search out broadcasts that fall into three main categories: broadcast, clandestine, and amateur or utility. Broadcasts consist of music, cultural, religious, and political programming. "Pirate" and other unlicensed radio stations, including some anti-government broadcast material, fall into the clandestine category. Utility broadcasts include weather information, world clocks, Morse code, and radio teletype.

Chapter Summary

◆Much of the early history of radio, during the second half of the 19th century, is the story of inventors and scientists making sense of invisible waves and how they could be harnessed to carry sounds and voice.

◆In the early 1900s, David Sarnoff, an employee of the Marconi Company, had a vision of radio as a home entertainment device. The first commercial radio station began broadcasting in 1920, leading to the first golden age of radio in the 1930s and 1940s.

◆In the 1920s, individual radio stations began pooling their resources to create economies of scale."

The first major networks that emerged were the Red Network and the Blue Network, which evolved into the National Broadcasting Company (NBC) and the American Broadcasting Company (ABC). The Columbia Broadcasting System (CBS) and a fourth network, Mutual Broadcasting System (MBS), followed in the 1930s.

◆ Radio became an important news medium during World War II when broadcasts from Europe by Edward R. Murrow set a new standard for broadcast reporting. That style of news broadcast on the radio later influenced television news.

◆ With the introduction of high-fidelity audio, more listeners began tuning in to FM stations for music. Talk radio revived AM. After the Fairness Doctrine was repealed, early talk radio hosts such as Rush Limbaugh provided a model for aspiring shock-jocks.

◆ Radio licensing by the government requires broadcasters to serve the public interest. The Federal Communications Commission (FCC) regulates broadcasting to protect that interest, but deregulation under President Reagan in the 1980s culminating in the Telecommunications Bill of 1996 may have weakened the protections.

◆ Digital radio, satellite radio, and podcasting promise to alter radio listening because of the quality of sound and type of programs available. However, the advances will mean purchasing new equipment.

◆ As technology, regulation, and economic factors change, the radio business is changing and so are the employment opportunities in radio. Advances in technology and media consolidation are two contributing factors to the limited job growth in radio and television broadcasting.

◆ Shortwave radio signals allow radio stations to broadcast globally. Internet radio, such as the BBC's Internet broadcast, has become popular as another form of global radio.

Glossary

Audion—a device used to convert radio frequency into audio frequency, so sounds could be transmitted and amplified

AM radio—a broadcasting system using amplitude modulation; 535 kilohertz to 1.7 megahertz

antenna—a metallic rod or wire that radiates and receives radio waves

band—a defined range of radio frequencies

citizens band (CB) radio—26.96 megahertz to 27.41 megahertz

cyberjock—sometimes pejorative term for a disk jockey who hosts a radio show from a single locale that is broadcast widely and uses computer software to localize weather, traffic, and advertisements

daypart—a subsection of the day used in radio or television programming

economies of scale—the decreased per-unit cost as output increases; this is because some resources are less expensive in bulk

electromagnetic waves—movements of energy that can travel at the speed of light in a free space detached from wires

FM radio—a broadcasting system using frequency modulation; 88 megahertz to 108 megahertz

frequencies—the number of complete oscillations per second of energy (e.g., sound) in the form of waves

genre—a style

megahertz—one million cycles per second

narrowcasting—creating a media channel that is aimed at a niche audience

niche—a smaller subgroup with specific interests

oligopoly—control of the market by only a few, rather than many, companies

podcast—a digital recording of a radio broadcast or similar program, made available on the Internet for downloading to a personal audio player

radio—telecommunication modulated by electromagnetic waves; may also refer to radio programming, modern music radio, the radio industry, or radio stations in general

ratings—statistical measures of listeners or viewers of broadcast programming

satellite radio—radio created from digital signals sent through satellites in space; allows for commercial-free broadcasting over a broad geographical area

shock-jock—a slang term for a disk jockey or talk show host who pushes the boundaries of what is offensive

shortwave radio—5.9 megahertz to 26.1 megahertz

television stations—54 to 88 megahertz for channels 3 through6; 174 to 220 megahertz for channels 7 through 13

voice-tracking software—computer software used in radio programming that allows a DJ to hear the end of one song and the beginning of another so he or she can record the voice tracks so they sound live, though it is played back at a later time. After recording the "break", the song is encoded and can be transmitted anywhere on radio or Internet.

Discussion Questions

1. Why is radio regulated?
2. Are podcasts, Internet radio, and streaming music "radio"? Why or why not?
3. What effect will satellite radio and high-definition radio have on standard radio?
4. How did the Fairness Doctrine work to ensure AM radio stations would stay on air?
5. What are your thoughts on media consolidation? Has this practice had a positive or negative impact on radio?

Supplemental Web Sites

◆ Ironically, in 2006, Chuck Schaden, a radio buff who gathered "Old Time" radio programs from the "Golden Age" into his weekly "Those Were the Days," radio program celebrated a strange anniversary.[36] Schaden celebrated being on the air for 35 years and eight months. This is longer than any show from the golden age lasted. "Don McNeill's Breakfast Club," aired for 35 years and six months when it signed off from the Allerton Hotel in Chicago on Dec. 27, 1968.[37] It had been longest-running radio show from the pre-television era. "Those Were the Days" with Chuck Schaden is still on the air. Listen to it at http://www.wdcb.org/personalities_detail.lasso?who=24712740082625700.

◆ For more on the Hutchins Commission and their suggestions for the improvement of radio, visit http://www.nieman.harvard.edu/reports/99-4_00-1NR/Hutchins_Freedom.html.

◆ Mark Crispin Miller analyzed the problems created by media consolidation for *The Nation* in 2002, and their online guide to "The Big Ten" provides a guide to these media cartels at http://www.thenation.com/special/bigten.html. The "Who Owns What" online database of media owners and companies that is maintained by the Columbia Journalism Review lets you search media ownership by station, type of media, or corporate parent. Visit http://www.cjr.org/tools/owners/.

◆ In a feature story about talk-show host John Ziegler, writer David Foster Wallace takes us inside the studio and alternately explains and illustrates how talk radio works. You can click to read the definitions and notes that Wallace has embedded for the reader. We get the meaning of "churn" which refers to the host's opening monologue where the nightly topics are introduced and the host aims to get listeners emotionally stimulated so they don't switch away. Wallace also addresses the difference between news and talk radio. If information isn't simply "spin," then the danger of talk radio lies in turning "democratic discourse" from a ""battle of ideas" to a battle of sales pitches for ideas" where the truth doesn't matter as much as a glib pronouncement about what someone believes." Visit http://www.theatlantic.com/doc/prem/200504/wallace.

◆ The BBC Web site has a timeline and multimedia clips highlighting the history of BBC radio and TV. Visit http://www.bbc.co.uk/heritage/story/.

◆ One of the most complete research sites about jobs in broadcasting has been done by Vernon Stone, Professor Emeritus, Missouri School of Journalism, and it provides information on broadcast careers and job mobility and more. Visit http://web.missouri.edu/~jourvs/.

Endnotes

1. "Heinrich Rudolf Hearst," Physicists' biographies at *http://phisicist.info/hertz.html*, Accessed July 17, 2008.

2. Helen Briggs, "Profile: Marconi, the wireless pioneer," *BBC News Online*, December 11, 2001, at *http://news.bbc.co.uk/2/hi/science/nature/1702037.stm*.

3. "De Forest, Lee," *Encyclopedia Britannica*, at *http://search.eb.com/eb/article-9029588*, Accessed July 21, 2008.

4. "The Complete Lee de Forest," *Perham Collection*, History San Jose, 2003, at *http://www.leedeforest.org*. Accessed July 17, 2008.

5. Armstrong, Edwin H," *Encyclopedia Britannica*, at *http://search.eb.com/eb/article-410*, Accessed July 22, 2008.

6. "broadcasting," *Encyclopedia Britannica*, at *http://www.britannica.com/EBchecked/topic/80543/broadcasting*, Accessed July 21, 2008.

7. "About RCA: Linking the Nation," *RCA*, at *http://home.rca.com/en-US/PressReleaseDetail.html?Cat=RCAHistory&MN=7*, Accessed July 16, 2008.

8. "National Broadcasting Co., Inc.," *Encyclopedia Britannica*, at *http://www.britannica.com/EBchecked/topic/404533/National-Broadcasting-Co-Inc*, Accessed July 22, 2008.

9. "CBS Corporation," *Encyclopedia Britannica*, *http://www.britannica.com/EBchecked/topic/100876/CBS-Corporation*, Accessed July 22, 2008.

10. "History of Radio," *http://history.sandiego.edu/GEN/recording/radio.html*, Accessed July 22, 2008.

11. Steven Schoenherr, "Golden Age of Radio 1935–50," *Recording Technology History*, July 6, 2005, at *http://history.sandiego.edu/gen/recording/notes.html*.

12. "modulation," *Encyclopedia Britannica*, at *http://www.britannica.com/EBchecked/topic/387402/modulation*, Accessed July 22, 2008.

13. *Historical Dictionary of American Radio*, edited by Donald G. Godfrey and Frederic A. Leigh (Greenwood Publishing Group, 1998).

14. "State of the News Media 2008: Audience," The Project for Excellence in Journalism, *Journalism.org*, at *http://www.stateofthenewsmedia.org/2008/narrative_radio_audience.php?cat=2&media=10*, Accessed July 17, 2008.

15. Christopher H. Sterling, "U.S. Policy: The Communications Act of 1934" *U.S. Museum of Broadcast Communications Archives*, at *http://www.museum.tv/archives/etv/U/htmlU/uspolicyc/uspolicyc.htm*, Accessed July, 17, 2008.

16. Fritz J. Messere, "U.S. Policy: Telecommunications Act of 1996," *U.S. Museum of Broadcast Communications Archives*, at *http://www.museum.tv/archives/etv/U/htmlU/uspolicyt/uspolicyt.htm*, Accessed July 17, 2008.

17. Clear Channel Communications Homepage. *Clear Channel Communications, Inc.*, at *http://www.clearchannel.com/*, Accessed July 17, 2008.

18. Jeff Perlstein, "Clear Channel: The Media Mammoth that Stole the Airwaves," *CorpWatch.com*, November 14, 2002, at *http://www.corpwatch.org/article.php?id=4808*, Accessed July 28, 2008.

19. Paul Davidson, "Looser media rules tossed," USA TODAY, June 24, 2004, at *http://www.usatoday.com/money/media/2004-06-24-fcc-overturned_x.htm*, Accessed July 28, 2008.

20. "SIRIUS XM Radio Provides Merger Update," September 9, 2008, SIRIUS Satellite Radio News Releases, *http://investor.sirius.com/ReleaseDetail.cfm?ReleaseID=333252&cat=&newsroom=*, Accessed September 12, 2008.

21. "Almost 70 Million Consumers Will Have Either an HD or a Satellite Radio by 2012," *Reuters*, January 8, 2008, at *http://www.reuters.com/article/pressRelease/idUS204500+08-Jan-2008+PRN20080108*, Accessed September 12, 2008.

22. WBBM 780 homepage, at *http://www.wbbm780.com/*, Accessed July 18, 2008.

23. "podcast," *New Oxford American Dictionary*, at *http://www.bbn.com/utility/glossary/p*, Accessed July 18, 2008.

24. About Arbitron. *Arbitron, Inc.*, at *http://www.arbitron.com/about/home.htm*, Accessed July 18, 2008.

25. Podcasting News homepage, at *http://www.podcastingnews.com/*, Accessed July 17, 2008.

26. Lou Pickney, "Variety Hits-History of the Format," at *http://www.varietyhits.com/variety/history.shtml*, Accessed July 17, 2008.

27. Anna Wilde Matthews, "Clear Channel Uses High-Tech Gear To Perfect the Art of Sounding Local," February 25, 2002, at *http://stayfreemagazine.org/public/clearchannel.html*.

28. BBC Radio homepage, at *http://www.bbc.co.uk/radio/i/*, Accessed July 17, 2008.

29. "The BBC Story: History of the BBC, the 1920s" at *http://www.bbc.co.uk/heritage/story/index.shtml*, Accessed July 17, 2008.

30. "BBC internet radio users up 70% on 2004," *BBC Press Office*, February 28, 2005, at *http://www.bbc.co.uk/pressoffice/pressreleases/stories/2005/02_february/28/radio.shtml*.

31. "News Analysts, Reporters, and Correspondents," Occupational Outlook Handbook, 2008-09 Edition, *U.S. Department of Labor, Bureau of Labor Statistics*, December 18, 2007, at *http://www.bls.gov/oco/ocos088.htm*.

32. "Announcers," Occupational Outlook Handbook 2008-09 Edition, *U.S. Department of Labor, Bureau of*

Labor Statistics, December 18, 2007, at *http://www. bls.gov/oco/ocos087.htm.*

33 "Broadcast and Sound Engineering Technicians and Radio Operators," Occupational Outlook Handbook 2008-09 Edition, *U.S. Department of Labor, Bureau of Labor Statistics*, December 18, 2007, at *http://www.bls. gov/oco/ocos109.htm.*

34 Ibid.

35 Ibid.

36 "Chuck Schaden," *Radio Hall of Fame*, at *http://www .radiohof.org/musicvariety/chuckschaden.html*, Accessed July 16, 2008.

37 Rich Samuels, "The Breakfast Club," at *http://www. richsamuels.com/nbcmm/bclub.html*, Accessed July 16, 2008.

9

MUSIC INDUSTRY AND A SHARED IMAGINATION

Raul Reis

Chapter Objectives:

◆ Understand the invention of sound recording.

◆ Identify various recording formats.

◆ Discuss the evolution of music since the early 20th century.

◆ Discuss the role of rock and roll in American culture.

◆ Identify controversies in the modern music industry.

Introduction

Imagine you are in a crowded train, then a library, and then a gym. What do you see in each scene? Aside from people, you probably also see portable music devices, such as iPods and MP3 players. Music is an essential part of human life. We make music, we listen to music, and music surrounds us in most commercial settings. Music is a big business.

History of the Music Industry

One basic method of music recording came through the use of symbols. **Musical symbols,** such as sheet music, were handwritten accounts of musical notations. The drawback to this form of recording was that it could only be performed by trained musicians who understood the notations. Other methods of production included the manipulation of wind or air and clockwork. The invention of the phonograph in 1877 by Thomas Edison made these previous reproduction methods obsolete.

The earliest form of the **phonograph,** or record player, was in the shape of a cylinder. Edison realized that sound could be recorded through the use of a horn, a stylus (needle), and a pliable material, such as tinfoil. The horn was connected to the stylus, and the stylus touched the tinfoil. When sound entered the horn, it caused the stylus to vibrate, which in turn created grooves in the tinfoil. In order to record the grooves, Edison spread the tinfoil around a wax cylinder. As sound entered the horn, the cylinder rotated to record the sound markings. In order to play back the sounds, a separate stylus moved through the path of the grooves and converted the vibrations into sounds. The first reproduction of a voice was not a great musical line; instead, it was Edison simply saying, "Mary had a little lamb." After Edison was satisfied with the phonograph, he sent word about the invention to prominent scientists throughout the United States and Europe. The cylindrical phonograph took off in Europe, and by the end of the 19th century, a phonograph factory in Paris had already cataloged 12,000 recordings.[1]

When Edison realized the potential for phonographs to provide entertainment, he opened phonograph parlors where patrons could listen to a recording for a nickel.[2] Soon phonographs became a popular attraction and were popping up in arcades. These amusement areas for recordings, and later on films, became known as **nickelodeons.**

THE GRAMOPHONE

Soon after Edison's achievement, Emil Berliner, a German immigrant who lived in Washington D.C., expanded on the phonograph by taking away the cylinder and instead recording the vibrations onto a flat disc. In addition to changing the format, Berliner also realized that copies of the recording could be made by creating a negative mold of the original recording and using this mold to create copies. The copies became known as **records** and could be played on a specialized machine known as a **gramophone.**[3]

Once Berliner introduced the method of recording onto a disk, he helped found the Victor Talking Machine Company along with Eldridge Johnson. The company trademarked advertisements featuring a dog, Nipper, listening to a gramophone with the slogan, "His Master's Voice." This is one of the most famous mascots in advertising history. The Victor Company prospered and went on to create the **Victrola,** a record player with a hand crank that was designed to look like a piece of furniture. The popularity of the Victrola cemented the disc as a superior format compared to the wax cylinder.

RADIO

During this period before radio, major news stories were sometimes "re-enacted" and recorded on wax cylinders to give the audience a sense of far away events. David Sarnoff's idea of the radio as an entertainment device that would be found in every house in America was a visionary one that came true. Prior to this, radios were generally used for emergency and for voice communications, such as from ship to shore. Sarnoff wrote that:

> . . . a radio telephone transmitter having a range of, say, 25 to 50 miles can be installed at a fixed point where the instrumental or voice music or both are produced. . . . The receiver can be designed in the form of a simple "Radio Music Box" and arranged for several different wavelengths, which should be changeable with the throwing of a single switch or pressing of a single button.[4]

The Radio Corporation of America (RCA) was founded in 1919, and radio as an entertainment device exploded during the 1920s and 30s. By 1938, 82% of American homes had a radio and by 1950 it was 91%. The mix of music and news was usually about 80% to 20%, although news programming increased during wartime.[5]

During the 1930s and 40s, music on the radio was the major form of popular entertainment. Musicians—not singers—dominated broadcasts in the early days of recorded music because early microphones couldn't capture the nuances of singing and the human voice with enough fidelity for the radio. With demand for music on the rise from radio stations, inventors were tinkering with every aspect of the recording process. As the quality of recordings improved, pre-recorded music was used more and more as a major part of radio programming.

RADIO STRIKES

When radio stations began playing records on air instead of having live performers, this angered many

Music and the Recording Industry

Despite the strong link of popular music to the medium of radio, it is a disservice to popular music to study it only as a subsidiary of the broadcasting business. Today, recorded music is heard in elevators, airports, dentists' offices, and the ears of joggers running through the park. Songwriting today is closely linked with the film industry, with many major hit songs being written to fit the needs of the movie soundtrack. As reflected in the popularity of the Grammy Awards show, music has come into its own as a major entertainment medium.

Development of the Music Recording Industry

Could Thomas Edison ever have imagined in 1877, when he built the first recording device in his Menlo Park, New Jersey, laboratories, that the legacy of his inventive mind would be compact discs, MTV, the GM-Delco auto sound system, Dolby theater stereo, the Sony Walkman, and the iPod? Certainly John Philip Sousa, the March King, realized by 1906 that recording devices would change the way people enjoyed music. He proclaimed that the day would come when nobody would sing or play the piano because it was easier to listen to a professional artist perform on a recording.

In the early days of recorded music, the bulky "Victrola" took up one corner of the living room and became a center of family entertainment. Later it was supplanted by suitcase-like portable equipment with a phonograph in the bottom half and the speaker in the top. The inexpensive portable phonograph made it possible for young people to buy records for playing in their own rooms. This development expanded the market for records, and the sound-recording revolution was under way.

Bell Improves on Edison's Invention. The Edison Speaking Phonograph Company was formed in 1878, just a year after Edison invented his machine, by a group of businessmen that included one of Alexander Graham Bell's relatives. Demonstrations of the marvelous new machine were held in theaters, concert halls, and tents at county fairs.

There were no "practical applications" for the machine, however, since nobody had yet produced information to be played on it. Edison was preoccupied with his work on the electric light, so it was up to Bell's family to continue development of the concept of recording and playing back sound. As the work of the Bell group progressed, Edison's interest was rekindled, and both parties poured their separate energies into perfecting the phonograph.

Still, the new invention was viewed mainly as a novelty, with early phonographs being set up in rows at carnivals and penny arcades so that people could hear recordings at a nickel a play. Each machine held one tune, and so listeners moved from machine to machine with their nickels if they wanted to hear several numbers.

By 1900, however, the home phonograph came on the market with the familiar configuration of a turntable on a box, a tone arm, and an amplifying horn—the device made familiar by Victrola's "His master's voice" logo with the attentive little dog. The device was "acoustical," meaning that it involved no electric power. The turntable was run by a spring that had to be hand-wound.

Early Recordings. Edison's recordings were cut into wax cylinders in so-called "hill-and-dale" grooves, and his system was adopted by the preeminent Columbia Phonograph Record Company. Emil Berliner, who also worked in New Jersey, where many sound recording innovations arose, developed disc recordings with "zig-zag lateral-cut grooves." Berliner formed the National Gramaphone Company to market disc players, and in 1901 he was the founder of the Victor Talking Machine Company, a forerunner of RCA Records.

Consumers had to choose between the cylinder and the disc, and gradually they moved toward the easy-to-handle, though breakable, shellac discs. Edison continued to stick by his cylinder, even after Columbia saw which way the market was heading and dropped the cylinder. Thus Edison closed himself out of the market he had created.

It is interesting to note parenthetically that the concept of "dual technologies" battling it out in the marketplace is one we will discuss in the chapter on television, with CBS and NBC stubbornly pushing different color television systems. Similarly, incompatible Beta and VHS formats confounded consumers in the early years of videocassette recordings. The introduction of compact discs was a rare instance of the industry achieving consensus before introducing a new technology.

By the 1920s, music was pressed on both sides of the Victor discs, the prices of recordings came down, and the public clamored for popular music.

Radio and Records. After the original patents on recording machines elapsed during the 1920s, production mushroomed and records became the most popular form of home entertainment. But a competitor loomed on the horizon: radio. When radio replaced records as the preferred form of home entertainment, records had to adapt. Reluctantly at first, but then quickly in order to keep pace with the new technology, the recording industry changed over from *acoustical* (mechanical amplification) recordings and playback systems to *electric* systems that were compatible with radio. (Again, we can see parallels today, as the industry moves to "digital" information that brings new fidelity to recordings of both aural and visual information.)

Because not everybody could afford electric playback equipment for their homes, in the 1930s companies began to introduce jukeboxes for playing records in public places such as bars and restaurants. For a nickel a play, the huge Wurlitzer next to the door would put on quite a show: the light tubes bubbled with color, the moving arm selected the records, and the full range of the sound spectrum boomed from the huge speakers. Even after personal, portable phonographs became the vogue, jukeboxes continued to be popular because they livened up public places.

As radio increasingly became the outlet for delivering recorded music to the public, musicians became alarmed because their livelihoods were in jeopardy. At one time the radio networks maintained studio bands to provide theme music for the shows. The live "Big Band" variety shows were among the most popular programs on the air. But radio soon discovered that it could dispense with the live musicians and use recordings over and over again. The American Federation of Musicians demanded restrictions on the use of recorded music, but neither the recording companies nor the radio networks and stations were willing to agree.

In 1942, the union went on strike and forbade its musicians to make recordings. The musicians' strike came at a time when World War II created a need for solidarity. As the strike dragged into its second year, President Franklin D. Roosevelt issued a plea for the musicians to return to help the nation's morale. But union leader James C. Petrillo was adamant. He demanded recording royalties that would compensate musicians for work lost because of jukeboxes and the use of recorded music on the radio. Eventually the recording companies were forced to comply.

One of the casualties of the strike was the Big Band era. But one of the benefits was the tradition of donations of free music by local unions for nonprofit community events, paid for by funds from the musicians' recording royalties.

ASCAP and BMI License Use of Music. The American Society of Composers, Authors, and Publishers (ASCAP) began collecting fees for the playing of its members' music in 1914, before the advent of radio. In the early 1940s, when some radio stations began to play recorded music all day as the main part of their programming, ASCAP doubled its fees. Many radio stations refused to pay the higher price, even though it meant not playing the works of ASCAP artists. That created the climate for a rival licensing organization, and Broadcast Music, Incorporated (BMI) was formed for the sole purpose of developing new artists to provide music "product" for the radio industry. ASCAP became the licenser of "old" artists and BMI developed the "new." By the 1950s BMI had become such a dominant force in licensing music for radio play that its near-monopoly status was investigated by Congress.

Ever-Improving Technology. In addition to the effects of the strike, the recording industry was dealt two other economic blows. The Great Depression that began in 1929 meant that records became an unaffordable luxury for many people. Then World War II in the first half of the 1940s made it impossible to get the materials necessary to make records or to manufacture phonographs.

Despite these setbacks, the producers continued to improve the technology. In 1948, Columbia Records introduced the 33-1/3 revolutions per minute "long-play" record (as opposed to the industry standard of 78 rpm). The vinyl discs were unbreakable and had 23 minutes of information on each side. Albums of 78 rpm records had consisted of several discs, meaning the program had to be interrupted periodically so that records could be turned over or dropped onto the turntable. Now it was possible to put on one record an album with several songs by one artist or a complete symphony. At the same time, the small 45 rpm disc was introduced, primarily for selling single recordings of hit songs to young people, who played them on portable machines they kept in their own bedrooms and hauled around to parties—the beginning of a concept we now take for granted: that every teenager and college student needs a personal recorded music system, which we now see in the iPod. At about the same time, "hi-fidelity" equipment that approximated studio or concert-hall sound was introduced. In 1958, a decade after the introduction of the long-play album, stereophonic records with two separate channels recorded in the same groove appeared on the market. It was almost another decade before multi-channel tape cassettes appeared, and just about another decade passed before compact discs were introduced.

Thus each decade brought a quantum jump in the quality of sound reproduction and the convenience of using the product. Sound recording, perhaps more than any other information industry, seems to have been able to capture consumers' interest with continuous development of its technology. When the compact disc, or CD, was introduced in 1983, the $1,000 price tag for a player suggested that it was not aimed at the ordinary consumer. However, the quality and flexibility of the system helped build a market, and the price came down in just a few years. The same has been true of MP3 players like the iPod and the Zune.

The CD format was established as a world standard, meaning any disc can be played on any player. Each digitally encoded disc is less than five inches in diameter, and the information on it is read by a laser beam rather than a needle. There is no contact between disc and player, eliminating wear, damage, and distortion. In addition to unparalleled sound reproduction, it offers the listener random song selection—a distinct advantage over both tape and phonograph records. Three years after their introduction, only two percent of American homes owned CD players. The switch from phonograph records to CDs has meant a shot in the arm for the classical music branch of the industry as collectors decide to replace their worn records with CDs. Yet some aficionados continue to insist that the music sounds warmer and more authentic from a traditional analog phonograph and vinyl album.

people in the music industry who didn't receive compensation. The American Society of Composers, Authors, and Publishers (ASCAP) was organized in 1914 to help license and collect fees for musicians and composers, such as **royalties,** which are payments made to the author of a work for sales and live performances. By the 1940s, recordings had become the biggest segment of the money collected by ASCAP. Radio stations argued that they shouldn't have to pay for playing pre-recorded music because it was free advertising and would generate larger sales, and thus benefit musicians and composers.

James Petrillo, the head of the American Federation of Musicians (AFM), began to work with ASCAP to make sure the stations would have to pay for radio play. He led two musician strikes that kept the airwaves quiet for several years in the mid 1940s. The matter went to court. When the courts finally ruled that radio stations must pay a licensing fee for playing records on the air, a system of paying fees for playing recorded music on the radio was instituted.

Strikes and labor issues weren't the only reasons for the shift from live musicians to recorded music and the eventual rise of the vocalist as the dominant musical artist. Recording technology in the form of better microphones and better shellac for the surface of records was changing the way records sounded. As recordings sounded more "live," the need for live musicians on radio was reduced. Today, the occasional live musician heard on the radio is a notable special programming feature.

IMPROVEMENTS IN TECHNOLOGY

At the end of World War I, the popularity of the recording industry had declined. In an effort to attract buyers, the industry began using radio technology to produce electronic recordings. This helped the sound quality improve; unfortunately, by the Great Depression, money was too tight for many people to buy records.

The technology behind record making steadily improved as well. In 1915 the standard record was a 78-rpm. The 78 record spun at 78 revolutions-per-minute and could hold four-and-a-half minutes of a recording per side. Columbia Records introduced the long-playing (LP) record in 1948. The LP had fine grooves that could hold approximately 30 minutes

of a recording per side and ran at 33.3-rpm. However, it didn't take long for additional improvements to be made. By the 1950s, RCA Corporation introduced the two-sided single to the market. These singles, or 45s (45-rpm) could hold up to 8 minutes of a recording per side. Stereophonic systems were also introduced which allowed one groove to hold two channels of information. By 1958, LPs, 78s, 45s, and stereos were all commercial items available for public consumption.[6] This technology was the primary mode of reproduction until the 1980s when cassette tapes and compact discs (CDs) took over.

Just as the 78 replaced the wax cylinder, the 45 replaced 78s. In the 1960s and 70s, the LP began to replace 45s. These changes were obvious to consumers because each new song or album was another purchase. On the home front, these also required listeners to upgrade the "hardware" used to play the recordings. Victrolas gave way to turntables. At the height of the 45, turntables that could stack several records and play them sequentially were the mode. As the LP album gained popularity, record players featured dual speeds to play 45- or 33-rpm records.

After World War II, the recording industry grew. Developments that had not achieved commercial success during difficult financial times were given the opportunity to prosper. In 1927, the Automatic Music Instrument Company (AMI) created the first coin-operated electric record player that played selected records. This invention is also known as the coin-operated **jukebox.** During the war, jukeboxes were popular in underground bars and taverns, and after the war, popularity exploded. Jukeboxes spread to diners, drugstores, and bars across the country.

STEREO AND FORMAT WARS

More hardware changes resulted from the introduction of stereo sound in the early 1960s. Stereophonic sound, or **stereo,** is the reproduction of sound using multiple audio channels, such as speakers. The development of stereo led to a more natural sounding recording. With the introduction of concept albums and expensive turntables with stereo speakers, audiophiles shifted away from listening to music on AM radio due to poor sound quality.

In the golden years of analog recording, from the 60s to the 80s, the format of audio transformed quickly from records to audio tape. The high-end reel to reel decks audiophiles sought in the 50s and 60s were made obsolete by cassette tape. Cassette tape, with less audio quality but better marketing of its hardware (players) and tapes, won the battle for consumer dollars over the 8-track tape and its hardware. Yet by 1988, CD sales surpassed LP sales for the first time in history.

Muzak: It's Not Your Father's Elevator Music Anymore[8]

Technology makes it possible to tailor and deliver an unending stream of popular music to almost any environment. Technology is also putting the listener in control in ways that were not possible in an analog age. Movies aren't just for watching anymore, and music isn't just for listening to. The entertainment giants are looking for synergy between the content in various media in ways that would have been impossible to pursue in an age of analog sound.

Think for a moment how most commercial spaces—stores, shopping malls, elevators, doctors' and dentists' offices—provide occupants with a soundtrack. Today, the ubiquitous music environment formerly known as "elevator music" has been re-imagined for today's consumer society as an "acoustic pheromone" designed to attract or repel shoppers according to their psychographic profile. In the article "The Soundtrack of Your Life," David Owen describes how Muzak, the nondescript elevator music of the 1950s, has moved into the "realm of retail theater."

Muzak sells about 80 pre-packaged programs and designs customized programs as part of its global business. The company has created a digital music inventory they call "the Well." In the Well are millions of commercially recorded songs classified by genre and even subgenre—jazz, shag, heavy metal, and more.

Today's Muzak is an expression of "brand." The company hires program designers who attempt to identify the psychological associations of songs and then connect the songs into an aural tapestry that appeals to the emotions of a shopper. The idea is to create an emotional soundtrack for a bar or retail store that affects a customer like an "aural pheromone." The sounds should attract some customers while repelling others in order to reinforce its emotional impact.

The program designers, called audio architects, alter the rhythms and song connections to get different moods going at different times of the day. The soundtrack gets louder and pushier around closing time. There is also different music for after hours when the customers are gone.

Because music makes emotional connections with us, the audio architectures Muzak creates are powerful and compelling whether we are conscious of it or not. Their biggest competitor, according to their marketing department, is silence.

Technology disrupted the music recording establishment with digital recording, which freed "content" from "medium" more profoundly than had ever been done before. **Digital recording** involves breaking down a recording into numerical code using 0s and 1s, and recording this code onto magnetic tape or optical discs. Prior to this, **analog recordings** recorded sound waves directly onto records or cassettes. This change led to even more format changes. The Sony Walkman, introduced in 1979, rocked the world of music recording. In 1984, Sony's Portable CD player sent another technological tremor through an industry that wasn't sure where its future lay. With the introduction of the MP3 in 1997 and Napster's first incarnation in 1999, there had been a revolution in music and recording whether the music business knew it or not. With the first iPod shipment from Apple in 2001, it seemed that music producers and record companies were finally aware that business wouldn't be the same anymore.

Rapid and incessant change creates what Marshall McLuhan described as "disruptive technology."[7] Today the music industry is unsettled because its long-time economic models are being challenged on several fronts. There are more ways for people to listen to music than ever before. There are new ways for artists to connect with audiences that cut out traditional roles played by the big recording companies. Corporate consolidation means that recording companies might be owned by defense contractors. Artists and the creative work they produce are no longer evaluated on the basis of musical content, but are just another "widget" to corporate accountants and stockholders.

POPULAR MUSIC

Prior to the phonograph, people still enjoyed music in their homes. Although they weren't able to listen to a song on a record player, people were able to play songs from sheet music. A small area in New York near Broadway, **Tin Pan Alley,** became a popular source for sheet music at the time. The name Tin Pan referred to the large number of musicians in the area who pounded on pianos in an attempt to sell their songs to producers.[9] At the time, sheet music was in such high demand that the terms "popular music" and "tin pan" became practically interchangeable. However, the name could also be considered derogatory in reference to the cheap pianos used by

musicians. Unfortunately for the musicians and songwriters of Tin Pan Alley, once the record player and radio became staples in homes and businesses, the demand for sheet music sharply declined and the Tin Pan Alley era was over.

One of the most influential genres during the period of early radio was jazz. **Jazz** is an improvisational form developed from ragtime and blues. **Ragtime** is a musical style that displaces regular accents by emphasizing weak beats, and **blues** is a style of African-American folk music that expresses emotions rather than telling a story. Jazz was developed by African Americans and is constantly evolving, making a specific definition tricky. It is generally characterized as being improvised with deviations of pitch and syncopated rhythms, which emphasize beats that are normally not accented. However, this is not always the case.

During the 1930s and 1940s, jazz was extremely influential and dominated radio and record sales. Some of the most popular jazz musicians of the time include Louis Armstrong, Duke Ellington, and Benny Goodman. These musicians are still popular today.

ROCK AND ROLL

By the end of the 1940s, six record labels controlled the majority of the music industry: Capital, Columbia, Decca, Mercury, MGM, and Victor. During this time period, labels pushed for a sentimental style that popularized songs such as "How Much Is That Doggy in the Window?" By the 1950s, rock and roll exploded onto the music scene. Early rock and roll was a combination of country music and rhythm and blues that was fueled by black culture and white spending power.[10]

Rhythm and blues (R&B) played a central role in the formation of rock and roll. In fact, many legendary rock bands, such as the Rolling Stones and the Who advertised themselves as rhythm and blues bands. **R&B** itself is a combination of blues and **big band,** which is a harder, but slower form of jazz. By the middle of the 1950s, R&B simply meant black popular music not focused on teenagers.[11]

Disc jockeys, such as Allan Freed, Dewey Phillips, and William Allen, helped create rock-and-roll radio, which spread this new musical style. White teenagers immediately gravitated to a sound that was sexy and exciting compared to performers of the 1940s and early 1950s. In fact, the term "rock and roll" was an expression used by African Americans to mean sex.

In 1954 the recording industry found a face that would further popularize the genre: Elvis Presley. Presley's appeal came from the fact that he was an attractive white man with the voice of a black man. It was this combination of cultures that acted as a catalyst for the rise of Elvis, but also of rock and roll. Elvis dominated the music charts from 1956-1958 and sent girls into a frenzy with his gyrations. Often when Elvis appeared on television shows, his entire body wasn't shown to the viewing audience. Instead, he was shown from the waist up.

Elvis was discovered by Sam Phillips, a disc jockey from Memphis who some have called "the man who invented rock'n'roll."[12] Phillips was willing to work with any performing artist, no matter their color. Because of this he was able to work with B.B. King and with Jackie Brenson and the Delta Cats. Phillips owned a recording service that allowed people to create their own records for a small price. He discovered Elvis Presley when Elvis came into the shop to make a present for his mother.[13] Phillips went on to open Sun Records and produced records for Johnny Cash, Jerry Lee Lewis, and Roy Orbison.

Phillips worked on combining the various musical styles of the South, such as blues, country, and gospel. This combination was one of the first versions of rock and roll, called rockabilly.[14] Elvis, Fats Domino, Little Richard, Buddy Holly, and Jerry Lee Lewis all performed rockabilly. **Rockabilly** is essentially a combination of rock and roll and hillbilly music. These performers appealed to teenagers across the country looking to rebel against the clean cut culture of early 20th century. In addition to music, teens embraced other rebellious figures such as James Dean and Marlon Brando. While the youth of America felt like they had found their own soundtrack, other cultural leaders condemned the style, going so far as to claim that rock and roll was "devil music."[15]

The intensity that rock and roll started with didn't last long. By 1959, Elvis was drafted into the army, Little Richard left rock and roll for gospel, Buddy Holly died in a plane crash, and Jerry Lee Lewis was condemned for marrying his 13-year-old cousin. After the loss of so many stars so fast, rock was at a crossroads. Knowing the potential for record sales, labels frantically searched for the next crop of

stars. However, the labels' interpretation of rock and roll was tame compared to the scene of the 1950s. In the early 1960s, the stars of rock and roll were Ricky Nelson, Frankie Avalon, Annette Funicello, and Connie Francis. These performers did not have the same impact as the performers of the 1950s.

THE BRITISH INVASION

In 1964, the Beatles took the United States by storm. Compared to the toned down sound of rock and roll in the early 1960s, the Beatles brought innovation and style. Up until then, British bands were unsuccessful in replicating American rock and roll. However, by the beginning of the 1960s, many British teens were becoming well versed in the genre. The British invasion was in full swing by 1964. Along with the Beatles, England could also claim the Rolling Stones, the Who, the Animals, the Kinks, and Dusty Springfield. Whereas the Beatles were beloved by audiences and television, the Rolling Stones were a more polarizing group. The Rolling Stones were darker and more sexual than the clean-cut Beatles. These two roles eventually split rock and roll and changed the genre to simply rock. Both groups continued successfully performing and selling albums, but the Rolling Stones influenced hard-rock performers whereas the Beatles influenced a softer sound based on melody. The British Invasion helped changed the face of American rock and roll. The Frankie Avalons were replaced with Steven Tylers, and the Annette Funicellos were replaced with Janis Joplins. The wholesome, clean-cut image of American rock stars evolved into an image of someone more intimidating.

FOLK MUSIC

During the turbulent political times of the 1960s and 70s, with the Civil Rights and women's movements and the Vietnam War, music naturally became politically expressive. Although all genres were inspired by the state of the times, folk music spoke the loudest with regard to activism. Folk music originated from an oral tradition in rural areas. Songs were passed down through generations and learned through hearing. Modern **folk music** is characterized as having a political agenda and using traditional, often acoustic, instruments.

In the early 20th century, during the Great Depression, Woody Guthrie was the first major composer of protest music, including "This Land Is Your Land" and "Union Maid." By the middle of the 20th century, folk music branched out to blend with other genres, such as rock and pop. Folk rock emerged through Bob Dylan, and folk pop gained popularity with the group Peter, Paul, and Mary.

Folk rock eventually split into two camps: folk rock from the United States and folk rock from Britain. Folk rock in the United States was characterized as youthful, rebellious protest music. Popular artists include the Mamas and the Papas and Simon and Garfunkel. On the other hand, British folk rock stuck more to tradition. Artists took established folk music, sometimes centuries old, and blended it with modern sounds. More recent folk rock and folk pop can be heard in the music of Bruce Springsteen, Tracy Chapman, and 10,000 Maniacs.

ALTERNATIVE ROCK

Similar to the situation in the early 1960s, by 1970, rock was once again at a crossroads. With the breakup of the Beatles and the deaths of Jimi Hendrix and Janis Joplin, rock would eventually split into smaller movements that would appeal to more specific audiences.

In the 1970s, the development of **punk,** an aggressive form of rock characterized by confrontational, socially aware lyrics and a sped-up style of music, tried to reawaken the energy that followed the early years of rock and roll. Punk acted as an urban celebration after years of hippie style and music. However, at the heart of punk rock was a rebellious attitude that went against the commercial nature of popular rock of the time. Even though punk never gained the widespread popularity of traditional rock, you can still see the impact and influence of early punk rockers on culture. Look around and you can probably spot one or two Ramones or Sex Pistols t-shirts. Another contribution made by punk rock was that it was able to usher in a sound that would help shape yet another movement in rock: grunge.

Grunge appeared in the early 1990s as a combination of heavy metal/hard rock and punk rock. The grunge movement emerged at an independent record label in Seattle, Sub Pop. Sub Pop helped launch the careers of Mudhoney, Screaming Trees,

Soundgarden, and Nirvana. The popularity of grunge can be directly attributed to the release of the single "Smells Like Teen Spirit" from Nirvana's *Nevermind* album. After the suicide of Nirvana front man Kurt Cobain and Pearl Jam's rejection of commercial popularity, the popularity of grunge faded by the end of the 90s.

Alternative rock provided categorization for musical groups that went against the norm of the glamorous rock style of the 1970s, with David Bowie, and the hair metal of the 80s and 90s, with Poison and Motley Crue. It provided a landscape that would launch such long lasting groups as U2 and Green Day. Many alternative rockers appealed to a specific audience of white males, which left a void in musical options for many blacks. This void helped to spur a musical revolution in the 1980s: rap and hip-hop.

HIP-HOP, RAP, AND GANGSTA RAP

Hip-hop can be defined as many different things. It is the background music used for rap. It is a musical style all on its own that blends rhythmic beats and rhyming lyrics. Hip-hop also refers to a culture that includes deejaying, rapping, graffiti, and B-boying, which is a combination of dance, style, and attitude.

The hip-hop genre originated in the Bronx section of New York. DJ Kool Herc was one of the first major hip-hop deejays.[16] The Jamaican immigrant used two turntables to blend fragments of older songs with popular music, which created an almost endless flow of music at parties. Hip-hop deejays of the time were also famous for isolating a record's break beat, the part of a dance record where the drumbeats are the only sounds that remain. These break beats encouraged dancing and dance contents where break dancing was a popular style. Another famous hip-hop deejay, Grandmaster Flash, led innovations in turntable manipulations, such as needle dropping and scratching.

Rap, a vocal style characterized by rhythmical speaking, emerged when hip-hop deejays spoke over records. DJ Kool Herc is known as the father of modern rap.[17] However, there are many other influences that led to the modern sound of rap, such as talking blues songs, jailhouse toasts (poems reminiscing about misdeeds), dozens (an oral game exchanging insults), and toasting (a style of rhymed speech from Jamaica).

The first nationally recognized rap song was Sugarhill Gang's "Rapper's Delight" (1979). Other pioneers of old school rap include Grandmaster Flash & the Furious Five and the Cold Crush Brothers.

In the 1980s, the introduction of MTV and a crop of new rappers spread the genre to many new listeners. Run-D.M.C. helped bring rap into the mainstream by combining rap with hard rock; the Beastie Boys, a trio of white rappers, helped broaden the audience even more for rap; the group Public Enemy rapped about socially conscious topics and black political ideology; and female rappers Salt-N-Pepa and Queen Latifah provided a balanced view of hip-hop culture by countering the misogynistic views of many male rappers.

By the end of the 1980s, Los Angeles responded to New York's rap and hip-hop sounds by further pushing the boundaries with a new style called gangsta rap and with the group N.W.A. (Niggaz With Attitude), who included Ice Cube, Eazy E, and Dr. Dre, among others. **Gangsta rap** is a form of hip-hop that provides a window into the lifestyle of poverty and drug use in many inner cities. Gangsta rap often contains hyperrealism, thoughts of immortality, and a romanticized image of the outlaw. N.W.A.'s album *Straight Outta Compton* provided a graphic perspective of the life of violence that permeated many inner cities. Gangsta rappers, such as Tupac Shakur, were praised for telling the truth about life for many people, but criticized by others for glorifying a criminal lifestyle. Gangsta rap in the 1990s became a dangerous showdown for East Coast and West Coast rivals. After the murders of West Coast Tupac Shakur and his East Coast rival Notorious B.I.G., many thought the genre had gone too far.

During the last 90s and the early part of the 21st century, hip-hop, which is often synonymous with rap, emerged as the most popular musical genre in the United States. Rappers, such as Jay-Z and Sean Combs have transcended music to become moguls who design clothes, fragrances, and beverages. Rappers, such as OutKast, Kid Rock, and Rage Against the Machine, have also incorporated rock and pop into their music similar to Run-D.M.C. Although many genres of music have become diluted and commercialized for profits, many argue that rap has been able to withstand these temptations due to listeners' demand for authenticity.[18]

Modern Music Industry

The modern music industry is composed of people who develop and distribute music to the general public. With the rise of file sharing the in the early 1990s, the entire business plan for the music industry was turned inside out. Control over manufacturing, distributing, and promoting artists was lost to the Internet. Music was available for free (albeit illegally) on the Internet, and it was also unregulated. There was no worry of parental advisories or censorship.

RECORD LABELS

During the 1980s and 90s, record labels were shuffled around and consolidated leaving four major labels to produce 85% of all recordings in the United States: Universal Music Group (Geffen, Interscope, Motown), Sony BMG Music Entertainment (Arista, Columbia, Epic), EMI Group (Capital, Virgin), and Warner Music Group (Asylum, Atlantic, Reprise).[19] The remaining 15% of U.S. record production came from various independent labels.

Many artists start off with or develop their own independent label. An independent label, or **indie,** is a record label that is independently funded and not connected to a major label. They can range from a label with one artist that is run out of the artist's home to a large business that helps put a spotlight on up-and-coming acts. Because indie labels have limited funding, they do not have the same power and influence as one of the four major labels. However, one advantage of indie labels is their willingness to take a risk on an unknown artist. Major labels have reason to be skeptical of unknown artists because even seasoned performers can be unprofitable for the label. In 2001, Mariah Carey signed the largest contract of that time, an $80-million-dollar deal with Virgin Records. After Carey had a public meltdown, Virgin released her from her contract in 2002, along with $28 million dollars.[20]

RECORDING ARTISTS

The most well recognized member of the recording industry is usually the recording artist. The recording artist is the person or group that struggles, often for years, trying to get discovered and gain a large audience. This is the name on the CD, download, and music video.

Profit Controversy

In 2000, rocker Courtney Love made a speech at the Digital Hollywood Online entertainment conference giving support to online downloading while bashing recording label practices. Love claimed that, "The system's set up so almost nobody gets paid."

Love presented a fictitious example of a band that ends up making a huge deal with a record label that includes a 20-percent royalty rate and a one-million-dollar advance on their contract. This may sound like the band in question has hit the jackpot; however, that million dollars doesn't line the musicians' pockets as one may think. Love breaks down the way this money is used to help jump start the band's album.

Love claims that $500,000 of that money is used to record an album. Then, out of the remaining $500,000, the band needs to pay their manager a 20-percent commission. That's another $100,000. Then, the band's lawyer and business manager are paid $25,000 each. This leaves $350,000 to be split among the band members. Let's assume there are four members. After $170,000 is taken out for taxes, that leaves $180,000 left for the group, or $45,000 each. This is the band's income for the following year until their album gets recorded and released.

It's not over yet. Now the band has to promote their album. Let's say the album is a huge success, sells a million copies, and the band releases two singles, both of which require videos. The combined total cost for the videos is one million dollars. The record label pays for this; however, 50 percent will be recouped by the label out of the royalties. Now the band needs to go on tour to further promote the album. This costs $200,000, which is again initially paid for the by label but is 100 percent recoupable. Love also claims that the record company will spend another $300,000 on independent radio promotion, which the band will eventually have to pay for. Plus, let's not forget that the band has to pay back the original one-million-dollar advance. This leaves the band in debt to the record label for $2 million.

However, what about all those records that were sold? Love says that if all one million records were sold at full price and the band received 20 percent of the royalties, they should receive approximately $2 million. Because this the amount the band owes the label, they are left with nothing except the satisfaction of being popular and heard on the radio. In this situation, Love claims that the record label grosses $11 million. After subtracting expenses, the label stands to profit approximately $6.6 million.

Successful recording artists need to be more than just good musicians. They also need to be negotiators aware of the business side of the music industry. Recording artists should be conscious of financial matters, such as contracts, copyright laws, and royalty payments. Infamous bankruptcy cases involving huge stars, such as M.C. Hammer, TLC, and Toni Braxton, are a reminder that dealing with record companies can be a very complicated process. Some artists, such as rocker Courtney Love, have been outspoken when it comes to record companies and payments. Love claims that record companies design contracts so that artists pay for the production of records. After the labels recoup these expenses, take their designated profits, and the artists pay their managers and lawyers, there is practically nothing left for the artist.[21] (See "Profit Controversy" sidebar.)

Artists must also be confident in their sound-while straddling the line of being marketable. Kelly Clarkson gained fame by winning *American Idol* and releasing pop-infused songs such as "Since U Been Gone." On her third album *My December*, released in the summer of 2007, Clarkson took artist control of the album and went in a darker direction. After a public feud with record label head Clive Davis, who questioned whether the record was a hit, less than expected record sales, and a cancelled tour, Clarkson quickly went back into the studio to work on a new album that was released in March of 2009. Clarkson's fourth record, *All I Ever Wanted*, returned to the pop sound that helped make her a star.

While talent shows such as *American Idol* and *America's Got Talent* have been extremely popular with viewers, the vast majority of artists are discovered by A&R (artist & repertoire) representatives. **A&R representatives** are essentially talent scouts that are on the lookout for the next big artist. They listen to demo, or demonstration, tapes and go to live shows. A&R representatives may also work with artists in the recording studio, helping to develop the artist's sound or helping to produce or manage the artist.

THE PRODUCTION STAFF

A **record producer** has many jobs. The producer manages resources and budgets for equipment and background musicians and runs the recording sessions. Producers can also have some creative control over a record. The producer can make decisions

to have an artist sing a track again or even delete a track from an album altogether.

Aside from the producer, there is also a staff of technical experts, such as audio engineers and sound mixers who work to make a record sound the best it can. These technical experts are managed by the record producer, so the work they do is based on requests by the producer.

Whereas the artists themselves are important to the sound of a track, the production is also highly important. Modern record production is more complicated than simply recording an artist singing or a band playing. Now different aspects of the track are recorded on separate audio tracks and then blended together. Once all of the tracks are recorded, the technical staff edits them. This can help explain why some of your favorite bands or singers don't sound as good performing live compared to the songs on their albums. Although there are other factors that contribute to this, it's difficult to produce a piece of live music that sounds like a track that had been labored over for hours.

While an artist is hard at work recording an album, a team of marketing experts is busy planning the marketing and promotion of that artist. This process includes organizing radio air play and advertising campaigns, such as television appearances, videos, and print advertisements. The marketing and promotion team is also responsible for coming up with catchy posters and displays.

SELLING THE MUSIC

The two primary modes of distribution are retail sales and online sales. Direct music retailers, such as f.y.e., are focused solely on selling music and music accessories. Other retail shops, such as Best Buy and Target, sell music but are not focused solely on its sale. Stores like these use **rack jobbers,** or contractors hired by retail stores to stock and order music for the store. This frees up a store's staff to focus on other, potentially more important, merchandise.

Online stores, such as Amazon and iTunes, have gained considerable popularity over the past 10 years. This has caused some direct retailers, such as Tower Records, to claim bankruptcy. Benefits of online stores include a large variety of options and the ability to preview a song or album prior to purchasing it. Shoppers also often have the option to purchase individual songs for less than $1. Online stores can charge a relatively inexpensive amount because there is no physical item to create. There is no expense for a CD, a case, liner notes, etc. There is also less potential to lose money due to excessive amounts of overstock.

Other less significant modes of sale are music clubs and specialty CDs, which can be sold through television, such as the compilation CD *Ultimate Power Ballads*.

Controversies in the Music Industry

Since 2000 and the rise of Napster, piracy has been a considerable problem for the music industry. **Piracy** is the illegal duplication of copyrighted works. A **copyright** is a law that gives the creator of the work ownership over that work. In the music industry, the artist is not necessarily the copyright holder of a song. Ownership can also be held by the record label or by an individual, such as a producer. For example, pop star Michael Jackson has partial copyrights to most of the Beatles' catalog of songs and receives a percentage of the royalties that these songs generate.[22]

During the rise of online pirating, from 1999-2002, music sales declined 31%.[23] Since then, the news for physical album sales in the United States has only gotten worse. The year 2000 was the pinnacle for physical album sales, selling 785.1 billion. In 2008, album sales were only 54 percent of that figure. However, downloads are not making up the difference.[24] According to the International Federation of the Phonographic Industry (IFPI), there were billions of illegal files swapped in 2007, and the ratio of unlicensed to licensed tracks downloaded is approximately 20:1.[25]

In an attempt to gain control of rampant piracy, the Recording Industry Association of America (RIAA) categorized peer-to-peer (P2P) file sharing as illegal and began suing people engaged in the activity. Many people assume that because something is able to be downloaded that it is legal. This is not the case. Since the early 21st century, copyright holders have allowed particular websites legal access to music downloading. However, many illegal sites still exist.

CENSORSHIP

Censorship is nothing new. It has been around since the invention of the radio and the record. In 1939, Billie Holiday's song "Strange Fruit" was banned from the radio for protesting the lynching of blacks.[26] In 1966, the cover art for the Beatles' record *Yesterday and Today* album was changed by their record label. The original art depicted the band members sitting among butchered meat and decapitated baby dolls; it was replaced with a stock photo of the group.[27] In the 80s and 90s rap groups such as 2 Live Crew and N.W.A. dealt with censorship issues concerning explicit content. In 2006, country trio the Dixie Chicks remarked at a concert in London, "Just so you know, we're ashamed the president of the United States [George W. Bush] is from Texas."[28] This comment alienated many country music fans, and conservative radio stations went so far as to ban the group from having airplay. Now, after years of hindsight, many recognize these musicians as classic artists in their respective genres.

Musical censorship is a controversial issue that is still not resolved. How far can lyrics push the envelope before they become too explicit and potentially detrimental to the listener? How far can labels and stores go to censor albums before they are infringing on the artist's freedom of speech? There are no clear cut answers to these questions; however, here are a few of the arguments for and against musical censorship.

Those in favor of censorship often support traditional family values. They argue that children and teenagers should not be exposed to explicit, offensive, or violent lyrics. They point out artists such as Eminem and Marilyn Manson as influential artists who are causing impressionable children to turn to bad behavior. Parents claim that parental warnings such as "Explicit Content" are inadequate warnings regarding the content of the record. Advocates of censorship also suggest that record labels specifically target teens and tweens in order to boost sales and that explicit lyrics are included or added to records as a marketing strategy. Some groups, such as the American Family Association (AFA), claim to not specifically support censorship; however, they do

Can Music Be Dangerous?

In October 1984, 19-year old John McCollum committed suicide while listening to an Ozzy Osbourne record. In December of the following year, 18-year old Raymond Belknap and Jim Vance spent six hours drinking beer, smoking marijuana, and listening to Judas Priests' *Stained Class* album. Both men then attempted suicide; only Vance survived. Following these incidents, the victims' families filed lawsuits against the bands claiming negligence, liability, and intent.

In the case of Osbourne, his albums do contain songs about suicide and death. However, the Court of Appeals ruled that even though Osbourne's songs contained these themes, they did not stress immediate action. Music is still covered under the First Amendment—even music that propagates the idea of suicide—as long as it does not convey immediate action of the message.

Because of the ruling in the Osbourne case, prosecutors in the Judas Priest case claimed that Bleknap committed suicide because of a subliminal message on the album saying, "do it, do it," which suggests immediate action. Although the judge pointed out that there was a subliminal message that sounded like "do it, do it" on one song, he ruled that the message was the accidental noise of a guitar part.[31]

Another famous case of critics questioning the safety of music is the 1992 controversy involving the song "Cop Killer" by the band Body Count and released by Time Warner. Body Count was a heavy metal band fronted by gangsta rapper Ice-T. The genres of heavy metal and rap have generally been followed by controversy; however, the timing of this release co-incided with the beating of Rodney King by police officers and the Los Angeles riots that followed the ruling acquitting the police officers of criminal charges. The song "Cop Killer" is a first person account of a person angered by the King ruling and by police brutality. The song also became a hot issue during the 1992 presidential election, getting slammed by the candidates and police organizations. The attention and pressure, including death threats, became so overwhelming that Ice-T held a press conference to announce that any further reproductions of the album would not include the song "Cop Killer."[32]

Many people claim that violence in music contributes to violence in real life. However, others claim that a person's response to themes like sex and violence are instilled in them by their family. However, it is difficult to make blanket statements about the effects of media on people because research on this topic is ever changing.

encourage advertisers to only support "quality programming." This way entertainment that goes against traditional values does not have the financial support it needs to be successful.[29]

The other side of the argument is led by the RIAA. Often those who are against censorship use the First Amendment as proof that censorship is unconstitutional. Censoring music can also create a slippery slope that can lead to censorship of books, newspapers, and other artistic forms of media. Those who oppose censorship claim that music acts as a reflection of the current culture. Therefore, if music is filled with sex and violence, perhaps there are other, bigger problems that need to be addressed before censorship comes into play. Additionally, opponents argue that it is not the responsibility of an artist or the music industry to prevent a child from listening to an album. That is the responsibility of a child's parent or guardian. Obviously, some songs are not appropriate for everyone. This is why the RIAA has taken the opportunity to label certain records as having "Explicit content." The RIAA also suggests that music can act as the starting point for talking with children about themes in music and what these themes mean.[30]

Careers in the Field

The music industry is a good fit for competitive people who have knowledge of various software programs and who are willing to work evenings, weekends, and holidays. The nature of the industry creates many specialized occupations, such as sound engineers that include audio technicians, sound mixers, and re-recording mixers.

Sound engineers set up and operate equipment that can record, synchronize, mix, and reproduce sound. They are also responsible for connecting the appropriate wires and cables and setting up mixing boards. Because recordings are now digital, understanding the equipment used in sound recording is vital. Specialized equipment has been replaced with computer software that can be found on your computer, and audio tapes have been replaced with computer hard drives.

Often, audio skills are learned through on-the-job training, but having some formal education is beneficial. If possible, take a few classes in electronics or computer engineering, volunteer to work at your school's radio station, or start building electronic equipment as a hobby. When you start in the field, don't expect to work for a major label. Most large stations and labels only look for technicians with experience, so focus the beginning of your career on on-the-job training.

Chapter Summary

◆ The first version of the phonograph was cylindrical, but it was eventually replaced with a flat disc, called a record.
◆ Radio was the first mass media after it became a major form of entertainment in the 1930s and 40s.
◆ The switch from analog to digital recording was revolutionary in freeing recorded content from the restrictions of various mediums.
◆ The music of rock and roll acted as a catalyst for teenage rebellion against the clean cut culture of the early 20th century.
◆ The combination of rock and roll and folk music led to the evolution of alternative rock, which included punk and grunge.
◆ The rise of alternative rock created a void for black listeners. This void led to the rise of hip-hop and gangsta rap.
◆ Controversies in the current music industry include piracy and censorship.

Glossary

musical symbols—handwritten accounts of musical notations

phonograph—earliest form of the record player

nickelodeons—parlors that allowed patrons to listen to recordings for a nickel

records—copies of sound recordings that are in the shape of a flat disc

gramophone—early record player that played flat discs

Victrola—record player with a hand crank designed to look like a piece of furniture

royalties—payments made to the author of a work for sales and live performances

jukebox—coin-operated electric record player that plays selected records

stereo—or stereophonic sound; reproduction of sound using multiple audio channels, such as speakers

digital recording—recording method that breaks down a recording into numerical code using 0s and 1s and records this code onto magnetic tape or discs

analog recording—recording method that records sound waves directly onto records or cassettes

Tin Pan Alley—area in New York, near Broadway, that was a popular source for sheet music before the popularity of radio and the record player

jazz—improvisational musical form developed from ragtime and blues

ragtime—musical style that displaces regular accents by emphasizing weak beats

blues—style of African-American folk music that expresses emotions rather than telling a story

R&B (rhythm and blues)—musical form that is a combination of blues and big band and was influential in the formation of rock and roll

big band—musical form that is a harder, but slower, form of jazz

rockabilly—musical form that is a combination of rock and roll and hillbilly music

folk music—musical style that uses traditional, often acoustic, instruments and has a political agenda

punk—aggressive form of rock music characterized by confrontational, socially aware lyrics and a sped-up style of music

grunge—musical form that is a combination of heavy metal/hard rock and punk rock

hip-hop—musical style that blends rhythmic beats and rhyming lyrics; the background music for rap

rap—vocal style characterized by rhythmic speaking

gangsta rap—form of hip-hop that acts as a window into a lifestyle of poverty and drug use in inner cities; characterized by hyperrealism, thoughts of immortality, and a romanticized image of the outlaw

indie—or independent record label; record label that is independently funded and not connected to a major label

artist & repertoire (A&R) representatives—record company talent scouts

rack jobbers—contractors hired by retail stores to stock and order music for the store

piracy—illegal duplication of copyrighted works

copyright—law that gives the creator of a work ownership over that work

Discussion Questions

1. Describe the mechanics of the original phonograph invented by Thomas Edison.
2. What led multiple musicians to strike in the 1940s?
3. What is digital recording? How is it different from analog recording?
4. Examine the origin of hip-hop. How was it formed? Who contributed to its popularity?
5. Describe the arguments for and against musical censorship. Where do you stand on the issue?

Supplemental Web Sites

Recording Industry Association of America: http://www.riaa.com/

International Federation of the Phonographic Industry: http://www.ifpi.org/

The American Society of Composers, Authors, and Publishers: http://www.ascap.com/index.html

The American Federation of Musician: http://www.afm.org/

The Rock and Roll Hall of Fame and Museum: http://www.rockhall.com/

National Hip-Hop Museum and Hall of Fame: http://nhhm.org/index.htm

Free Muse: World Forum on Music and Censorship: http://www.freemuse.org/sw305.asp

Endnotes

1 music recording. (2009). In *Encyclopædia Britannica*. Retrieved February 25, 2009, from Encyclopædia Britannica Online: *http://search.eb.com/eb/article-9110130*.

2 "The Thomas Edison Papers: Wax Cylinder Phonograph," Rutgers University, *http://edison.rutgers.edu/cylinder.htm*, Accessed February 25, 2009.

3 Phonograph. (2009). In *Encyclopædia Britannica*. Retrieved February 25, 2009, from Encyclopædia Britannica Online: *http://search.eb.com/eb/article-9059766*.

4 TK from author.

5 TK from author.

6 Phonograph. (2009). In *Encyclopædia Britannica*. Retrieved February 25, 2009, from Encyclopædia Britannica Online: *http://search.eb.com/eb/article-9059766*.

7 TK from author.

8 David Owen, "The Soundtrack of Your Life," *The New Yorker*. April 10, 2006. *http://www.newyorker.com/archive/2006/04/10/060410fa_fact*. Accessed March 9, 2009.

9 Tin Pan Alley. (2009). In *Encyclopædia Britannica*. Retrieved February 26, 2009, from Encyclopædia Britannica Online: *http://search.eb.com/eb/article-9072549*.

10 Rock and roll. (2009). In *Encyclopædia Britannica*. Retrieved February 26, 2009, from Encyclopædia Britannica Online: *http://search.eb.com/eb/article-9105870*.

11 Rhythm and blues. (2009). In *Encyclopædia Britannica*. Retrieved February 26, 2009, from Encyclopædia Britannica Online: *http://search.eb.com/eb/article-9063492*.

12 "Sam Phillips: Rock'n'Roll Guru," BBC News, *http://news.bbc.co.uk/2/hi/entertainment/827057.stm*, *Accessed February 26, 2009*.

13 "Sam Phillips: Rock'n'Roll Guru," BBC News, *http://news.bbc.co.uk/2/hi/entertainment/827057.stm*, *Accessed February 26, 2009*.

14 "Sam Phillips," The Rock and Roll Hall of Fame and Museum, Inc., *http://www.rockhall.com/inductee/sam-phillips*, Accessed February 26, 2009.

15 Rock and roll. (2009). In *Encyclopædia Britannica*. Retrieved February 26, 2009, from Encyclopædia Britannica Online: *http://search.eb.com/eb/article-9105870*.

16 Hip-hop. (2009). In *Encyclopædia Britannica*. Retrieved March 3, 2009, from Encyclopædia Britannica Online: *http://search.eb.com/eb/article-9117537*.

17 Hip-hop. (2009). In *Encyclopædia Britannica*. Retrieved March 3, 2009, from Encyclopædia Britannica Online: *http://search.eb.com/eb/article-9117537*.

18 Hip-hop. (2009). In *Encyclopædia Britannica*. Retrieved March 3, 2009, from Encyclopædia Britannica Online: *http://search.eb.com/eb/article-9117537*.

19 Bill Lamb, "Top 4 Major Pop Record Labels," About.com: Top 40/Pop, *http://top40.about.com/od/popmusic101/tp/majorlabels.htm*, Accessed March 3, 2009.

20 Jason Ankeny, Artist Biography—Mariah Carey, *Billboard*, *http://www.billboard.com/bbcom/bio/index.jsp?pid=48340*, Accessed March 3, 2009.

21 Courtney Love, "Courtney Love Does the Math," Salon, *http://archive.salon.com/tech/feature/2000/06/14/love/index.html*, Accessed March 3, 2009.

22 "The Rights Stuff," Snopes.com, *http://www.snopes.com/music/artists/jackson.asp*, Accessed March 3, 2009.

23 Peter Feuilherade, "Online Piracy Devastates Music," BBC News, *http://news.bbc.co.uk/2/hi/technology/3532891.stm*, Accessed March 4, 2009.

24 Geoff Duncan, "Nielsen: U.S. Album Sales Down 14 Pct." Digital Trends, January 2, 2009, *http://news.digitaltrends.com/news-article/18791/nielsen-u-s-album-sales-down-14-pct*, Accessed March 6, 2009.

25 International Federation of the Phonographic Industry, "IFPI Digital Music Report 2008," *http://www.ifpi.org/content/library/DMR2008.pdf*, Accessed March 6, 2009.

26 "1900–1949," USA/Canada, Free Muse, *http://www.freemuse.org/sw20536.asp*, Accessed March 4, 2009.

27 "1960–1969," USE/Canada, Free Muse, *http://www.freemuse.org/sw20694.asp*, Accessed March 4, 2009.

28 Peter S. Canellos, "Furor over country band echoes a nation's cultural discord," *The Boston Globe*, June 20, 2006, *http://www.boston.com/news/nation/articles/2006/06/20/furor_over_country_band_echoes_a_nations_cultural_discord/*, Accessed March 4, 2009.

29 "General Information," The American Family Association, *http://www.afa.net/about.asp*, Accessed March 4, 2009; "Analysis," *http://www.geocities.com/musiccensorship/analysis.htm*, Accessed March 3, 2009.

30 "Tools for Parents and Educators," The Recording Industry Association of America," *http://www.riaa.com/toolsforparents.php?content_selector=&searchterms=censorship&terminclude=&termexact=*, Accessed March 4, 2009; "Analysis," *http://www.geocities.com/musiccensorship/analysis.htm*, Accessed March 3, 2009.

31 Deflem, Mathieu. 1993. "Rap, Rock, and Censorship: Popular Culture and the Technologies of Justice." Paper presented at the annual meeting of the Law and Society Association, Chicago, May 27-30, 1993, *http://www.cas.sc.edu/socy/faculty/deflem/zzcens97.htm*, Accessed March 4, 2009.

32 Deflem, Mathieu. 1993. "Rap, Rock, and Censorship: Popular Culture and the Technologies of Justice." Paper presented at the annual meeting of the Law and Society Association, Chicago, May 27–30, 1993, *http://www.cas.sc.edu/socy/faculty/deflem/zzcens97.htm*, Accessed March 4, 2009; Barry Shank, "Fears of the White Unconscious: Music, Race, and Identification in the censorship of 'Cop Killer,'" *http://www.emayzine.com/lectures/rap.htm*, Accessed March 4, 2009.

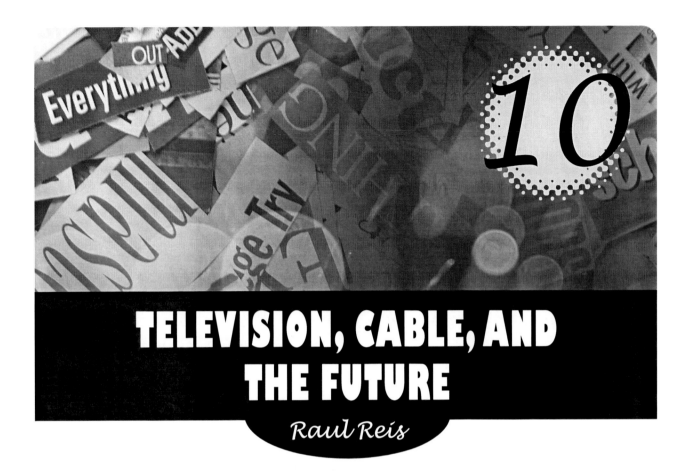

10

TELEVISION, CABLE, AND THE FUTURE

Raul Reis

Chapter Objectives

◆ Understand how the television set and television broadcasting was developed

◆ List the different types of television programming

◆ Describe how television networks develop programming

◆ Understand how cable television was developed

◆ Give examples of future trends in the television industry

Introduction

Since television entered people's homes in the 1940s, it has been a primary source of entertainment for many American families. Whether you watch one hour or 20 hours of television a week, the medium most likely plays some sort of role in your life. You may have learned your ABCs from a children's program, watched your favorite sports team win a championship, or witnessed the Twin Towers go down on September 11th through the power of the television screen. Imagine if you were unable to connect to the world in this way. How would you stay informed or entertained? While newspapers and radio can provide adequate information, they do not have the multi-sensory effect of television. You can listen to a space shuttle launch on the radio and hear the command tower count down to blast off. In a newspaper, you can see an amazing picture of thick smoke building up beneath the shuttle as it lifts into the sky. However, television has the power to bring sight and sound together to create an experience that makes viewers feel like they are witnessing an event in person.

Television often gets a bad rap. It has been given names like the boob tube or idiot box, and those who are avid television watchers are often categorized as couch potatoes. But television is much more than meaningless images with synchronized sound. It is a portal to a world that one would not see if not for the connective power of television. It is also an amazing piece of technology that required the efforts of many innovate individuals.

To understand how television became such an important part of our culture, let's review the birth of the medium, examine how programming is developed, and discuss how new technologies have transformed how we watch television.

The Advent of Television

Television has taken many different shapes over the last century. Like many forms of media, it started as merely a concept and was developed into an industry. This industry was almost overlooked, as many individuals felt society had no use for television.

THE EARLY STAGES

While developing the technology to bring live pictures to a screen was a long and meticulous process, one of the first inventions that made television broadcasting possible came about accidentally. In 1872, English telegraph worker Joseph May made an unusual discovery about the element selenium. While examining materials for use in the transatlantic cable, the first telegraph cable to cross the Atlantic Ocean, May randomly placed a strand of selenium wire on a table near a window. As beams of sunlight passed through the window onto the wire, May noticed that the sunlight caused the electric conductivity of the selenium wire to change. Upon further investigation, he realized that the amount of electricity produced by the wire was in direct relation to the amount of light that fell on it. While this discovery was only of minor importance at the time, it provided the foundation for **photo-electricity**, or turning light into an electric signal.

Over the next few years, various inventors such as George R. Carey attempted to use this discovery to create electric images. They used selenium cells to break up a picture and sent the pieces over a wire

to small electric lamps. Once the selenium cells reached the electric lamps the image would be recreated in a mosaic. A **mosaic** is a television tube that consists of many tiny photoelectric particles that convert light to an electric charge.[1] To recreate the image, the electric lamps would be turned on, turned off, intensified or dimmed. The more lamps used in the mosaic, the more detailed the picture. However, this process required an outrageous amount of wiring and an impractical setup of electrical lamps. To reach the level of detail in a modern day 23 inch television, it would take 350,000 lamps, each no more than one-fortieth of an inch in diameter.[2]

In 1884, German inventor Paul Nipkow avoided the problems of a mosaic device by applying the principle of scanning. **Scanning** involves viewing all the elements of a picture successively, rather than all at once, and sending them in a specific order over a single circuit. In this principle, a photoelectric cell would scan, or look over, only one portion of a picture at a time—going right to left then down a row, just as a person would read a book. Nipkow developed a rotating disk, called a scanner disk or Nipkow disk, which allowed information-filled cells to be sent from a transmitter to a reception point where the original image is recreated line by line. At the time, this technology was viewed as impractical. However, the concept of using a single wire to transmit an entire image became, and still remains to be, the basis of all television.[3]

More than forty years later, the concept of scanning was used to create the first successful televisions. While the machines may not be considered televisions by today's standards, they could transmit pictures. In 1922, Charles Francis Jenkins of the United States created a machine that sent still pictures through radio waves, but perhaps the more true form of television was created by John Baird in 1925. Baird's machine created a transmission of a live human face. The inventions of Jenkins and Baird were not immediately hailed as revolutionary technology. Critics felt the cost of building such systems would never be repaid and that the world did not have much use for television. Still, Jenkins and Baird, as well as companies like American Telephone and Telegraph Company (AT&T) and General Electric Company (GE) worked to further develop television technology. In 1928, Jenkins began to sell television kits that allowed consumers to build their own

Television

The word *television* was coined by a Frenchman named Constantin Perskyi at the 1900 Paris Exposition. On August 25, 1900, he read a paper to the International Electricity Congress and used the word to describe a device that could send images through electricity. Strangely enough, at the same exposition, a set of trading cards, titled "In the Year 2000" displayed images of inventions that were expected to emerge by the year 2000, one of which resembled a television. Little did they know that the *television* would reach their homes in only a few decades.[4]

televisions. He also established his own television station and produced animated programs. In 1929, the British Broadcasting Corporation (BBC) allowed Baird to produce and broadcast a half-hour television show. These programs were made for extremely small audiences, as very few people owned television sets. However, in the following years, audiences would grow from tens to thousands as viewers were purchasing or constructing their own television sets just to catch a glimpse of a few flickering images on a dim receiver screen.[5]

STEADY PROGRESS

Determining who invented the television is a difficult task, as the efforts of many inventors played a role in the development of technologies used in a television system. However, two individuals played a major role in developing television into a mechanically sound and economically viable system. Vladimir Zworykin was a Russian immigrant who worked at Westinghouse Electric Company, a subsidiary of Radio Corporation of America (RCA) in Pittsburgh, Pennsylvania. In 1923, while working for the company, Zworykin filed a patient application for an all-electronic television system. Despite the fact that Zworykin was unable to build and demonstrate the system due to lack of funding, he managed to convince David Sarnoff, vice president of RCA, to provide $100,000 in funding on the promise that in two years he would produce a usable electronic television system. As Zworykin worked on building his system, another inventor by the name of Philo Taylor Farnsworth was demonstrating his basic version of an electronic television system called an Image Dissector. Farnsworth was an ambitious young man from Utah with only a high-school education. He learned about electronics though technology magazines and his own experimentation. Farnsworth secured funding for his project by gathering investors who hoped to gain a profit from marketing an affordable television system that was consumer friendly. While Farnsworth was able to develop his system for only $5,000, a fraction of Zworykin's cost, it would take many years and nearly $50 million dollars before anyone could create a television that was profitable.[6]

With the initial funds provided by RCA, Zworykin developed the Kinescope, a cathode-ray receiver that could project images onto a glass tube. **Cathode rays** are beams of electrons used to project images on to florescent screen inside a vacuum tube. Meanwhile, Farnsworth worked on perfecting his Image Dissector. A functional television could have been created more quickly and for less money if the two men were able to collaborate, but competition between RCA and Philco, Farnsworth's partnering company, kept the two innovators apart.

In 1930, RCA attempted to purchase the patent to Farnsworth's Image Dissector for $100,000, but was turned down. RCA and Zworykin were able to learn enough from the Farnsworth's Image Dissector to develop the Iconoscope camera tube, which became their first working electronic television system.

This development created conflict between RCA and Farnsworth. In 1932, both parties met in court to determine who invented the electronic television. After a long process, the court eventually ruled in favor of Farnsworth, and in 1939 RCA agreed to pay royalties to Farnsworth Television and Radio, Inc, the firm Farnsworth created after leaving Philco. Still, RCA was able to gain a fair share of the credit for the television through its various publicity events. Later that year, RCA demonstrated its system at the 1939 World's Fair in New York City. At the official opening ceremonies, Franklin Delano Roosevelt became the first US president to be televised. Some media outlets hailed television as a technology that would change the American home, but others, including *The New York Times*, described it as a gimmick without useful applications.

TELEVISION REACHES THE PUBLIC

In 1941, the Federal Communications Commission (FCC) decided that the technology was well developed enough to bc introduced to the public. In that year, fewer than 10,000 regular viewers were able to receive television transmissions from a handful of stations. Television sets were a very significant investment for a middle class family. A black-and-white receiver with a 5 inch screen cost about $1,000, at a time when a Chevrolet cost $2,000. Still, the public was growing curious about television. Unfortunately, the attack on Pearl Harbor and World War II greatly delayed the widespread adoption of television by the public, partly because most electronic companies diverted their resources for the war effort. Many American television stations reduced their schedules or simply went off air. American electronic companies such as Bell labs, General Electric, and Westinghouse focused their efforts on using television to guide missiles, long-range reconnaissance, and other military endeavors. RCA's David Sarnoff proclaimed to President Franklin Roosevelt that, "all

our facilities and personnel are ready and at your instant service."[7]

The war ended in 1945, and television expanded rapidly. By 1948, nearly 70 television stations were on air. The expansion was quickly halted by a second delay. Due to concerns regarding the limited space available in the VHF (very high frequency) band, the FCC administered a 4-year freeze on all new station licenses. In 1952, the organization opened the UHF (ultra high frequency) band to allow more space for television transmission and resumed issuing new licenses. By 1955, the cost of a television began to drop thanks to mass production and competition in the industry. That year, nearly 67 percent of Americans were equipped to receive programs in black-and-white. That figure grew to 87 percent by 1960.[8]

TELEVISION IN COLOR

Just like black-and-white television, color television gained popularity slowly. In the 1940s, Peter Carl Goldmark of the Columbia Broadcasting System (CBS) introduced the first color television system. Subsequently, RCA developed a technique for color broadcasting that, unlike CBS's version, would be compatible with black-and-white broadcasting. This type of compatible broadcasting was approved by the FCC in 1953. Within the next year, RCA started to manufacture color television sets known as the CT-100 color receiver. The high price and questionable quality of color television sets caused the majority of consumers to stick to black-and-white sets. But over the next ten years, the price of color TV sets dropped and the quality improved dramatically. By 1967, color television sets outsold black-white-televisions for the first time, and in 1973 more than half of American households had a color set. Today, 98 percent of Americans have a color TV in their home.[9]

TELEVISION GOES DIGITAL

In December 2005, the US Congress approved new legislation forcing broadcasters to end all analog transmission of television signals. As of February 2009, any viewer using an antenna to receive television signals would need to acquire a converter box in order to receive programming. Digital TV transmission, already a reality for many cable and satellite service providers and consumers, promises better image and sound quality. The approved legislation also allocated up to US $ 1.5 billion for consumer purchase of converter boxes that will allow all analog TV sets to receive the new digital signal.[10]

Digital television transmission, coupled with technological innovations on the receiving end, such as high definition television (HDTV), liquid crystal display (LCD) and plasma screens, and high quality audio systems, are poised to revolutionize the way most people watch TV. These new technologies have prompted a growing number of consumers to set up sophisticated home-theaters—entertainment centers comparable to the best theater-going movie experience.

The development of the technology behind television sets and television broadcasting took many years and numerous people to perfect. Similarly, the development of programming for television was, and still is, a painstaking process.

The Formation of Television Programming

While creating the technology that made television possible was a tremendous feat, deciding what should be broadcast on television was an equally challenging task. After the initial excitement of seeing live people appear on a screen wore off, it was apparent that quality programs would have to be developed if the medium was going to continue to grow and surpass radio.

FROM RADIO TO TELEVISION

Early radio programs—variety shows, dramatic productions, comedies, and quiz shows—were performed live for simultaneous transmission throughout the country. So important was the supposed dynamic of a "real" event that announcers at one radio network were required to wear tuxedos; the management was convinced that this made them speak with distinction and moreover it both impressed the studio audience and sparked their earnest participation.

When many of the popular radio programs and formats moved to television, the tradition of presenting them live continued, if for no other reason than because it was quicker and cheaper than filming and editing them. Newscasters had to learn to look at the camera from time to time, but basically they were the same radio news readers with a microphone and a sheaf of papers in front of them, with little in the way of graphics or film footage to illustrate what they were reporting.

TELEVISION AS ENTERTAINMENT

Variety shows were a natural for television. Whereas radio had been limited to presenting musical acts that could be appreciated by the ear alone, television could use baton twirlers, jugglers, tap-dancers, wire-walkers, puppeteers, and animal acts. **Variety shows** were presented live, sometimes from a hastily refurbished Broadway theater with an announcer standing in front of the curtain and ballyhooing the next act much as a vaudeville host might have done. Ed Sullivan's *Toast of the Town* long reigned as television's quintessential variety show. *Arthur Godfrey and His Friends* was an extended family of young performers chaperoned by a father-figure host, while Milton Berle's popularity stemmed from the comedian's willingness to go to any extreme to pull off a ridiculous skit. These types of programs paved the way for modern sketch comedy programs. **Sketch comedy shows** often contain a series of short comedy scenes, referred to as sketches. Sketches are about five to ten minutes long and typically performed by ensemble casts. NBC's *Saturday Night Live* is an iconic sketch comedy show that has aired for over 30 years. Variety shows have made a bit of a comeback in recent years with shows such as *American Idol* and *America's Got Talent*, but modern shows have added a competitive twist to the formula.

Dramatic television also made a smooth transition from radio to television. Radio drama had been fairly simple to produce live, because actors only needed to sound like the characters they played, and sound effects took care of setting the scene. Nonetheless, drama made the move to television with considerable success. A new generation of playwrights, directors, designers, and actors presented **anthology dramas**, high-quality original hour-long and 90-minute plays weekly on such shows as

General Electric Theater, Playhouse 90, and *Studio One.* Eventually these live dramas were replaced with pre-recorded dramatic programs.

Some lament the passing of live dramatic television. But a look at those old shows reveals that their production values were quite basic, and the look was flat in texture. Today we expect more polish and excitement from prerecorded programs.

Still, some entertainment programs such as talk shows maintain a live or partially live format. NBC pioneered the talk show format, wherein personalities provided a blend of entertainment, information, and service material. *Today* was the prototype for the early morning news-weather-feature-chatter wake-up format, and *The Tonight Show* paved the way for countless desk-and-couch late-night programs in which a genial host does an open monologue, interviews a handful of celebrities, banters with the band and the audience, and bumbles through a topical comedy sketch.

Early television broadcasting was carried for only a few hours each day, mainly in the evening when whole families could watch. As programming was expanded into the daylight hours, children's programming was added. **Children's programming** consists of television shows that are appropriate and often educational for children under the age of 12. Sitting on bleachers or benches in tiny, cramped studios, an audience of a few dozen kids would be entertained by puppets, perpetually cheerful adults, a clown, and a few zany characters. Buffalo Bob was the host-sidekick to the freckle-faced *Howdy Doody,* in one of the earliest children's programs. It became the forerunners of popular children's programs such as *Sesame Street, Barney,* and *The Wiggles.*

The situation comedy is a staple of television programming. A **situation comedy, or sitcom,** is a program that typically consists of a group of characters placed in a familiar setting or situation that ultimately generates humorous activity. Traditional sitcoms are filmed in front of a live studio audience and allow viewers to hear the emotional reactions of audience members. *I Love Lucy,* a popular situation comedy of the 1950s, was the first television program to be filmed and then broadcast at a later time. The show pioneered the three-camera set-up, with one camera in the center used for the establishing shot of the Ricardos and their neighbors in the living room, and the other two focusing on the faces of Lucy and the person with whom she was speaking.

Today, notice how often the "situation" in a situation comedy revolves around a family or group of characters gathered around a familiar setting—the living room or a bar or an office or a coffee house—and the three-camera set-up moves the action along swiftly in a manner that is easy to follow on the small screen. This classic form of situation comedy is used in shows such as *Two and a Half Men* and *Everybody Loves Raymond.* Other shows such as *The Office* and *Scrubs* have scrapped the studio audience and added more cameras to create a program that is more like a movie than a television show.

Other popular programs that have evolved over the years have been detective shows and westerns. The shows are typically filmed on location and edited into a one-hour format, with commercial breaks nicely worked in at planned pauses in the action. Crime dramas joined sitcoms as the main programming for prime-time television. Networks and their advertisers wanted to train audiences to watch the same programs regularly, so they encouraged producers to develop familiar and likable characters who could be shown in standardized yet slightly different situations week after week.

Game shows were popular programs on radio, but they became even more popular on television as the agony or glee of the contestants could be seen in all its human glory. Easy and cheap to produce, the games became not only words, bells, and buzzers, but giant boards with flashing lights, handsome hosts, and maybe even beauty queens modeling or presenting the prizes.

For a short while game shows disappeared from television when it was discovered that some contestants on the most lucrative prime-time shows, including *The $64,000 Question,* had been coached in ways that prepared them to answer difficult or obscure questions. The quiz show scandals of the 1950s shook the public's confidence in the integrity of television programming. While it may have taken longer to win back the public's trust, games shows returned to television after four years. Today nationally syndicated shows such as *Jeopardy* and *Wheel of Fortune* are still extremely popular, attracting large audiences on a nightly basis. In the late 1990s, US networks successfully imported and adapted European game shows such as *Who Wants to Be a Millionaire,* which gained daily slots on ABC's prime-time schedule, and even topped the most-watched charts for a short time.

Quiz Show Scandal of 1959

The most notorious case of game show rigging occurred in 1959 on the show *Twenty-One*. The program required contestants to go head-to-head in a trivia contest and answer enough questions to reach 21 points in order to receive a cash prize. Charles Van Dorean, an English professor at Columbia University, was a celebrated winner on the popular game show, winning more than $130,000 and many admiring fans, but he soon found himself in the center of controversy. Around the time of Van Dorean's win, rumors began to spread that game show executives feed certain players answers to questions in an effort to heighten drama and allow a more likeable contestant to win. During a congressional investigation, which was coordinated to examine the rumors, Van Dorean admitted to cheating during his 15-week run on the show. The scandal followed Van Dorean for many years, forcing him to retire from his position at Columbia and publish books under a pseudonym.[11]

Another format that made the transition from radio to television was the soap opera. **Soap operas** are serial stories told through a series of characters, usually in installments. Named "soaps" because their earliest sponsors were often personal hygiene and house cleaning products and companies, these radio dramas thrilled generations of listeners before making their move to television. Initially, because of their storylines and daytime broadcast schedule, the characters and plots were of interest mainly to young and middle-aged women. But as storylines diversified and diverse characters were brought in, many men became big fans of television soaps as well.

The addition of visual components to the soap opera meant that several story lines could be followed at once. Along with the usual middle-aged characters developed in the radio format, television added plots involving more glamorous young people. Soap operas became so popular for a while that, in the 1980s, producers and networks moved to nighttime with dramas such as *Dallas* and *Dynasty*, which explored more mature themes. Many of the weekly one-hour prime-time dramas that were created in the 1990s such as *Melrose Place* and *Dawson's Creek* and up to today, such as *Desperate Housewives* and *Gossip Girl*, were heavily influenced by the original soap opera format and language.

TELEVISION AS AN INFORMER

In the early stages of development, many supporters viewed television as a revolutionary way to inform and educate the masses. Today we take for granted the ability of network and local news departments to provide complete (and many times live) coverage of presidential elections, natural disasters such as the 2004 tsunami, space shuttle launches, terrorist attacks, sport events, wars, inaugurations, and just about any other newsworthy event. Yet, these news functions were developed and perfected in little more than one generation.

Early television was capable of providing little more than the 15-minute reading of the news that radio offered. Gradually, film footage and then live transmissions were added. Because of the addition of visual images, news broadcasts were allotted more time. By the end of the 1960s, first with the civil rights movement and then with the Vietnam War,

Telenovelas

Soaps operas are popular not only in America but around the world. Latin American countries have been very successful developing their own brand of soaps, called *telenovelas*. These serial dramas, developed in countries such as Brazil, Mexico, and Venezuela, are exported all over the world, and shown on prime-time in countries as diverse as China, Turkey, or Italy.

Televised sporting events are one of the main features that set television apart from all other mediums. Sports events are complicated in terms of camera placements, following the action, and cutting from close-ups to the entire field of action. But they were quickly embraced by television programmers because they attracted large audiences; they were fairly inexpensive to produce; and advertisers liked the tie-in with popular hometown teams. In addition to baseball, which radio had covered for decades, television elevated professional football to new stature. It also brought wide popularity to boxing, professional wrestling, bowling, and even marginal sports-entertainment attractions such as the roller-derby competition.

Reality programming is one of the newer forms of television programming and has become a very successful genre. The term **reality TV** is generally applied to describe programs that focus on non-actors that produce unscripted dialog. The format has been so victorious on TV that it has gained its own Emmy category. Although many question the label itself, since it has revealed several circumstances in which reality was tweaked to produce more desirable results, reality shows have made a strong mark on the network's schedules, and at least at this point don't seem to be losing steam.

Ranging from the prosaic—talent shows such as *American Idol*—to the bizarre—survival shows such as *Survivor* and *The Amazing Race* that test contestants' mental and physical strength. These reality shows are relatively cheap to produce and generate enough buzz to gain their own free publicity. Many analysts have also credited their success to the fact that they give audiences the sense of being able to watch themselves through the eyes and experiences of "real people."

television news had guaranteed a significant, permanent, premium (and much longer) space in the networks' schedules.

Coverage of the political nominating conventions marked the 1950s and made the careers of seasoned journalists such as Edward R. Murrow, David Brinkley, Mike Wallace, and Walter Cronkite, who had all migrated to TV from traditional media such as radio and newspapers. The presence of TV cameras in those conventions made them not only more relevant for the audience, but also made the medium much more attractive as a workplace for those seasoned reporters. Television made the nominating conventions a prime-time show, just like the World Series of baseball or the Miss America Pageant.

Because of their prominence at historic events, the network anchors were elevated to positions of power and respect unusual for anyone in American society. That's why Walter Cronkite, who consistently had the highest believability ratings before his retirement from the anchor seat in 1981, came to be known as "Uncle Walter" for the American public. The viewers felt he not only brought them the news, he in fact embodied the news.

In one decade or so, the era of the news reader was over. The all-powerful anchor and the participant journalist were now the norm on TV. The same way cameras, and later transmission dishes, made images and live transmissions an essential part of television journalism, it quickly became apparent that the anchors and other on-air personalities didn't have to remain tied to the New York or Washington studio. Instead they could be expected to travel with the President to a summit, attend the Olympic Games, and even visit the war front as Cronkite and others memorably did during the Vietnam War.

Some news programs began to take an unlikely turn in the 1980s, as infotainment became a hot new format. **Infotainment** is a form of programming that combines current news and feature stories. Programs such as *Entertainment Tonight*, and *Extra*, presented soft celebrity or crime news. The fast-moving, easily digestible format blended the structure of a news program with the easygoing style of a talk show. The anchorpeople are encouraged to be personalities themselves, and to feature the same stars that the audience read about in *People* and other similar news-gossip magazines.

It was just a matter of time before the success of such infotainment shows rubbed off into the traditional news shows. Currently, even the networks' serious news shows, such as *60 Minutes* or *Primetime Live*, have either generated their own spin-offs or incorporated many of the blended features popularized by infotainment. As recently as ten years ago, no one could imagine that the traditional news magazines would be racing to scoop each other on topics such as celebrity infidelity, Britney Spears, or New York socialites. Many in the news business defend themselves by pointing toward the audience, and saying that they are only giving the public what it wants.

Similarly, many news talk shows and news segments have become glorified soap boxes for celebrities to promote their latest films, books, or CDs.

Shows such as the highly successful *Today* and *Good Morning America*, which are currently competing for the top morning ratings spot, have also incorporated infotainment into their format, transitioning easily from serious news segments to celebrity talk to cooking and fitness tips.

Since the events of September 2001, as the general public turned once again to the networks for reliable information, broadcast TV's news audience seems to have stabilized, after a brief increase in numbers. The competition from 24-hour news channels such as CNN and Fox News spurred the networks to reinvest in their coverage, a fact that became clear during the first stages of the Iraq War, when every single major news outlet had their own ground crews—and sometimes their anchors and star reporters—in the battlefield.

Television Networks and Public Broadcasting

Each of the major radio networks entered the television business in the late 1940s, with NBC and CBS signing up affiliates in most of the 100 major markets, while ABC and Dumont—the long-forgotten fourth network—lagged far behind. Dumont dropped out of competition in the mid-1950s, and ABC became the dark horse in the network field, a role that it would hold until its ascendancy in the 1970s as the premier sports network.

EARLY NETWORK PROGRAMMING

In the early stages of the medium, there was insufficient programming for round-the-clock broadcasting. Typically, the station of the late 1940s and early 1950s came on the air with a "test pattern" around 5 p.m., carried one or two local programs, including the reading of the news in the early evening, and then joined the affiliated network for three hours of programming—the beginning of the concept of prime time. That paralleled radio network programming, and the format remained the heart of the network-affiliate concept even after the networks began to provide soap operas and game shows during the daytime hours.

Because the art of television production would take time to develop, each network carried movies that filled almost the entire three-hour prime-time slot at least one or two evenings a week. Each network began to work with advertisers and film producers to develop continuing half-hour and one-hour programs. Soon certain nights took on a distinctive flavor. Saturday emerged as comedy/variety night, with CBS's popular *The Jackie Gleason Show* and NBC's *Your Show of Shows*. CBS established several situation comedies on Tuesday night and the other networks accepted its domination in that segment of programming, much the way in which the other networks conceded in the 1990s and early-2000s that Thursday nights were NBC's "Must-See TV" nights, where the network reigned unchallenged with its popular sitcoms.

The networks gradually developed the capability of filling every night of the week with original programming, and they had to do it 52 weeks of the year because they had no ability to store and reuse television programs. Filmed "kinescopes" of television programs were useful for archival purposes, but they were not of broadcast quality. The introduction of the videotape—an electronic means of recording and storing television programs—meant that the networks could make just 26 episodes of a weekly program and show "reruns" during summer months.

By the 1960s, the networks had developed the practice of introducing most of their new shows one or two weeks in the middle of September. Shows that did not find an audience fairly rapidly were canceled and replaced with other programs whose pilot

Network Affiliates

Companies such as NBC, owned by RCA, transposed the radio network system to the newly-developed medium of television. The very profitable and accommodating corporate parent-affiliate relationship proved to be an even greater success on TV. In the largest and most profitable markets, such as New York and Los Angeles, the corporate parent also owned the station, but ownership limitations imposed by the FCC left the ownership of most stations to local, and at the time family-owned, companies.

The affiliation system has survived for so long because it is based on a symbiotic relationship beneficial for both parent network and affiliates. Through this system, local stations receive network programming from the parent station (which they rebroadcast for a fee); produce local programs such as regional newscasts; and also purchase nationally syndicated programs, which help to fill the stations' daily schedule. In return, besides paying fees for the shows they receive, affiliates also pay to the parent network a percentage of the income generated by local advertising, and receive a percentage of the nationally broadcast commercials. In many cases, particularly in special programs and sporting events such as the NFL season and the Olympic Games, network and affiliates strike deals on how to finance the costs and divide the profits. These deals are not always easy to arrange, but the survival of the affiliation system speaks for its mutually beneficial aspects.

episodes shown the summer before did not win them a slot in the opening fall line-up. This practice is still used by the networks, with the possible difference that now unsuccessful shows typically get canceled much faster than they did before.

FCC EXAMINES THE ROLE OF NETWORKS

Ever-mindful of its mandate to prevent monopoly control of the information carried on the public airwaves, the Federal Communications Commission began the first of several inquiries into program production and distribution in the late 1950s. In 1970 the FCC passed the "Financial Interest and Syndication Rules," a document that forced the networks out of the business of syndication. A network could no longer control the profits from reruns of its shows. Shortly thereafter, the federal government filed antitrust suits aimed at curtailing network control of programming. By the end of the 1970s, all three networks had signed consent decrees that limited the number of programs they could own. Syndication and program control were profitable for the networks, so the FCC limitations, while they prevented a monopoly in the production and distribution business, also precipitated the decline of network revenues.

Indeed, by the beginning of the 1990s, as the share of audience and the revenues from the networks plummeted, the FCC began to relax its restrictions on the networks. The Fox Broadcasting Company, bidding to become the fourth network, was granted a waiver by the FCC to program 18 1/2 hours a week without being subject to the syndication rule.

In 1991, the FCC made some concessions to the networks, allowing them to keep resale rights to as much as 40 percent of the programming they produced, and to earn royalties on reruns of other programming. From 1991 on, the FCC has reviewed many of its ownership rules in a way that greatly benefited the networks and the parent companies that own them.

NETWORKS LOSS PROFITS

The networks began the 1980s with a combined share of 91 percent of the television viewing audience. By the early 1990s they had about 60 percent. By the turn of the century, the networks had lost 44 percent of the 1980 nightly TV audience to other media such as basic and premium cable as well as satellite, dropping their combined share to approximately 50 percent of the audience.[12] This decline translates into lost advertising revenues, because shrinking audiences put the advertisers in a much stronger bargaining position when they haggle with networks over "upfront" sponsorship of shows—committing themselves in advance to pay for advertising that will put a show on the air.

The networks have struggled hard not only to stop this audience decline but to regain some of the lost market share. They have also tried to find different ways of increasing their profitability. Inventing or "reinventing" genres and formats such as reality TV and game shows has been one of these tactics. By creating or betting on these formats that are cheaper to produce and seem to attract new viewers, networks hope to stop some of their losses.

Another area that has seen a lot of investment—and a great deal of return for television channels—is DVDs and digital media files. These pieces of technology are a cash cow for networks and cable channels, as well as the programs' producers. They are very cheap to produce and release—recent and even "classic" sitcoms, dramas, miniseries, and TV movies have already been produced and only have to be repackaged. In some cases, programs are loaded with extras and bonuses, such as cast commentaries and deleted scenes. The costs involved usually relate additional copyrights and bonuses for the cast, creators and producers, as well as marketing and publicity.

PUBLIC BROADCASTING

Not all forms of television broadcasting seek to make a profit. **Public broadcasting**, unlike commercial broadcasting, is meant to be used as resource for the public, not a means to turn a profit for a corporation. The advent of television was hailed as an opportunity for new and unparalleled efforts to educate the masses with the new technology. Unfortunately, commercial interests were so strongly opposed to reserving part of the spectrum for educational television that educational forces had to pressure the FCC in a systematic and sustained way. Once the network licensing freeze was over in 1952, the FCC agreed to reserve one channel out of every eight for noncommercial use.

While noncommercial programming does not produce money, it still costs money to produce. Therefore, funding is an essential part of its survival. Universities sponsored the first educational television stations, but financial support was difficult to find. The Ford Foundation, which helped educators put pressure on the FCC, continued its support by underwriting National Educational Television (NET), a consortium of nonprofit stations that formed their own sort of network. Rather than feeding programs electronically from a central location, as the commercial networks did, they merely mailed or delivered recorded programs to one another to rebroadcast.

By the late 1960s, there were nearly 200 educational television stations, and it was apparent that they needed to be put on sounder footing. The Public Broadcasting Act, passed by Congress in 1967, created the Corporation for Public Broadcasting (CPB) to foster the growth of nonprofit radio and television stations and facilitate their linkage for the purpose of sharing production costs. Two years later, the Public Broadcasting Service (PBS) was created specifically to facilitate nonprofit television programming. The CPB is a primary supporter of PBS.

The Public Telecommunications Financing Act of 1978 requires the CPB to submit to the president and Congress a "comprehensive and detailed inventory of funds distributed by federal agencies to public telecommunications agencies." Up until the 1980s, the federal agencies contributed the most to CPB's budget. Then, federal support for public television was seriously cut back. More and more, public television turned to funds from viewers and the business community. Pressured by a lagging income, in 1988 PBS changed its rules to permit the mention of one specific product or service each time a corporation received credit for funding a program. Today, only about 14 percent of the funds that support public broadcasting come from the federal government. The rest is spread among state governments, the business community, and the general public, through personal donations.

PRESSURE ON THE NETWORKS

The chief programmer at each of the major broadcast networks spends a lot of time studying the scheduling board on the office wall that shows the three

hours of prime-time programming—8 to 11 p.m. in the East and West, 7 to 10 p.m. elsewhere—for seven nights a week—22 hours (Sunday nights carry an additional hour of prime time) for each network to fill, 88 hours of programs for the four major networks combined. Because about half will be 30-minute episodes of situation comedies and dramas, and each network offers at least one 2-hour movie each week, the total number of prime-time programs each network offers at any one time is around 30.

Trying to decide what will constitute an effective lineup of shows each night in terms of holding an audience from one show to the next is complicated enough. The problem is compounded by the necessity of competing with other major networks, independent stations, public broadcasting, cable, DVDs, Internet, video games, and other distractions. But *scheduling* is only part of the complex business of network programming. There are other pressures on the chief programmer, all of them pushing the network toward decisions that result in "lowest common denominator" programming that makes it difficult for anything but mediocre programs to survive the process.

Among the groups that affect the networks' decisions are:

◆ Advertisers

◆ Affiliated stations

◆ Government regulators

◆ Advocacy groups and television "watchdogs"

◆ The competition—all television, not just other networks

◆ Packagers—studios and independent producers of programs

◆ Artists and creative people, many of whom control their own shows

◆ The viewers

Any of these groups, when and if they become actively involved, have a veto power over the network. When you are dealing with such a large audience and such high production costs, you cannot afford to ignore or offend any segment of society. That's a dilemma that confronts network television more than any other medium.

Advertisers want popular programs that attract everybody and offend nobody. The stations that affiliate with the network have much the same outlook. In addition, the affiliates often have concerns that are regional: Stations in the conservative, religious regions of the country are more likely to drop a network show with too much emphasis on sex and violence or controversial topics, while outlets in the major urban centers might complain about programs that do not provide enough thought-provoking material.

Network Ratings

Every mass medium has a method for measuring the size and composition of its audiences. Audited circulation figures enable advertisers to know how many people read a newspaper or magazine, and surveys provide specific information about which people make up the audience. Box office figures measure theater attendance, and theater producers can observe the house to know which segments of the audience are responding to the program.

But broadcast media, as we saw previously, pose a special problem because the consumers can change the station they are watching from minute to minute, and there is no way for the broadcaster to observe or calculate which family members are in the audience for particular programs. A special form of research, then, is needed to measure who is watching what. In order for the information to be useful, it has to be quantified quickly for programmers and the advertisers they must satisfy.

WHAT IS A RATING?

The firms that measure the reach and penetration of television programming know how many homes in the country have television. It is against this total number of potential viewing units that the ratings are calculated. The ratings for a given half-hour never add up to 100 percent, since 100 percent of homes with television aren't viewing at any one time. The top program in prime time may have a 30 rating, and all of its competitors in that time slot may have a combined 40 rating, for a total of 70—meaning that 30 percent of the sets in the area measured were not turned to any program.

Ratings are most significant in evening prime time, when most people are likely to be at home and free to watch television. This is the period when the major manufacturers of consumer goods and services want to reach the largest possible audience. Ratings are far less significant in the middle of a weekday morning, when as few as 5 percent of households use television.

At times of the day other than prime time, the measurement known as the **share** is more significant. It is possible for a local show to have a rating of only 7, which means that 93 percent of the area homes with television were not tuned in. But the show could have a 40 share, meaning that 4 out of every 10 sets that *were* turned on at that time were tuned to the program.

National advertisers of cars, soaps, and soft drinks that want to reach every consumer probably will not be impressed with a 40 share when they discover that it is coupled with a 7 rating. But a station that has the most popular program in the cheaper time slot will attract plenty of local and specialized advertisers.

DEVELOPMENT OF THE RATINGS SYSTEMS

The first ratings systems, developed for radio use in the 1930s, involved telephone interviews ("What program are you listening to at this time?"), face-to-face interviews at the door ("What stations have you listened to in the past 24 hours?"), and even postcard reply surveys ("Please check off which stations were listened to this past week, and by which family members"). All of the systems relied on the cooperation of those who responded, and on their recall ability. Clearly a system that monitored broadcast consumption as it occurred would be preferable.

The AC Nielsen Company acquired the rights to a device, invented by two professors at MIT, called the **audimeter**, which could record when a radio set was turned on and to which station. When a family agreed to be one of the 1,000 Nielsen families across the country, they were visited monthly by a technician who removed the punched tape carrying the listening information. The data might be nearly two months old by the time Nielsen could assemble them for use by broadcasters and advertisers.

By the time television was introduced for home use, however, the audimeter had been improved so that the consumer could remove the tape and mail it in. Nielsen shifted from radio measurement to rating the television programs, and by the 1960s the technology had improved to the point where data was automatically fed to the company over phone lines, making the data available to the producers within a few days. Today, both Nielsen and its main competitor, Arbitron, supplement electronic data with the phone surveys in major markets when instant information is demanded by the industry.

Critics of the Nielsen technique point out that a television set may be put in use merely to provide background sound, to keep a pet or baby company, or to convince burglars that someone is home—with nobody really *watching* television; and thus no consumer paying attention to the advertising messages.

The rival Arbitron system for a while required family members to make notations in a diary concerning the times when the set is on; to which channel, and, most importantly, which members of the family were watching. Critics questioned whether the diaries were kept carefully and accurately.

Neither method measured "why" or "how intently" the program was watched, or what value the audience put on the message after they had watched it. That is why the ratings firms augment their usual measurements with telephone surveys that go into greater detail.

Cable Television

The concept of *broad*casting is an exciting because information is beamed out for anyone to receive—a true and democratic *mass* communication system. Still, there are problems with broadcasting. The

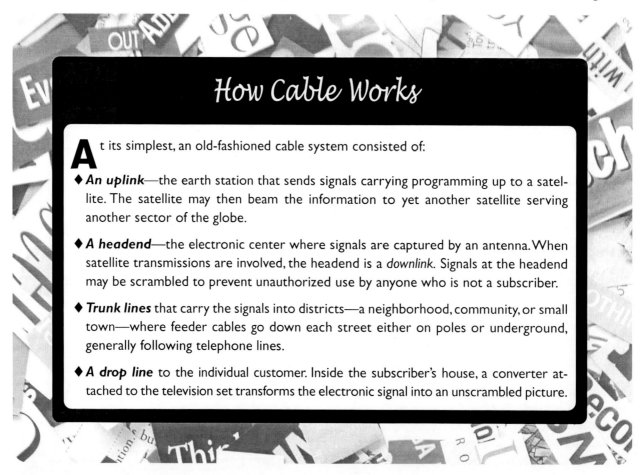

How Cable Works

At its simplest, an old-fashioned cable system consisted of:

◆ *An uplink*—the earth station that sends signals carrying programming up to a satellite. The satellite may then beam the information to yet another satellite serving another sector of the globe.

◆ *A headend*—the electronic center where signals are captured by an antenna. When satellite transmissions are involved, the headend is a *downlink*. Signals at the headend may be scrambled to prevent unauthorized use by anyone who is not a subscriber.

◆ *Trunk lines* that carry the signals into districts—a neighborhood, community, or small town—where feeder cables go down each street either on poles or underground, generally following telephone lines.

◆ *A drop line* to the individual customer. Inside the subscriber's house, a converter attached to the television set transforms the electronic signal into an unscrambled picture.

signal goes only so far, depending on the power of the transmitter. Signals can be lost if mountains or tall buildings intervene. Perhaps more importantly, the number of signals that can be carried on local airwaves is limited. Within 30 years of the advent of broadcasting, it was clear that technical improvements were needed in order to ensure that clear and adequate signals could be supplied to every consumer, and that many more choices could be added to the average consumer's television "menu."

Transmissions take barely a fifth of a second, and thus **superstations**—broadcast stations that decided to serve the entire country instead of just their local broadcast area by offering themselves to cable operators—in Atlanta, Chicago, and New York can be viewed in places thousands of miles away. Entertainment and news services also are fed to foreign countries, so the same movie, sports event, or 24-hour news can be viewed simultaneously in Detroit, Seattle, Cancun, or Calgary.

CABLE BEGINS AS CATV

By 1950, **community antenna television (CATV)** was bringing signals to remote areas and those previously cut off from broadcast centers by intervening terrain, such as the mountains of Colorado. CATV entrepreneurs erected tall antennas to capture distant or blocked signals, and then ran coaxial cable to the homes of subscribers who were happy to pay for the service. Eventually CATV operators began to "import" programs from beyond the area served by their antenna, and the concept of cable television began to develop.

The first technical problem occurred when the fledgling cable companies went to string their wires. Some planned to run the cables from house to house, but that was feasible only in areas of dense settlement. The obvious solution was to use the poles owned by the telephone company, as other utilities have done. But telephone companies set rates in many areas that added greatly to the cost of cable. Managers of the AT&T system forecast correctly that cable—far from being just a means of improving the television signal—was an alternative means of bringing many kinds of information into homes electronically. That put the cable companies in potentially competitive conflict with the phone companies.

CABLE GROWTH

The flurry of interest in cable distribution of programming in the 1950s led some to predict that the entire nation would soon be wired. However, 50 percent penetration of American homes was not realized until 1988. One hundred percent cable availability was not a reality until the 1990s, when alternative systems such as satellite TV began to cover areas that were previously bypassed by traditional cable. Just as it did with broadcast television, the FCC has had to work its way through several difficult issues to ensure that all customers are served adequately and fairly, and to guard against domination of the field by any one economic group or interest.

In 1959 a US Senate subcommittee considered legislation to require licensing of CATV operators, who were not regulated by any agency. Lacking information about the scope of cable and unsure of the many ramifications of the new technology, the legislators argued the bill furiously. At that point, states and municipalities jumped into the regulation of cable, forcing owners to obtain local franchises in order to string wires through or under the streets and requiring them to return a percentage of the income to the municipality in return for that franchise. The borough of Manhattan was among the first areas to be served by cable because its tall buildings make broadcast reception difficult. Many areas of New York City took longer to adopt cable because of the high costs. This situation was symbolic of the chaos and uncertainty of cable distribution.

REGULATING CABLE

The FCC did not get involved in regulating cable until 1965, when it ruled that programs imported from more than 60 miles away could not duplicate any local broadcast in the preceding or following 15 days. That restriction prohibited a cable operator, for example, from using a satellite to pick up a concert that was broadcast live in another market but that was scheduled to be shown on tape locally at a later date. This "syndicated exclusivity" regulation pleased the broadcasters but angered the cable operators, who joined forces to lobby against it. They succeeded in convincing the FCC to shorten the exclusivity period to just one day. It was the first event in an ongoing struggle that saw the cable operators gaining strength and forcing the FCC not to automatically favor the entrenched broadcasters.

In 1968, the US Supreme Court rejected the argument by cable operators that cable was not interstate and therefore not subject to regulation by the federal government. Moreover, it said FCC regulation of cable was necessary in order to carry out the mandate of congress to develop the dissemination of electronic information in the best interests of the public. That decision laid the foundation for the FCC's heavy involvement in regulating cable.

In the 1970s, cable companies began to offer original programming, and they broadened the information they could offer by receiving signals from satellites. Now homes wired to cable could receive programs from anywhere. When cable differentiated itself as the "multi-channel medium" with the most variety to offer, it became attractive even to those in populated areas who did not need CATV in order to receive a signal.

THE 1972 REGULATIONS

The FCC issued a set of regulations in 1972 that put cable's house in order, superseding earlier decisions as well as a jumble of state and municipal regulations. Among the most important provisions were the following:

◆ **Certificate of Compliance.** While municipalities could still franchise cable owners, each system operator was required to obtain a "certificate of compliance" from the FCC. The granting of the certificate was virtually automatic, but the process alerted the FCC to verify that the operator was capable of providing service and that the municipality stayed within guidelines in setting reasonable franchise fees.

◆ **"Must Carry" Rule.** To ensure that cable operators would not carry just the most popular and profitable programs, all local signals had to be carried on cable if it is requested by a local station. The **must-carry rule** was popular with stations but unpopular with cable operators who preferred to pick and choose among local stations to maximize their profitability.

◆ **Importation of Signals.** Cable operators were permitted to import signals in order to carry all three major networks and adequate independent stations. There were several rules governing how many stations could be imported, and operators could not bring in a network affiliate hundreds of miles away that was available closer to the home region.

◆ **Anti-siphoning.** Cable systems were allowed to offer pay channels carrying movies, sports, and concerts. However, siphoning of events and programs that previously appeared free on broadcast television was prohibited. The FCC administered a rule in 1968 to prevent popular broadcast programs such as the Super Bowl, the World Series, and the Olympic Games from being expropriated by pay television.

◆ **Multiple Ownership.** Owners of television stations could not operate a cable franchise in the same community, and the television networks were prohibited from owning cable channels.

◆ **Local Origination.** Cable operators were required to provide local origination programming. In the 100 largest markets, these included "access" channels available to individuals or groups who wanted to get their information on the air.

The 1972 regulations required cable operators to provided original material "to a significant extent," but start-up costs made it difficult to build and equip studios. In the large markets where local access was required, franchisers provided little more than a rented storefront equipped with one or two cameras and tape recorders supervised by a single technician. Long-winded speeches by minor politicians, artistic presentations by those with marginal talent, and low-budget news programs have been carried by the public access channels in some large cities. On the positive side, schools and colleges have been encouraged to create and broadcast programs using their own television production facilities and crews.

DEREGULATION GIVES CABLE GREATER FREEDOM

The 1984 Cable Communications Act eased regulation on the industry. It came after lobbyists for cable owners successfully convinced congress to shield them from controls by municipalities and states. The owners argued that the prime responsibility of the operator should be to the subscribers of cable television, not to government bodies, and that the market would determine the prices people wanted to pay for various services.

In 1985, the must-carry rule was struck down by a federal court and the FCC did not fight the move. The chair of the FCC said the decision "takes the first step toward a true marketplace for the distribution by cable systems" and "represents a positive step toward full First Amendment protection for all forms of electronic media." The demise of the must-carry rule occurred after Supreme Court Chief Justice Warren Burger refused to heed the call of broadcasters, especially owners of the smaller UHF stations, who wanted to ensure that cable had to carry their programming. The president of the National Association of Broadcasters called the action, "a blow to the localized system of broadcasting in this nation." Even some FCC staff members feared that greedy cable operators would ignore local needs and offer only the most profitable programming. New York City cable operators immediately dropped the New Jersey public broadcasting channel, although many New Yorkers work or travel in New Jersey and could be interested in news and programs from their neighboring state.

Cable operators proclaimed they would continue to fight regulation by the FCC and other authorities on the grounds that they should have all the freedoms accorded to the print media. They argued that they must have the flexibility to find programming that is different from broadcast fare. They also wanted to explore the concept of **narrowcasting**—offering channels for specialized audiences such as children, rock music fans, sports enthusiasts, and hobbyists.

In 1988, the Reagan Administration released a report by the Commerce Department's National Telecommunications and Information Administration that called for even further deregulation of cable in order to foster more competition. The report was aimed at ensuring that a few large companies would not dominate the industry. While it did not suggest that telephone companies should be allowed to enter the cable industry, it did suggest that telephone lines could be used as common carriers to help more cable companies gain access to information.

RE-REGULATION OR CONTINUED DEREGULATION?

In 1990, the head of New Jersey's Board of Public Utilities claimed that cable television in the state of New Jersey was a monopoly and suggested that permitting more than one cable company to operate in a town would benefit subscribers by giving them a choice of providers and lower rates. Cable companies argued that federal deregulation precluded states and communities from interfering with their franchises. While cable rates and programming policies cannot be dictated by states or communities, local authorities can set service requirements for utilities. New Jersey has strengthened rules that require quicker response to service outages and billing credit when service outages occur.

Bills working their way slowly through Congress at the beginning of the 1990s would allow cities to regulate rates in areas without two or more cable operators, limit the number of subscribers nationally that any one cable operator could serve, regulate the prices of premium channels, and reinstate the must-carry rule. Cable operators, who argued that they spent extraordinary amounts of money to develop almost a million miles of system in just one decade, nevertheless prepared themselves for some form of re-regulation. In the summer of 1991 the FCC reinstated local rate regulations for many cable operations. Working in favor of the cable companies was the fear on the part of many in congress that allowing states and municipalities to control rates and decide on the number of franchises would lead back to the corruption and chaos that marked the early days of cable regulation.

In the fall of 1992, the pendulum continued its swing back toward regulation of cable when both houses of Congress passed a bill to regulate rates for basic cable services and spur competition. Consumer groups and broadcasters were among the biggest supporters of the measure, which passed with sufficient majorities in both houses to override the expected veto from President Bush. Nevertheless, in January 1992, the Senate handed cable operators a setback by passing legislation that would strengthen both local and federal regulation in order to limit the increases in cable rates. Siding with broadcasters, the legislators wrote into the law a requirement that cable operators pay for programming produced by the broadcasters.

CABLE MATURES AS A BUSINESS

Through the 1980s, the popularity of cable grew at a tremendous rate. More than 4,000 new systems were launched in that decade—a new system virtually every day. Initially many were owned by local entrepreneurs. Some had media experience, others were businesspeople eager to make a buck, and still others were engineers who had expertise in the technology. Eventually many of those that didn't have an understanding both of the technology and the business sold out to companies that did. Many of the new owners were parts of chains, and some of the largest chains were owned by large communication companies.

Westinghouse, the electric manufacturing company, for example, entered the cable business in 1981 by purchasing Teleprompter, the firm that wired the northern half of Manhattan in New York City. Just five years later Westinghouse put Teleprompter's parent company, Group W Cable Inc., up for sale and turned a profit. Westinghouse management had decided to concentrate on broadcasting, where the investment offers a quicker return to stockholders. Warner Communications (now part of Time Warner) formed Warner Amex, but a few years later bought out American Express's share in order to form a new cable venture with Viacom. Ownership patterns were in a state of flux throughout the 1980s as communication companies tried to figure out whether cable belonged in their mix.

Eventually chain ownership became the norm. The government's encouragement of further deregulation at the end of the 1980s was based partly on a concern that a few companies were cornering a large segment of the market. The largest, Telecommunications Inc., had 20 percent of the nation's 42 million cable customers. Deregulation was seen as encouraging more players to enter the market.

CABLE BECOMES PROFITABLE

Among the largest cable services, only one was profitable in 1983: TBS, the Atlanta-based Turner superstation. Five years later, however, most of the top advertiser-supported services made money, led by TBS, Turner's Cable News Network (CNN), and ESPN. In fact, each of those top three cable services made more profit than CBS and ABC combined.

Under deregulation, the networks were free to enter into ventures with cable services, and so the combination of players was constantly shifting throughout the 1990s and into the new century.

Cable's profitability can be exemplified by the increased costs of cable subscriptions. At one time the average consumer paid less than $10 a month for cable. Now, many subscribers pay a basic rate over twice or three times that much and add premium services that may bring the monthly bill to over $100, when taxes, fees and Internet services are added.

Eventually—assuming that the FCC decides to require competition in the market—cable will approach 100 percent penetration of the American market and consumers will draw the line on how much they are willing to pay and how many services they need. When that happens, the cable industry will "shake out," meaning that many companies will exit because they cannot make a profit, and the remaining companies will solidify their holds over the segment of the market they control. Rather than being producer-driven the industry will be equally consumer-driven. There will be a balance that involves information being created, priced, and delivered by the producers according to the needs and interests of the consumers.

USERS SHAPE THE MEDIUM

Most mass media have to poll their audiences to find out what they like and don't like. Cable gets constant indications of the popularity of its services. Subscribers call to add the Disney Channel or drop HBO. They write letters to say that they would like to see their service add C-Span, which covers Congress, or perhaps an additional Spanish language station. They realize they have more control over the information they receive than they do with most other mass media.

Some cable operators questioned the concept of offering a basic service for a fixed rate. The basic service system provides consumers with 20 to 30 channels for one standard price. Each additional premium channels cost more. Instead, cable companies started to sell channel packages, which meant that subscribers had to choose between groups of channels and options, without the option to ungroup them.

Recent research, however, indicates that consumers are not staying in their niches. In fact, many viewers are watching the broadcast network-type programming on such services as USA Network and the TNT more heavily than the narrowly focused programming designed for well-defined audiences. Convinced that consumers really do like network-type shows, TBS and other cable channels have experimented with running sitcoms in blocks when the broadcast networks are showing news or public affairs programs, so that viewers who want light-hearted entertainment can find it on cable when it isn't on the networks.

The Future of Television

As broadcast and cable networks lose revenue to other forms of media, it has become clear that television must reinvent itself in order to survive in the future. This reinvention may require altering traditional methods of programming and adapting to new technology.

MARKET SEGMENTATION

Market segmentation seems to be one of the strategies devised by the networks to survive and prosper in the television business. In the 1950s, 1960s, and 1970s the networks remained unchallenged in the market, and had to design their schedules in a way that reached the widest and largest audience possible. This attitude helped to solidify the idea that the networks should always provide **general programming**—shows that included a mix of dramas, comedies, sports, news, game shows, variety, talk shows, and other genres aimed at the widest general audience possible.

With the advent of cable and satellite technologies, and the market fragmentation we have witnessed since the late 1970s, the networks began to question if their old market strategy was still sustainable. During the 1980s, the three networks resisted and delayed the necessary changes as much as they could. However, Fox emerged in the early 1990s as a viable network exactly because it dared to mess with the formula. Originally aiming its programming at ethnic minorities and younger audiences, it claimed niche markets obviously underserved by the traditional networks.

Despite the fact that, as Fox grew and solidified in the 1990s it also veered toward a more traditional general programming format, beefing up its sports and news divisions, for example, its initial success shook up the market, and made it clear for the three major networks that adaptation to the new reality was crucial for their survival. The market segmentation and experimentation by the networks seen in the 1990s and 2000s might be considered a direct effect of both Fox's emergence and the necessity to respond to the market segmentation introduced by cable television.

As a result, the networks have toyed with new ideas and formats since the mid-1990s. Instead of targeting the widest, broadest general audiences possible, these formats have been clearly designed to attend particular segments or niche markets, an unthinkable idea 15 years ago. Thus, CBS and ABC have alternated between trying to reach younger and older, urban and rural, and liberal and conservative audiences, with short-lived programs that are dropped the next season. At least CBS's and ABC's market segmentation have paid off, as the networks enter the 2006-2007 season with high ratings. Tellingly, NBC, the network that has most resisted market segmentation and experimentation, has been struggling with dipping ratings for the past two seasons.

TELEVISION ON DEMAND

In order to stay up-to-date with the desires of the public, broadcast networks and cable networks need to adapt the content of their programming to the match the likes and dislikes of the public and adjust program scheduling to adapt to the viewing habits of the public. With the arrival of the Internet, we have turned into an on-demand society. Many people don't wait for the morning paper or the nightly news to learn about a breaking news story, they go to the Internet to pull up the information when they demand it. Similarly, many viewers do not sit down and watch a television show during its scheduled time. Through the use of Digital Video Recorders (DVRs), viewers can record a program, shut off the set or watch a different program, and then watch the recorded program whenever they choose.

Other forms of on-demand viewing are available on the Internet. Most major networks have full episodes available for free on the networks' Web sites or for sale on Web sites such as Amazon and itunes. While using the Internet to keep up with on-demand culture will be an important part of network television's survival, it also opens the industry up to more competition. YouTube and other video sharing Web sites offer thousands of hours of original programming that can pull viewers away from network programs that are available on television and on the Internet. To keep viewer's eyes on network television programs, networks such as CBS and BBC have partnered with YouTube to provided collaborative programming to viewers.[13]

In the future, television programs may permanently move from the television screen to the computer screen, couch potatoes may turn into mouse potatoes, and audiences may become their own programmers. But just as it has for the last 100 years, television will continue to grow and evolve with technology.

Careers in the Field

When a television show ends and the credits begin to scroll, many viewers change the channel and move on to a new program. However, those who stay tuned will notice the numerous roles involved in producing a television show. Positions like director, camera operator, and costume designer may be self-explanatory, but other potions such as key grip, gaffer, or vision mixer may be a mystery to those outside of the television business. Television offers a wide range of career opportunities to people with various talents and interests. On screen talent may experience the more glamorous side of television, but the true magic occurs behind the scenes. Behind the scenes positions occur in four different areas: pre-production—producers, casting directors, and writers; production—floor managers, boom operators, and technical directors; control room—television director, video tape operator, and graphics operator; post-production—sound editor, composer, and special effects operator. The size of a television crew depends on the complexity of the production.

If you are interested in a career in television it is important to decide on an area in which you would like work so you can tailor your education and build the proper experience. A great way to discover which area you are most interested in is to find an internship or entry-level position at a television station or production company. Positions such as runners and production assistants (PAs) are sometimes available to individuals with little or no experience. If you are outside of a major city, look to your local cable station or university station for opportunities.[14] If you are technically savvy, you can build experience by producing your own show though a podcast over the Internet.

Getting your foot in the door in the television industry may be a difficult process, but positions are available to those who are willing to work their way up the ladder. Whether you aspire to be a technical director or an executive producer, knowing as much as you can about the medium will only help you in your journey. Who knows, in only a few years, maybe television viewers will see your name scroll across the screen at the end of a program.

Chapter Summary

◆ The development of television technology started in the late 1800s and involved with the invention of the cathode-ray tube, scanning disk, and Image Dissector.

◆ Many of the first television programs were based off of radio programs. Over time such as situation comedies, prerecorded dramas, and reality television emerged.

◆ Cable television created more competition for broadcast networks and more options for television viewers.

◆ Television programs are slowly moving to the Internet to attract more viewers

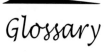

Glossary

anthology drama—high-quality original hour-long and 90-minute plays that aired weekly, often aired live

audimeter—a device that can record when a radio set or television set is turned on and to which station

cathode rays—beams of electrons used to project images onto a florescent screen inside a vacuum tube

children's programming—television shows that are appropriate and sometimes educational for children under the age of 12

community antenna television (CATV)—a method of broadcasting that uses tall antenna towers to reach remote areas that are cut off from broadcasting centers

general programming—shows that included a mix of dramas, comedies, sports, news, game shows, variety, talk shows, and other genres aimed at the widest general audience possible

infotainment—a form of programming that combines current news and feature stories

mosaic—a television tube that consists of many tiny photoelectric particles that convert light to an electric charge

must-carry rule—a FCC regulation stating that all local signals had to be carried on cable if it is requested by a local station.

narrowcasting—the act of offering channels for specialized audiences such as children, rock music fans, sports enthusiasts, and hobbyists

photoelectricity—the act of turning light into an electric signal

reality TV—programs that focus on non-actors that produce unscripted dialog

scanning—the act of viewing all the elements of a picture successively, rather than all at once, and sending them in a specific order over a single circuit

Share—a measurement that is used to express a network's percentage of the viewing audience

situation comedy—a program that typically consists of a group of characters placed in a familiar setting or situation that ultimately generates humorous activity

sketch comedy shows—a program with a series of short comedy scenes

soap operas—serial stories told through a series of characters, usually in installments

superstations—broadcast stations that decided to serve the entire country instead of just their local broadcast area by offering themselves to cable operators

Variety show—a live show that features numerous acts such as dancers, musicians, and comedians

Discussion Questions

1. Name two individuals that played an important role in the development of the television. What contributions did these individuals make?
2. What is infotainment? How has it affected news programs?
3. How is public broadcasting different from other forms of broadcasting?
4. What was the purpose of the must-carry rule? How did it affect cable operators?
5. How has the Internet affected television?

Supplemental Web Sites

❖ PBS: http://www.pbs.org/wgbh/amex/quizshow/ sfeature/quiz.html Learn more about the Quiz Show Scandals of the1950s and play *Twenty One.*
❖ Museum of Broadcast Communication: http:// www.museum.tv/ Learn more about television history and view old programs.
❖ YouTube: http://www.youtube.com Examine future trends in television.

Supplemental Reading

❖ *Tube: The Invention of Television* by David E. Fisher, Marshall Fisher
❖ *Defining Vision: The Battle for the Future of Television*, by Joel Brinkley

Endnotes

1 Mosaic. (2008). In *Merriam-Webster Online Dictionary.* Retrieved November 13, 2008, from *http://www.merriam-webster.com/dictionary/mosaic*
2 Christopher H. Sterling, John M. Kittross, *Stay Tuned: A history of American broadcasting.* Lawrence Erlbaum Associates: 2002.

[3] **Television.** (2008). In *Encyclopedia Britannica.* Retrieved November 13, 2008, from Encyclopædia Britannica Online: *http://www.britannica.com/EBchecked/topic/1262241/television*

[4] Television History: The First 75 Years. (2006). TV History. Retrieved from *http://www.tvhistory.tv/1890s%20Victorian%20Trade%20Card.htm*

[5] **Television.** (2008). In *Encyclopedia Britannica.* Retrieved November 13, 2008, from Encyclopædia Britannica Online: *http://www.britannica.com/EBchecked/topic/1262241/television*

[6] Ibid.

[7] RCA Press Room, About RCA – Television, Retrieved at *http://home.rca.com/en-US/PressReleaseDetail.html?Cat=RCAHistory&MN=9*

[8] *http://www.history.com/encyclopedia.do?articleId=203824*

[9] Associated Press. "Color TV Hits 50th Anniversary in US" *USA Today*, March 24, 2004. Retrieved from *http://www.usatoday.com/life/television/news/2004-03-24-color-tv_x.htm*

[10] Digital TV 2009

[11] The American Experience, Quiz Show Scandal, People & Events, *Public Broadcasting System.* Retrieved from *http://www.pbs.org/wgbh/amex/quizshow/peopleevents/pande02.html*

[12] Ratingscirculation.pdf in ch. 3 articles folder

[13] Thom Patterson, "Is the Future of Television on the Web" *CNN.com* Retrieved from *http://www.cnn.com/2008/SHOWBIZ/TV/05/01/tv.future/index.html*

[14] Dave Owen, "How to Get a Job in Television" *Media College.* Retrieved from *http://www.mediacollege.com/employment/television/find-job.html*

MUSIC, MOVIES, THEATER, SPORTS, AND EVOLVING ENTERTAINMENTS

Barbara Iverson

◆ The entertainment industry performs many of the same roles as the news media—informing, marketing, correlating society and serving the ritual needs of consumers.

◆ The music recording industry, in addition to providing much of the content for the radio medium, has important links with the film and electronic gaming industries and provides powerful marketing tools for other products.

◆ Advances in technology have the effect of constantly renewing interest in music though digital technologies and are challenging the existing business models in the music industry.

◆ These industries adopt parent rating systems, warning labels and other self-policing strategies to avoid direct governmental regulation.

◆ The "blockbuster" mentality was the basis of filmmaking by business conglomerates, but technological changes are challenging this paradigm, and

new methods of filmmaking and distribution as well as viewing are springing up.

◆ Electronic games—video games and especially online massively multiplayer role-playing games—are evolving forms of mass entertainment.

◆ Because they are "one too many" in nature and part of the marketing mix, live theater, sports events and theme parks function as forms of mass communication in our society.

The music recording industry, the motion picture industry, live theater, sports, newer mass media like electronic gaming (video and online) and popular theme parks mirror and comment on the larger society. The products created for these industries encapsulate slices of cultural history. They provide models for understanding the values and lifestyles in a culture. These media provide jobs and opportunities in art, communications, marketing and advertising. It is important to understand the interaction between these media that can both define and reflect social trends and our mass society. These are not news media, but they serve some of the same purposes as the news media.

Roles of the Entertainment Industry

The music recording industry, the motion picture industry, live theater, sports, electronic gaming (video and online) and theme parks inform the public, act as marketing tools, reflect changes in society and satisfy our need for ritual activities. This is not entirely different from the role of news media. And as we have discovered in our study of the "serious" mass media, digital technologies are transforming the "fun" mass media—the mass media of entertainment—at a very rapid rate. As these media transform and converge, the interrelationship of the entertainment and news media grows. "Business as usual" isn't usual when digital technology transforms how industry creates, distributes, markets and regulates entertainment and how society ultimately consumes and understands it on an almost daily basis.

The entertainment industries become the news as new technologies, new products and new business models transform how we amuse ourselves. Further-

Entertainment That Reflects Society

♦ *TOMMY* (music album, rock opera, motion picture)—deals with war, disability, emotional isolation, gaming and music

♦ *V FOR VENDETTA* (graphic novel, motion picture)—addresses ideas of government repression and terrorism

♦ *THE SOPRANOS* (Cable TV, DVD)—long-running serial about an American family whose breadwinner just happens to be a mafia chief

♦ *GRAND THEFT AUTO* (video game)—one version included pornographic images that one could unlock after purchasing the game. This feature was removed after the ESRB challenged the game company.

♦ *THE WARRIORS* (motion picture, video game)—a cult film hit from the '70s, considered ultraviolent at the time. Now a video game that contains "Blood, Intense Violence, Sexual Themes, Strong Language, Use of Drugs and Alcohol" according to the ESRB

♦ *HAIRSPRAY* (motion picture, live musical theater)—a wacky reminiscence about growing up in Baltimore where teens integrate the local amusement park

♦ *THE HOLY LAND THEME PARK* —"Visit Jerusalem in Orlando" featuring musical productions, live shows, rides and shopping

Entertainment as Social Critique

- *JFK* (released on December 20, 1991) (motion picture)—This film by Oliver Stone sets out to tell the history surrounding the assassination of John F. Kennedy, President of the United States. The film won two Academy Awards and was nominated for eight, including Best Picture, which it did not win. It made Roger Ebert's list of the top ten films of the decade.

- *THREE KINGS* (1999) (motion picture)—This film by David O. Russell is set at the end of the Persian Gulf War. Four soldiers steal gold that was stolen from Kuwait, but they end up helping the victims of an oppressive regime and the Persian Gulf War.

- *THE PASSION OF THE CHRIST* (2004) (motion picture)—This film by Mel Gibson shows the last twelve hours of the life of Jesus Christ, known to Christians as "the Passion." It was nominated for three Academy Awards. The film's dialogue is in Latin, Hebrew and Jesus' native tongue, Aramaic. It was released with subtitles.

- *BOWLING FOR COLUMBINE* (2002)—This documentary by Michael Moore explores the roots of America's predilection for guns.

- *GOOD NIGHT, GOOD LUCK* (2006) (motion picture)— This film by George Clooney is a biographical treatment of Edward R. Murrow's confrontation with notorious bully Senator Joseph McCarthy.

more, entertainment productions reflect such social issues as gender, religion, bias, disease, crime, terrorism and politics in myriad ways that inform, educate and provoke discussion of these issues. Popular entertainment often pushes the envelope of what is socially acceptable.

Some entertainment goes beyond comment; its design produces a social critique and possibly spurs us to action in our real world. It thus serves the correlation function of media.

Entertainment that produces discussion or controversy can energize people to take action outside the world of entertainment. Interest groups or individuals frequently attempt to try to put political pressure on legislators or regulators urging that media

be censored, regulated or otherwise altered owing to its perceived effects on society.

The Southern Baptist Convention (SBC) ended an eight-year boycott of Disney parks in 2005. The SBC boycott aimed at ending Disney's policy of extending benefits to homosexual employees and sponsorship of "Gay Days." The boycott had no discernable financial impact on corporate profits or policy and ended when Disney studios and Miramax films split up.

The reaction to Janet Jackson's "wardrobe malfunction" during the Super Bowl pre-game entertainment program by various consumer groups caused the FCC to re-evaluate its stance on nudity and offensive language. You can evaluate this famous fifteen seconds for yourself at *http://www.ifilm.com/ifilmdetail/2533319?htv=12.*

Fines and threats of fines, have led to network self-censorship. Howard Stern's move from broadcast radio to subscription satellite radio was motivated in part by his reaction to FCC fines and his network's attempts to tone down his program.

Electronic game companies started the Entertainment Software Rating Board (ESRB) to head off government regulation of violent or sexually explicit content in games. They modeled the game rating system on the Motion Picture Association of American (MPAA) movie ratings. The Recording Industry Association of America (RIAA) also rates music in a voluntary system.

The American Academy of Pediatricians carefully details information about each of the rating systems and how these ratings should guide parents and others in guiding entertainment choices for children and teens (*http://www.aap.org/family/ratingsgame.htm*). According to the AAP,

> Ratings have become more common because research has shown how much children are influenced by what they see and hear, especially at very young ages. The effects don't seem to go away as the child gets older. One study of 8-year-old boys found that those who watched violent TV programs growing up were most likely to be involved in aggressive, violent behavior by age 18 and serious criminal behavior by age 30.

The current system of regulating the content of mass media is a mixed bag. The ratings for movies, music recordings, electronic games and television programs are currently voluntary, and industry groups control them, not regulators. Violations are under that aegis of retailers and manufacturers that respond to consumer pressure or congressional warnings on their own. The FCC is in charge of regulating what is transmitted over the airwaves; it has jurisdiction over broadcast radio and television and has shown an increased vigilance in catching any network violations of their code of conduct and in assessing large monetary fines for networks that violate the standards.

Music Industry and a Shared Imagination

Music is an elemental part of human life. We make music, we listen to music, and music surrounds us in most commercial settings today. Music is big-business. Here are some facts and figures that demonstrate the importance of the music industry as an influence on our lives.

◆ Record company revenues (trade revenues) reached $1.1 billion in 2005—a threefold increase over 2004 ($380 million).

◆ Digital music (online and mobile) represents approximately 6 percent of overall music sales, but it is increasing.

◆ Mobile music sales (music for cell phones) are not far behind online, with revenues roughly split 60–40 between them.

◆ People downloaded 420 million single tracks in 2005 globally—more than double the number downloaded in 2004 (156 million).

◆ In the U.S., people downloaded 353 million single tracks (up from 143 million) [Nielsen SoundScan].

◆ The number of users of subscription services, such as Rhapsody and Napster, increased from 1.5 to 2.8 million globally in 2005.

◆ Online song catalogues doubled to over 2 million tracks on the major services.

◆ Globally there are now over 335 legitimate online services, up from 230 in 2004 and from 50 two years ago.

◆ Mobile sales in Japan totaled $211 million, or 96 percent of digital sales in the market, in the first nine months of 2005. Single track downloads reached 4.3 million during the period.

◆ Mobile phone subscriptions reached 1.5 billion in 2005—a 50 percent increase on 2002.

◆ Satellite radio subscriptions reached over 9 million in the U.S. alone—three times as many as the number of global subscription services users. Over 475 million people globally receive Digital Audio Broadcast services (DAB).

◆ The estimated number of infringing (illegal) music files available on the Internet at any one time is 885 million. By contrast, broadband uptake rose by 26 percent in the past year. Total infringing music files are down 20 percent on the 1.1 billion peak in April 2003 according to Dave Pelland's estimates for KPMG Technology Insider.

The recording industry has a long history, and from its beginnings tension has existed between the creative "content producers," the musicians and composers and that part of the industry that recorded, packaged and marketed recorded music. The first commercial music recordings are wax cylinders that feature Edison's name and company logo, not artist information.

Thomas A. Edison (1847–1931) one of America's most prolific inventors, is famous for the light bulb, but at the beginning of the twentieth century, he was better known for the phonograph wind-up "record player." It actually played music recorded on wax cylinders. Edison would go camping with a group of men that included Henry Ford (inventor of the Ford automobile) and Harvey Firestone, Luther Burbank the naturalist and occasionally President Warren Harding. They once went roughing it on a vacation to the rural south where Ford expected recognition because his Model T had taken America by storm. But in poor rural America where roads were few and cars beyond the means of most people, no one knew Ford, but everyone recognized Edison for his phonograph.

In this time before radio, publishers sometimes "re-enacted" major news stories and recorded them on wax cylinders to give the audience a sense of faraway events. The San Francisco earthquake of 1906 is one of these, and you can listen to and see what wax cylinders look like (*http://www.npr.org/templates/*

story/story.php?storyId=5352622). Initially used for emergency and voice communications, such as from ship to shore, David Sarnoff's idea of the radio as an entertainment device that every house in America would have was a visionary one that came true. Sarnoff wrote that

> . . . a radio telephone transmitter having a range of, say, 25 to 50 miles can be installed at a fixed point where the instrumental or voice music or both are produced . . . The receiver can be designed in the form of a simple "Radio Music Box" and arranged for several different wavelengths, which should be changeable with the throwing of a single switch or pressing of a single button.

Radio Corporation of America (RCA) was founded in 1919, and radio as an entertainment device exploded during the 1920s and '30s. By 1938, 82 percent of American homes had a radio, and by 1950 it was 91 percent. The mix of music and news was usually about 80–20, though news programming increased during wartime. During the 1930s and '40s, music on the radio was the major form of popular entertainment, and radio was the first of the mass media.

Musicians, not singers, dominated broadcasts in the early days of recorded music because the early microphones couldn't capture the nuances of singing and the human voice with enough fidelity for the radio. With demand for music on the rise from radio stations, inventors were tinkering with every aspect of the recording process. As the quality of recordings improved, radio programming used pre-recorded music more and more.

The American Society of Composers Authors and Song-Writers (ASCAP) organized in 1914. ASCAP licenses and collects royalties and fees for musicians and composers on sales and live performances of their works. By the 1940s, recordings had become the biggest segment of the money collected by ASCAP. The radio stations argued that they shouldn't have to pay for playing pre-recorded music because it was free advertising and would generate larger sales and thus benefit musicians and composers.

As the head of the American Federation of Musicians (AFM), James Petrillo began to work with ASCAP to make sure the stations would have to pay for radio play. He led two musician strikes that kept the airwaves quiet for several years in the mid 1940s. The matter went to court.

When the courts finally ruled that radio stations must pay a licensing feel for playing records on the air, a system of paying fees for playing recorded music on the radio became instituted.

It is interesting to note that "webcasting" or Internet radio faced a similar situation. The Register of Copyrights for the government set up a Copyright Arbitration Royalty Panel (CARP) that made recommendations to the Librarian of Congress who has the ultimate responsibility to set the rate for webcasting and what are called ephemeral recordings. The Librarian of Congress set the per play song fee at 7 cents. The government posts the rates at *http://www.copyright.gov/carp/webcasting_rates_final.html.* The musicians went on strike for several years, but eventually they got the recording companies and radio networks to agree to their terms. Dr Billy Taylor, noted musician and music scholar, observed that

> After the strike, all of the instrumental musicians were taken off the radio. We were on the radio, and everywhere you went they had radio orchestra music and people danced to it. All of a sudden, about a year [later] or maybe a little longer, that was cut off. [Instrumentalists], as artists, never returned. From that point on, the dominant artists were vocalists and it's been that way ever since, for all these years.

Behind the shift from live musicians to recorded music and the rise of the vocalist as the dominant musical artist lay more than strikes and labor issues. Recording technology in the form of better and better microphones and better shellac for the surface of records was changing the way records sounded. The need for live musicians on radio decreased as recordings sounded more "live."

Today, the occasional live musician heard on the radio is a notable special programming feature. As the 78 RPM recording replaced the wax cylinder, the 45 RPM replaced the 78 RPM recording. In the 1960s and '70s, the LP began to replace 45s. These changes were obvious to consumers because each new song or album was another purchase. On the home front, this also required listeners to upgrade the "hardware" used to play the recordings. "Victrolas"

gave way to turntables. At the height of the 45, turntables that could stack several records and play them sequentially were the mode. As the LP album gained popularity, record players featured dual speeds to play 45 or 33 RPM records.

More hardware changes resulted from the introduction of stereo sound in the early 1960s. With the introduction of concept albums and expensive turntables with stereo speakers, audiophiles shifted away from listening to music on the radio, at least on AM radio, because the sound wasn't as good.

In the golden years of analog recording, from the '60s to the '80s, the format of audio transformed quickly from records to audio tape. Except for collectors, cassette tape made obsolete the high-end reel to reel decks audiophiles sought in the '50s and '60s. Cassette tape, with less audio quality but better marketing of its hardware (players) and tapes, won the battle for the consumer dollar over the eight-track tape and its hardware. Yet by 1988, CD sales surpassed LP sales for the first time in history.

Technology disrupted the music recording establishment when digital recording let the music genie out of the bottle, freeing "content" from "medium" more profoundly than ever before, but not for the first time. The Sony Walkman, introduced in 1979, rocked the world of music recording. In 1984, Sony's Portable CD player sent another technological tremor through an industry that wasn't sure where its future lay. With the introduction of the MP3, the memory-saving and quality-providing digital format in 1997, and Napster's first incarnation in 1999, there was a revolution in music and recording, whether the music business knew it or not.

With the first iPod shipment from Apple in 2001, it seemed that music producers and record companies were finally aware that business wouldn't be usual anymore.

Rapid and incessant change creates what Marshall McLuhan described as "disruptive technology." Today the music industry is unsettled because there are challenges on several fronts to its long-time economic models. There are more ways for people to listen to music than ever before. There are new ways for artists to connect with audiences that cut out traditional roles played by the big recording companies. Corporate consolidation means that defense contractors might own recording companies.

People no longer evaluate artists and the creative work they produce on the basis of musical content, but it is just another "widget" to corporate accountants and stockholders.

Economies of scale in this business environment favor a single artist who sells millions of records and does product endorsements. A corporation can feature that artist on the cover of a magazine it owns. It also owns the recording company at the expense of the quirky but brilliant artist/performer who can sell thousands of records and whose music will influence the culture. To learn about the business, you can watch "Money for Nothing" on the Website.

Muzak: It's Not Your Father's Elevator Music Anymore

Technology makes it possible to tailor and deliver an unending stream of popular music to almost any environment. Technology is putting the listener in control in ways that were not possible in an analog age. Movies aren't just for watching anymore. Music isn't just for listening; the entertainment giants are looking for synergy between the content in various mediums in ways that an age of analog sound would have found impossible to pursue.

Think for a moment how most commercial spaces—stores, shopping malls, elevators, doctor's and dentist's offices—provide occupants with a soundtrack. Business has re-imagined the ubiquitous music environment formerly known as "elevator music" for today's consumer society as an "acoustic pheromone" designed to attract or repel shoppers according to their psychographic profiles. In *The Soundtrack of Your Life* author David Owen describes how Muzak, the nondescript elevator music of the 1950s, has moved into the "realm of retail theater."

Muzak sells about eighty pre-packaged programs and designs customized as part of its global business. The company has created a digital music inventory they call the "Well." In the Well are millions of commercially recorded songs classified by genre and even subgenre—jazz, shag, heavy metal and more.

Today's Muzak is an expression of "brand," and it hires program designers that attempt to identify the psychological associations that songs have and then to connect the songs into an aural tapestry that appeals to the emotions of a shopper. The idea is to create an emotional soundtrack for a bar or a retail store that affects a customer like an "aural pheromone." The sounds should attract some customers while repelling others in order to reinforce their emotional impact.

The program designers, called audio architects, alter the rhythms and song connections to get different moods going at different times of the day. The soundtrack gets louder and pushier around closing time. There is different music for after hours when the customers are gone.

Because music makes emotional connections with us, the audio architectures that Muzak creates are powerful and compelling whether we are conscious of it or not. Their biggest competitor, according to their marketing department, is silence.

Digital formats mean information is information, and how the producers serve it up to us is more fluid than it previously was. We listeners, we content users, are gaining control over the "how and when" of our entertainment experiences, and the entertainment producers are slow to cede this control.

Motion Picture Industry: From Pictures to Pixels

The film industry is subject to a tsunami of changes in how it creates, produces, markets and distributes its creative content. The very name, "film industry" may soon become a charming artifact. The industry shoots movies with DV cams (Spike Lee's *Bamboozled*) or HD cams (George Lucas' *Star Wars Episode II: Attack of the Clones*).

New blockbusters are available on DVD and for download the same day they open in theaters (Steven Soderberg's *Bubble*). Change is the new norm in the film or movie industry.

In the early days of motion pictures, studios and movie theaters operated independently. As the industry matured, the studios moved to acquire control beyond the ownership of the talent, production facilities and titles. They began to buy up movie theaters, from small town shows to the grand movie palaces. We call this "vertical integration" because one company controls a product from its inception to its final form.

Vertical integration enables a movie studio to set prices and policies from top to bottom. Independents at any level—actors to directors, writers, producers and theater owners—become dependent on the large consolidated studios for work and to get their work out to audiences.

From its beginnings, Hollywood movie production moved toward consolidation. By the 1930s, Warner Bros., Paramount, 20th Century Fox, Loew's (MGM) and RKO (Radio-Keith-Orpheum) were the major players and had achieved vertical integration. Along with "The Little Three"—Universal, Columbia and United Artists—studios that made pictures but that lacked one of the crucial elements of vertical integration, these companies operated as a mature oligopoly. Eight companies essentially controlled the entire market.

When their pictures came out, the studios exploited their vertical integration to force independent theaters to do "block booking" where they paired popular pictures with "B" list films that the independents had to accept and screen, often sight unseen, as part of the deal.

In 1948, independent movie producers and exhibitors challenged the monopolistic behavior of the major studios, and that year's federal decree of *United States v. Paramount* ordered the studios to divest themselves of their theaters.

The studios complied, and this opened up the market. However, the rise of the post-war boom in television beginning in 1950 further disrupted the economic model that had prevailed in the movie industry from the 1930s.

Hollywood's Golden Age, when those eight companies had control of 95 percent of all film rentals and close to 70 percent of all box-office receipts, came to an end.

There are parallels between that time and today. Hollywood and the movies suffered through a dire time when many predicted an end to movies in the face of the "new media" of that time—broadcast television.

It is ironic that the "Big Three" television corporations, ABC, CBS and NBC, established near-monopolistic control of television broadcasting only to face similar challenges to their hegemony with the rise of cable television and the expansion of the number of channels available for programming.

While the current rapid growth of video on demand and the availability of television content on various kinds of digital playback devices such as cell phones and iPods are still unsettled and in search of economically viable business models, the situation is transforming the television industry further.

The movie industry perceives this move to "unbundle" content from any particular method of delivery as a threat. The motion picture industry lobbies Congress to "dumb down" playback devices and to add "flags" and other copy-protection to some forms of content in an attempt to shore up analog business models in a digital world.

Meanwhile technology marches forward on other fronts for the movie industry. New digital formats designed for theater use can make the viewing experience more real just as HDTV is doing in living rooms everywhere. Refitting theaters with new projectors and sound systems is costly. The theater owners must find a price point where audiences will pay more for a better viewing experience in order to make the transition to digital projection systems work.

The Bureau of Labor Statistics noted in 2006 that:

> Most motion pictures are still made on film. However, digital technology and computer-generated imaging are rapidly making inroads and are expected to transform the industry.
>
> Digital technology also makes it possible to distribute movies to theaters through the use of satellites or fiber-optic cable, although relatively few theaters are capable of receiving them in that manner right now. In the future, however, more theaters will be capable of receiving films digitally, thus sharply reducing the costly process of producing and distributing bulky film.

This matter of fact observation is causing major concern throughout the movie business. The move to digital production and projection means new methods of making pictures. Digital moviemaking will replace old jobs with new ones. The entire industry needs to retool its equipment across production, distribution and presentation in the transition to digital.

Disney, Fox, MGM, Paramount, Sony Pictures Entertainment, Universal and Warner Bros. Studios created Digital Cinema Initiatives in March 2002 to ". . . establish and document voluntary specifications for an open architecture for digital cinema that ensures a uniform and high level of technical performance, reliability and quality control . . . and to help spur deployment of digital cinema systems in movie theaters."

Theater owners fear the expense of the changeover. Audiences anticipate better images, but they may resist higher box office prices. The Digital Cinema Report follows the digital cinema scene from the perspective of theater owners (*http://www.digitalcinemareport.com/*).

Actors fear that animations or digital versions of themselves could replace them. Will they receive fair compensation for their work in a movie that plays on the big screen, the television screen and on little screens of iPod or mobiles? The Screen Actors Guild (SAG) has spoken out about this. On February 27, 2006 SAG president Alan Rosenberg accused ABC of selling *Lost* and *Desperate Housewives* for digital download to iPods without first bargaining with the Screen Actors Guild. ABC intends to pay residuals to performers based on the videocassette formula, which SAG doesn't believe is fair. SAG is going to take action to challenge ABC's decision.

Directors have to adapt their vision to the new medium. In the analog world, television and motion pictures were different media, and each had its own aesthetic. From crew to cast to director and writers, working in the movies was similar but quite distinctive from working in television. When "filming" a production or live event happens digitally, what is left to distinguish a motion picture from a television show or even from a news package? The resulting "product" is a set of moving images recorded, edited and packaged in a digital medium. Is it a film when not captured on filmstock? Is it television if it's a movie that one can play back equally well in a theater, on a television set or on a computer screen?

The seemingly straightforward move from one medium, like film or videotape, to another, like digital video, is unintentionally disruptive to the status quo. Technology itself might be neutral and devoid of value judgments, but its use and implementation become human choices that involve values and invoke judgment calls.

It is an open question what kind of compensation content producers will receive when audiences view a work simultaneously on many platforms in a world where they have more control over the where and when of viewing. However, we can look at how the music recording and radio industries worked out similar issues at the height of analog recording.

In an era when prerecorded music was becoming a staple on radio, musicians and composers, as well as the radio stations and networks, faced fundamental changes in how things were done. This gave rise to disputes about fees and residuals. In 1914, "Tin Pan Alley" songwriters joined up with ASCAP (American Society of Composers and Publishers), whose function it was to set up and then collect a royalty each time a licensed song was played.

Initially, most of the revenue ASCAP collected came from the sale of sheet music, variety shows, dance band programs and the like that aired on radio. With the introduction of prerecorded music, this became the biggest slice of ASCAP's revenues and thus that of musicians and composers.

Photography as a Communication Channel

We live in an increasingly visual culture. If this weren't the case, then MP3 players that brought us music would be enough. But in the early part of the twenty-first century, video looks like one of the "killer apps" that drives businesses and consumers into a spending frenzy.

Images are basic in a visual culture. The modern "picture press," began in 1842 with the *Illustrated London News* and took a form we recognize as modern after World War I. Public interest in stories told with pictures, the brief rise of a free press in Germany after the War and technology in the form of small, light, easy-to-use cameras gave rise to more photos in print.

World War II was the impetus that drove many European photographers and photo editors to

America. They gathered in New York City where Henry Luce ran the publishing empire that included *Life*, a showcase for photographers from advertising and journalism. The picture story captured the American imagination at the same time that it helped form America's idea of itself and enabled it to present its face to the world. Many classic photos and *Life* covers are viewable at *http://www.life.com/Life/lifephotos.html*.

Many modern photographers who produced photographs we regard as art, such as Margaret Bourke-White (*http://xroads.virginia.edu/~CLASS/am485_98/coe/maggie.html*) and Edward Steichen, produced journalistic and advertising images with equal ease. You can view Steichen's photographs of the Pacific in the Second World War at *http://www.airandspacemagazine.com/ASM/Mag/Supp/FM06/srpg.html*.

In the 1930s, these photographers as well as film-makers and writers began to work in a style called "documentary." This spare, strong and sharply focused work looked with a critical eye on social issues like poverty and injustice. Writer and critic Walter Benjamin made the distinction between an art photo without a news caption and "responsible image making." The art photo can transform poverty or pain into something beautiful to behold, but the photojournalistic image uses words to anchor the photo's meaning as a commentary on the world.

In the pre-television era after World War II, people read pictorial magazines eagerly, and they flourished in major cities around the world as well as in America. The stories in these magazines became the narratives that helped to create national consciousness in war-wracked nations.

The popularity and growth in the number of magazines that featured photo stories made it easy for successful photographers to become freelancers and to leave their jobs at publishing houses. The independence of freelancers from strict editorial directives led to an era of creative, individualistic work.

During the '50s and '60s one of the most influential mass media were photographic images in narrative stories and in advertising were. The gradual ascendance of television, also a visual medium, and especially the Vietnam War, began to draw viewers from print to the television screen.

The large national magazines like *Look* and *Life* couldn't compete with the six o'clock news and the visceral imagery of the ongoing casualties and process of the war. Color television became ubiquitous and hungry for images that moved viewers.

The modern influential image-makers began to work in television and the movies. The montage replaced the large format photo-magazine as the place making images as art and responsible images, and theaters and TV sets became the media through which images connected with audiences. The meteoric rise of MTV, which is a twenty-four-hour smorgasbord of images in frenetic movement, is another indicator of the increasingly visual orientation of our mass media and of ourselves.

The popularity of television news over print news and television entertainment series surrounds us in images that speak to our eyes and engage our emotions if not our conscious thought. This ranges from the popular but transient "reality shows" to critically recognized series like *The Sopranos* and *Deadwood*, as well as to big-screen productions like *Moulin Rouge*, the *Star Wars* epics and *Brokeback Mountain*.

Live Performance: From Theater to Touring

Theater is entwined with American history. The information that theater producers present to consumers tells us much about the values and interests of the people at each stage of the nation's development.

Like any mass medium, live theater entertains, educates and mirrors society. Theater as business evolves in response to its audience. It adjusts to changing conditions that influence the balance between all mass media and how people decide to allocate their attention as well as their dollars.

Theater in America was star-driven when it began. Theater companies had their own playhouses in cities across America. They developed a set of plays, a repertory, to showcase their stars. As conditions shifted economically and in reaction to the rise of other mass media, such as silent and then talking films and later, radio, live theater production altered too.

A collaborative system arose where a producer and a director assembled a team including writers, actors and stage designers to produce a play that would have a long run. These productions were typically large-scale. They often began on Broadway and then moved out of New York to other cities and regional theaters.

By the 1960s the heyday of Broadway was over. Playwrights from Chicago, Los Angeles and other cities were writing plays produced outside New York. August Wilson, David Huang, Wendy Wasserstein, Des McAnuff, David Mamet, Tony Kushner and Peter Sellars are typical of these modern authors. For them, New York is an important place to show off their work, but it isn't the ultimate destination. Theater is alive and well in America these days, though there are fewer theaters and performances going on today than there were in the 1900s. At that time, there were fewer other media to compete with live theater for an audience.

Today Broadway features often develop from books or movies that were bestsellers or blockbusters. A success on Broadway frequently translates into plans for a movie version for popular plays and musicals.

Large media corporations look for what they call "synergy" in entertainment properties. In the 1980s, businesses began to grow by combining with other diverse businesses into "conglomerates." A single corporate entity would consist of many smaller businesses that did not all specialize in the same commercial enterprise.

If a corporation can purchase the rights to a good story in the form of a book that it can then adapt for screen and stage and also make it into a show or a ride at a theme park plus spawn an electronic game and drive the market for retail merchandise like dolls, toys, costumes and such—that's synergy. The synergy builds additional profit opportunities for large corporations from a single entertainment property. It isn't risky to build on a sure thing the way it is to take a chance on a new artist or a property or a piece of controversial art.

Disney's *Lion King, Beauty and the Beast* and *Mulan* are examples of this type of corporate undertaking. The entertainment "products" include books, coloring books, videos, animated films, lavish traveling musicals, shows at ice-arenas and features at theme parks.

Since the 1970s, performing arts production has changed with the introduction of computer-controlled lighting and stages. One technician with a computer console can do the work a team of stagehands used to do. "Vari-lites" let one person control lighting effects and projected scenery, replacing a crew. The expense of the technology becomes a tradeoff when stage work requires fewer people hired.

The AIDs epidemic that surfaced in the U.S. in the 1980s swept through the performing arts community and led to the premature deaths of many theatrical luminaries. The themes of modern productions have reflected its impact. One example is *Angels in America* by Tony Kushner, presented on Broadway and in major theaters across America, which has a version broadcast on television and that is available on DVD.

New Mass Media Entertainment: Can We Have Your Attention, Please

Theme parks, sports and electronic games represent new kinds of mass media that have been attracting growing audiences and experiencing revenue growth since the 1970s.

The Disney theme parks are an important part of the corporate focus on synergy and for creating demand for entertainment products inside and outside the gates of the theme park. Other popular theme parks include Kraken, Knott's Berry Farm, Legoland, the various Six Flags sites, and Paramount's Kings Point. The Website, Theme Park Insider *http://www. themeparkinsider.com/*, lists parks ranked by attendance. The site provides an award-winning consumers' guide to theme parks in the United States and other nations.

It includes ratings and reviews of the world's best theme and amusement parks and allows readers to post about accidents and other problems at most of the major theme parks in the United States. In 2004, theme park attendance was 328 million. Researchers expect it to increase to 358 million in 2009, pushed up in part as "Baby Boomers" become grandparents.

When the Entertainment and Sports Programming Network (ESPN) launched the first all sports cable channel on September 7, 1979 its success was by no means a sure thing. Bill Rasmussen, formerly a semi-pro hockey team's PR man, fought to create the network, using Getty Oil money to get it started. In its early years, ESPN nearly went broke and bust.

A limited budget and no connections to major sports programming forced ESPN to carry rarely watched sporting events in its early years. Unable to afford to carry football, baseball or any of the other major sports, ESPN concentrated its efforts on its news programming. This proved a good decision.

ESPN put its resources into its news show, Sportscenter, and network executives turned college basketball games and the National Football League draft into television events. They used marketing masterfully and built audiences for sports in new ways.

By 1995, ESPN was the first cable network to make it into 70 percent of homes. Sports programming continues to be popular, and in 2006 ESPN reached more than 80 million homes or 78 percent of American homes with television

ESPN features more than sixty-five sports. Its properties include ESPN, ESPN2, ESPN Classic Sports, ESPNews and ESPN The Magazine. ESPN Original Entertainment has developed the sports game show, ESPN's *2-Minute Drill* and the documentary *The Season* and continues to create new sports-based programming.

Old Media Are Finding New Uses in New Media

Global spending on entertainment media dipped in 2000 after the dotcom boom but has steadied and is expected to reach $690 billion by 2009. Demand for digital distribution of music, books, films and video games is increasing.

The availability of high speed broadband is a "major catalyst" behind this trend according to industry analysts. Threats to growth in entertainment industries lurk in rising interest rates and skyrocketing energy costs. The demand for this kind of entertainment is increasing in developing countries, especially in China. This will continue to push overall spending on these media upward.

Video games, online film rentals, digital distribution of music, music for mobile devices, e-books, video on demand and satellite (subscription) radio accounted for about $160 million in 2000. By 2004 this had risen to $11.4 billion.

As demand for the electronic forms of media grows, sales of physical media continue to fall. Physical music (CDs), home video rentals and PC games are examples of content that one can deliver as physical or electronic media, and consumers favor electronic delivery.

In the 1970s and '80s, arcade games like "Pac-Man" and "Pong" by Atari were popular in bars and restaurants. In 1972 Magnavox introduced the Odyssey game console that connected to a television set and played "Pong." The Odyssey system came with "Pong," but the player could remove its program cards, similar to such modern game systems as X-box.

The system was primitive by today's standards, but over 80,000 of them sold in 1972. Another 250,000+ Odyssey machines sold between 1973 and late 1975, bringing the total to 350,000+ Odyssey sales. Stores removed the system in fall 1975 and replaced it with a new, simpler model: the Odyssey 100.

As simple as it was, the Odyssey set the stage for increasingly sophisticated game boxes and online games like the massively multi-player "World of Warcraft."

In 2005, video games brought in a record $10.5 billion in sales of hardware, software and accessories. Electronic games played on "game boxes" initially connected to video outputs and stayed limited to players who were together in time and space. "Mario Bros," "Pong," "Donkey Kong" and games of this generation had colorful animations and catchy background music loops. Players took turns competing against characters in the game.

Multiple player games developed so that several players could compete against each other and against the game. Before the World Wide Web and broadband, there were a variety of games that let players compete with each other online. The history of these games goes back to the time before the World Wide Web when players played text-based games like

"Zork" and "StarTrek" via CRTs, using mainframe computers. Wikipedia has an interesting detailed history of massively multiplayer online role-playing games or MMORPG that allows readers to update the information there by adding details (*http://en.wikipedia.org/wiki/MMORPG*).

"EverQuest" was introduced in 1991, and it was the most commercially successful MMORPG in the United States for five years. Before concerns about social life in MySpace ever arose, EverQuest was the subject of articles in *Time* and other mainstream magazines, which explored what virtual social life was like and looked at online addiction and other questions inspired by its popularity. In the '90s, the major MMORPG games were "Ultima Online," "EverQuest" and "Asheron's Call."

In these games, players take on roles and find themselves in a perpetual world maintained on servers supplied by the game company. Other characters are a mix of those controlled by other humans and characters generated within the game.

While playing, players may step out of character and chat or engage with each other in character. The commercial games charge a fee for time spent in the game world, often charging by the month.

The number of these games has expanded since the 1990s, and many of them now have fan Websites that provide information about the games, fan art, discussion forums and even video and audio "mash-ups" where fans use images from screengrabs and audio from the games to create their own videos and MP3s.

U.S. consumer spending on online games jumped about 20 percent from $73 million in 2003 to $88.8 million in 2004, and it was $54.4 million for the first half of 2005. The Online Publishing Association predicts spending for online games will continue to climb higher.

Some games allow players to create "mods" or modifications to the game code so that they can extend the game world. The game designers do not create mods; the public does. With mods, players can create new items like weapons, characters, enemies, models, modes and textures. Some games let players add levels and storylines to games. By allowing and even encouraging "modders," the game company fosters a sense of community among players. The mods are a sort of virtual investment on the part of players that probably encourages them to keep playing the game.

At the base of these games are quests, monsters, treasures, levels and "experience points." Gaining in-game experience lets a player's "avatar" (character) grow or change. There are economies in the games so players can trade items and currency. In many games players join clans or guild organizations, and these also build a sense of community.

Some of the games have developed economies in the real world where expert players sell game loot or points for real money on e-Bay. There are instances of seeming addiction to the games, and there was one man in South Korea who collapsed and died after allegedly playing for many hours without eating, drinking or resting. Employers have fired employees caught playing at work.

The attraction of these worlds is based on their interactivity and the way they evolve into social communities. With each improvement in computer graphics or broadband speed, the games become more entertaining and sophisticated.

Laurie Karpman, now a composer for Sony Online, wrote the score for "EverQuest" and sums up the current online gaming situation like this: "Middle-aged women will be playing (ABC's) *All My Children* games. You'll play, 'I'm Conducting the Berlin Philharmonic' games or 'I'm Laurence Olivier in *Hamlet*' games. We're still doing fancy *Lord of the Rings*-type games or first-person shooters, but that's only the beginning. It's going to move into all kinds of things." You can read more on the Website (see article at the end of this chapter.)

While the pleasures and problems of MMORPGs and virtual entertainments are digital and different than traditional entertainments that occur face to face in the real world, such as sporting events, concerts, plays or casinos, they appear no better or worse than traditional entertainments.

And the Future Will Bring . . .

Studies of people in their teens indicate that they are heavy users of all media, which is not surprising, but the degree to which they multitask, that is watch television while they type a paper on their computer and instant message with friends, represents something new in mass media. Media professionals who must connect with people to get their message across, whether news, entertainment or advertising, say we are in an "attention economy."

The message doesn't just need to get into the media; it has to break through a barrage of media to capture someone's attention. When individuals had fewer choices in mass media, media producers were the information gatekeepers who controlled what the viewers or listeners could tune into and when. Those times are gone.

Analog technologies that made it difficult to combine content from different media are easier to work around and are being replaced in a world of digital information. The public audience is no longer a bunch of passive consumers. They are media makers, the editors and program directors in the "We Media" or "Me Media" environment today.

What lies ahead for mass media entertainment? More choices, more user control, more competition for attention and more fun as the existing businesses and industries adapt to our digital century or go the way of the kinescope.

PUBLIC RELATIONS

Raul Reis

Chapter Objectives:

◆ Trace the development of the public relations industry, from inception to present day.

◆ Discuss the contributions of pioneering figures in the field of public relations, including P.T. Barnum, Ivy Lee, and Edward Bernays.

◆ Identify the four PR models, and outline their major elements.

◆ Discuss the components involved in implementing a PR plan.

◆ Identify and discuss the varied roles and functions of public relations in the contemporary global marketplace.

◆ Understand the skills necessary for professionals to succeed in the public relations industry.

Introduction

In 2000, Turkcell, one of the three main mobile phone providers in Turkey, learned from a customer survey that its subscribers wanted to see the company more involved in the community, particularly when it came to supporting educational projects. As a result, the company joined nonprofit organizations in launching a campaign, "Contemporary Girls of Contemporary Turkey," that aimed to increase educational opportunities for Turkish girls, especially in impoverished rural areas.

As part of this ongoing public relations campaign, scholarships were offered in the first year to 5,000 girls in 28 rural areas. Because of the campaign's dramatic success, those numbers were increased in successive years, reaching 35 areas and benefiting thousands of girls who would have not been otherwise able to attend primary and secondary schools.

For Turkcell, the campaign changed people's general views of the company, earned them three major social responsibility awards in the program's first three years, and generated not only positive publicity, but also popular support and goodwill toward the organization.[1] In 2007, the program won the prestigious Golden World Award from the Institute of Public Relations.[2] This campaign provides an excellent example of how companies are using **public relations**—that is, the business of bringing about public understanding and goodwill toward a person or organization—to improve their image and build a more positive relationship with consumers.

Early Public Relations: A Historical Overview

THE ORIGINS OF PUBLIC RELATIONS

While the term public relations probably is barely over a century old, one finds ample instances of such activity among the ancients. Aristotle's *Rhetoric*, for example, is considered by some to be one of the earliest volumes on public relations. In this work, the ancient Greek defined rhetoric as the "art of oratory, especially persuasive use of language to influence the thoughts and actions of listeners"— a primary concern in any public relations campaign, past or present. Moreover, the authors of the first major public relations textbook indicate that "Caesar carefully prepared the Romans for his crossing of the Rubicon in 49 B.C. by sending reports to Rome on his epic achievements as governor of Gaul.[3] Others suggest that the gospels (*gospel* means "good news") were written "more to propagate the faith than to provide a historical account of Jesus' life."[4]

The groundwork for much of modern public relations thought can likewise be traced to the American colonial era. Founding fathers, including Benjamin Franklin, Thomas Jefferson, and John Adams, used propaganda techniques familiar to today's public relations practitioners. Samuel Adams spelled them out:

◆ Formation of an activist organization

◆ Using many media

◆ Creating events and slogans

◆ Orchestrating conflict

◆ Sustaining an information campaign over time until the minds of the public were won over to the cause.[5]

Although conceived of during the eighteenth century, these public relations tenets remain relevant today, particularly within the political arena.

FROM PRESS AGENTRY TO PUBLIC POLICY

Politics remained an integral venue for the development of public relations throughout the 1800s. Andrew Jackson, the first "common man" to assume the presidency (from 1829–1837), felt more responsible to the masses than had previous presidents. Distrustful of those who traditionally held power, he surrounded himself with a "kitchen cabinet" of advisors more in tune with his populist views. Among his confidants was Amos Kendall, a former newspaper editor who took on many of the duties now associated with the White House press secretary.

Kendall's approach was that of a press agent— catering to the needs of the press. He wrote speeches for Jackson to deliver, conducted straw polls on public opinion, and built Jackson's image as an honest and resourceful president. By shaping the way Jackson was represented in the press through words, action, and the strategic release of information, Kendall became a model for public relations practitioners to follow for years to come.[6]

P.T. Barnum can be credited with translating the nascent public relations industry, and its reliance on press agentry, into the world of entertainment. Barnum not only catered to the press, but in fact courted them with bold, sensational stunts and spectacles meant to capture the world's attention. And he became, indeed, a master of publicity: exhibitions at his American Museum, ranging from the "mermaid woman" to Siamese twins to "General Tom Thumb," a man only 25 inches tall, sold millions of tickets.[7] And he is perhaps best known for proclaiming his eponymous circus to be "the greatest show on earth."

By the beginning of the twentieth century, the term public relations had come into use. It generally was interpreted to mean the way business explained itself to the people and attempted to convince them that it was working for their general welfare. American Telephone & Telegraph Company (AT&T) president Theodore Vail gave the term legitimacy when he directed that the company's 1908 annual report be titled "Public Relations." The publication focused on the firm's responsibility to make a fair profit, to treat its employees well, and to answer any questions that could reduce conflicts between itself and its publics.[8]

IVY LEE: INFORMING THE PUBLIC

As the twentieth century began, American business was under attack as a force that dominated society and trammeled individuals. Magazine muckrakers took industry to task for dehumanizing the workplace and putting worker comfort and safety second to profits. As a result, unions organized and legislators began to enact laws to limit business practices. A former New York newspaper business reporter, Ivy Ledbetter Lee, saw the need for industry to do a better job explaining itself to society. Lee's message to business was: "Let the public be informed!"

Business had always tended toward secrecy, but Lee advised business leaders that openness could help win the support of distrustful publics, including legislators. Lee opened one of the first publicity agencies specializing in providing information about business to the media. Lee centered his agency's services around his Declaration of Principles, which spelled out how his firm intended to give editors accurate, complete information and to answer inquiries from the press as swiftly as possible.[9]

One of Lee's greatest PR successes occurred within the coal industry. Lee provided news on behalf of the coal operators to counter information supplied by local labor unions. He convinced John D. Rockefeller to visit the family's mines in Colorado to offset criticism in a labor dispute. Eventually he was able to change the senior Rockefeller's image of detached aloofness to one of a charitable and concerned leader of business.

EDWARD BERNAYS: SHAPER OF THE PROFESSION

While Ivy Lee is considered a pioneer in the PR field, the name Edward L. Bernays is synonymous with the shaping of public relations as we know it today. More than any other work, his *Crystallizing Public Opinion*, published in 1923, ushered in the era of scientific persuasion within the public relations realm. Scientific persuasion effectively replaced Ivy Lee's construct of public relations as the simple dissemination of information, which had previously supplanted press agentry—the hype and hoopla associated with P. T. Barnum.

Born in Vienna and a nephew of Freud, Bernays once was a press agent—the person who contacts the media to promote theatrical events—for the great tenor Enrico Caruso. A journalist by training, he was called to serve on the American government's Creel Committee for Public Information during World War I, which gave him a better understanding of the workings of **propaganda**—information deliberately spread to help or hurt the reputation of an individual, organization, or country.

His second book, *Propaganda*, published in 1928, was based on the concept that "the conscious and intelligent manipulation of the organized habits and opinions of the masses is an important element in democratic society. Those who manipulate this unseen mechanism of society constitute an invisible government which is the true ruling power of our country."[10]

Bernays coined the phrase "engineering public consent" as a synonym for proactive public relations. He argued that facts and events could be arranged and presented to convince an audience that one course of action was preferable to another. His textbook *Public Relations* was published in 1952, and he continued as a spokesperson and advocate for public relations past his hundredth birthday in 1991.

Bernays, who died in 1995, also coined the phrase "public relations counsel" and suggested that it was a profession, not merely a craft or trade.[11] Unlike press agents and publicists, who care only about getting publicity for their clients, Bernays suggested that the public relations counsel should use the techniques of the social sciences to understand how public opinion is created and thus how public opinions can be swayed through scientific, ethical, and socially responsible techniques.

Modern Public Relations: Models, Concepts, and Program Basics

PR MODELS

As with many subfields of mass communication, it can be helpful to conceptualize public relations in terms of theoretical models. Two leading public relations scholars and theorists, James E. Grunig and Todd Hunt, characterize Edward Bernays as responsible for developing two new models of public relations, which joined two earlier models.[12] P. T. Barnum personified the **press agent/publicity model**, with his shameless promotions based more on fancy than fact. Ivy Lee, in contrast, represented the **public information model**, with his emphasis on one-way (source-receiver, or producer-consumer) dissemination of truthful information.

The writing and practice of Bernays led to the development of what Grunig calls the **two-way asymmetric model**. This model uses formative research—research conducted before beginning an information campaign—to ascertain the attitudes of the target publics. While the flow of information is imbalanced in favor of the producer, feedback from the consumer can and does influence the producer. The two-way model represents a necessary way of conceiving public relations when the actions and behaviors of consumer publics affect the actions and behaviors of producers in the competitive business system.

As Bernays worked with educators and professional leaders, he came to realize that in businesses subject to heavy government regulation, or where the activist consumer has as much influence as the producer, balanced communication is necessary to adapt the organization to the realities of society. Grunig calls this fourth situation the **two-way symmetric model**. Examples might include an energy utility wishing to open a nuclear power plant, or a pharmaceutical company hoping to introduce an experimental drug. Consumer feedback and, ultimately, approval, is critical in such situations in order to ensure success for the business.

With the popularization of the Internet and other media technologies that facilitate the speedy dissemination of information, it is possible to say that consumers and clients have attained a new level of power over all realms—business, politics, and entertainment. Nowadays, it is virtually impossible for most industry sectors to succeed without fully taking into account the opinions, needs, and desires of their target publics. In this sense, the two-way symmetric model has become the most important and widely used public relations model.

Table 12.1 summarizes the characteristics of the four models of public relations. Note that the development of the models follows public relations history over the last century.

Although the two-way symmetric model tends to dominate the field in today's age of information, all four models still coexist. The astute public relations practitioner is the one who knows how to choose the correct one to fit the situation at hand. Your own college or university, for example, might use publicity to sell football tickets, public information to tell about a research project, two-way asymmetric public relations

Table 12.1   THE FOUR MODELS OF PUBLIC RELATIONS

Model	Characteristics
Press agent/publicity	Emphasis on promotion, sensationalism, persuasion and/or manipulation of public, sometimes at the expense of facts
Public Information	Emphasis on one-way dissemination of truthful information
One-way asymmetrical model	Emphasis on formative research to determine wants, needs, and attitudes of target consumers
Two-way symmetrical model	Emphasis on balanced communication between producer and consumer

when dealing with student protesters, and the two-way symmetric model when trying to convince a foundation to fund a major grant.

FACILITATING THE FLOW OF INFORMATION

Preceding chapters have examined the functions of specific news and entertainment media. However, the subject of this chapter, public relations, as well as the topic of Chapter 13, advertising, are not media in themselves. Instead, they may be conceptualized as **media facilitators.** That is, public relations and advertising make the creation and distribution of mass media possible because, directly or indirectly, they underwrite the cost of disseminating information cheaply to large audiences.

Advertisers, as we shall see in the next chapter, provide the cornerstone of financial support by purchasing time or space in the mass media. Public relations, on the other hand, bestows what some have called a "subsidy" because it involves the supply of information, which the media otherwise would have to pay to gather, for free. In fact, without the financial support of public relations and advertising, the forms of media that we consume on a daily basis would be astoundingly expensive—a newspaper might cost a couple of dollars, instead of 25 or 50 cents, and magazines might run $15 each.

In addition to providing financial support, PR has, over the past few decades, transformed from a "behind the scenes" entity to a powerful, highly visible, and influential industry at the forefront of media, culture, and business. In his 1986 book *Goodbye to the Low Profile*, Herb Schmertz, former vice president of public affairs at Mobil Oil, highlighted and described this rapidly changing role of public relations.[13]

Schmertz had once been considered controversial among public relations practitioners because of his willingness to inject his own forceful personality into the debate on oil companies and their policies. For years, it had been assumed that PR people worked quietly behind the scenes, avoiding conflict and perpetuating the fantasy that events happened naturally without the assistance of public relations. As the title of his book suggests, Schmertz believed it was time to reinvent the popular concept of public relations, acknowledging the role of PR in fostering open and full debate on public issues.

While not all PR professionals agree with his assertive techniques, most appreciate that public relations, once considered an apologist and publicist for big business, has become a force for building alliances, influencing discussion of public issues, and facilitating the flow of information between producers and consumers of products, services, and ideas. Public relations clients in today's global marketplace thus need, and demand, sophisticated, multi-faceted PR programs that require and depend on astute research and novel, persuasive devices.

PROGRAM IMPLEMENTATION

The implementation of a modern PR program is a complex operation that varies greatly, depending on the account and client. However, a few components tend to remain consistent across all situations.

Identifying Subpublics. These days, PR professionals realize that modern consumers have effects on the producers that are as important as the effects producers hope to have on consumers. The mass public rarely acts in a unified way. As a result, one key component in implementing a PR program for any organization or purpose is to determine the characteristics and behaviors of the target consumer, or **subpublics.** This is not a totally new concept: magazines and radio, responding to the competition from television, learned to tailor their messages for specialized audiences with specialized information needs and interests.

Some of the subpublics a large organization such as a corporation must identify and plan communication programs for might include:

- Employees

- Consumers of products or services

- Other individuals or organizations providing raw materials or services to the organization

- The surrounding business community and local chambers of commerce

- Stockholders in a company or members of an association

◆ Municipal governments and state and federal regulatory and legislative bodies that can pass laws affecting the organization

◆ Political and activist groups

◆ Professional groups that determine norms and standards for a field

◆ Minorities

◆ Voters

◆ The news media

◆ Trade publications serving a particular industry

Each of these categories of subpublics can be further divided. Employees, for example, would include part-time workers, blue-collar personnel, clerical staff, managers, and supervisors. Catering to the information needs of every group complicates the job of public relations agents in an organization.

At your college or university, for example, the PR staff working for the administration or development office likely divide the alumni subpublic into smaller categories. Alumni subpublics might include:

◆ Wealthy graduates of 50 years ago who might just come forth with a few million dollars if buildings were named for them

◆ Football fanatics whose loyalty depends largely on the win-loss record of this year's team

◆ Parents who are thinking of sending their children to the school from which they graduated

◆ English majors who now head corporations and think the school should offer a degree in business

◆ Engineers who work for industry but return to campus occasionally for refresher courses

◆ Scholars who earned Ph.D. degrees and are now college professors

Each subgroup is potentially helpful and influential, and thus the PR staff likely works hard to carefully target their messages and requests to each one.

For example, a university may develop a dozen different publications catering to these subpublics, rather than relying on a single alumni magazine to satisfy everyone's needs and interests.

Setting Objectives. When implementing a program, PR professional must also set clear goals and objectives. Press agent/publicity and public information specialists are concerned mainly with getting information to consumers. Thus their objectives are relatively simple and obvious: "Fill the stadium on Saturday" or "Let people know about the many uses of our products." In the two-way models, however, objectives are more complex: "Gain compliance with the new recycling laws" or "Help our employees find educational resources that will promote their career advancement."

Whatever the model, public relations people have to set specific objectives—the number of people reached or the number of consumers behaving in a certain manner—and specific time frames and deadlines so that the effects of the public relations program can be measured and demonstrated to management in numerical terms.

Planning the Program. To ensure that they have followed all the steps in implementing a successful public relations program, many professionals follow a plan modeled after John E. Marston's **RACE formula**.[14] The letters stand for research, action, communication, and evaluation. Since evaluation at the end of a program is a kind of research that may lead to modifications or changes in the public relations program, the formula can be seen as a spiral that continually renews the process of analysis, program design, and communication.

Research includes measuring public opinion, analyzing all information currently available to publics, considering options, pretesting messages, assessing the impact of information channels, and making qualitative assessments of ideas that may prove effective. *Action* means laying out the program that will get the message across—planning events and organizing information that will persuade the consumer to accept the views (or product or candidate) put forth by the organization. *Communication* means putting the messages into the channels of information. *Evaluation* means assessing the effect of those messages on the target audience.

The Roles and Functions of Public Relations in Today's Global Marketplace

In today's global marketplace, where communication is lightning fast, new technology is constantly developing, and many organizations aim to reach consumers all over the world, public relations continues to grow in prominence and importance. Moreover, the roles and functions of public relations continue to expand and evolve in response to these changes and challenges. Indeed, public relations today fulfills a variety of functions within a diverse set of contexts. While the following discussion is not exhaustive, it is a useful sampling of some of PR's most important roles.

CRISIS MANAGEMENT

In the last few decades, one of the most important roles PR departments have played in many large organizations has been within the context of crisis management. Developing crisis communication plan comprises one of the most important responsibilities of many PR bodies.

Crisis communication consists of two important phases. The first is called **damage control**. It involves finding out what has happened and how it has negatively affected the public's perception of the organization. The immediate task is to demonstrate that the organization is taking responsibility and has the means of solving the crisis.

The second phase involves moving the organization from the crisis footing to one of **issues management**. While it may not be possible to undo the effects of the crisis or make it go away, it is possible to demonstrate to the public that the organization is working to solve or alleviate the problem through cooperation or negotiation with other organizations.

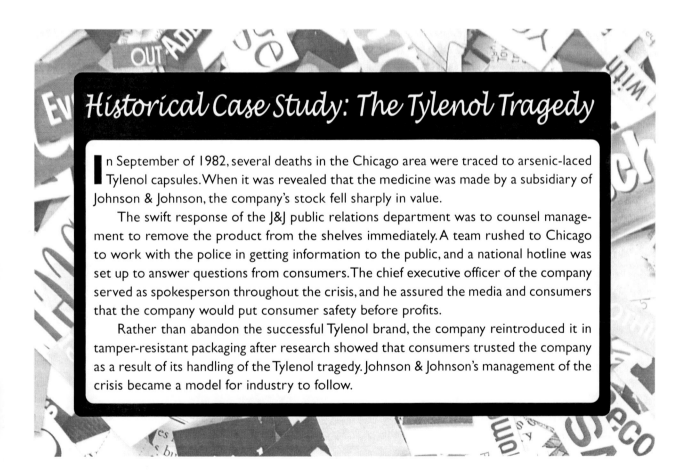

Historical Case Study: The Tylenol Tragedy

In September of 1982, several deaths in the Chicago area were traced to arsenic-laced Tylenol capsules. When it was revealed that the medicine was made by a subsidiary of Johnson & Johnson, the company's stock fell sharply in value.

The swift response of the J&J public relations department was to counsel management to remove the product from the shelves immediately. A team rushed to Chicago to work with the police in getting information to the public, and a national hotline was set up to answer questions from consumers. The chief executive officer of the company served as spokesperson throughout the crisis, and he assured the media and consumers that the company would put consumer safety before profits.

Rather than abandon the successful Tylenol brand, the company reintroduced it in tamper-resistant packaging after research showed that consumers trusted the company as a result of its handling of the Tylenol tragedy. Johnson & Johnson's management of the crisis became a model for industry to follow.

An example is the exposure of a nonprofit charity organization whose executive director has been discovered misappropriating contributions and putting them to personal use. The damage control phase consists of showing that the wrongdoing has been stopped and the wrongdoer has been relieved of duty. The issues management phase consists of a program to reassure contributors that their money is being applied to the charitable programs for which it was intended, and that those programs continue to be worthy of public support.

High profile examples of poor crisis communication— the 1979 Three-Mile Island nuclear power plant accident, for instance, in which the federal government and plant operators took three days to effectively address the public—have set examples for today's corporations on how such crises *should not* be handled. As a result of these historical failures, many corporations nowadays specifically mandate how quickly media requests for information must be met in the event of a crisis, as well as which officer will serve as spokesperson for the company when a catastrophe occurs.

Case Study: A "Green" Oil Company?

British Petroleum (BP), a major oil and chemicals company that operates across six continents to the tune of $277 billion in revenues in 2007, has tried, at least since the mid-1990s, to clean up its image and brand itself as the "environmentally responsible" oil company.[16] Its advertising and public relations campaign, which in the U.S. had adopted slogans such as "bp: beyond petroleum" and "bp: better petroleum," has been largely successful in changing the company's image.

BP's rebranding effort can be traced to the mid-1990s, years before the company's purchase of Amoco, a competing oil giant, and several years before its incorporation of ARCO, another major player. In 1996, BP resigned from and distanced itself from the Global Climate Coalition, a lobbying group that ridiculed the science behind global warming and tried to undermine the Kyoto treaty discussions. The move coincided with the promotion of John Browne as BP's CEO.

In 2000, BP hired Ogilvy & Mather Worldwide, one of the largest global advertising and PR firms, to design and launch the $200 million public relations and advertising campaign responsible for the "bp: beyond petroleum" slogan and the company's new yellow and green sun logo.[17] BP's public relations effort also includes publicizing the company's research into alternative energy sources, as well as its attempts to cut greenhouse gases emission levels in its refineries.

Despite some recent setbacks—in July 2006, BP had to shut off its gigantic Prudhoe Bay oilfield in Alaska, after a corroded and poorly maintained pipeline caused an oil spill in the area; in 2005, an explosion at a Texas BP refinery killed 15 workers—the BP rebranding effort has been mostly successful. In a field where consumers are hard pressed to find "good guys" among many perceived villains, BP has been able to elicit positive reactions from the general public.

In 2007, after many of their toys were discovered to contain dangerous levels of lead paint, Mattel Inc. found itself mired in a serious crisis. In response, CEO Robert A. Eckert issued a direct apology on the company's Web site. The company then enacted a recall, followed by a revised safety plan that required more rigorous inspections for its products.[15] As Mattel demonstrated, effective public relations planning can mitigate a crisis, winning support for an organization by showing its willingness to talk openly about its mistakes. In following, a poor PR response to crisis can result in total loss of public trust and, potentially, loss of business for a company.

CORPORATE REBRANDING

Another important role of public relations within a corporate context involves **rebranding**—that is, implementing initiatives that cause consumers to associate an organization with a new and improved identity. In some instances, rebranding may overlap with or follow crisis management, serving as a means to rehabilitate and change the image of a company marred by scandal or tragedy. In other cases, rebranding may represent an organization's attempt increase their appeal to consumers, and in turn, their potential profits.

Case Study: Reducing Violence in Central America

Since the late-1990s, public weapons buyback and exchange programs have been successfully implemented in Central and South America in an attempt to reduce societal violence. In countries such as Panama and El Salvador, which pioneered these programs, the campaigns' success can be largely credited to well-executed public relations campaigns set up by local and federal governments, in collaboration with social institutions and private companies.

In the mid-1990s, the United Nations warned that small weapons posed a very significant threat in developing (and developed) countries that had a history of civil unrest. Working with nonprofit organizations such as Rotary International and the Ford Foundation, the U.N. called for a "microdisarmament" that would reduce this threat.

Countries such as Panama and El Salvador were quick to respond to this call and set up comprehensive public relations and education campaigns that called on the general public to give up their guns in return for toys, food, or even cash. The public relations campaigns included public announcements in the mass media; press conferences with the organizers; paid advertisements in newspapers, radio and television; and flyers, among other tactics.

As a result, some areas that implemented the program in Panama registered a drop in violent crime from 5,124 cases to 1,588 cases in one year. In El Salvador, the United Nations observer mission collected more than 10,000 weapons, and the Guns for Goods exchange program collected 9,527 weapons, 3,157 magazines and 120,696 rounds of ammunition over four years.[19]

The demonstration of **corporate social responsibility**, or CSR, is at the heart of many PR rebranding efforts. The Turkcell case study that opened this chapter is just one among many examples of how companies today use PR to revamp their images, benefit society, and augment their bottom lines.

In recent years, the burgeoning Green Movement—an increased concern on sustainability and environmentally-friendly practices—has incited many organizations to emphasize their products or practices as environmentally altruistic. Critics refer to this PR tactic as **greenwashing,** and accuse organizations of exaggerating their environmental contributions or misrepresenting their practices for PR and monetary gain. In some instances—the development of a hybrid locomotive by GE as part

Historical Case Study: Selling Kitchens . . . and Nixon

The American public's opinion of Vice-President Richard Nixon in the 1950s soared when he visited an American exhibition in Moscow. He was shown forcefully lecturing Soviet Premier Nikita Khrushchev about the benefits of the American way of life in front of a model American kitchen. One might suspect that Nixon's staff arranged the event. But it was the public relations man for the kitchenware firm who created the moment spontaneously. "Right this way, right this way!" he shouted at the two leaders as they moved through the exhibit. They moved toward the kitchen, and Nixon made an assertive gesture toward the American hardware. An Associated Press photographer tossed his camera to the public relations man inside the exhibit, who took the famous "Kitchen Debate" photos.[20] The public relations man, William Safire, became President Nixon's speechwriter a decade later, and now is a respected syndicated columnist.

Moreover, crisis management also comes into play frequently in politics. When a scandal emerges surrounding a key political figure, PR people spring into action with plans to contain the damage and move forward as quickly as possible.

PR fulfills a similar role within the entertainment sector. When a major celebrity is involved in a scandal or breaks the law, a publicist usually scrambles to release a statement explaining or apologizing for the behavior. Many celebrities employ a team of public relations professionals who help shape the image of their clients by coordinating interviews and television appearances, orchestrating photo ops, and ensuring that their client's projects receive ample press attention and coverage.

In both politics and entertainment, **spin**—a PR tactic in which a specific point of view of interpretation of an event is presented with the intention of influencing public opinion—often comes into play. Successfully convincing the public to see ideas or actions that they may not understand or agree with in a positive light comprises a key preoccupation of many PR practitioners.

of their Ecomagination initiative, for example—companies do seem to be making valid, and valuable, efforts to improve the environment.[18] Other cases, such as the BP example outlined above, remain more ambiguous. Regardless, greenwashing will surely remain a key issue in the public relations for years to come.

GOVERNMENTS AND GOODWILL

The work of public relations is not limited to the business sector; public relations practitioners are key players at government agencies at the local, state, and federal level alike. Building strong ties with the community through programs and initiatives, keeping citizens informed about government issues, decisions, and services, and encouraging the public to participate in government-sponsored activities are a few of the varied functions of public relations within this realm.

Public relations officers at local and state health departments, for example, might foster goodwill within the community by promoting free health screenings or information sessions. In addition, public information specialists at a given government agency might explain the reasons for controversial policies or decisions to affected citizens. On a national level, PR programs have been implemented by governments in response to a variety of societal issues, from the deterring alcohol and drug use, to preventing forest fires, to reducing violence through weapons buyback programs as mentioned in the case study from Central America.

POLITICS AND ENTERTAINMENT

One need look no further than the 2008 U.S. Presidential election campaigns for evidence that public relations and politics go hand in hand. Interestingly, many of the principles applied to business apply to politics as well, albeit in slightly different ways. Politicians are often "branded" and "rebranded" in the hopes of capturing the public's attention and allegiance—John McCain and Sarah Palin, for example, were "mavericks," while Barack Obama and Joe Biden represented "change." Developing a strong image for politicians is a key concern for PR people within this realm.

Skills and Tactics of the PR Professional

Because of the diversity of the field, today's PR professionals must possess a multitude of skills, employ a variety of tactics, and stay informed about key issues in the field.

RELATIONS WITH THE NEWS MEDIA

The most critical skills for public relations practitioners are those necessary for placing stories in the news media. Editors must be convinced that a story is interesting, factual, and relevant. While the advertising agency pays to insert its message in commercial space or time, the public relations counsel ethically cannot pay to control what goes in the news columns. The apparent newsworthiness of the item is what wins it credibility.

Not surprisingly, many of today's successful public relations professionals are former journalists who understand the workings of the newsroom. Fundamental skills for dealing with the press include:

◆ Writing an interesting news release following the journalistic format and style used by the news media.

◆ Explaining to a busy editor on the phone in just a few minutes why a story is interesting and important.

◆ Providing the contacts or resources the journalist needs to write a story; helping the journalist get through to the spokespeople for your organization.

◆ Arranging a press conference that is well-timed for the media and produces useful information.

◆ Understanding the special needs of the print and broadcast media, which often have different priorities.

Two-Way Benefits. When we discussed the creation of news in Chapter 5, we acknowledged the special relationship between the press and public relations professionals. Former Mobil vice-president for public affairs Herb Schmertz, to whom we referred early in this chapter, counsels public relations professionals to maintain good relations with reporters and editors because "information is currency. If you build a good relationship with a reporter, you may find you'll learn as much from him as he'll learn from you. . . . when you talk with someone who's well-informed, not all of the information flows in the same direction."[21]

That special relationship between journalists and public relations people suggests they can be placed simultaneously as producers and consumers of information. For example, a public relations person may have information for a journalist about a company's efforts to comply with new pollution standards set by the state government. The reporter's questions in response to the briefing may reveal what the reporter has heard about another company's efforts to forestall enforcement of the new regulations. That information, in turn, may help the public relations person to advise management about the climate of opinion surrounding the issue.

MANAGEMENT BY OBJECTIVES

In recent years, public relations has borrowed a business management technique known as **MBO**—management by objectives—in order to clearly demonstrate the worth and impact of their programs. In the past, when public relations departments made such promises as to "improve our organization's image" or "celebrate the organization's contribution to the community," they found it difficult to show their contribution to the bottom line of the organization. That is to say, they could not show that they enhanced the making of a profit or, in the case of nonprofit organizations, that they served the main goal of the organization.

However, by adopting MBO, public relations people developed the ability to demonstrate the worth of their programs in terms business people can understand. Today, PR professionals can use MBO to state the impact of PR program through quantitative measurement. Here is an example: "The information project reached 40,000 residents, and over half of them requested our information packet—three times as many as last year, when there was no information program."

RESEARCH APPLICATIONS

The typical public relations professional of a generation ago was a former news reporter or editor hired to deal with former colleagues in the press. Today's public relations practitioner needs an important new skill: the ability to use research to understand how a public thinks and behaves in regard to issues that affect a client organization.

Just as the advertising industry became more sophisticated when it learned to measure the consumer's preferences and needs, so too has the public relations industry evolved as it has realized the importance of consumer research. Understanding the attitudes of consumers is critical to effectively reach target publics with a message and persuade them to change their behaviors.

As with advertising, the survey or **public opinion poll** is a major research tool for public relations people. Another is the **focus group interview**, in which small groups of selected consumers are interviewed in a formal but open-ended way that allows them to make known to the researchers their interests, preferences, and concerns. Studying behaviors and quantifying them is another valid technique: How many people of what types attended an event, and how many of them subsequently requested information using the phone number provided?

The rise of research by public relations practitioners relates directly to the increase in MBO techniques. Research is needed to demonstrate exactly how and why an objective was set, and whether or not it was achieved.

WRITING: THE ESSENTIAL SKILL

Critics of public relations practitioners assume that the chief talent of the "PR person" is the ability to talk a good line, coupled with a propensity to "like other people." This limited view assumes that persuasion is accomplished by overwhelming another person with one's personality and depth of conviction.

In truth, persuasion is best accomplished by presenting factual data in a comprehensible, interesting, compelling, and believable manner. Consumers of the information should have the opportunity to think about the arguments, weigh the evidence, and persuade themselves that the idea or cause presented is the best one.

This is why writing is the basic skill of public relations. And this is also why, historically, so many public relations people have come from the ranks of reporters and editors. A premium is put on the individual who can gather information accurately, organize it coherently, and present it in a straightforward manner.

Journalistic writing, both feature articles and hard news reporting, provides the models that public relations people imitate when attempting to place a client's stories in the news media. The closer they come to the ideal, the greater the chances of placement. Because public relations also involves supporting the marketing of products and services,

Careers in the Field

A compelling reason for studying public relations is that the field, far from being static in terms of growth as many other mass media fields are, provides increasing numbers of entry-level jobs for college graduates. Opportunities abound in a variety of areas, including government, education, nonprofit and social programs, business, politics, and entertainment.

Some organizations handle all public relations in-house, meaning they put together their own publications, do their own lobbying with legislative bodies, and prepare campaigns aimed at diverse external publics, from stockholders to customers to community groups. Most corporations, however, and also many government bodies and trade associations, give several important segments of their public relations work to specialized agencies. These organizations often turn to agencies for campaigns aimed at promoting specific products, lobbying, community relations, and media relations.

Some agencies specialize by topic: politics and public affairs, health care, insurance, environmental concerns, or new product introductions. Other agencies specialize in types of service: video news releases, special events, publications, or crisis communication. Small agencies may consist of a principal and one or two assistants, while freelancers may handle only two or three accounts; the largest agencies, with dozens of account teams, serve dozens of clients in a variety of ways.

In public relations, the quest for credibility has raised questions about the need to accredit or even license practitioners, much as lawyers are admitted to the bar, doctors are licensed to practice, and accountants must pass exams in order to pursue their trade. The Public Relations Society of America (PRSA) and the International Association of Business Communicators (IABC) both offer accreditation exams. However, because accreditation is not necessary to practice public relations and because the majority of practitioners do not join either organization, professional accreditation is not yet as meaningful as it is in the fields of law, medicine, and accounting. Accredited or not, today's public relations practitioners find that the field is maturing, gaining acceptance, and taking an increasingly important role in the management of complex organizations that depend on the support of consumers in order to survive.

promotional writing modeled after advertising copy is a specialized writing skill that may prove helpful. Similarly, writing for the ear and following tight time formats are desirable specialized skills for public relations people who target the broadcast media.

CAPITALIZING ON EMERGING TECHNOLOGY

PR professionals need not only be skilled in media relations and writing, but also in the strategic use of the newest, cutting-edge technologies. Blogs and personal media such as Facebook provide forums for both research for and implementation of PR programs. Many corporate executives maintain blogs on their corporation's Web sites in order to appear accessible to consumers, for example, just as many actors, actresses, and music artists maintain personal pages or fan sites to promote their projects. In addition, podcasts, e-mails, and text messages can be keys to success in PR programs, keeping consumers informed and helping them to feel connected to a given cause or organization. In future years, the importance of emerging technology will likely only grow within the field of public relations.

Chapter Summary

◆ The concepts central to modern public relations can be traced to ancient texts, including Aristotle's *Rhetoric* and the Bible, as well as to the ideas of the founders of the United States.

◆ Amos Kendall and P.T. Barnum may be considered two of the earliest press agents; Barnum, in particular, was known for enacting elaborate publicity stunts. Ivy Lee pioneered the concept of public relations as a tool for businesses to gain support from consumers. Edward Bernays, with his emphasis on proactive public relations and astute analysis of target publics, shaped public relations as we know it today.

◆ The press agent/publicity model, public information model, two-way asymmetric model, and two-way symmetric model comprise the four theoretical constructs for approaching public relations. Although the two-way symmetric model tends to dominate in the contemporary landscape, all four models continue to coexist and may be used to achieve specific PR goals.

◆ The modern public relations industry is a media facilitator. Identifying subpublics, setting objectives, and implementing Marston's RACE formula are key components of effective PR programs.

◆ Public relations plays key roles in crisis management, corporate rebranding, government, politics, and entertainment.

◆ Cultivation of media relationships, management by objectives, research, writing, and the use of emerging technologies are integral skills for success in the public relations field.

Glossary

corporate social responsibility (CSR)—the actions or programs adopted by organizations that reflect an interest in and concern for social and environmental issues

damage control—the first phase of crisis communication in which PR practitioners identify how the crisis has negatively affected the public's perception of the organization and demonstrate that the organization is taking responsibility and has a plan for solving the crisis

focus group interview—a research tool in which small groups of selected consumers are interviewed in a formal but open-ended way that allows them to make known to the researchers their interests, preferences, and concerns

greenwashing—the practice of companies expressing environmental concerns and/or making their products appear to be environmentally sound

issues management—the second phase of crisis communication in which PR practitioners aim to demonstrate to the public that the organization is working to solve or alleviate the problem through cooperation or negotiation with other organizations

MBO—management by objectives, a technique used by professional managers and borrowed by public relations professionals; it involves laying out specific, quantifiable goals for PR campaigns

media facilitators—industries, such as public relations and advertising, that make the creation and distribution of mass media possible because, directly or indirectly, they underwrite the cost of disseminating information cheaply to large audiences

press agent/publicity model—a PR model, favored by P.T. Barnum, that emphasizes promotion and publicity with little regard for facts

propaganda—information deliberately spread to help or hurt the reputation of an individual, organization, or country

public information model—a PR model, favored by Ivy Lee, that emphasizes one-way (source-receiver, or producer-consumer) dissemination of truthful information

public opinion poll—a research tool in which a large group of randomly selected consumers are surveyed on their opinions on a given topic

public relations (PR)—the business of bringing about public awareness, understanding, and goodwill toward a person or organization

RACE formula—John E. Marston's construct for the implementation of a successful public relations program involving four steps: research, action, communication, and evaluation

rebranding—the process through which a product, service, or organization is marketed and associated with new, different, and improved identity

spin—PR tactic in which a specific point of view of interpretation of an event is presented with the intention of influencing public opinion

subpublics—specialized audiences with specialized information needs and interests that PR professionals must identify before implementing and specifically targeting a program

two-way asymmetric model—A PR model in which formative research is used to ascertain the attitudes of the target publics before a PR plan is implemented; it recognizes that the actions and behaviors of consumer publics affect the actions and behaviors of producers in the competitive business system

two-way symmetric model—A PR model most often applied to businesses subject to heavy government regulation, or where the activist consumer has as much influence as the producer; it recognizes that balanced communication is necessary to adapt the organization to the realities of society.

Discussion Questions

1. Discuss the ethical implications of the press agent/publicity model favored by P.T. Barnum. Is the predominance of hype over truth ethical? Why or why not? What contemporary examples illustrate this potential conflict?
2. Analyze the factors that have contributed to the predominance of the two-way symmetrical model in PR communications in recent years. What advantages does this model offer over other techniques? What potential problems can occur as a result of its use?
3. How would you characterize the "special relationship" that exists between public relations professionals and the media? How can it be helpful, and/or detrimental, to both parties? What about the public? Explain your response.
4. Consider how you would design a PR program to rehabilitate the image of an organization in crisis. If possible, choose a current example from the news to illustrate your ideas. What steps would you take? What objectives would you delineate? How, and why, would your program be effective?
5. What impact have technological, political, economic, and/or cultural developments of the past decade had on the PR industry as a whole, and, more specifically, on the skills necessary to succeed in the industry?

Supplemental Web Sites

Bureau of Labor Statistics, Occupational Outlook Handbook for Public Relations Specialists: http://www.bls.gov/oco/ocos086.htm

Public Relations Society of America: http://www.prsa.org/

Public Relations Student Society of America: http://www.prssa.org/

International Association of Business Communicators: http://www.iabc.com/

Institute for Public Relations: http://www.institute-forpr.com/

Center for Media and Democracy: PR Watch: http://www.prwatch.org/

Ogilvy Public Relations Worldwide: http://www.ogilvypr.com/

The Museum of Public Relations: http://www.prmuseum.com/

Council of Public Relations Firms: http://www.prfirms.org/

Douglas Rushkoff: Technology, Media, and Popular Culture: http://rushkoff.com/

Frontline: The Persuaders: http://www.pbs.org/wgbh/pages/frontline/shows/persuaders/

Endnotes

1 Aydemir Okay and Aylar Okay, "Contemporary Girls of Contemporary Turkey: Case Study of a Public Relations Campaign." In *The evolution of public relations: Case studies from countries in transition*, Judy VanSlyke Turk and Linda H. Scanlan, eds. pp. 23–33. Gainesville, Florida: The Institute for Public Relations Research and Education, 2004. Available at *http://www.instituteforpr.org/files/uploads/Int_CaseStudies.pdf*.

2 Turkcell, Communication Activities. "IPRA Golden World Awards, 2007 Competition." Available at *http://www.turkcell.com.tr/c/docs/ic/TURKCELL_SNOW-DROPS.pdf*.

3 Scott M. Cutlip and Allen H. Center. *Effective public relations.* Englewood Cliffs, New Jersey: 1952.

4 Source info TK

5 Source info TK

6 Source info TK

7 Irving Wallace, "P.T. Barnum." *Encyclopædia Britannica.* 2008. Encyclopædia Britannica Online. Available at http:// search.eb.com/eb/article-9013431.

8 Source info TK

9 Source info TK

10 Edward L. Bernays. *Propaganda.* New York: Horace Liveright, 1928.

11 Source info TK

12 James E. Grunig and Todd Hunt. *Managing Public Relations.* New York: Holt, Rinehart, Winston, 1984.

13 Herb Schmertz, *Goodbye to the Low Profile: The Art of Creative Confrontation.* New York: Little Brown, 1986.

14 John E. Marston. *Modern public relations.* New York: McGraw-Hill, 1979.

15 Nicholas Casey and Nicholas Zemiska, "Mattel Does Damage Control After New Recall" August 15, 2007, *Wall Street Journal* [Online Edition]. Available at *http://online.wsj.com/article/SB118709567221897168.html?mod=googlenews_wsj*.

16 Fortune Global 500 2007. *fortune* [Online edition at cnn.money.com] Available at *http://money.cnn.com/magazines/fortune/global500/2007/snapshots/6327.html*.

17 Sourcewatch, "BP." Available at *http://www.source-watch.org/index.php?title=BP*.

18 "GE Ecomagination: Hybrid Locomotive" GE Corporate Web Site. Available at *http://ge.ecomagination.com/site/#hybr*.

19 Mark Hucklebridge and William Godnick, "Public Relations Campaigns Reduce Violence in Panama and El Salvador." In *The evolution of public relations: Case studies from countries in transition*, Judy VanSlyke Turk and Linda H. Scanlan, eds. pp. 135–147. Gainesville, Florida: The Institute for Public Relations Research and Education, 2004. Available at *http://www.institute-forpr.org/files/uploads/Int_CaseStudies.pdf*.

20 Source info TK

21 Herb Schmertz

ADVERTISING

Barbara Iverson

Chapter Objectives:

◆ Explain how the advertising industry has evolved over the last three hundred years

◆ Describe how advertisements are used in mass media

◆ Explain how advertisements benefit the consumer and media outlets

◆ Understand how the government regulates advertisers and how advertisers regulate themselves

◆ List four future trends in the advertising industry

Introduction

From the moment you wake up in the morning until the time you go to sleep at night, how many commercial messages do you think you are exposed to? If you watch TV or read the newspaper regularly,

you many think you are exposed to a hundred or so messages. If you rarely give attention to major forms of mass media, you may think the number is even lower. The reality is that the average American is exposed to 3,000 commercial messages a day, that's over one million a year.[1] That number may seem inflated, however, if you really think about the words and images that are communicated to you over the course of a day you can see the truth behind this staggering number. As you get ready to leave the house in the morning you may flip on the radio or morning news and hear numerous broadcast commercials. When you pour your cereal, you may notice a promotion for an unrelated product printed on the back of the box. On your way to work or school you are exposed to hundreds of messages: the billboard for a vacation package alongside the road, a sign for a brand of shampoo on the side of a bus, or a bumper sticker on the car in front of you. You may be exposed to some commercial messages without even noticing: the Nike logo on your friend's shirt, the Starbucks coffee cup on your neighbor's desk, or the Jansport label on your backpack.

Commercial messages are all around us, and corporations are making it increasingly difficult to avoid them. Nearly $450 billion is spent annually to lure customers to certain products or services. Promoting commercial messages is called advertising. **Advertising** is essentially the act of calling the public's attention to a product, service, or need. Advertising is commonly found in different types of mass media in the form of radio or television commercials, newspaper spreads, or billboard announcements. However, as we discovered earlier, advertisements can be found almost anywhere.

Advertising before the 21st Century

Advertising has existed in the United States for over three hundred years. The first known advertisement was placed in a newspaper, the Boston News-Letter, in 1703. The advertisement, or ad, publicized the sale of an estate in Oyster Bay Long Island. Years later Benjamin Franklin began running advertisements in the *Pennsylvania Gazette.* The first true pioneer of advertising did not emerge until 1833. Printer Benjamin Day found a way to bring advertising to the masses by creating the first successful penny newspaper, the *Sun,* in New York. Within four years of its first edition, the publication's circulation reached 30,000, making it the most widely read newspaper in the world. As the 19th century progressed, advertising became an important part of business development for major companies. Advertising agencies formed, companies hired full time advertising copywriters, and major corporations invested unprecedented amounts of money in ad placements. In 1882, Procter & Gamble Co. started an advertisement campaign for Ivory soap with an $11,000 budget, an amount that was unheard of at the time.

Modern advertising began to emerge in the 1900s with products such as Kellogg's cornflakes. In 1906 WK Kellogg created a widespread campaign by placing its advertisements in six Midwestern magazines. By 1915 Kellogg was spending more than one million dollars a year on national advertising, creating a benchmark for the future of advertising. By 1921, RJ Reynolds was designating $8 million to advertising, most of which was spent on promoting Camel cigarettes. The investment proved to be successful as by 1923 Camel controlled 45% of the US cigarette market.

As advertising became more popular, the government became involved in the process. The

Advertisers and Athletes: The start of a love affair

In 1905, three-time National League batting champion Honus Wagner became the first person to sign an endorsement contract. Wagner's deal with bat company Hillerich & Bradsby, Co. allowed the company to engrave his signature on Louisville Slugger bats and sell them to eager fans. Since 1905, more than 7,000 endorsements deals have been created between Louisville Slugger and professional baseball players. Wagner's deal sparked an ongoing trend in endorsement relationships between corporations and professional athletes that is highly prevalent in the advertising world today.[3]

Section 5 of the Federal Trade Commission Act, passed in 1914, declared that that the Federal Trade Commission (FTC) can issue cease and desist orders against any company that engages in dishonest or misleading advertising. Companies were now liable for any claims made in advertisements. Cigarette companies found themselves in hot water because of this act.[2] We will learn more about tobacco advertising and government regulations later on in this chapter.

A CHANGING MARKET

As public preference changed, so did the approach of advertisers. During the early part of the 20th century radio emerged as a popular form of media. Soon companies opted to spend their advertising dollars on the airwaves rather than print pages. By 1938, radio exceeded magazines in advertising revenue. But again, the market changed. Advertisers turn to television as a new way to reach consumers. On July 1, 1941, NBC's WNBT aired its first telecast. A close-up view of a Bulova watch opened and closed the telecast, marking one of the first instances of product placement on television.

Other changes in advertising occurred around this time. The US government started to use advertising to help build support for World War II. The War Advertising Council gained free advertising for public service messages. Popular campaigns such as "Buy War Bonds" and "Loose Lips Sink Ships" were placed in magazines and radio broadcasts across the United States. After the war, the War Advertising Council was renamed the Advertising Council and proceeded to advertise public service campaigns such as Smokey the Bear, McGruff the crime dog, and "Just Say No" to drugs.[4]

Advertiser's approach to choosing the perfect medium for their products changed with the emergence of AC Nielsen's machine-based rating system for television. The system made it possible to track how many households view certain television programs. Nielsen's machine allowed companies to find out on which programs their advertising dollars would be most wisely spent.

As the 20th century progressed, advertising companies became more methodical about where, when, and how they placed certain ads. Advertisements were no longer just used to persuade consumers to buy a product; they were used to

encourage the public to embrace a brand. "The Pepsi Generation" was an advertising campaign initiated in 1963. It projected the image that all those who are young, or young at heart, should drink Pepsi brand cola.[5]

Soon after the MTV era introduced new, flashier forms of advertising during the 1980s, the Internet introduced new, high-tech forms of advertising in the 1990s. By 1993, the Internet enlisted five million users and emerged as a profitable medium for advertisers. Before the end of the century, well over $2 billion was spent on Internet advertising. Today over $24 billion dollars is spent on Internet advertising adding to total of $450 billion spent on advertising worldwide.[6] To understand why so much money is spent on advertising, let's examine why we need it.

A Culture of Consumerism

With billions of dollars being spent every year to convince consumers to buy certain products, one must question the necessity of advertising. Why can't the consumer just decide what products and services to purchase on their own? That question cannot be properly answered without understanding consumerism. **Consumerism** is the theory that an increase in the consumption of goods and services will benefit the economy.[7] In short, the more we buy the more we thrive. Americans adopted a culture of consumerism at the start of the 20th century. People began to work less hours, acquire higher paying jobs, invest in the stock market, and buy luxury items like cars, washing machines, and expensive clothing.

The culture of consumerism is clear in today's society. Americans purchase more than $6 trillion dollars in goods and services each year, and they rely on advertisements to inform them about new products. Gone are "mercantile days" when each shopkeeper waited on every customer by taking and filling their order personally, acting as clerk, cashier and then often as salesman, describing new products and discussing the merits of various goods. How does the consumer today learn about the amazing plethora of goods and services available in today's expanding marketplaces? For better and worse, this is where advertising comes in.

ADVERTISING AND THE CONSUMER

Advertising may not seem like a benefit because of the negative connotations connected to the practice. Consumers sometimes feel that advertisers are always trying to sell them something they don't need. However, in many cases advertisers are promoting goods and services that support our basic needs. Food, clothing, shelter, and other goods that aid us in our daily lives are products that are advertised. Sure, we may not need brand name clothing, but a Gore-tex jacket may help you keep warm in the winter. Without advertising, consumers may never learn about new product that can improve their health and well being.

Advertising also has financial benefits for the consumer. Advertising promotes competition within the market, which drives down prices and increases product availability. It also helps consumers decide where to get the best price and what products have the best value.

ADVERTISING AND THE MEDIA

Advertising is the foundation of the economic health of our nation's media. Broadcast television and radio arc solely supported by the revenue brought in by advertising. Newspapers, magazines, cable television, and Internet outlets rely on subscription fees as well as advertising revenue to support their businesses. Without revenue from advertising many media outlets would not exist and those that could survive would come at a substantially higher cost to the consumer.

Because advertisers allow media outlets to function with little to no cost to the consumer, more outlets are able to flourish, giving consumers more choices in news and entertainment. For example, in the 1950s television viewers were only offered three broadcast networks. Today, they have their choice of six broadcast networks and hundreds of cable channels. Advertising had the same effect on print media. In 1960 there were 312 morning newspapers, and today there are over 700. The number of consumer magazines has increased as well. In 1988 there were almost 13,000 publications, and today that number is more than 18,000.[8]

Advertising is also an integral part of the Internet. Paid advertisements make many of the most popular sites such a Google, Mapquest, and You Tube free to Internet users. Without revenue from advertisers there would be little incentive for Web site administrators to develop new Web sites. But when it comes to advertising and the Internet, the benefits run both ways. As we will discuss later on in the chapter, the Internet has become a large part of the future of advertising.

Now that we know why advertising is important to the consumer and the media, let's see how it is used.

The Many Faces of Advertising

Traditionally, advertisements appear in media in the form of print or broadcast. Print advertisements usually contain pictures or photos, catchy headlines, and occasionally coupons and can appear in newspapers, magazines, or flyers. Broadcast advertisements consist of brief 15-20 second audio and/or video pieces designed for television or radio. In addition to traditional advertising, methods such as direct mail, outdoor signage, and point-of-sale advertising can also make a big impact on consumers.

DIRECT MAIL

Direct mail, sometimes referred to by consumers as junk mail, consists of advertisements sent through the postal service. Direct mail advertisements typically promote special sales or offers to select consumers. It can be a very useful form of advertising because companies can create mailing lists that only target consumers that are most likely to purchase their goods or services. Grocery store circulars and "pre-approved" credit card offers are common direct mail pieces. While direct mail pieces often receive a bulk rate for postage costs, it can still be rather expensive. The advertisements can also be viewed as a nuisance and be thrown away unopened.

POINT OF SALE

Point of sale advertising is the placement of products, promotions, or other offers on or near a checkout counter. The candy in a grocery store checkout line and the flyer asking you to try a new style of burger on the counter of a fast food restaurant are both forms of point of sale advertising. Point of sale advertising has become high tech in the last few years. At coffee retailer Aroma Espresso Bar, customers who approach the counter may be greeted by a cashier and video screen that displays images of the various breakfast items available for purchase. Through this type of advertising, customers who entered the shop with the intention of only purchasing a cup of coffee may be encourage to also pick up a croissant or muffin.

Point-of-sale advertising can be very beneficial to advertisers because most purchasing decisions are made in the store and advertisers have a chance to appeal to consumers' impulses.[9] However, point-sale-advertisements, especially the kind that involves technology, can be expensive and sometimes overlooked.

OUTDOOR ADVERTISING

Outdoor advertising is another way to reach consumers outside of their homes. Traditionally thought of as billboards signs, outdoor advertising has changed a lot in the last ten years. Outdoor media now includes park benches, public transit vehicles, or bus shelters that are wrapped with images and text promoting various products.

Some outdoor advertisings methods can range from silly to bizarre. In Time Square in New York City a glass elevator was designed and built to simulate an Oreo cookie being dunked into a glass of milk. In London, a group of individuals were paid to walk on to a subway train wearing jackets with video screens in the arm pits. When a person would raise their arm, a video ad for Right Guard deodorant would play for the whole crowd in the train to see. While this method of advertising may sometimes be viewed as precarious, advertisers are willing to spend big, $7.3 billion in 2007 according to the Outdoor Advertising Association of America, in order to get their message out to the public.[10]

THE INTERNET

While advertisers are getting more creative with the way they execute advertising in traditional mediums, nothing has shaken up the advertising world more than the Internet. As we discussed in chapter 11, the Internet is becoming a dominate force in media. In many ways the Internet works like a television or a newspaper. Advertisers can place an electronic banner ad, similar to a print ad in a newspaper, on a home page or a select page of a Web site. They can also place a pop-up or side bar video, similar to a television commercial, on a partnering Web site. These types of advertisements are increasing as more people are looking to the Internet to read up on the latest news or watch their favorite TV program.

The Internet also offers advertisers other ways to reach consumers that are unmatched by newspapers or television. Paid search and pay-per click advertising has come forward as one of the fasted growing methods of advertising. **Paid search** is a form of advertising used on a search engine Web site, which allows companies to have a brief advertisement placed on top or next to search results when certain keywords are used. For example, when a user types in the keywords "hair salon Miami" a small add for Gabriella's Unisex Salon in Miami may appear at the top of the search results page under a paid advertisements section. In **Pay-per-click** advertising, Web page administrators allow outside companies to place advertisements on their Web pages in exchange for a small fee, which is paid to the Web site administrator, when a user clicks on the ad. For example, Sarah Hawkins has a Web site for her event planning business. To make some extra cash for her business, Sarah allows Larson's Limousine Services to place a small ad on her Web page. Sarah may receive about 10 cents from the limo service every time a user clicks on the ad.

Paid search and pay-per-click were first implemented and mastered by Google founders Sergay Brin and Larry Page. Called AdWord (paid search) and AdSense (pay-per-click), these forms of advertisements are a key part of what has made Google the multi-billion dollar company it is today.[11] In 2007, Google made over $16 billion in advertising revenue and that number is projected to grow even larger in the next few years.[12]

Companies are drawn to this type of advertising because it allows advertisers to more accurately measure how many potential customers they are reaching, and it also guarantees that consumers are actively viewing the advertisement. Unlike a television commercial that can be missed when a viewer

Political Advertising: The Living Room Candidate

During election season in the United States, television viewers may notice more ads for political candidates than ads for fast food restaurants. Since the 1950s, television has changed the game for political candidates. Through television, candidates can enter voters' homes and influence their decision making through images, slogans, and rhetoric. The use of television ads for political advertisings was not in vogue until the 1952 election between Dwight D. Eisenhower and Adlai Stevenson. Previous candidates such as Governor Thomas Dewey viewed political television ads as "undignified" and refused to use them in his 1948 campaign.

Diverging from this view, Eisenhower embraced television ads, creating several 30 seconds spots titled "Ike for President" that featured animated characters, songs, and the now famous slogan, "I like Ike." Eisenhower's campaign merchandised the candidate just as a corporation would merchandise a new product. So it is not surprising that the same ad agency that created M&M's slogan "melts in your mouth not in your hand," developed the "Eisenhower Answers America" ad series. In these television ads Eisenhower responded to questions from ordinary citizens. Forty spots, recorded in one day and then broadcast throughout the campaign season, aired before popular shows such as *I Love Lucy*. The spots helped Eisenhower enter his constituents' living rooms on a nightly basis and be viewed as a man of the people.

Stevenson never warmed up to the idea of using television to market a candidate. He publicized his disapproval of the process with the statement: "I think the American people will be shocked by such contempt for their intelligence. This isn't Ivory Soap versus Palmolive." Stevenson created television spots promoting his campaign; however they were often long and dull and aired during late hours. Viewed as nothing more than on-camera radio spots, Stevenson's television ads did little for his campaign.[13]

Dwight D. Eisenhower won the 1952 election by a large margin. His campaign changed the way Americans view their candidates, but also the way candidates make their appeal to the American people. In the 2008 presidential campaign, candidates spent nearly $3 billion on political television ads.[14] Whether they are used to promote a candidate's views and proposed policies or to portray competitors in negative light, political television ads have become an important part of the election processes.

Advertising Agencies

The forerunner of the advertising agency as we know it today was founded in 1841 by Volney Palmer, whose Philadelphia brokerage service specialized in buying advertising space from newspapers at a volume discount, then selling parts of that space to individual advertisers at a markup. To this day advertising agencies gain part or all of their compensation through the discount they receive from publishers bringing in ads. It is a service to the publishers to have large blocks of ads coming in without having to work with individual merchants or manufacturers.

It was not until the 1870s that advertising agencies emerged to serve manufacturers who needed advice on how to package their products and promote them to consumers. The N. W. Ayer and Son Agency, also of Philadelphia, was among the first to provide the service of studying a product and developing a "campaign" or strategy, for making that product familiar and desirable. The Ayer agency is responsible for many of the advertising slogans that have become part of our cultural lexicon, like "Diamonds are forever," and "When it rains it pours."[15]

leaves the room or a print ad that can easily be passed by, paid search and pay-per click advertising is actually initiated by the consumer, increasing the chances that the ad will be thoroughly viewed.

Monitoring Advertising Information

As we discovered earlier in this chapter, advertisers will go to great lengths to draw consumers to their products. However extreme, silly, or idiotic the ploy, advertisers still have to adhere to certain standards set by the advertising community and the federal government. Unscrupulous advertising is a major concern for media outlets and consumers alike. Publishers, networks, and other communication companies must be sure not to align themselves with companies that

make false claims or promote dangerous products. False advertising cannot only damage the reputation of a media outlet, it can also harm the consumer. In the following section we will look at how Americans have monitored advertising using a mixture of government surveillance, consumer advocacy, media self-regulation, and industry self-regulation.

GOVERNMENT REGULATIONS

The first casualty of government regulations in advertising was the pharmaceutical industry. Fed up with false claims and dangerous ingredients, the medical community joined with consumers and publishers to press Congress for the passage of the Pure Food and Drug Act in 1906. The law prohibited claims of undocumented cures, forbade manufacturers to misrepresent the efficacy of their products, and required all ingredients to be identified on the product label. This act particularly exposed the use of alcohol and drugs such as morphine in many pharmaceuticals. While these products apparently produced miraculous effects, more serious problems of addiction or complications were likely to follow the initial relief.

Soon after the Pure Food and Drug Act, the Federal Trade Commission (FTC) was established in 1914. The agency was authorized to regulate advertising and prevent deceptive practices. The FTC monitors and corrects claims of products that "cure" the common cold, guarantee "permanent weight loss," or "reverse baldness." As the FTC grew stronger, it became more proactive in its supervision of advertising practices; rather than merely handling complaints, the agency studied abuses and issued reports that attacked deception and the dissemination of misleading information.

In the 1950s, the FTC began to crack down on "bait and switch" ads that lure consumers with a "low-ball" price. **Bait and switch** is a method of fraudulent advertising in which a company advertises a product at an unprofitable price then reveals to a potential customer that the product is unavailable. The FTC charged that many merchants used pressure sales tactics to convince the consumer to "move up" to higher-priced products after claiming that the advertised items were out of stock or not really of satisfactory quality. The FTC also investigated the misuse of the word free in advertisements for products that weren't really free but required the purchase of other goods.

Beginning in the 1970s, the FTC took a hard look at "Brand X" ads, which compared a sponsor's product with an unnamed competitor. The government agency pushed advertisers to (1) name the competitor so the consumer would know which two products were being compared; and (2) cite impartial research data as proof that one product is better or more effective than another.

In order to protect the rights of companies and consumers, the FTC can issue a cease and desist order or can levy a fine against advertisers whose messages it feels have injured another firm or a consumer. In the 1970s, the agency began to require "corrective advertising" to offset the effects of long-running campaigns that had misled the public. Profile bread was required to explain to consumers that its claim of having fewer calories per slice was true only because its slices were thinner than those of the competitor, and that using the product would not cause weight loss. The FTC forced Profile to spend one fourth of the company's advertising budget to correct this misleading claim. Some companies have used sneaky maneuvers to sidestep FTC rulings. Ocean Spray, the maker of various juices, was imposed with an order to spend a portion of the company's advertising budget of the current year to correct a false claim. The company simply decided not to advertise that year. They rested on the claim that one quarter of zero dollars is zero dollars.[16]

More than 20 US government agencies are empowered to regulate one or more forms of advertising. The US Postal Service screens catalogs and other direct mail advertising for information that would constitute "using the US mail to defraud." The Securities and Exchange Commission keeps an eye on any claims that would tend to create undue expectations for the rise in the value of a stock. The Food and Drug Administration oversees the dissemination of any information concerning foodstuffs, health care products, cosmetics, and drugs. A current area of concern for the FDA is the proliferation of health claims that seek to take advantage of the public's concern about fitness and dieting. In 1991, the agency announced new rules that would curb claims like that of Quaker Oat Bran, which allege to "reduces cholesterol," unless such claims could be substantiated by independent authorities such as the Surgeon General or the National Academy of Sciences.

Manufacturers and the advertising industry constantly pressure government agencies to ease up on regulations for fear that regulations will become as stringent as they are in some other countries. In Malaysia, television ads that show a car driving fast and even flying through the air—a common way of demonstrating the handling of an automobile in American ads—are prohibited because uneducated viewers might attempt to emulate the behavior. Malaysia's strict code controlling TV ads also stipulates that speakers in commercials must use the correct pronunciation of the official Maylay language, not dialects of Chinese or Indian.

Most Americans value their right to receive information without interference. They would not welcome or tolerate government control of entertainment or educational information for reasons of cultural purity or governmental preference. On the other hand, they place great value on receiving accurate information, especially about health and personal

Subliminal Messages

Surely one of the most pervasive hoaxes of the twentieth century was the notion that "subliminal" advertising was used to make people desire an alcoholic drink, buy a certain make of car, or dash off to a restaurant lusting for a plate of clams. Gullible people with little understanding of psychology—including some state legislators who have introduced bills that would ban "subliminal" ads—fall prey to books and articles suggesting that words hidden in ice cubes, shapes concealed in the folds of a garment, or symbols worked into pictures of food have the power to make the consumer jump up and rush to the store, controlled by some unknown force.

In fact, in certain New Jersey theaters in the 1950s, movie audiences were exposed to images superimposed over the last scenes of films, exhorting them to "Drink Coca-Cola" and "eat popcorn." That caused newspaper editorialists to raise a hue and cry against the "alarming and outrageous" mind-fooling technique they supposed would put consumers in a trance. But it doesn't take much to stimulate a movie audience to get up and move to the refreshment stand during intermission. The "subliminal" trickery was hardly necessary.

Psychological research indicates that intense stimuli have a much greater effect than subtle stimuli. Messages hidden within other images certainly are far too subtle to equal the effects of obvious and overt advertising techniques. Despite these finding, legislators in the US government proposed a ban on subliminal advertising in all forms of media.[17]

products. That is why there has been little or no protest from citizens as legislative and regulatory bodies have become more stringent with advertisers.

THE ATTACK ON CIGARETTE AND LIQUOR ADVERTISING

Because of the wealth of information regarding the health problems caused by cigarette smoking and second hand smoke, cigarettes have been under attack in the United States for nearly half a century. In 1965, a series of findings by the Surgeon General led to required warnings on all cigarette packages and advertisements.

In 1971, after a long congressional debate, cigarette advertising was prohibited from the broadcast media by the federal government, which has more direct control over broadcast media than over print media. The tobacco industry and the broadcast industry maintained—and continued to argue—that the ban was unconstitutional. The temporary setback in advertising revenues for the broadcasters was a gold mine for the print media, which had lost billions of dollars to television over the preceding decade.

Pushed by the American Medical Association in the mid 1980s, Congress debated whether cigarette ads should be banned from the print media as well. The growing number of regulations imposed by the industry on smoking in the workplace and the decision by the military to restrict smoking helped fuel the spread of anti-smoking information. The industry responded with its own arguments that smokers should be allowed to choose whether to use the product and whether to receive information about it.

Lawyers for the RJ Reynolds Tobacco Company, for example, successfully fought the Federal Trade Commission's decision that one of the firm's advertisements misrepresented the results of a government study of smoking. The ad said that the results of the study were inconclusive. RJ Reynolds contended that the company's interpretation of the study was corporate opinion, and was thus protected by the First Amendment. The FTC simply saw the ad as one of many false claims about a scientific study by the tobacco industry.

Research shows that today more college women than college men smoke cigarettes, which researchers attribute to the fact that the tobacco industry is successfully linking smoking by women with images of glamour, success, and equality, as well as a means of staying thin and attractive. All of these charges are denied by the tobacco industry, which maintains that cigarette advertising is now directed only at people who already smoke.

The drive to prohibit all advertising of harmful substances such as tobacco and alcoholic beverages is being spearheaded by the medical community. Ironically, it came shortly after the medical professional societies finally altered their own ethical standards to permit "tasteful and restrained" advertising for doctors and medical institutions—a practice long prohibited by the profession.

The national debate over the effects of advertising on people who abuse substances has become heated and emotional. A former "Winston man" quit smoking and testified before Congress stating: "My

Joe Camel

During the 1990s, Joe Camel, the cartoon spokesman for Camel brand cigarettes, was one of the most recognizable characters in American culture. With his dark sunglasses, slick clothes, and entourage of gorgeous friends, Joe Camel stood for all things cool. The Camel cigarette dangling from the corner of his mouth connected the cigarette brand to a favorable image. The fact that Joe Camel was an animated character concerned many consumers. Opponents of the character felt RJ Reynolds Tobacco Company, maker of Camel cigarettes, was using Joe Camel to appeal to children and young teens. A study conducted in 1991 by *The Journal of the American Medical Association* showed that 6-year-old children were just as familiar with Joe Camel as with Mickey Mouse.[18] The study also showed a connection between the Joe Camel campaign and an increase in teenage smoking. RJ Reynolds denied that it tailored its advertisements to children and conducted its own studies that contradicted those of the American Medical Association.

Still, in 1997 the FFC declared that the Joe Camel campaign violated federal law because of its harmful effects on minors. RJ Reynolds decided not to fight the ruling and chose to replace Joe Camel with a realistic non-animated outline of a camel.[19] Today the stylish image of Joe Camel can only be seen in back issues of magazines or faded billboards, however the character's impact is still visible in the demographics of today's smokers.

job was to encourage, entice, and lure. I became a high-priced accessory to murder." The National Association to Prevent Impaired Driving, a coalition of a hundred traffic safety, health, and public policy groups, issued a study titled "Beer and Fast Cars" that criticized the brewing companies for sponsoring auto races and putting their emblems on cars. The practice, said the report, targets young blue-collar men, the group with the highest incidence of auto accidents and arrests for driving under the influence of alcohol.

A study conducted for *The Wall Street Journal* showed that US citizens overwhelmingly opposed the illegalization of alcoholic beverages and tobacco products, but their attitudes toward dissemination of information about the substances are quite different. By a substantial majority, the respondents favored banning beer and wine ads from television (hard liquor was already banned) and banning all alcohol and tobacco advertising from print media as well.

Consumers with a Voice

In 1989 advertisers including Ralston Purina, General Mills, and Domino's Pizza canceled their advertising on NBC's controversial sketch comedy show "Saturday Night Live" at the urging of a religious group that viewed the show as objectionable. "It's a difficult time for advertisers," said an NBC spokesperson. "There are a lot of pressure groups out there."

Pepsi discovered that statement to be true when it presented a commercial featuring recording artist Madonna shortly after the controversial music video for her song "Like a Prayer" hit the airwaves. Some religious groups opposed Madonna's use of Christian symbols and deemed the video and the artist distasteful and offensive. Pepsi canceled the Madonna ad feeling its association with the artist would create negative publicity. Pepsi found itself in the same situation again in 2002. However, it only took a complaint by one person to cause the company to change its advertising campaign.

On his news show *The O'Reilly Factor* political commentator Bill O'Reilly questioned Pepsi's use of rapper Ludacris as a company spokesperson, claiming the rapper espouses violence, degrades women,

and promotes substance abuse.[20] Pepsi later dropped Ludacris as its spokesperson, but still received negative responses from consumers, and the rapper, who were disappointed that the company gave into pressure from one conservative figure.

It is not the options of well know figures that truly concern advertisers, it is the opinion of the American people. Irate individual consumers have always fired off letters and e-mails complaining about ads, but it is when special interest groups get involved that advertisers begin to worry. Groups such as the American Family Association's OneMillionMoms.com often participate in large-scale letter writing campaigns that aim to encourage advertisers to pull spots from television or radio shows that are considered immoral, violent, vulgar, or profane. The group takes credit for convincing large retail chains such as Lowe's to pull advertising from popular, but morally questionable, shows such as ABC's Desperate Housewives.[21] Organizations such as the American Family Association petition the advertisers of "distasteful" entertainment in attempt to pull funding from shows the organization finds offensive. A reduction in the number of paid advertisers may cause the entertainment industry remove certain content from their products.

Today more than ever, advertisers have to walk a fine line in order to avoid offending one or another side of almost any issue. Advertisers must sometimes choose to alienate one segment of the population in order to appeal to their target audience. Still advertisers keep their ear to ground when it comes to the opinion of the American consumer. A tarnished brand image can result in a major loss in revenue for advertisers.

MEDIA SELF-REGULATION

Mass media producers usually exercise their rights to refuse advertising that is in bad taste or that makes questionable claims and they are also in the position to reject spots that touch on controversial political issues. On the night of the 1984 presidential election, the WR Grace Company began running an "issues" spot on network television that depicted a baby crying when it was handed a bill for $50,000—the child's share of the national deficit. Two of the networks accepted the ad, but one rejected it. In 1986, the company submitted a new version of the

ACT against Predator Advertising

Action for Children's Television (ACT), a grass-roots organization formed by Peggy Charren in 1968, was created out of concern regarding the lack of suitable television programs for children. The group also had concerns about the type of advertising shown within children's programming. In 1989, ACT served as a consultant to the Consumers Union's holiday special, a program aimed to educate parents and children on the seduction of toy advertisements around the holiday season. "Buy Me That!", broadcasted on HBO, dissected several misleading techniques, including the implication that toys can walk and talk, the suggestion that a toy house or gas station comes with all the people and cars shown in the ad, and the failure to make clear that "some assembly required" may mean that an adult has to build a toy from parts before a child can play with it. The program also revealed how ads that show children happily bouncing around on Pogo Balls and tossing Flip Balls with the ease of Olympic athletes are the results of editing, and it is unlikely that most kids will be able to perform with the same happy satisfaction as those depicted on the screen.[22]

ACTs most successful campaign occurred when the organization help pass the Children's Television Act of 1990, which increased the quality of educational and informational on television. Shortly after the act was passed, Charren closed ACT and suggested that it was now up to parents to police the airwaves and decide for themselves what type of programs are best for their children.[23]

ad to the networks depicting an elderly man on trial in the year 2017 for failing to do anything to halt the growing national debt. This time all three networks would not accept the ad, stating that it was too controversial and exposed the networks to possible complaints under the **Fairness Doctrine,** a policy created by the FCC that required the coverage of all controversial issues to be fair and balanced.

J. Peter Grace, chairman and chief executive officer of the firm, responded: "They sell commercial time to advertise detergents, lingerie, hamburgers, appliances, and beer. Can it really be argued that selling time for conveying facts or ideas on important public issues will be detrimental to the interests of the country or the three networks?" Grace scoffed at the networks' contention that their news departments could do a better job of covering political issues than could business interests using advertising as a tool of information.

Most of the American advertising industry agreed with Grace and saw the network move as an attempt to pressure the Congress to do away with the Fairness Doctrine. In other words, the issues ads were being used as bargaining chips by the networks in their quest for less regulation. In 1987, the FCC finally did abolish most provisions of the Fairness Doctrine, but the regulatory body announced that it would continue to enforce the provision stating that issues currently the subject of voter referenda come under the Fairness Doctrine. Thus, opponents have to be given free air time to respond to statements made by another side on the issue.

For a long time the National Association of Broadcasters code was another media mechanism that affected what advertisers could do. First drafted in 1929, the code did not have the force of law; it was accepted by individual stations as a condition of membership in the NAB. When a suit resulted in the 1982 court decision that such a code unduly restricted the freedom to communicate information through advertising, the NAB withdrew it. Nevertheless, many of its provisions had been adopted as part of the standards and practices followed by individual stations, and thus they survive today.

The NAB code prohibited or limited the presentation of some products, which is why you never see hard liquor in commercials, and nobody actually *drinks* the beer or wine being advertised. Actors in commercials are permitted to be shown only lifting the glass or bottle toward or away from their lips. The film editor cuts away from the action during the moment when the liquid ostensibly is being guzzled.

Without the authority of the NAB code, broadcast stations are finding it more and more difficult to explain what messages are acceptable for commercials or public service announcements, and why. For example, a station had a long-standing policy of refusing messages advocating birth control, explaining that "controversial issues" were not suitable for ads and were more properly covered by public affairs discussion programs. The station decided to accept condom ads, however, if they were presented as part of a campaign to slow the spread of HIV/AIDS or other sexually transmitted diseases.

Most media will not accept an anonymous advertisement that discusses a public issue or in any way takes a political stand. The name of at least one sponsoring person must be placed in the ad. The media will refuse the ad if they cannot verify that the sponsoring name is a valid one. The media also rejects advertisements they feel may open them to libel suits; in the eyes of the law it is the media who publish the defamation and thus share the responsibility for it, even if the damaging words were written by the sponsor.

INDUSTRY SELF-REGULATION

In order to forestall regulation, the business community and the advertising industry try to prevent abuses that might lead to public outrage and government interference. Most advertisers support their local Better Business Bureaus in the campaign to warn consumers about fraudulent claims and deceptive practices. The local telephone company's yellow pages will not accept advertising it deems to be misleading, and merchants must prove claims they are the "best" or the "only" before the telephone book will carry those words.

The National Advertising Review Council (NARC) was formed by the national Better Business Bureau, the American Advertising Federation, the American Association of Advertising Agencies, and the Association of National Advertisers—in short, the major forces in the advertising industry—for the purpose of self-regulating advertising. The investigative body of the NARC is the National Advertising Division (NAD), which is empowered to initiate inquiries into deceptive or misleading advertising and to hear complaints from both consumers and advertisers.

In a typical complaint to the NAD, Orville Redenbacher popcorn charged that General Mills' Pop Secret cheese flavored microwave popcorn claimed consumers preferred its product to Orville Redenbacher's cheese flavored popcorn, but the test was taken before Redenbacher had reformulated its product and the ad was run after the new product was on the market. In a later test, Redenbacher claimed, its popcorn scored higher. General Mills said its ad had completed its run, and new ads would not be run until after further testing. Case closed.

A more exotic complaint was lodged by the Children's Advertising Review Unit of the NAD against a copying machine company whose ads showed frustrated business people throwing their copiers out of windows. The complaint said that the dangerous act of throwing things out windows might lead impressionable children to imitate the practice, and the scenes of copying machines crashing on the sidewalk might cause anxiety in young children. The sponsoring firm agreed to consider those concerns when planning new ads.

The NAD does not have the power to censor ads, impose fines, or bring any other sanctions. But both the act of review and the publication of the results in the leading trade publications are instructive to the advertising community and help prevent future abuses or excesses. In practice, the NARC and NAD have been effective forces in serving the information needs of the consumer.

The Future of Advertising: Keeping Current

With the introduction and expansion of new media, the advertising industry will have to continue to evolve. While traditional media such as television, newspapers, and radio will still be important outlets, advertisers must look at the cultural trends to determine the best way to reach consumers.

NEW TECHNOLOGY

Since a growing number of people are looking to the Internet to stay up-to-date on news and entertainment, advertisers are going to look to the Internet to spend large portions of their budgets. Paid search and pay-per-click advertising is just the beginning. Viral videos and blogs will emerge as an effective way to reach consumers.

Mobile phones have also changed the game for advertising. As a device that people rarely leave home without, mobile advertising is riding on the heels of the Internet as the newest way to deliver commercial messages to consumers 24 hours a day.

Predictions about Advertising

◆ The 30-Second Spot will finally die. The funeral will be attended by the 60-Second Spot, the Radio Ad, the Infomercial, and the Bumper Sticker.

◆ Blogs will change everything. For marketers, the blogosphere will prompt them to think very seriously about their business models.

◆ The consumer will be boss.

◆ The FDA will crack down on illegal drug marketing via the Internet.

◆ Advertising "one-stop shops" will thrive. As marketers are pressed to find ways to reach consumers, advertising holding companies like WPP and Interpublic will continue to evolve into "one-stop shops" for everything from advertising to guerrilla marketing to package design.

◆ The Hispanic consumer will arrive. After years of treating the Hispanic segment as an afterthought, marketers will shift more money to addressing the demographic with a much greater amount of TV, print, and online ads featuring Latinos.

◆ Marketers will continue to fear Google.

Todd Wasserman

After seeing a commercial have you ever thought to yourself, I could come up with a better way to deliver that message? If so, perhaps you should consider a career in advertising. The field of advertising can be very exciting for creative and managerial types alike. However, advertising involves more than just coming up with catchy jingles or clever slogans. It involves a high level of research, analysis, and at the heart of it all, salesmanship. There are different facets of advertising that job seekers might find interesting. On the administrative side, positions include account management, media planning, and market research. When hiring for these positions, agencies look for candidates with a strong business mind, effective communication skills, and leadership experience. On the creative side, openings are in copywriting and art direction. Agencies typically look for copywriters and art directors with the ability to think outside of the box and come up with innovative ideas that will benefit the client and the consumer. Jobs in advertising are a bit scarce and competition for positions, especially on the creative side, can be tough. However, if you have the right combination of business sense and creativity, you might just stand out in the crowd.[25]

Today's mobile phones are far more advanced than the two-pound clunkers introduced in the 1980s. With the ability to browse Web pages and send e-mails, mobile phones are like handheld computers. Now that many cell phone makers are creating phones with flash technology, it can be possible to send full length commercials to thousands of consumer via their mobile phones.

PRODUCT PLACEMENT

When you watch episodes of your favorite TV show or movie you may notice the main character is drinking a Vitamin Water and wearing a Ralph Lauren Polo shirt. Those items were not randomly placed in the scene; they were put there by advertisers. Advertisers hope that consumers see a character wearing or using a certain product then want to emulate that character's choices.

The practice of inserting advertising into film and television entertainment came under scrutiny when consumers started to take notice. The executive director of the Center for Science in the Public Interest used the op-ed page of The New York Times as a forum for alerting the public to the amount of advertising that is finding its way into the movies we pay to see. In one movie, "Bull Durham," he counted the presence of Miller beer products or signs 21 times, along with obvious plugs for a soft drink, a brand of bourbon, and even Oscar Mayer wieners—a total of 50 brand names on screen for an average of one every two minutes.

Today, some television shows can have up to 7,500 instances of product placement in a single season. TV executives may worry that too much product placement may harm the integrity of a show, but as more and more advertisers are choosing the Internet over TV, they welcome the revenue. For advertisers looking to continue marketing products on television, product placement will be an increasing force.

GUERRILLA MARKETING

Traditional advertisements like the 30 second commercial and the newspaper insert will soon take a back seat to more exciting and cost-effective forms of advertising formulated by guerrilla marketing. **Guerrilla marketing** is an unconventional form of advertising that attempts to get the maximum result from minimal resources. Examples of this type of advertising could involve a person running the New York City Marathon in a chicken suit and sign advertising a new fast food restaurant chain. The gimmick may cost a few hundred dollars, but the message could reach over one million spectators and possibly get news coverage.

Guerrilla marketing is not always used for a cheap laugh; it can sometimes call attention to serious issues. At Taiba Hospitals in Kuwait, administrators painted pink strips on a speed bump at the entrance of the hospital. A sign next to the speed bump said, "Feel the bump? Have your breasts checked." The ad was a high impact way to remind women to get a yearly breast examination.[24]

In the next decade we will see a lot of changes in the way advertisers deliver their commercial messages and the number of commercial messages we are exposed to will continue to grow. Whether these changes and increases will benefit us as consumers or saturate our lives with unneeded products is unclear. However, good or bad advertising will still remain an integral part of our economy and culture.

Chapter Summary

◆ Americans are exposed to thousands of commercial messages a day from various types of media outlets
◆ Advertising has evolved over the years to adapt to the changes in mass media
◆ Advertisers go beyond standard television and radio commercials to advertise products. They use methods such as direct mail, point of sale advertising, outdoor signage, and the Internet to promote their message.
◆ Government agency, community groups, and the media regulate advertisements to ensure they are not dishonest, misleading, or distasteful
◆ Advertising is a continuous force in our economy, and advertisers are finding new and inventive ways to reach consumers

Glossary

Advertising—the act of calling the public's attention to a product, service, or need
Bait and switch—a method of fraudulent advertising in which a company advertises a product at an unprofitable price then reveals to a potential customer that the product is unavailable
Consumerism—the theory that an increase in the consumption of goods and services will benefit the economy
Direct mail—a type of advertisement sent through the postal service
Fairness Doctrine—a policy created by the FCC that required the coverage of all controversial issues to be fair and balanced
Guerrilla marketing—an unconventional form of advertising that attempts to get the maximum result from minimal resources
Outdoor advertising—the placement of ads outside in the view of the general public, typically on billboards, signs, or other outdoor objects
Paid search—a form of advertising used on a search engine Web site, which allows companies to have a brief advertisement placed on top or next to search results when certain keywords are used
Pay-per-click—a form of advertising in which Web page administrators allow outside companies to place advertisements on their Web pages in exchange for a small fee, which is paid to the Web site administrator, when a user clicks on the ad
Point of sale advertising—the placement of products, promotions, or other offers on or near a checkout counter

Discussion Questions

1. How aware are you of the advertising in your environment? Do you think you have ever been swayed to purchase a product without being aware of the commercial message that prompted your purchase?
2. Do you think you benefit from advertising? Do you use it to help make decisions about what products to buy?
3. Do you think that banning the tobacco advertising is against the first amendment? Should tobacco companies have the same rights as other companies?
4. Do you think advertising has become too intrusive? Would you be willing to pay more money to media outlets if they removed advertising?
5. What examples of guerrilla marketing have you noticed in the last few years?

Supplemental Web Sites

The FCC Web site: http://www.fcc.gov/

Find information on current policies, ongoing campaigns, or violations regarding the regulations of advertisements. You can also learn how voice your own opinion.

Political advertisements: http://www.livingroom-candidate.org/

Search through television commercials for political candidates from the last fifty years. Discover how politics have changed since the introduction political advertising.

Google advertising: http://www.google.com

Learn about the different ways Google uses advertising to generate revenue.

Endnotes

1. Brenda O'Neill, "Can you feel sorry for an ad man?" *BBC News* November 21, 2005 at *http://news.bbc.co.uk/2/hi/uk_news/magazine/4456176.stm*.
2. "Advertising Age: The Advertising Century" *Ad Age* at *http://adage.com/century/timeline/index.html*.
3. Scot Mondore "One Hundred Years of Player Endorsements: Honus Wagner and Louisville Slugger" The National Baseball Hall of Fame and Museum February 19, 2007 at *http://www.baseballhalloffame.org/news/article.jsp?ymd=20070219&content_id=859&vkey=hof_news*.
4. The Advertising Council, "Ad Council: The Story of the Ad Council" at *http://www.adcouncil.org/timeline.html*. Retrieved October 10, 2008.
5. *http://wehner.tamu.edu/mgmt.www/v-buenger/466/Coke_and_Pepsi.pdf*.
6. "Mobile Advertising" *The Economist* October 4, 2007 at *http://www.economist.com/business/displaystory.cfm?story_id=9912455*.
7. Merriam-Webster at *http://www.merriam-webster.com/dictionary/consumerism*
8. "The Role of Advertising in America" Association of National Advertisers at *http://www.ana.net/advocacy2/content/advamerica*.
9. Jennifer L. Schenker, "Point-of-Sale Advertising Goes High Tech" BusinessWeek September 22, 2008 at *http://www.businessweek.com/globalbiz/content/sep2008/gb20080922_109810.htm*.
10. Stephanie Clifford, "Summer Silliness Brings a Pizza Field and a Giant Oreo" The New York Times August 1, 2008 at *http://www.nytimes.com/2008/08/01/business/media/01adco.html?pagewanted=1&_r=1*
11. Google Web site at *http://www.google.com/ads/*.
12. Google Web site Investors' information at *http://investor.google.com/fin_data.html*.
13. "The Living Room Candidate: 1952 Eisenhower vs. Stevenson" Museum of the Moving Image at *http://www.livingroomcandidate.org/commercials/1952*.
14. Mark Preston, "Political television advertising to reach $3 billion" CNN October 15, 2008 at *http://www.cnn.com/2007/POLITICS/10/15/ad.spending/*.
15. N.W. Ayer & Son. (2008). In *Encyclopedia Britannica*. Retrieved October 17, 2008, from Encyclopedia Britannica Online: *http://www.britannica.com/EBchecked/topic/1349123/NW-Ayer-Son*
16. Anthony Pratkanis, Elliot Aronson *Age of Propaganda*.
17. Chris Sharp, "Subliminal Messaging: A life changing phenomenon" Helium at *http://www.helium.com/items/383493-subliminal-messaging-a-life-changing-phenomenom*
18. Jane E. Brody, "Study Ties Women's Brands To Smoking Increase for Girls" *The New York Times* February 23, 1994 at *http://query.nytimes.com/gst/fullpage.html?res=9405E5DB113BF930A15751C0A962958260&sec=health&spon=&pagewanted=all*.
19. "Joe Camel Advertising Campaign Violates Federal Law, FTC Says" Federal Trade Commission Press

Release May 28, 1997 at *http://www.ftc.gov/opa/1997/05/joecamel.shtm*.

20 Bill O'Reilly "Challenging Pepsi" *The O'Reilly Factor* August 28, 2002 at *http://www.foxnews.com/story/0, 2933, 61546,00.html*.

21 Frank Rich "The Great Indecency Hoax" *The New York Times* November 28, 2004 at *http://www.nytimes.com/2004/11/28/arts/28rich.html?pagewanted=print&position*.

22 Walter Goodman, "TV VIEW; A Cautionary Guide for Little Customers" *The New York Times* December 3, 1989 at *http://query.nytimes.com/gst/fullpage. html?res=950DE1D61030F930A35751C1A96F948260&sec=&spon=&pagewanted=all*.

23 William Richter, "Action for Children's Television" The Museum of Broadcast Communication at *http://www.museum.tv/archives/etv/A/htmlA/actionforch/actionforch.htm*

24 "Taiba Hospital: Feel the bump? Have your breasts checked" *www.Jazzarh.net* March 18, 2008 at *http://www.jazarah.net/blog/taiba-hospital-felt-the-bump-have-your-breasts-checked/*

25 "Guide to Careers in Advertising" Advertising Educational Foundation at *http://www.aef.com/industry/ careers/1422#3*.

LAW AND ETHICS

Genelle Belmas

Chapter Objectives:

◆ Define and distinguish among law, policy, and ethics.

◆ Understand the history, theories, and interpretations of free speech and free press in the United States.

◆ Identify legal, ownership, and regulatory issues faced by the mass media.

◆ Understand the ways in which ethics is relevant to individuals in the media, as well as to media organizations.

Introduction

In theory, the laws of society are based on the ethical morals and values of the people living in it. For the most part, this theory is true, and many laws uphold what most of us know to be fundamentally wrong, such as murder and theft. Other laws, however, are commonly broken. When was the last time you drove a car above the legal speed limit? Traffic laws are among those that many of us break—and usually feel little remorse for doing so. The gray areas between these extremes reflect the fact that we all have our individual beliefs about right and wrong, and we often disagree about legal matters. Controversial moral issues such as immigration, abortion, and the death penalty have been issues of contention in the United States for decades. While legislative decisions determine the legality of these issues, members of society continue to argue about the ethics of them.

On a smaller scale, individuals work out their disputes about who is right and who is wrong in small claims and divorce courts. Our litigious society is so rife with these squabbles that we can even watch as other people's petty tiffs are mediated on television by the likes of Judge Judy. According to the National Center for State Courts, state trial courts averaged about one incoming civil, domestic relations, criminal, juvenile, or traffic case for every three American citizens in 2003. That's over 100 million cases in state systems alone![1]

Lawsuits aren't only born of the disputes between individuals; media and other organizations also contribute to this case crunch. The Recording Industry Association of America reported that it brought suit against 8,650 file sharers in 2005, many of them students using university high-speed connections. This organization alone brought to court an average of over 700 lawsuits a month. While the debate over the legality of file-sharing may have some ethical concerns, this controversy highlights how disputes about morality may be veils for disputes about money and the competing interests not of consciences, but of cash.

In this chapter we will look at the landscape of media law and ethics, how they interact, and how they affect media organizations and professionals.

Law, Policy, and Ethics

While legislation often overlaps with our morals, it is important to recognize the different definitions for terms involved in a discussion of these issues. **Policy** is an overarching plan or goal of a country

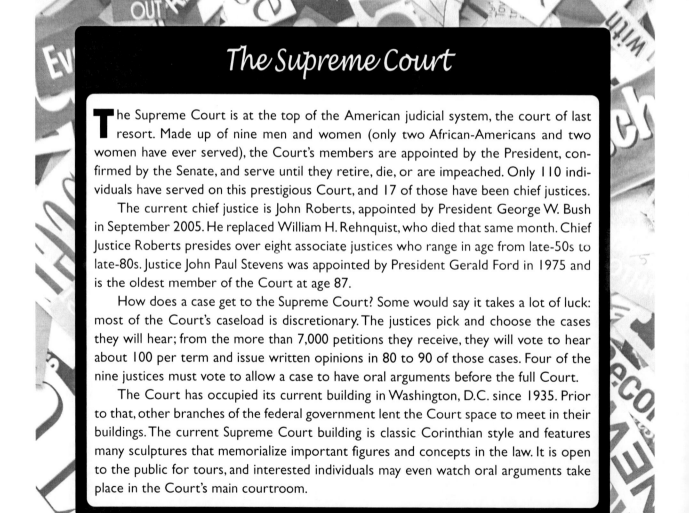

The Supreme Court

The Supreme Court is at the top of the American judicial system, the court of last resort. Made up of nine men and women (only two African-Americans and two women have ever served), the Court's members are appointed by the President, confirmed by the Senate, and serve until they retire, die, or are impeached. Only 110 individuals have served on this prestigious Court, and 17 of those have been chief justices.

The current chief justice is John Roberts, appointed by President George W. Bush in September 2005. He replaced William H. Rehnquist, who died that same month. Chief Justice Roberts presides over eight associate justices who range in age from late-50s to late-80s. Justice John Paul Stevens was appointed by President Gerald Ford in 1975 and is the oldest member of the Court at age 87.

How does a case get to the Supreme Court? Some would say it takes a lot of luck: most of the Court's caseload is discretionary. The justices pick and choose the cases they will hear; from the more than 7,000 petitions they receive, they will vote to hear about 100 per term and issue written opinions in 80 to 90 of those cases. Four of the nine justices must vote to allow a case to have oral arguments before the full Court.

The Court has occupied its current building in Washington, D.C. since 1935. Prior to that, other branches of the federal government lent the Court space to meet in their buildings. The current Supreme Court building is classic Corinthian style and features many sculptures that memorialize important figures and concepts in the law. It is open to the public for tours, and interested individuals may even watch oral arguments take place in the Court's main courtroom.

or an organization, and **laws** are put into place to implement a policy plan or goal. Laws can take the form of statutes passed by legislative bodies at federal, state, or local levels; administrative mandates from agencies like the Federal Communications Commission (FCC); or rulings handed down by judges—**common law**. **Ethics,** on the other hand, often informs law but, more specifically, involves balancing competing interests to determine the "right" or "correct" course of action.

As an example, the United States has a policy that government should be generally open to its constituents. In other words, most governing should not take place in secrecy: the House and Senate are presumed to have open sessions unless there is a need to close them, and all states have open meetings and records laws. Ethics informs the open government idea by suggesting that having "government in a fishbowl" is morally correct in a democracy, where the rulers rule with the consent of the governed. In the case of executive agencies, like the FCC, the Food and Drug Administration, and the Federal Aviation Administration, the policy of openness of records is codified into law by the federal Freedom of Information Act (FOIA). The FOIA requires agencies to make requested records available to the public unless the records fall under nine exemptions to openness, such as harming national security interests.

In the United States, the highest judicial body is the Supreme Court. Made up of nine men and women and based in Washington, D.C., the Supreme Court is responsible for deciding some of the most controversial and morally charged cases. Unless Congress passes a law or a Constitutional amendment is passed to contradict the Court's ruling, these decisions are final and make up the body of common law, also referred to as case law.

History of Free Speech and Press in America

The Constitution of the United States contains a Bill of Rights, which gives important protections to individuals in America. It reads, "Congress shall make no law respecting an establishment of religion, or prohibiting the free exercise thereof; or abridging the freedom of speech, or of the press; or the right of the people peaceably to assemble, and to petition the government for a redress of grievances." Within that amendment are five discrete rights: free speech, free press, freedom of religion, freedom of assembly, and freedom to petition the government. We will focus primarily on the free press aspect, although a free press is of course closely related to freedom of speech.

As we will see, even though the First Amendment explicitly says that "Congress shall make no law . . . abridging the freedom . . . of the press," Congress makes laws affecting the media all the time. Most of the body of First Amendment law is made up of limitations on governmental power to regulate speech and press.

THE ZENGER TRIAL: THE IMPORTANCE OF TRUTH

A significant landmark for free speech and press occurred in 1735, when John Peter Zenger's newspaper, the *New York Weekly Journal*, criticized William Cosby, governor of New York. The governor put Zenger in jail for violating the law of **sedition,** which was quite clear at the time: Criticism of the government or its officials, even if true, that aroused the sentiments of the people against the government or the officials would be considered seditious libel, and there was no defense.

Zenger hired renowned Philadelphia attorney Andrew Hamilton, who took a unique approach to the problem. He knew that Zenger had, under the law, libeled Governor Cosby. Instead of trying to argue that Zenger had not libeled the governor, Hamilton instead attacked the law itself. He asked the jury to consider whether truth should not be considered to be a defense to libel: "I hope it is not our bare printing and publishing a paper that will make it a libel. You will have something more to do before you make my client a libeler. For the words themselves must be libelous that is, false, scandalous, and seditious or else we are not guilty." To drive home the point, Hamilton added, "Truth ought to govern the whole affair of libels."[2]

The jury went into deliberation and returned a verdict of not guilty, and Zenger was freed. The Zenger case remains important for several reasons.

It is one of the earliest and most famous jury nullifications, in which the jury gives a "not guilty" verdict despite the fact that they believe the defendant was responsible for the action because they believe the law itself is wrong; and second, it is a strong statement of the importance of truth in American media law.

EARLY THEORIES OF FREE SPEECH AND PRESS

There have always been individuals hostile to attempts by the government to regulate their speech, either through **prior review**—forcing material to be shared with the regulating body prior to its publication or broadcast—and **prior restraint**—banning the publication or broadcast of the material after reviewing it—or **censorship**—prohibiting the publication or broadcast of certain material. In England in 1644, John Milton wrote *Areopagitica: For the Liberty of Unlicensed Printing* in response to a licensing order from Parliament. The order required authors and creators to submit their works to licensors for permission to publish. In the pamphlet, Milton denounced the licensing arrangement and called for government to hold publishers and authors accountable for what they wrote after it had been published, instead of engaging in prior review. Milton too supported truth as the ultimate goal of publication: "And though all the winds of doctrine were let loose to play upon the earth, so Truth be in the field, we do injuriously by licensing and prohibiting to misdoubt her strength. Let her and Falsehood grapple; who ever knew Truth put to the worse in a free and open encounter?"

In 1859, John Stuart Mill, an English philosopher and theorist, added his book *On Liberty* to the lexicon of defenses of free speech. He proposed a "harm principle," in which he suggests that the only legitimate way in which society can interfere with the free action of another is to prevent harm: "The sole end for which mankind are warranted, individually or collectively, in interfering with the liberty of action of any of their number, is self-protection. That the only purpose for which power can be rightfully exercised over any member of a civilized community, against his will, is to prevent harm to others."[3] Mill argued that free speech is necessary for a self-governing nation. Without free discourse, truth may never emerge and individuals will never be able to examine their beliefs with an open dialogue to be sure that those beliefs are correct.

Mill's writings form the foundation for the **marketplace of ideas** theory of free speech and press. Under this theory, all ideas should be permitted to be published and disseminated so that consumers may pick and choose, culling through the falsities and bad ideas to find the good ones. Thus, the government should not engage in censorship because it is important to a free flow of information and ideas that all ideas, no matter how farfetched, dangerous, or seditious, must be allowed to be distributed.

Early Interpretations of the First Amendment

Although the Bill of Rights was ratified in 1791, it was not until the early 1900s that the First Amendment would first be interpreted—and in the context of free speech, not press. In several cases during World War I that involved individuals opposed to the draft (*Schenck v. United States* and *Abrams v. United States*, both in 1919) the **clear and present danger doctrine** was suggested. Under this doctrine, the government may only punish a speech act if it invokes a clear and present danger of harm. For example, if an individual falsely shouts fire in a crowded theater and causes a panic when patrons trample each other to the exits, the government may punish the shouter for causing a clear and present danger. This doctrine is still in use today, although it was modified in 1969 in *Brandenburg v. Ohio* to become the **imminent lawless action doctrine,** whereby the government may only punish speech that directly provokes imminent lawless action. In *Gitlow v. New York* (1925), the Supreme Court made the First Amendment applicable to the states via the Fourteenth Amendment.

More important for the press, however, was a 1931 case that made the press nearly immune from most censorship. Jay Near published a rabblerousing newspaper called *The Saturday Press* in Minneapolis. The paper was anti-Semitic, anti-black, anti-labor, and anti-Catholic, and Minneapolis officials ordered the paper shut down under a nuisance law. Near appealed, and his case went to the Supreme Court.

In *Near v. Minnesota* (1931), the Supreme Court said that in most cases, prior restraint would be illegal in all but three instances: the publication of troop movements during wartime could be subject to prior restraint, as could obscene speech and incitements to violent overthrow of the government. This case had the ultimate effect of barring most censorial actions by the government on the media, and its ruling was relied upon in the famous "Pentagon Papers" case of the 1970s (*New York Times Co. v. United States*, 1971), which permitted the *New York Times* to publish classified information about the war in Southeast Asia that the government had not proven would cause "grave and irreparable" damage to national security concerns.

Legal Issues Facing the Mass Media

With great freedom, as the American press has, comes great responsibility. As noted above, the courts and Congress regularly make laws that affect the media. These laws exist to protect consumers and give them recourse if they have been harmed by the media in some way. Many of the laws are a check on the media's power to harm—either through falsities, shabby reporting, invasion of individual privacy, or infringement of intellectual property rights.

American broadcasters operate under a more restrictive regime of laws than newspapers, magazines, and other print media. Under this dual system of regulation, the broadcast media—over-the-air "free" television and radio—are subject to additional regulations on what they may or may not do. These restrictions were originally put into place because the broadcast media are trustees of what was believed to be a scarce, public resource (the airwaves). Now, as cable, satellite, and high-definition TV and radio are becoming more and more popular, these regulations have outlasted the original justifications for them.

Issues of ownership and access have been important areas of concern for both media professionals and the public. Who gets to participate in the marketplace of ideas, and whose ideas will not see the light of day? How is media concentrated, and who owns what? All of these questions are important to understanding the role of mass media in a modern age. Despite the rise of Web 2.0 and the participatory Internet community, many individuals still get their news and information through traditional media like television and newspapers, and the owners of these media have a large, and arguably disproportionate, ability to affect what we believe to be important.

Advertising is also regulated in small and large ways. The Supreme Court has developed the **commercial speech doctrine** to determine when and how advertising can be regulated, and the advertising industry has an active self-regulatory system in place to police itself and its participants.

We first turn to areas of First Amendment jurisprudence that affect all forms of mass media, regardless of message or technology.

LIBEL

Any media organization, whether news, advertising, public relations, or entertainment, may be sued for **libel**—an untruthful, defamatory statement about someone that is published or broadcast through the media. Organizations are wary of libel suits. According to the Media Law Research Center, the average award for plaintiffs who won libel suits between 1980 and 2006 was $560,092.[4] The highest award against a media organization was $222.7 million, against the Wall Street Journal in 1997 (*MMAR Group, Inc. v. Dow Jones & Co.*, 1997). Because of the cost involved, media organizations of all types take libel actions very seriously.

The libel with which Zenger was charged is much different from libel actions of today. Of course, the media have many more protections than they did in Zenger's time, and now the burden rests on the aggrieved party to prove not only that his or her reputation was harmed (defamation), but also that the publication was false and that the harm resulted in some compensable damage that the court can remedy.

Prior to 1964, libel operated in the common law, and under the common law of libel, a person who believed that he/she had been libeled had only to prove that his/her reputation had been harmed, the information had been published, and he/she had been sufficiently identified in that publication. But in the case of *New York Times v. Sullivan* (1964), arguably one of the most important First Amendment cases in history, the Supreme Court changed the rules.

In that case, L.B. Sullivan, a police commissioner in Montgomery, Ala., argued that he had been identified and defamed in an advertisement taken out by civil rights groups in the *New York Times*. Sullivan was never mentioned by name but said that the text of the ad, which criticized the actions of the police, criticized him as well. The Alabama Supreme Court agreed and awarded Sullivan $500,000 in damages. The *Times* appealed, and the United States Supreme Court reversed the award and developed a new test to determine if public officials like Sullivan have been libeled and are entitled to monetary compensation.

The Court stated that public officials should be open to criticism and that debate on issues of public importance should be "uninhibited, robust, and wide-open" and may contain harsh attacks on public officials. Those public officials may only recover damages for libel under certain limited circumstances. Public officials, in addition to proving defamation, identification, and publication under the common law, must also prove that the media organization acted with **actual malice**—either knew the information it was publishing was false and published

The Food Lion Story

Imagine flipping on your television and watching an investigative program that suggests that your local grocery store, to maximize its profits, was bleaching old meat and reselling it, selling spoiled potato salad, or forcing its employees to work additional hours without paying them. You'd be unlikely to shop at that store again!

In North Carolina in 1996, a jury awarded a $5.5 million verdict against ABC News for a 1992 *PrimeTime Live* investigation on Food Lion, a Southern grocery chain. Food Lion alleged that ABC's journalists had gotten jobs in Food Lion stores by creating fraudulent resumes that lied about grocery work experience and had trespassed with hidden cameras to film behind-the-scenes work at several Food Lion stores. Moreover, Food Lion claimed that the footage had been edited to suggest things that were not true: a clip about an employee telling an ABC reporter disguised as her colleague that a deli product had soured was cut before the employee instructs the reporter to throw the product away. The verdict was later reduced on appeal.

ABC defended its actions by saying that it was deceiving for a greater good: to reveal dangerous and illegal activities by Food Lion. Food Lion never sued ABC for libel, so the truth or falsity of the broadcast was never considered in court. The case raises issues in both law and ethics. Does the end ultimately justify the means? Should hidden cameras ever be permissible under any circumstances? Should lying to get to the truth be an acceptable ethical approach? Should the law punish truthful information gained by deceptive means?

it anyway, or acted with **reckless disregard** as to truth or falsity, that is, it didn't care if what it was publishing was true or not. This requirement made it much harder for public officials—and later, public figures like celebrities and professional sports figures—to recover damages for libel. A 1974, *Gertz v. Welch*, set the bar lower for private individuals, who must only prove **negligence** (journalistic sloppiness) rather than actual malice in order to recover for libel.

Libel doesn't just exist on newsprint and over the airwaves. Individuals and companies who libel someone online are subject to the same rules as those who libel in traditional media. However, internet service providers like NetZero or Earthlink are not liable for damages for the distribution of the libelous material, thanks to a law that is part of the Telecommunications Act of 1996. Section 230, as it is often called, exempts internet service providers from liability for libel as long as they do not act as editors of the materials posted. For example, if one individual libels another on a public America Online (AOL) message board, the victim may sue the perpetrator of the libel but not AOL.

PRIVACY

In the age of identity theft and the omnipresent media, consumers are more concerned than ever about protecting themselves from intrusion into their private lives. Media law considers invasion of privacy to be a **tort**—an injury or wrong inflicted on one person by another person, who is legally responsible for any damages sought. The common law of privacy includes four torts: intrusion upon seclusion, publication of private facts, false light, and misappropriation. Each state may recognize one or more of the privacy torts as causes of action.

Intrusion Upon Seclusion. **Intrusion upon seclusion** is a physical invasion of one's personal space or property—think of your cranky neighbor's NO TRESPASSING sign. Media professionals are not permitted to trespass on private property to get a story or to use telephoto lenses to peer through a window. Jacqueline Kennedy Onassis obtained restraining orders against a photographer who hounded her and her children in search of their images to sell to media publications (*Galella v. Onassis*, 1973).

Publication of Private Facts. As you may have guessed, publication of private facts occurs when the media obtain private facts about a person and publish them. Oliver Sipple experienced this tort when he saved the life of President Gerald Ford from an assassin's bullet. Sipple was gay and active in the San Francisco gay community, a fact that his family and employer did not know. When the local newspaper found out that he was gay, it hailed him not only as a hero but a gay hero, resulting in his estrangement from his family. Sipple sued the newspaper and lost; the court reasoned that because he was "out" in San Francisco and active in his local gay community, the fact that he was gay was not really private (*Sipple v. Chronicle Publishing*, 1984).

False Light. Similar to libel, **false light** occurs when the media distorts or falsifies information and implies untruths about someone. This tort is perhaps best typified by the story of Linda Duncan, who was filmed walking down the street by a Washington, D.C. news station. A shot of her face accompanied a voiceover for the news story about a possible new cure for genital herpes which said, "For the 20 million Americans who have herpes, it's not a cure." Duncan, who did not have herpes, sued the television station and won because the court said a reasonable person viewing the newscast would assume that the juxtaposition of the voiceover and Duncan's image meant that she had herpes (*Duncan v. WJLA-TV, Inc.*, 1984).

Misappropriation. **Misappropriation** occurs when someone uses someone else's name or likeness for commercial gain without consent. Late-night talk show host Johnny Carson successfully sued for misappropriation when a company whose business was to rent and sell portable toilets called its products "Here's Johnny Portable Toilets" without Carson's consent. The defendants admitted they would not have chosen the name without the association to Carson and his famous introduction phrase, "Heeeeeeeeeeeeere's Johnny!" which is strongly associated with him and his nightly program (*Carson v. Here's Johnny Portable Toilets*, 1983).

INTELLECTUAL PROPERTY

In the information age, rather than buying and selling wheat and cotton, we trade in information, which has become an important commodity. A large legal practice has arisen around the protection of this kind of property, including written work, music, company product names and logos, and inventions. The Constitution offers protection for intellectual property "to promote the Progress of Science and useful Arts, by securing for limited Times to Authors and Inventors the exclusive Right to their respective Writings and Discoveries."

Intellectual property law can be divided into three different areas: copyright, trademark, and patent law. **Copyright law** protects original creations, either published or unpublished, when they are set down in fixed form (like written on paper or saved as a computer file). **Trademark law** shields consumers from confusion by protecting words, symbols, or phrases used to identify products from each other. **Patent law** gives inventors exclusive rights to benefit from their inventions for a limited time; patents can be granted to inventions that are novel, useful, and not obvious.

Copyright. Copyright is protected only by federal law. While creators don't have to register their copyrights on their creative works to have protection, doing so gives the creator additional protections and benefits. At the same time, just because a work is copyrighted does not mean that it cannot be used by anyone else for any reason. The **fair use doctrine** provides for some uses of copyrighted materials without the permission of the copyright holder. For example, a newspaper reporter reviewing the latest bestselling novel may quote briefly from the novel to support claims about the book. Courts use the fair use doctrine to assess the nature of the use of the copyrighted work, the nature of the work itself, the amount of the use, and the effect of the use on the market value of the work. The doctrine protects uses like reviews, educational and non-profit endeavors, and research.

Sharing music online is not a fair use, and most individuals who engage in file-sharing understand that much of what they are downloading and sharing is in fact copyrighted. The Recording Industry Association of America (RIAA) has been active in pursuing file-sharers. The Supreme Court has also said that services that encourage users to engage in illegal file-sharing can be shut down. In *MGM v. Grokster* (2005), the Court said that "one who

distributes a device with the object of promoting its use to infringe copyright, as shown by clear expression or other affirmative steps taken to foster infringement, is liable for the resulting acts of infringement by third parties." In other words, Grokster had encouraged the use of its software to infringe the copyrights on protected songs. Similar lawsuits drove the popular music-sharing software company Napster to bankruptcy in 2002. In October 2007, the RIAA successfully sued a Minnesota woman for $220,000 for copyright infringement of 24 songs through file-sharing, in the first piracy case to go to trial.

Copyright is also protected online by a law called the *Digital Millennium Copyright Act* (DMCA), which was signed into law in 1998. The DMCA did several important things. First, it criminalized any attempt to circumvent copyright protections. Second, it provided protection for online service providers against copyright infringement lawsuits if the online service provider adheres to a set of guidelines and removes allegedly infringing material from its website upon notification.

Trademark. Trademark law, which can be protected at both the state and federal levels, exists primarily to protect the consumer. If, for example, a consumer purchases a brand-name cola product, that consumer expects that cola to taste the way it always has. Trademark law protects symbols, pictures, words, slogans, and even shapes and colors. The owner of a trademark has the exclusive right to use that trademark in whatever manner he/she likes in relation to the products it identifies. The term "trademark" applies to goods, like shoes, computers, or bread; "servicemark" applies to services like banking, insurance, or airline travel; and the generic "mark" is used to refer to either. If a trademark or servicemark is registered with the U.S. Patent and Trademark Office, it may use the registered symbol, ®. If not, the terms ™ or ℠ may be used prior to legal registration.

The strongest marks are "fanciful" or "arbitrary": they bear no obvious connection to the goods or services they identify. The word "Apple" and its corresponding fruit-shaped logo is an arbitrary mark for computer products, as most individuals would not have thought of apples in connection with computers. In fact, legal disputes between Apple Corps

Ltd., the commercial guardian of iconic rock legends The Beatles, and Apple Inc., Steve Jobs's computer juggernaut, have persisted for nearly three decades. The original settlement allowed Apple Inc. to use the name and logo with the proviso that the company would not enter the music business. When it began selling iPods and offering digital music downloads on iTunes, Apple Corps filed additional trademark suits, which have led to millions of dollars of settlements and have kept surviving members of The Beatles from allowing their music to be available on iTunes.

Fanciful marks are invented or made up, like Xerox or Kodak. The best marks develop a secondary meaning associated with their use; for example, even though first names are not usually distinctive enough to gain trademark protection, marks like Tiffany for jewelry and Ben & Jerry's for ice cream have enough name recognition to have developed secondary meanings. Most people can easily conjure an image of a Tiffany lamp and will likely think of ice cream when someone says Ben & Jerry's. If you are looking to develop a new trademark, think first of fanciful or arbitrary marks that are easily distinguishable and easy to register.

Patent. Patents protect inventions for a limited amount of time by granting exclusive rights to the inventor. New patents are generally protected for 20 years. The owner gets "the right to exclude others from making, using, offering for sale, or selling" the invention. There are three types of patents. Utility patents may be granted to anyone who invents or discovers new and useful processes or machines. Design patents may be granted to anyone who invents a new, original, and ornamental design for a product. Plant patents can be granted to the inventor or discoverer of any distinct and new variety of plant. An idea or concept may not be patented; only an invention that uses the idea may be patented.

FREEDOM OF INFORMATION

As noted earlier, the policy of the United States government is one of openness. To that end, the federal government has two major laws that are meant to ensure open meetings and access to government records. The Government in the Sunshine Act of 1976 provides that all meetings of executive agencies must be open to the public unless they are specifically required to be closed under 10 exemptions (for example, high-level national security or ongoing lawsuits). Minutes of those meetings must also be made available.

The Freedom of Information Act of 1966, as discussed earlier in this chapter, assumes openness for records of those same executive agencies unless the records fall under one of the nine exemptions, which are similar to the Sunshine Act's exemptions. The act was amended in 1996 to encourage the collection and dissemination of electronic records as well as traditional paper records and files. At the end of 2007, President Bush signed an amendment to the FOIA creating a system to track the status of FOIA requests, establishing a hotline for problems faced by federal agencies, and offering ombudsmen as alternatives to litigation in disclosure disputes.

The FOIA not only allows news organizations access to the information they need to ensure the accuracy of the news they disseminate, but it also, therefore, allows individuals access to the truth. In 2008, the Federal Government approved a $1.5 trillion bailout for financially fledgling banks. Although the Federal Reserve agreed to transparency when doling out the cash, it was sued by Bloomberg news organization when the Fed refused to disclose the names of the companies set to receive cuts of this chunk of taxpayer money. Bloomberg relied on the FOIA to make its case.

BROADCAST REGULATION

Over-the-air television and radio broadcasters do not receive the same level of protection as print media. The rationale for this different treatment is that because broadcast media is uniquely accessible. While you can choose whether or not to read a news article, children or anyone else within hearing range of a broadcast may not always be able to avoid hearing it, so broadcasters must be regulated more strongly.

Regulation of the broadcast media can be traced back to the sinking of the ship RMS *Titanic*. In the aftermath of the April 1912 disaster, during which many deaths could have been avoided had all ships been using their wireless systems, Congress passed the Radio Act of 1912, which required all ships to have a 24-hour wireless watch. As more and more individuals and companies began to broadcast, the airwaves became crowded and chaotic. The Radio Act of 1927 created the Federal Radio Commission and gave that commission the power to grant broadcast licenses and assign frequencies to radio stations. This act considered "public interest, convenience and necessity" as it formed the foundation of the dual system of regulation that exists today; no such mandate exists for print media. The Radio Act of 1927 was replaced by the Communications Act of 1934, which created the FCC and gave it broad regulatory powers. The Telecommunications Act of 1996 augmented the Communications Act and will be discussed later. Below are some of the elements of the broadcasting regulatory scheme.

Political Advertising.

As part of their service to the public, broadcasters must provide access to their television and radio stations for political advertising purchased by candidates. The "equal time rule," Section 315 of the Communications Act, says that if a broadcaster permits the purchase of airtime by any candidate for local or state office, that broadcaster must permit all other candidates the option to purchase airtime as well. Broadcasters may deny all candidates for state or local office the ability to buy airtime, but Section 312 of the Communications Act mandates that all candidates for federal office must be permitted to buy airtime if they request it. Moreover, all airtime sold to candidates for political advertising must be sold at the lowest rates the broadcaster charges to any of its regular advertisers.

The V-chip.

In response to concerns that broadcast television was becoming more sexual, more violent, and more profane, the Telecommunications Act of 1996 contains a mandate that all new televisions 13 inches or larger manufactured after 1999 have installed V-chip technology. This technology makes it possible for parents to block access to undesirable television content from their children. Broadcasters were offered the chance to voluntarily rate and categorize their programs so that parents could choose to block or receive programming based on these ratings. The ratings appear in Table 14.1. While the V-chip technology has been successfully implemented, a 2007 FCC report focuses on the failure of the V-chip to keep objectionable material away from children. Not only are producers free to set their own ratings, but the report also cites research that suggests that only 15 percent of all parents use the V-chip: many are unaware that their new TVs have the technology, and others are unwilling to navigate the sometimes confusing directions to use it.[5]

Obscenity.

In 1973, the landmark *Miller v. California* case decided that **obscenity** is not protected by the First Amendment and established a test to define obscenity for the purposes of regulating it. Known as the Miller test, the following three criteria must be met in order for material to qualify as obscene: (1) an average person, applying contemporary community standards, must find that the material, as a whole, appeals to the prurient interest (i.e., material having a tendency to excite lustful thoughts); (2) the material must depict or describe, in a patently offensive way, sexual conduct specifically defined by applicable law; and (3) the material, taken as a whole, must lack serious literary, artistic, political, or scientific value.[6] The government may ban the creation, distribution, sale, and possession of speech that it finds to be obscene.

Indecency.

Indecency regulations have been around since the 1920s. In the 1978 *FCC v. Pacifica Foundation* case, the Supreme Court established that indecency could not be broadcast during the hours of 6:00 a.m. to 10:00 p.m., when children are most likely to be in the audience. The case involved George Carlin's "Filthy Words" monologue, in which the comedian repeats "the seven words you can't say on television" ad nauseum. A radio station broadcast this monologue at 2:00 p.m. on a Tuesday afternoon in October 1973, and a man and his son heard the broadcast, were upset by it, and complained about it to the FCC.

Indecency is legally defined as material that, "in context, depicts or describes in terms patently offensive as measured by contemporary community standards for the broadcast medium, sexual or excretory activities or organs." Indecency is protected by the First Amendment; while it cannot be banned, its broadcast is regulated. An indecent monologue, such as Carlin's, would not be indecent—and certainly not obscene—if it were printed in whole in the daily newspaper or on a website. It would also be permitted to air between the hours of 10:00 p. m. and 6:00 a. m.

Table 14.1

V-CHIP RATINGS

TV-Y (All Children: This program is designed to be appropriate for all children.) Whether animated or live-action, the themes and elements in this program are specifically designed for a very young audience, including children from ages 2–6. This program is not expected to frighten younger children.

TV-Y7 (Directed to Older Children: This program is designed for children age 7 and above.) It may be more appropriate for children who have acquired the developmental skills needed to distinguish between make-believe and reality. Themes and elements in this program may include mild fantasy or comedic violence or may frighten children under the age of 7. Therefore, parents may wish to consider the suitability of this program for their very young children. Note: For those programs where fantasy violence may be more intense or more combative than other programs in this category, such programs will be designated TV-Y7-FV. For programs designed for the entire audience, the general categories are as follows:

TV-G (General Audience: Most parents would find this program suitable for all ages.) Although this rating does not signify a program designed specifically for children, most parents may let younger children watch this program unattended. It contains little or no violence, no strong language, and little or no sexual dialogue or situations.

TV-PG (Parental Guidance Suggested: This program contains material that parents may find unsuitable for younger children.) Many parents may want to watch it with their younger children. The theme itself may call for parental guidance, and/or the program contains one or more of the following: moderate violence (V), some sexual situations (S), infrequent coarse language (L), or some suggestive dialogue (D).

TV-14 (Parents Strongly Cautioned: This program contains some material that many parents would find unsuitable for children under 14 years of age.) Parents are strongly urged to exercise greater care in monitoring this program and are cautioned against letting children under the age of 14 watch unattended. This program contains one or more of the following: intense violence (V), intense sexual situations (S), strong coarse language (L), or intensely suggestive dialogue (D).

TV-MA (Mature Audience Only: This program is specifically designed to be viewed by adults and therefore may be unsuitable for children under 17.) This program contains one or more of the following: graphic violence (V), explicit sexual activity (S), or crude indecent language (L).

SOURCE: Federal Communications Commission website, *http://www.fcc.gov/vchip/*.

Profanity. The FCC also regulates the broadcast of **profanity**—words that are so highly offensive that their mere utterance alone may be considered a nuisance. Like indecency, broadcasts containing profanity are also restricted from airing between 6:00 a. m. to 10:00 p. m.

The controversy over indecency and profanity is not over yet: in 2007, the Second Circuit Court of Appeals said that a new FCC policy to punish "fleeting expletives" (one occurrence of the F-word or another profanity) was a change that was not permitted under administrative rules. The FCC has announced that it will appeal to the Supreme Court.

Children's Television. The Children's Television Act of 1990 was passed for the purpose of increasing the quantity and quality of educational broadcast

television programming for children. In particular, broadcasters were mandated to serve the "core" informational programming needs of children by providing weekly educational programs of at least 30 minutes in length and broadcast between 7:00 a.m. and 10:00 p.m. Programs like "VeggieTales" and "Care Bears" fulfill the educational and informational requirements. FCC rules also limit the number of minutes of advertising that may be shown during children's programming to 10.5 minutes per hour on weekends and 12 minutes per hour on weekdays.

MEDIA OWNERSHIP ISSUES

Despite the government's proclivity for regulation, it does seem to agree with the theory that more media voices mean more options and more participation in

"Bong Hits 4 Jesus"

The case had a graphic hook: a group of high school students holding up a large home-made sign reading "Bong Hits 4 Jesus" on a public street outside their high school. The less exciting *Morse v. Frederick* was the name of the case ultimately decided by the Supreme Court in 2007 that provided more limitations on student free speech rights.

High school senior Joseph Frederick came to school late on the day that his Juneau, Alaska high school was released from normal classes to watch the Olympic torch pass by in a parade in 2002. To get a little attention from television cameras, Frederick unfurled his homemade sign on a public street across from the high school. The high school principal, Deborah Morse, horrified at what she perceived to be a pro-drug message, crossed the street, tore the sign out of Frederick's hands and suspended him. Frederick took the case to court.

The appeals court said that Morse could be held personally liable for damages for abridging Frederick's free speech rights. The Supreme Court disagreed. Chief Justice Roberts wrote that it was reasonable for Morse to think that the banner was supporting drug use, even though Frederick claimed it was nonsense intended to grab television cameras. Moreover, even though Frederick had not been to school that day and did not display his sign on school property, the fact that the parade took place during school hours and that students were released to watch under administrative supervision meant that the event was "school-sponsored." Therefore, for Morse not to have taken action against the sign would have sent a signal that she was not serious about opposing drug use. The result: a broader interpretation of administrators' abilities to restrict student expression.

The Court was not unanimous. Justice Stevens, one of the more liberal justices on the Court, wrote that an administrator should not be permitted to punish student speech simply because the administrator disagrees with it. As for the idea that the banner would entice students to try drugs, Stevens scoffed, "Admittedly, some high school students (including those who use drugs) are dumb. Most students, however, do not shed their brains at the schoolhouse gate, and most students know dumb advocacy when they see it. The notion that the message on this banner would actually persuade either the average student or even the dumbest one to change his or her behavior is most implausible."

the marketplace of ideas. Monopolies are considered to be bad for consumers because they limit consumer choices and permit the monopolists to raise prices. The FCC has been inconsistent in promoting diver-

sity in the media marketplace. In December 2007, the commissioners announced rules to promote diversification of broadcast ownership by making it easier to obtain financing and licenses. On the same day, they also announced revisions to the newspaper/broadcast cross-ownership rule, amending a 32-year ban on one entity owning both a daily newspaper and a broadcast station in the same market and permitting cross-ownership in large markets containing what they consider to be sufficient competition.[7]

The Telecommunications Act of 1996, passed with great fanfare and hope, had as one of its major goals the increase of competition between telecommunications organizations in order to bring about reduced costs to consumers as the result of more competition. The act abolishes former restrictions on cross-market competition, letting cable industries compete to offer telephone service, for example. It also lifted broadcast ownership limitations, permitting one owner to own television stations with a maximum service area cap of 35 percent of the U.S. population and eliminating the cap on the number of radio licenses one owner can own. However, it left in place limits on the number of licenses that can be owned in specific markets.

Critics of the Telecommunications Act suggest that instead of getting lower prices and more competition, as was promised, consumers got more consolidation, higher prices, and less diversity. For example, the removal of ownership caps in the radio industry resulted in an extreme consolidation of radio ownership, as seen in Table 14.2. The "Big Six" media conglomerates—General Electric, Time Warner, Disney,

News Corp., Bertelsmann of Germany, and Viacom—control over 90 percent of the U.S. media industry.

REGULATIONS ON ADVERTISING

You might be surprised that the government may regulate even truthful advertising about legal products. Yet even this limited protection is more than advertising got when it was first considered by the Supreme Court in the 1940s. Over time, the commercial speech doctrine developed, giving limited protection to speech that advocates a commercial transaction.

The Supreme Court first considered whether advertising should have First Amendment protection in 1942 in *Valentine v. Chrestensen*. At issue in the case was a flyer that a submarine owner was passing out that advertised paid rides on his submarine on one side and, on the other, complained about the New York commissioner of docks forbidding him to store his submarine at New York piers. The Court dismissed the political speech on the reverse of Chrestensen's flyer, instead focusing on the advertisement and stating that speech of a purely commercial or advertising nature would be outside of the protection of the First Amendment.

Over the years, successive Courts chipped away at the total lack of protection for advertising until the case of *Central Hudson Gas & Electric Corp. v. Public Service Commission* (1980) established a legal test to

Table 14.2

NUMBER OF RADIO STATIONS OWNED BY TOP 10 BROADCASTING COMPANIES IN 2005

Rank	Owner	Total # of Stations	# of News Stations
1	Clear Channel	1184	132
2	Cumulus Broadcasting	300	31
3	Citadel Broadcasting	223	19
4	CBS Radio	179	22
5	Educational Media Foundation	161	0
6	American Family Association	128	0
7	Salem Communications	106	23
8	Entercom	103	15
9	Saga Communications	87	12
10	Cox Radio	78	6

SOURCE: Journalism.org, "State of the News Media 2007," *http://www.stateofthenewsmedia.com/2007/narrative_radio_ownership.asp?cat=4&media=9.*

determine whether a particular regulation on advertising was constitutional. That test looks at the legality of the product or service (illegal goods or services cannot be advertised), the importance of the state interest supported by the regulation, and the "fit" between the regulation and the state interest. Acceptable regulations cannot regulate too much or too little speech, and there must be a direct connection between the regulation and advancement of the state interest.

The current Supreme Court has several justices who would do away with this clumsy test, among them conservative justice Clarence Thomas, who has said that he would get rid of all regulations on advertising that keep consumers "ignorant in order to manipulate their choices in the marketplace." Thomas does not see a reason to protect commercial speech any less than political or other forms of speech. However, his perspective has not yet garnered sufficient support from other justices to be the rule of law. Thus, the *Central Hudson* test, as it is usually called, is usually used to determine whether a regulation on advertising is justified.

The administrative agency responsible for the regulation of advertising by the federal government is the Federal Trade Commission (FTC). The FTC is empowered to prevent unfair competition and enforce truthful advertising laws. It also investigates consumer and company complaints about advertisements. However, because it is a government bureaucracy, it moves much more slowly than the industry itself. As noted earlier in this chapter and in others, the advertising industry has developed a strong self-regulatory regime in which advertisers police each other and generally agree to abide by rulings of its self-regulatory bodies—the National Advertising Division (NAD) and the National Advertising Review Board, both part of the Better Business Bureau. The process of investigation and compliance is much faster and cheaper than that of the FTC, although the rulings of the self-regulatory bodies have no legal force. Although membership in and compliance with the bodies' decisions is voluntary, the Better Business Bureau reports that NAD has resolved more than 3,700 advertising cases and has a 96 percent compliance rate.[8]

Of particular note for public relations specialists is the FCC's 2007 fine against cablecaster Comcast for broadcasting a video news release (VNR) without providing sponsorship information as required by law. The product, "Nelson's Rescue Sleep," was included in a consumer issues segment, and the VNR contained many images and mentions of Rescue Sleep and said that "If you are one of the estimated 70 million Americans who have trouble sleeping, Rescue Sleep may be what you're looking for." Comcast argued that because it had not received any compensation for running the VNR, it should not have to disclose sponsorship, but the FCC disagreed and fined Comcast $4,000.

Media Ethics

While companies' advertising efforts usually have their own self-interest in mind, most journalists endeavor to provide consumers with an honest account of the stories they cover. They try to get all sides of a story, try to quote their sources accurately and in context, and work hard to get a truthful version of the story published under often-strict deadlines. They seek to eliminate bias and accept criticism from their editors and the public. All of these goals—truth, accuracy, objectivity, accountability, and responsibility—are part of media ethics.

Media ethics is an example of applied ethics; media organizations often find themselves facing ethical issues, and ethicists attempt to apply moral theories to real-life situations. The ethical imperatives of the law also apply to the media. For example, journalists strive for truth both to avoid libel claims against them and to enlighten the democratic society in which they live.

However, there is much more to ethics than simply "doing the right thing." Ethics refers not to a set of clearly established rules but, rather, involves weighing competing interests and considering moral standards and values as part of a decision-making process. The variables involved in answering an ethical question are rarely clear-cut, and there is almost never a solid right answer to an ethical question.

THE HUTCHINS REPORT

In 1947, American journalism was dealt a serious blow by the publication of *A Free and Responsible Press*, commonly known as the Hutchins report. The report was a landmark consideration of the role of an ethical press in American society. A searing indictment of the state of American journalism, the report outlined the many ills of the self-serving media and made four recommendations for how journalism could serve democracy: provide a truthful and comprehensive account of the day's events in a meaningful context, offer a forum for the exchange of comment and criticism, project the opinions and attitudes of the groups in a society to one another, and make available the currents of information, thought, and feeling to every member of society.

The Hutchins report was written by a commission of intellectuals without input from members of the media, and the report was met with immediate criticism and strong resistance. Despite this unfavorable reception, the report contained the genesis of what has become the **social responsibility model** of the media, which promotes the idea that the media have responsibilities as well as rights and should work toward fostering positive, informed self-governance. Many would also suggest that today's citizen journalism, public journalism, and participatory Web 2.0 are the progeny of the Hutchins report's call for a more diverse media.

PERSONAL ETHICS

While the law aims to reflect the widely accepted standards of society, ethics involves consideration of elements with much more complexity. Individuals are often faced with dilemmas of whether to take an action that is legal but may or may not be ethical. Imagine, for example, that you are a journalist reporting on an alleged rape, and you must decide whether or not to print the names of the alleged perpetrator and victim. Current legal doctrine says that if this information is part of the public record and a reporter accesses it, the reporter may legally publish it. But there may be more for you to consider than just the legal consequences of printing these names. How will the community treat the alleged perpetrator when this story goes public? Is it right to expose him to potential public ridicule before he has even been tried for a crime? What if the police are certain he committed the crime—does that make the decision to publish his name easier? Will you feel responsible if someone decides to take the law into their own hands, and he ends up hurt—or worse? What about the victim—should you expose this personal violation that

happened to her? Won't the community look at her differently too? Most reporters would probably choose not to publish this information, and most news organizations even have policies against such publication. In this case, the law permits something that most media professionals would choose not to do.

For situations that are not so clear-cut, Dr. Ralph Potter of Harvard Divinity School developed what has become a classic approach to ethical problem-solving. Dr. Potter's construct, known as the Potter Box, asks individuals to consider several areas and issues within the ethical problem and come to a decision only after balancing the competing interests contained within those issues.

The Potter Box approach requires consideration of issues in four different areas: facts, values, principles, and loyalties. First, determine what facts are important to the final decision. Then, consider the values that are important to you as a person, a professional, a family member—any role that you are playing in this situation. You may come up with terms like "honesty," "integrity," "responsibility," and "open-mindedness." Next, look at guiding principles from moral authorities or ethical theorists; for example, you may take the Kantian perspective that one should always tell the truth or the Aristotelian mandate that the best approach to any problem is to be found in the Golden Mean, not at any extreme. Finally, identify the people or ideas to which you are loyal. They may include family and friends, employers, customers, the public at large. After having considered—and in many cases, reconsidered—these four elements, you can then make your decision.

The Potter Box is one of many approaches to making ethical decisions, but most of them focus on the individual thinking about more than just the self or the obvious answer. Professor Lou Hodges of Washington & Lee University ends his discussions of ethical decision-making with the following question: "How would I feel if the results of my decision were printed on the front page of the *New York Times*?" If the answer is positive, the decision is likely to be morally defensible.

PLAGIARISM

Unlike other intellectual property violations, **plagiarism**—the presentation of someone else's exact or close words or ideas as one's own original work—is not regulated by the law. However, it is one of the most widely agreed upon ethical misdeeds that students and journalists can commit. Most universities have stringent codes against such academic dishonesty, and journalists whose plagiarizing ways have been discovered rarely keep their jobs for very long.

In 2003, *New York Times* journalist Jayson Blair resigned after he was accused of plagiarizing and fabricating stories. After his resignation, an investigation found that he had plagiarized or fabricated at least 30 of the stories he had written in less than a year at the paper. In an act of mea culpa, the *Times* printed a front-page story titled "Times Reporter Who Resigned Leaves Long Trail of Deception" that disclosed to the public what the investigation had uncovered. The news of this breach was quite a scandal for a paper with such a well established reputation of reliability that its masthead logo reads "All the news that's fit to print."

ORGANIZATIONAL ETHICS

It may seem a false division to separate individuals from the organizations they serve, but organizations have resources and power that individuals do not. We focus on three tools that organizations can use to be more socially responsible forces.

Codes of Ethics. One of the first ethics codes, a pledge to do the moral and correct thing, was the Hippocratic Oath traditionally taken by physicians dating from the 4th century B.C. From finance to engineering to real estate, many professions have codes of ethics. These codes are statements of the "best practices" of the industry, instructions to practitioners of that industry, and the values to which the industry adheres. Some ethics codes even have provisions for the loss of membership in the organization or industry if the code is violated.

Of particular importance to media professionals are the codes of the Society of Professional Journalists (SPJ) and the Public Relations Society of America (PRSA). The SPJ code is divided into four sections that exhort journalists to seek and report truth, minimize harm, act independently, and be accountable. Each section of the code provides detailed examples: to act independently, a journalist should avoid conflicts of interest, refuse gifts from sources, and disclose any conflicts that are unavoidable. The SPJ code does not have any legal author-

ity to fine or censure reporters in violation of it, but many news organizations have a copy of the code posted in their newsrooms and consider themselves ethically bound by its recommendations.

The PRSA code of ethics originally had an element of enforcement; a PRSA member who violated an element of the code of ethics faced grievance proceedings that ended with a punitive recommendation. In 2000, the code was revised to focus less on enforcement and punishment and more on encouragement and inspiration. It is a lengthy code with value statements including the importance of advocacy, honesty, expertise, fairness, and loyalty. PRSA members sign a pledge in which they promise "to conduct myself professionally, with truth, accuracy, fairness, and responsibility to the public; to improve my individual competence and advance the knowledge and proficiency of the profession through continuing research and education; and to adhere to the articles of the Member Code of Ethics 2000 for the practice of public relations as adopted by the governing Assembly of the Public Relations Society of America."[9] Members can still have their memberships revoked if they do not adhere to the elements of the code, but the code now focuses more on encouraging positive and ethical behavior rather than promoting fear of enforcement.

News Councils. Only a handful of news councils are in operation in the United States. News councils operate in Minnesota, Washington, Hawaii, and New England, based at the University of Massachusetts at Amherst. Minnesota's news council is the oldest of the four, having heard its first case in 1971. Internationally, there are dozens of news councils, from Canada to Peru to Germany to New Zealand.

When consumers bring grievances against the news media, news councils provide non-legal forums for resolution. Consumers may find this forum preferable to lawsuits, which are expensive and time-consuming—one study estimated that an average case takes four years and costs $250,000. Furthermore, many individuals are more interested in setting the record straight than acquiring financial gain. News councils accomplish several goals: they permit the aggrieved individual to make a case in public in front of the media organization, and they give the media organization a chance to defend the choices it made in the situation. The openness of the hearings provides an opportunity for all parties to learn. Some media organizations do not approve of news councils, which they criticize as an additional layer of bureaucracy or a threat to journalistic freedom. Critics claim that a venue for addressing consumer complaints already exists—in the courts.

Most councils are made up of a combination of media professionals and members of the public. In Minnesota, the staff of the news council works with the media organization and the complainant to resolve the case before a hearing takes place. If the issue cannot be resolved, a hearing is scheduled. No attorneys are permitted. Each side makes its case before the membership of the council, the issues are debated, and a decision is reached the same day.

The newest of the news councils, the New England News Forum, which was formed in 2006, does more than just run hearings for aggrieved individuals. The organization offers seminars and discussions on media ethics, does research on issues of media accountability and responsibility, and examines how the Internet and Web 2.0 are affecting traditional media.

Ombudsmen. Swedish for "representative," the ombudsman is not unique to media organizations. Ombudsmen are employed by companies, governments, and other organizations to serve as intermediaries between the public and the organization.

In the media, an ombudsman may also be called a reader representative or a public editor. The Organization of News Ombudsmen (ONO) is an international group of individuals who serve as ombudsmen for the media. An ombudsman receives complaints or concerns about media coverage or issues of fairness, truth, bias, and taste and investigates those complaints. He or she then responds to the complainant and may publish a column or article about it in the media outlet. Some ombudsmen organize forums for discussion with concerned members of the public or the community, some may supervise corrections, and, in small organizations, they may be called on to perform other news-related duties. They are often senior staff members with a lot of journalistic experience and the ability to relate to the public without being defensive but with sensitivity and concern.

Careers in the Field

If you think you could handle the ethical dilemmas that media professionals face and keep track of all the regulations and restrictions, there are a myriad of jobs you could consider. Reporters, writers, and investigative journalists aim to disseminate truthful information to the public, and their publishers, producers, and editors are first in the line of people ensuring they do so. Advancement opportunities might include administration work for a society of media professionals, where you might establish and write codes of ethics; mediation work for a news council; or attempts to popularize the ombudsman profession in the U.S. If you're more interested in the law, you could consider working for the American Civil Liberties Union (ACLU), which employs staff and volunteer advocates, community organizers, spokespeople, and lawyers to protect the right to free speech, among many other rights. For the most ambitious, you could aim for an appointment as a Supreme Court justice and play a major part in determining the common law.

The ombudsman position has yet to catch on in the United States, which has fewer than 40 media ombudsmen. Internationally, however, there are many more news ombudsmen, in India, Colombia, England, South Africa, Sweden, and Turkey. What does the lack of both ombudsmen and news councils in the United States, in comparison to the rest of the world, suggest about the American approach to media accountability and responsibility?

Chapter Summary

◆ Although laws are intended to reflect and uphold the moral values of society, many issues are not always agreed upon. Organizations may use policies to declare their particular stances on issues, and individuals may find themselves avoiding an action that is legal but which they feel is unethical.

◆ The First Amendment clearly states the rights of free speech and free press. However, the U.S. has a long and complex history of how these rights have been interpreted, legislated, and enforced. Some forms of speech are more protected than others, and the media are regulated in various ways. These areas of the law continue to change even today.

◆ Broadcast and print media are regulated differently. Some of the legal and ethical issues these media face include libel, privacy, intellectual property, plagiarism, obscenity, and ownership.

◆ Individuals and organizations face ethical questions involving competing interests with no clear-cut right answer. Codes of ethics and the Potter Box may help to determine the ethical course of action in a given situation.

◆ When individuals or organizations feel that their rights to free speech or press have been violated, many venues exist in which they can seek recourse, from media news councils and ombudsmen to appeals courts and the Supreme Court.

Glossary

Actual malice—the publication of information with the knowledge that it is false

censorship—the process of regulating speech by prohibiting its publication or broadcast

clear and present danger doctrine—a doctrine asserting that the government may only punish a speech act if it invokes a clear and present danger of harm

commercial speech doctrine—a set of Supreme Court mandates giving limited protection to speech that advocates a commercial transaction

common law—rulings handed down by judges

copyright law—statutes protecting original creations, either published or unpublished, when they are set down in fixed form

ethics—a set of principles and beliefs intended to guide people to act in a "right" or "correct" way

fair use doctrine—rules allowing for the use of copyrighted materials without permission of the copyright holder

false light—the effect caused by the media distorting or falsifying information to imply untruths about someone

imminent lawless action doctrine—a revision to the clear and present danger doctrine asserting that the government may only punish speech that directly provokes imminent lawless action

indecency—material, containing sexual or excretory content that does not rise to the level of obscene, that is protected by the First Amendment but regulated by the FCC

intrusion upon seclusion—a physical invasion of one's personal space or property

laws—statutes passed by legislative bodies at federal, state, or local levels; administrative mandates from agencies like the Federal Communications Commission; or rulings handed down by judges to implement policy plans or goals

libel—an untruthful, defamatory statement about someone that is published or broadcast through the media

marketplace of ideas—a theory of free speech and press asserting that all ideas should be permitted to be published and disseminated so that consumers may pick and choose from among them

misappropriation—the use of someone else's name or likeness for commercial gain without consent

negligence—journalistic sloppiness

obscenity—material not protected by the First Amendment and determined by the Miller test

patent law—statutes giving inventors exclusive rights to benefit from their inventions for a limited time if those inventions are novel, useful, and not obvious

plagiarism—the presentation of someone else's exact or close words or ideas as one's own original work

policy—an overarching plan or goal of a country or an organization

prior restraint—banning the publication or broadcast of material after prior review

prior review—the process of regulating speech by reviewing it in advance of publication

profanity—material, including words that are so highly offensive that their utterance may be considered a nuisance, protected by the First Amendment but regulated by the FCC

reckless disregard—the lack of media concern over the truth or falsity of the information they are publishing

sedition—criticism of the government or its officials

social responsibility model—the idea that the media have responsibilities as well as rights and should work toward fostering positive, informed self-governance

tort—an injury or wrong inflicted on one person by another person, who is legally responsible for any damages sought

trademark law—statutes shielding consumers from confusion by protecting words, symbols, or phrases used to identify products and distinguish them from each other

Discussion Questions

1. Can you think of a time when you experienced or observed what may have been a violation of the right to free speech? How might you think about or handle a situation such as this now that you have read this chapter?
2. How do you feel about the extent to which the media are regulated? Would you be in favor or more or less regulations?
3. Have you ever witnessed the broadcast of obscene, indecent, or profane speech that you felt should have been restricted?
4. What ethical questions have you faced? What methods did you use to solve them?
5. Discuss some examples of media actions that are legal but may or may not be ethical. What

decisions would you make in these situations, and why?

Supplemental Web Sites

American Civil Liberties Union: http://www.aclu.org

Media Law Resource Center: http://www.media-law.org

Federal Communications Commission: http://www.fcc.gov

Federal Trade Commission: http://www.ftc.gov

National Advertising Review Board: http://www.narbreview.org

United States Supreme Court: http://www.supremecourtus.gov/

Society of Professional Journalists' Code of Ethics: http://www.spj.org/ethicscode.asp

Radio and Television News Directors Association's Code of Ethics & Professional Conduct: http://www.rtnda.org/pages/media_items/code-of-ethics-and-professional-conduct48.php

American Society of Newspaper Editors' Statement of Principles: http://www.asne.org/kiosk/archive/principl.htm

New England News Forum: http://www.newenglandnews.org/

Organization of News Ombudsmen: http://www.newsombudsmen.org/

Copyright Information: http://www.copyright.gov

Reporters Committee for Freedom of the Press: http://www.rcfp.org/ogg

Stop Big Media: http://www.stopbigmedia.com/chart.php.

Endnotes

[1] National Center for State Courts, "*National Center for State Courts Overview*," retrieved November 12, 2008 from *http://www.ncsconline.org/D_Research/csp/2004_Files/EWOverview_final_2.pdf*, February 2005.

[2] Lief, Michael S. and Harry M. Caldwell. And the Walls Came Tumbling Down: Closing Arguments that Changed the Way We Live, from Protecting Free Speech to Winning Women's Suffrage to Defending the Right to Die. New York: Simon and Schuster, 2004.

3 Mill, John Stuart. *On Liberty*. Edited by David Bromwich and George Kateb. Binghampton: Vail-Ballou, 2003.

4 Media Law Resource Center, "Annual Study Of Media Trials Analyzes 14 Trials In 2006: 9 Wins, 5 Losses," *http://www.medialaw.org/Content/NavigationMenu/About _MLRC/News/2007_Bulletin_No_1.htm*.

5 Federal Communications Commission, "Report: In the Matter of Violent Television Programming and its Impact on Children," April 25, 2007, *http://www.firsta-mendmentcenter.org/PDF/FCC_TV_violence_2007.pdf*.

6 Federal Communications Commission, "Frequently Asked Questions," *http://www.fcc.gov/eb/oip/FAQ.html*.

7 Federal Communications Commission, "FCC Adopts Revision to Newspaper/BroadcastCross-Ownership Rule," December 18, 2007, *http://braunfoss.fcc.gov/ edocs_public/attachmatch/DOC-278932A1.pdf*. Federal Communications Commission, FCC Adopts Rules to Promote Diversification of Broadcast Ownership, December 18, 2007, *http://braunfoss.fcc.gov/edocs_public/ attachmatch/DOC-279035A1.pdf*.

8 *http://www.us.bbb.org/WWWRoot/SitePage.aspx?site= 113 &id=01a45f12-5b9a-45ab-8d78-49100a077b92*.

9 Public Relations Society of America. "Code of Ethics," *http://www.prsa.org/aboutUs/ethics/preamble_en.html*.